Surge to Freedom

SURGE TO FREEDOM

The End of Communist Rule in Eastern Europe

J. F. Brown

Duke University Press

Durham and London   1991

Third printing in paperback, 1992

Parts of, or ideas in, several chapters in this book are
based on work done by the author for The Rand
Corporation. Parts of chapter 9 appeared in the author's
chapter, "Conservatism and Nationalism in the
Balkans: Albania, Bulgaria, and Romania," in
William E. Griffith (ed.), *Central and Eastern Europe:
The Opening Curtain?* (Boulder, Colo., Westview Press,
1989). Reprinted by permission of Westview Press.
Library of Congress Cataloging-in-Publication Data
appear on the last printed page of this book.

For Alison and Julia

Contents

Preface

Whatever its original worth may have been, my book *Eastern Europe and Communist Rule*, published by Duke University Press in early 1988, soon failed, like the communist rule it purported to analyze, to withstand the momentous events that followed its publication. The book sought to examine the weaknesses of that rule, but it would have needed Nostradamus himself to have foreseen how soon those weaknesses would lead to the end of communist rule in Eastern Europe.

The present book, begun at the end of 1989 and finished six months later, looks back at the fall of East European communism. It not only analyzes the two years preceding the fall but, with the benefit of hindsight, seeks to uncover the more basic reasons for the system's precipitate end. In this sense *The Surge to Freedom: The End of Communist Rule in Eastern Europe* is both a companion volume to, and a revised, updated, version of, *Eastern Europe and Communist Rule*. Readers familiar with the earlier book will recognize how much it forms the basis of the new one.

An introduction giving a concise explanation of the immediate causes for the 1989 revolutions is followed by a longer chapter delving into their deeper reasons and posting the most important landmarks in the forty years of communist rule. A brief review of Gorbachev's revolution in Soviet policy toward Eastern Europe is followed by six "country" chapters devoted to the last period of communist rule in each of the Soviet Union's erstwhile East European allies and satellites. A chapter on Yugoslavia and Albania follows; in both of these countries, their independence notwithstanding, communist rule is also approaching its conclusion. Finally, there is a concluding chapter on the problems facing the new East European democracies. These are numerous and daunting. Whether they are ever solved, or even contained, might be the subject of another book in a few years' time. The appendix gives a chronology of the main events of *annus mirabilis* 1989.

More than a few people have helped me with this book. Undergraduates and graduates whom I taught at Berkeley, UCLA, and Rand challenged me to rethink and then shed "certainties" to which I had clung for too long. The Rand Corporation has provided a most congenial and liberal atmosphere in which to earn my keep. Colleagues at Rand like Ron Asmus, Keith Crane, Steven Popper, and Barbara Kliszewski deserve special mention. So do widely scattered friends like Barbara Donovan, Charles Andras, Vlad Sobell, Ron Linden, Olga Alexandra McCord, Bill Robinson, Anneli Ute Gabanyi, Jane Lester, Rada Nikolaeva, Louis Zanga, Milan Andrejevich, József Szabados, Michael Shafir, Keith Bush, Ken Jowitt, Gail Kligman, Ronelle Alexander, and Iwanka Rebet.

As with *Eastern Europe and Communist Rule*, Duke University Press has been prompt, professional, and civilized. Valerie Milholland, Dick Rowson, and Bob Mirandon could not have been better colleagues.

I owe another special debt to Radio Free Europe Research, the products and services of which continue to be invaluable. Hyung Seong typed the manuscript. She did it skillfully and patiently, and it was a privilege to work with her.

My wife, Margaret, realized my need to write this book; she gave every encouragement and made every allowance. It would not have been written without her and she has no idea how much I thank her.

J. F. Brown
Los Angeles
June 1990

Surge to Freedom

Introduction
1989: Year of the Avalanche

"89 bis," as the title of Andre Fontaine's comment in Le Monde put it on November 11, 1989. He was likening the German Democratic Republic's decision two days earlier to open its borders to the year 1789, when the French Revolution began its liberating, cataclysmic course. There were similarities: it was not just the neatness of the 200-year span between the French and the East European revolutions that prompted comparisons. Just over a month later when the Romanian Uprising toppled the old order, similarities were added that had not previously been present: violence, bloodshed, tyrannicide.

But the comparison with France in 1789 was not exclusive, or totally fitting. Eastern Europe 1989 has similarities with other great movements in European history, most notably 1848. Then the revolutions proliferated as they did in 1989. But the closest similarity between the two was in their intellectual component. In three countries—Hungary, Czechoslovakia, and the GDR—it was the intellectuals, in company with the young, who finally pushed through to liberty. And in Poland it was that most effective and secure alliance of all—between intellectuals and workers—that wore down and then broke down communist power. Amos Elon, writing in the New Yorker on January 22, 1990, saw the "Prague Autumn" (1848 par excellence) as the "victory of culture over power." Throughout Eastern Europe 1989 it was certainly the victory of dynamic and durable ideas over an ideology that had become impotent and hence ephemeral.

Between 1989 and 1848, however, there was likely to be one huge difference: the outcome. The intellectuals of 1848 soon went down against the military force of the Great Powers. If the intellectuals of 1989 could reverse economic decline and solidify their relations with large sections of their own societies, their victories would be permanent. Their problems were enormous—but, with proper Western help, not insoluble.

East Winds, West Winds

It was the sheer speed of events that left observers and participants, not to mention their victims, positively gasping. The eighteenth-century English diarist Horace Walpole wrote (with the chauvinism that was respectable then) that every day in 1759 when his countrymen woke up there was news of another victory. So it seemed in the second half of 1989. Almost every day another breakthrough, another downfall, another East European victory. "*Vents d'est*," a book of essays published in Paris in 1990, could not have had a more appropriate title. And these were not the east winds Chairman Mao used to wax poetic about. They were the winds of liberalism, of values and aspirations that communism may have submerged, but could never eradicate. They were, in that sense, "West winds."

The speed of events in 1989 became critical in itself, generating a dynamic that became an essential part of the process of change. It created an excitement, an expectancy, a sense of inevitability that affected everyone. The east winds assumed hurricane force. No analysis of these events, or their causes, can quite convey this surge. Brilliant journalism can, and there was a fair measure of that. So can creative literature, and the novels and poems of 1989 are already appearing. What this chapter does is itemize the main events that raced through 1989, seek their causes, and cover the interactive responses of the East European countries to them.

Why the Deluge?

The basic reasons for the collapse of the Soviet system in Eastern Europe go back to the imposition of communist rule more than forty years earlier. They have been analyzed by me as well as by many others and provide the backdrop to the more immediate reasons given below. In the following chapters these reasons are put in their national and transnational settings. What follows here is an introductory, basic assessment of a drawn-out and complex development.

The collapse of the house that Stalin built in Eastern Europe had six interrelating causes:

(1) The most obvious and all-encompassing was simply *forty years of failure*. It was a multifaceted failure in which the incompatibility between Soviet interests and East European national aspirations became increasingly evident. But this incompatibility might have receded, or become less corrosive, had the system been able to establish a rational and satisfactory economic basis, ensuring higher standards of living and meeting rising

popular expectations. As it was, the system was shot through with economic failure, and this already had become fatal during the second half of
the 1970s. By then it was obvious that this condition was not just another
periodic malaise but terminal. During the 1980s drastic remedial reforms
might have given the patient an extra lease on life (or another furlough from
death). But, failing this, the situation rapidly deteriorated beyond repair.
And this time the Soviet Union, in the past ready to prop up its faltering
satellites, was unable or unwilling to provide economic help; it had its own
terminal illness to grapple with. By the end of the 1980s the great economic
failure was pervasive. All the East European regimes, except the Romanian,
had tried to shelter their people from the worst effects of their ineptitude.
But now they could no longer do it.

(2) It was this failure that made the *illegitimacy* of communism inescapable. Basically, the communist regimes had been illegitimate from the start.
But, as discussed in chapter 1, they encountered only brief periods of active
opposition. Most of the more than forty years of communist rule in Eastern
Europe were characterized by popular passivity, signifying not so much
acceptance as resignation. But even Nicolae Ceauşescu, who qualifies, in the
face of severe competition, as the worst East European communist ruler, had
his moments of actual *legitimacy*. Toward the end of the 1980s, however, the
very notion of legitimacy in Eastern Europe was derisive. Economic failure,
of course, was not the sole cause of the all-embracing illegitimacy that now
isolated all the regimes. But it brought the other causes into focus; it was
tangible; and it was primary. Above all, while economic success might have
dulled the edge of the East European nationalist discontent, economic failure sharpened it and gave it coherence.

(3) This economic failure stimulated and consolidated *societal opposition* in most East European countries. It brought together, though in different degrees of unity and cooperation, intellectuals, many young people,
and many workers, the combination that was needed to challenge communist rule effectively and consistently. Elements of the civil society, therefore,
were emerging in some East European countries long before communism's
final demise. Just as important, economic failure turned away other sections
of society from supporting the regime (see chapter 1). Such support, however passive, self-interested, or reluctant, had sustained the regimes during
previous crises.

(4) It was hardly surprising, then, that the communist ruling elite,
challenged by its opponents and deserted by its supporters, intimidated,
too, by the immensity of its own failure, began *to lose confidence in its
ability* to rule and, more to the point, *to lose the willingness to use the*

means to maintain its rule. After 1968, the Prague Spring, and its abrupt termination, all notions about "communism's global mission" had evaporated. Twenty years later, even the will to stay in power had been sapped.

(5) However inexorably the East European states moved into the classic prerevolutionary situation, their progress was helped by "external factors." The *improvement in East-West relations,* begun in earnest in the late 1960s, gathering force in the 1970s, interrupted during President Reagan's "Evil Empire" engrossment, and then resurging in the mid-1980s, was important. Détente did not strengthen communist rule in Eastern Europe; it softened it. And, gathering force in the 1970s, it pounded a system already groggy from the body blow of 1968.

(6) The Western impact was as nothing, however, compared with that of the other "external factor"—the Soviet Union. Developments in the Soviet Union made the East European revolutions both inevitable and successful. The tinder was already there, but it needed Mikhail Gorbachev to light it (see chapter 2). Gorbachev's effect on Eastern Europe was at once galvanizing and demoralizing, depending on the perspective from which it was viewed.

(a) It was galvanizing for three elements in public life: opposition groups; the many sections of youth that were becoming politically conscious; reform elements, where they existed, inside the regimes themselves. These elements interacted. The opposition groups also began to cooperate with reform elements within the regimes: that is, where they existed— Poland and Hungary. It was not coincidental that change proceeded in these two countries, by no means slowly, but in a fairly orderly, predictable fashion. Elsewhere, change came abruptly and massively.

(b) It was demoralizing for regime conservatives everywhere. Shortly after Pius IX ascended the throne of St. Peter, in 1846, Metternich is reported to have said: "We bargained for everything except a liberal Pope." So the East European conservatives bargained for everything except a liberal Soviet leader. (And Gorbachev turned out to be far more liberal than *Pio Nono.*) The conservatives could live with Gorbachev in his early reorganizer-modernizer phase (see chapter 2), but, when he evolved into a systemic reformer, doom was not to be delayed.

(c) But for these same conservatives the most demoralizing thing of all about Gorbachev was what finally sealed their fate and that of the entire system. He kicked away their last prop of support by letting the Brezhnev Doctrine wither and expire. The reassuring creak of Soviet tanks to the rescue would be heard no more. Eastern Europe's leaders were left on their own with nothing between them and their subjects except the most incriminating thing of all: their own record.

It was then that the dominoes began to fall. They tended to fall in twos. Poland and Hungary went quietly in the second half of 1989, almost seeming to vie with each other in laying the first foundations of the "civil society." Then came the German Democratic Republic and Czechoslovakia, within a few weeks of each other, in September and October. With the one gone, the chain reaction started: the other could not survive. It quickly extended to Bulgaria: Zhivkov fell in early November. Then came the Rumanian Uprising in December. In neither Romania nor Bulgaria was the democratic revolution completed. But, despite the ensuing disappointments, tyranny had been overturned.

This was the pattern of pairing in the last half of 1989. But these were not quite the same pairings that initially formed in response to Gorbachev. Poland and Hungary were always together as the most responsive countries. The GDR and Romania teamed up as the least flexible, with Czechoslovakia and Bulgaria in between. The course of each country's response is traced in the individual country chapters that follow. But, generally, in those countries that initially responded the most fully to Gorbachev, the progress toward change became orderly, while where change was first resisted, it finally became overwhelming as in the GDR and Romania. In the beginning, to borrow Alpine terminology, Poland and Hungary had been "avalanche" states in relation to Gorbachev; Czechoslovakia and the GDR "thaw" states; and the GDR and Romania "glacial" states. But in the end it was precisely the "glacial" states that felt the full and abrupt force of cataclysm.

Gorbachev had not wanted cataclysm anywhere. But he became like the Sorcerer's Apprentice, unable to control what he started because he misunderstood what he was experimenting with. He wanted reform socialism, even transformed socialism. He got democracy, however unsure and faltering. He wanted little Gorbachevs in Eastern Europe, as Stalin wanted little Stalins. He got men like Václav Havel and Tadeusz Mazowiecki (and soon realized he could have got much worse). The situation simply ran away from him. The only thing for him was to run after it, and make the best of it— something he became very good at, through practice. At the end of 1989 he stopped running in Eastern Europe. He had lost the race and was accepting defeat with good grace. But now the race was on in the Soviet Union itself.

1 Millennium Becomes Memento Mori

Communism in Eastern Europe was doomed when it became irreformable. When was that? Opinions may differ.

Perhaps it was irreformable from the start. Illegitimate and unviable—politically, economically, and, above all, morally—communism was imposed by force and had to be maintained by force. In most of Eastern Europe it took on a fatal aspect of illegitimacy: it was imposed by *Soviet* force of arms. In this respect it was not irrelevant that in Yugoslavia and Albania, the only two East European countries where it was not Soviet-imposed, communism was still surviving by the end of 1989. But, even there, for how long?

For the rest of Eastern Europe the fact that communism was regarded as alien in essence and alien-imposed was a basic reason for its eventual failure. In some countries it might have stood a chance had it been a domestic product. But that "made in the Soviet Union" label added a fatal dimension to the inherent inadequacies.

Stalin put Eastern Europe into a straitjacket. More correctly, into eight separate, but identical, straitjackets. Although the prescribed model was of Soviet design, it was supposed to suit countries as varied as any in Western Europe. Nothing fit. But this did not deter Stalin. The straitjackets must fit; and, allowing for size, they must look alike. He knew what he was doing. The rules of international relations had changed, as he told Milovan Djilas. Supremacy now meant imposing your ideological system on territories taken.[1] *Cuius regio, eius religio* was back in its totalitarian twentieth-century variant.[2]

The Historical Background

Most East Europeans after World War II regarded communism as alien and Soviet-imposed, a new means through which Russia could fulfill old ambitions. But it was not wholly rejected. There was a general awareness that there could be no return to the prewar order.[3] Communism seemed to define, in political perspective, the most pressing social and economic problems of the day and promised their rapid solution. As such, it appealed to some intellectuals, workers, and many young people. Nowhere, ironically, was its following stronger than in the Czech Lands of Czechoslovakia (not in Slovakia), where a civil society, in the Western sense, had flourished before World War II. But the Nazi occupation, disillusion with the West over the "betrayal" at Munich in 1938, a strong working-class and intellectual left-wing tradition, sentimental Pan-Slavism, the Soviet Union's immediate postwar prestige unsullied by the brutalizing presence of the Red Army that had cast such a pall over much of Eastern Europe—for some, or all, of these reasons communism tended to attract many Czechs, especially of the younger generation.

East Germany—first the "Soviet zone" of Germany and then the German Democratic Republic—was a special case. Even the massive Soviet military presence, the atrocities, and the major and minor economic plundering did not totally discourage the solid core of Soviet ideological camp followers. Again, there were several reasons for such left-wing sentiment: the defeat in war; the revulsion from Nazism; the sympathizers trickling in from a West Germany occupied by the "capitalist" powers; the refugee communists from both the West and the Soviet Union. When the "first German socialist state" was established as the GDR in 1949, its support was narrowly based, but it was not totally unrepresentative. Stalin was to undo most of this support in just four years' time.

In Hungary there was strong sentiment for radical change after 1945, with some sympathy for the shortcut to which the communists were pointing. Just after World War I the ghastly experiences of the short-lived Soviet republic under Béla Kun had seemed likely to dim communism's attractions forever. However, the moral and material disasters into which Hungary's leaders led their people during World War II, together with the country's untenable social system, now made communism a realistic option for a small but not insignificant minority.

In Bulgaria, where communism had enjoyed its strongest following in the Balkans, where Pan-Slavism and Russophilism were widespread, and where Georgi Dimitrov, already a legend in his lifetime, was back in Sofia to lead the revolution, the Bulgarian communist party was a powerful force, by no means totally dependent on the victorious Soviet army.

Communism, no matter how vaguely defined, had the least support in Poland and Romania. In neither case was this due to much lingering satisfaction with the prewar order. Both countries were ripe for radical change, and had it not been for their historic grievances against Russia, communism probably would have been more attractive. But Poles remembered the partitions at the end of the eighteenth century that wiped their country off the map until 1918. They also remembered the Red Russian invasion of 1920, and the Hitler-Stalin carve-up of their country in September 1939, the mass deportations, and the postwar Soviet annexation of Poland's eastern provinces. Besides, Stalin had decapitated the leadership of Poland's small communist party in one of his "mini-purges" in 1938. It was he who summed up the situation with his classic quip: introducing communism in Poland was like trying to put a saddle on a cow.

In Romania, where the only viable philosophy had been nationalism, Russia and the Soviet Union had been considered a mortal enemy. After 1918 Greater Romania had included Bessarabia, taken from Russia. But the minuscule Romanian Communist Party, loyal to the Moscow-directed Comintern, had advocated Bessarabia's return to the new Soviet Union despite the fact that the clear majority of its inhabitants were, and preferred remaining, Romanian. In addition, the fact that the leadership was dominated by Jews, Hungarians, and Bulgarians, made the Communist Party seem un-Romanian as well as anti-Romanian. In 1940 Bessarabia and Northern Bukovina had been grabbed by Stalin in another deal with Hitler. After the war there was no prospect whatsoever of either being returned by a victorious Soviet Union. Instead, Romania became a Soviet colony and a source of Soviet booty—another good reason for rejecting communism and its local practitioners.

But such support as had existed in Eastern Europe for "communism," or for radical change along centrally directed lines, should not be exaggerated. In neither Bulgaria nor Hungary, for example, could the communist party get even 20 percent of the vote in free elections after the war. Most support there went to peasant parties, reflecting the still largely agrarian character of their societies. In 1946 in the Czechoslovak parliamentary elections the communists got about 38 percent of the vote in the strongly industrialized Czech Lands, the highest "honest" percentage of the vote a communist party ever received in Eastern Europe. Subsequently, communist support appeared to be dropping sharply in the Czech Lands, too, necessitating a change in strategy by the Czechoslovak Communist Party. Power was no longer to be achieved through the ballot box but through the quasiparliamentary coup of February 1948.

Domesticism and National Communism

Moreover, some of the electoral support for the communists at this time was due to their relative moderation and apparent identity with national aspirations. The wolves really did appear in sheeps' clothing. To woo their electorates, they effectively camouflaged some of their more dire intentions. In agriculture, for example, they spoke not of collectivization, but of land redistribution, and they gave little hint of any nationalization plans for small-scale industry. How much of this sweet reasonableness was genuine is open to question. There was precious little of it later on, which cast doubt on any earlier sincerity. But some hints of the former moderation did remain for a while. Zbigniew Brzezinski best described it by a term: "domesticism."[4]

It was domesticism that soon worried Stalin and prompted him to reduce the East European regimes to the status of total satellites. Domesticism did not mean conscious independence, or even autonomy. What it did mean was the regimes, or even the communist parties when still in opposition, going about their business, laying the foundations of socialism in a way they deemed as having some bearing on local conditions, and with a single-mindedness Stalin diagnosed as an unhealthy preoccupation. What Stalin wanted was not local spontaneity but controlled obedience, not specific solutions for specific problems but a standard formula, or straitjacket, devised by himself. The only norm for Stalin was the Soviet norm, his norm. And he was quick to recognize that the logical extension of "domesticism" was "national communism," where the East European national interests would brush up against those of the Soviet Union. Thus, even at this early stage in the communist history of Eastern Europe, "national communism" had begun to emerge. All communism tends to become national communism, as R. V. Burks inferred more than thirty years ago.[5] It was always true, whether those involved realized it or not.

The first crisis of national communism came in 1948 with the Tito-Stalin break. But there were other symptoms of domesticism that needed to be stifled before they went that far. Władysław Gomułka lost his leadership of the Polish Communist Party in 1948 and went into eight years of disgrace for looking at Poland's problems in a communist, but also in a Polish, way. In Bulgaria, Traicho Kostov, a ruthless communist like Gomułka, was put to death for acting mildly Bulgarian. These were just two examples, and there were others. Even Georgi Dimitrov, former secretary-general of the Comintern, who knew Stalin well enough to be terrified of him, made the mistake of acting as if Bulgaria existed. He paid for this with public humiliation by Stalin—some even say with his mysterious death in 1949.

Stalin used different means to reverse the drift toward national communism. He established the Cominform in 1947, the first international communist organization since the disbandment of the Comintern four years earlier. After the break with Tito he tried to destroy Yugoslav national communism by every means short of military invasion. But Tito resisted and, by doing so successfully, made history and altered it. Tito's reputation fell after his death in 1980. The Yugoslavia he created seemed close to disintegration and collapse. Yet by defying Stalin successfully, he shattered the twin myths of communist unity and Stalin's omnipotence, setting both a precedent and a level of aspiration for others. Just to have *attempted* what Tito did was a historic act. To have *succeeded* represented leadership of a *historic* order.

Having failed with Yugoslavia, then, Stalin did not intend to fail with the others. They were now subjected to a *Gleichschaltung* more thorough than anything Hitler ever achieved. Its aim was to stamp out all traces of national communism, domesticism, and spontaneity. Stalin spun a web of control through a system of bilateral treaties wrapping the satellites, first with Moscow and then with each other. Within each country Soviet officers and officials controlled every key sector of public life. In the East European communist leaderships themselves, "home" communists suspected of unreliability were purged, imprisoned, or executed. The "Muscovites" who replaced them, so-called because of their often long years of refuge and conditioning in the Soviet Union, were "safer." Many of them, indeed, knew little and cared less about the countries to which they now returned to rule. The fact that many of them were Jewish only increased their isolation from those they ruled, strengthening the myth that communism was a "Jewish conspiracy" and perpetuating anti-Semitism in a region which, because of the Nazi Holocaust, was now largely without Jews.[6]

The *Gleichschaltung* was cemented by terror. Those who went through it were marked for life, sometimes in ways of which they were unaware. Had Stalin not died as soon as he did, had he lived even a few years more, East European society would have become a wilderness, surviving perhaps, but barely, and with little hope of recall or revival. But, in historical perspective, the Stalinist period was brief. It did not eradicate either national consciousness or the will to resist; it only submerged them. And submergence was nothing new in East European history. In fact, within weeks of Stalin's death, pressure from society started pushing up again.

The Rebirth

In East-Central Europe—Poland, Hungary, and even Czechoslovakia and the GDR—this pressure had a real impact on future developments. It also began to be recorded by the Western media, and thus clearly remembered. The riots in 1953 in East Berlin and other cities in the GDR were the first example of worker militancy against communist rule and provided the first pretext for Soviet military intervention. But the pressure was not confined to *East-Central* Europe, the northern tier of Soviet control. There was some pressure in Romania and Bulgaria, too. These countries, however, were almost totally ignored by Western media.

Had the strikes in Plovdiv or Braşov in 1953 been covered by Western media, both Bulgarians and Romanians might have escaped some of the stigma for quiescence that dogged them right until 1989. The correlation between the presence of Western media and the incidence of unrest in Eastern Europe (or elsewhere) remains to be analyzed in detail. In the period of history covered by this book, however, its relevance and importance are unquestionable. Western television, certainly, became a vital factor in the East European struggle for liberty in the late 1980s. The level of societal unrest in Eastern Europe was obviously never determined by the degree of available Western media coverage. But the swelling ranks of the opposition, especially their leaders, knew they were now actors on the world stage, and they played their roles accordingly. (Nowhere more so than in Prague 1989, where the whiff of grease paint was never far away.) Western television may not have inspired this opposition, but it supplied an audience in the tens of millions. And that audience was vital because it protected them. Except in the case of Romania in 1989, where the regime was dedicated to savagery, media attention might well have deterred the authorities (in Czechoslovakia or the GDR, for example) from a severity that could have been decisive. Blanket coverage prevented blanket retaliation. In December 1981, after the declaration of emergency, the zomos ran amok through Poland's industrial centers, driving Solidarity underground in a matter of days. They could do this because martial law shut out the Western media. There was no shortage of zomos (or their ilk) throughout Eastern Europe in 1989, champing at the bit, or perhaps even frothing at the mouth. The Western media, in force and unhampered this time, gave their handlers pause for thought.[7]

Between Stalin's death in 1953 and the Hungarian Revolution and the Polish October of 1956, events occurred that were crucial to the course of communist rule in Eastern Europe. The dismantling of the Stalinist superstructure began. Though the institutions of Stalinism remained largely intact, their practices were modified. This process was uneven, varying by country. But terror, the cement of Stalin's monolith, started to crack. And in different parts of Eastern Europe, most notably in Hungary and Poland, signs of domesticism reappeared. Many members of the ruling elites were not unmindful of the popular restiveness and began trying to mend fences, efforts in which they were aided, however, inconsistently, by the new Soviet leadership. The "Muscovite" officials, for example, so recently imposed by

Stalin, were now weeded out and replaced by "home" communists. Some of these, like János Kádár, had been victims of the previous purges; others, like Todor Zhivkov, had only been in their apprenticeship when Stalin was alive.

Malenkov, in his walk-on role as Stalin's heir apparent, promoted the "new course" in Hungary, promising a change in economic priorities toward more food and consumer goods. Malenkov also helped Imre Nagy become Hungarian prime minister, temporarily cutting the power of the hated Rákosi regime and inadvertently reviving the domesticism that was to spawn the revolution in 1956. But it was Nikita Khrushchev, who toppled Malenkov in 1955, who changed both the strategy and the concept of Soviet rule in Eastern Europe. Though Stalinist to the core in his determination to preserve Soviet authority in Eastern Europe, Khrushchev knew it had to be done differently. Legitimacy was now the goal. Legitimacy would be the means to find and then maintain the right balance between cohesion and viability in Eastern Europe.[8] This shift in Moscow's approach required changes at both levels of communist rule: the *international*, encompassing the Soviet Union's relations with its satellites; and the *national*, involving relations between rulers and ruled within the satellites themselves.

The First Revolutions

From a Stalinist perspective the shift was quite revolutionary. Khrushchev and his advisers seemed to have been weighing it seriously already in 1955. But after the upheavals in Hungary and Poland the next year, they saw that a new approach was imperative if the same were not to happen again.

It was Khrushchev's secret speech at the Twentieth CPSU Congress in March 1956 that turned the post-Stalin stirrings into revolutionary momentum. The speech itself had very little to do directly with Eastern Europe. It was meant for domestic consumption, aimed at producing results inside, not outside, the Soviet Union. But its effects on an already destabilized situation in Eastern Europe were devastating. Exploding the Stalinist illusion, breaking the constraints it had imposed, it was seen by many East Europeans as signaling the end of the postwar order Stalin had established. They were soon to be disillusioned.

The Hungarian Revolution in 1956 brought down the curtain on the *first act* of the drama of Eastern Europe and communist rule. For a few of the nineteen days the revolution lasted, deliverance seemed in sight, and not just for the Hungarians. Indeed, had the Soviet Union not intervened, in a short time there would have been little left of communism anywhere in Eastern Europe. What happened thirty-three years later would have happened then. The Hungarian Revolution was a catalyst in the history of Europe as well as that of Hungary. For the first time it demonstrated, graphically and tragically, the fundamental truth about Eastern Europe after World War II: the incompatibility between Soviet interests in the region and East European national aspirations. That was the leitmotiv of the history of communist Eastern Europe—basic, simple, conclusive.

Many expected the Soviet suppression of the Hungarian Revolution to turn back the clock to Stalinism. Instead, it set the stage for a period of progress and pragmatism unequaled until the arrival of Gorbachev. The progress even bred certain hope—hope, though, within the limits established by the crushing of the Hungarian Revolution in 1956. The Soviet Union was in Eastern Europe to stay and, as long as it stayed, communism would stay. And there would be no deliverance from the West; hopes of that support had been definitely put to rest.

East Europeans were now faced with the choice: give up all hope, or delve into their inner resources and rediscover the basic realism that had sustained them across the centuries. This would help them not just to survive, but also cope, hollowing out oppression to an extent permitting at least some collective and individual self-respect. They opted for self-respect. For the East Germans the choice was postponed till the building of the Berlin Wall in 1961. Until then, their special escape hatch to the Federal Republic had remained open and they could put off their appointment with reality.

The East Europeans' lot was made easier because the worst they had feared did not happen. There was fierce repression in Hungary after the revolution, culminating in the obscenity of Imre Nagy's secret trial and execution. There was serious persecution in Romania, mainly against the large Hungarian minority that had sympathized with the revolution. This persecution marked the beginning of the end of the institutionalized distinctiveness accorded the Hungarian minority in Romania after World War II. Soon, their self-governing institutions were whittled down and they themselves subject to the myriad indignities and chicaneries of the assimilation process.

Despite repression, however, Eastern Europe was on the threshold of better things. Khrushchev was the key. After denying the East Europeans liberty in 1956, he tried to mitigate their subjection. This policy gives him his niche in East European history. To realize that reform must continue *after* the Hungarian Revolution, with the risks involved, not least to his own position, and to create the conditions for it, suggests not just leadership, but statesmanship. With his peculiar amalgam of political pragmatism and ideological fantasy, Khrushchev set to his task. He was convinced that socialism, properly applied, could reconcile Soviet interests and East European aspirations. He was wrong, but Eastern Europe benefited from his illusions.

In Eastern Europe he was prepared to allow domestic reform, with more autonomy in external affairs—some leeway in relations with Moscow itself, as well as in opening relations with the West. In Poland and Hungary he also was fortunate in his choice of post-1956 leaders. János Kádár, despite his services in helping to defeat the Hungarian Revolution, seemed a risky choice to Hungarian and Soviet dogmatists alike, all of whom wanted not reform, but reaction. He was known as an enemy of the former Stalinist regime, which had persecuted him. But Kádár quickly won and kept Khrushchev's trust, establishing a relationship with him that was subordinate but not subservient. He was soon to pursue a policy of "reform and reaching out" that paid dividends for years to come. Until the turn of the 1980s the Kádár era seemed able to reconcile the notions of Hungarian progress and Soviet supremacy.

In Poland, as a result of the October, Władysław Gomułka was not so much chosen by Khrushchev as forced on him. His role in the crisis was the opposite of Kádár's: that of people's tribune swept back into power to break with Stalinism and restore Polish self-respect. For the numerous Polish dogmatists, as well as their Soviet counterparts, this change was dangerously unacceptable. To them, Gomułka looked too much like Imre Nagy for comfort. Khrushchev was aware of the possible similarities. He only finally accepted Gomułka because he could not afford bloodshed in Poland like that in Hungary. From the Soviet standpoint it turned out to be an inspired decision. Gomułka, never the "liberal" or even the reformer many had thought (or wanted) him to be, closed down the precarious gains of the Polish October inside four years and presided over Eastern Europe's first "normalization" process. In doing this he wrecked whatever chances of genuine progress communist Poland might ever have had, nipping in the bud incipient pluralism and market socialism, the plans for the latter already prepared by Oskar Lange and his brilliant coterie of reformers. Gomułka gave Poland the "small stability," as it was called, for fourteen years, but it was a stability mired in stagnation.

Gomułka was not like Imre Nagy at all. He was more akin to Gustáv Husák, who "normalized" Czechoslovakia for twenty years after the crushing of the Prague Spring. The basic difference was that Gomułka had the chance of building on the promise of October, whereas Husák was charged with ministering the last rites to the Prague Spring. There were few hopes of Husák, but many of Gomułka. He was not without his shorter- and longer-term value in the light of subsequent Polish history (see chapter 3). But he chose to ignore his historic opportunity. Had he taken it, East European history might have been changed and 1989 postponed.

Comparisons between East European leaders invite the most arresting comparison of all: Khrushchev and Gorbachev. A closer analysis of Gorbachev's East European policy follows in the next chapter. What needs to be mentioned is the similarity between Khrushchev's policy right through to his removal in October 1964 and that of Gorbachev during his first twenty months of power. In that period Gorbachev, like Khrushchev, seemed bent on repairing the Soviet alliance, projecting a similar dynamism and energy. He seemed ready, also like Khrushchev, to interfere in the internal affairs of the East European states to prod their leaders into reform. Change was not incumbent on them, but it was strongly recommended. Above all, Gorbachev seemed determined to make multilateralism a workable reality. Between March 1985 and late 1986 he seemed to be taking up where Khrushchev left off.

Khrushchev saw the Soviet alliance as greater than the sum of its parts. Building on the bedrock of bilateralism inherited from Stalin, he became the first champion of multilateralism. The Warsaw Pact, created in 1955, became not just the means of integrating the East European military into the Soviet war effort, but an important instrument of bloc control, consultation and political unity. Comecon (the Council for Mutual Economic Assistance), founded in 1949 by Stalin but then virtually ignored by him, became Khrushchev's most important multilateral instrument, with the aim of making the bloc economically viable and challenging the capitalist European Economic Community that opened its doors for business in January 1958.

But the more Khrushchev proceeded with his plans for multilateralism, the more he realized the need to go one step farther—toward supranationalism. He was probably influenced by the workings of the European Economic Community which, for all the communist predictions of doom, had made an auspicious start. The problem was to get supranationalism accepted by the East European members of Comecon, especially those for whom the new "international socialist division of labor" would mean modifying, or even reversing, some established aspects of their economic development. The very fact that Khrushchev had such a problem showed how the alliance had changed since 1953. Supranationalism was implicit in Stalinism; it needed neither explanation, consultation, nor legislation.

The situation was now radically altered. Khrushchev had to bully, lobby, cajole, and wheedle. The socialist camp, after all, was supposed to be the "socialist commonwealth," a concept first floated in 1955.[9] But the crucial difference was that fear was no longer the basic instrument of Soviet policy. The Soviet Union still dominated, but it could not terrorize into submission.

The Romanian Contribution

Not only had the pall of terror lifted. Other factors were eroding Moscow's authority—the Sino-Soviet dispute, for example. Beijing (Peking) was becoming an alternative center of power and ideological dispensation to Moscow, which gave the East European parties and states wider room for maneuver in their relations with the Soviet Union. It also deterred Moscow from taking too hard a line against offenders. With Mao watching, and the communist world watching them both, Khrushchev could prescribe but not proscribe; he could coerce but not fully compel.

China had become active in East European affairs in 1956, playing a not uninfluential role as counselor in both the Hungarian Revolution and the Polish October. In 1957 it played a major role in helping pick up the pieces of socialist unity and pulling them back into a coherent whole, what Zbigniew Brzezinski called the "Maoist effort to reconstruct a center."[10] But even in the course of these constructive exertions, China was fomenting the "antagonistic contradictions" that caused the split between itself and the Soviet Union. The former allies became rivals, then enemies, competing for support among the world's ruling and nonruling parties. For some, Moscow was no longer even primus inter pares.

The only East European state to bolt the Soviet camp and become a Chinese client was Albania. The Albanian party, under Enver Hoxha, was virtually read out of the world communist movement (Soviet segment) by Khrushchev at the Twenty-second CPSU Congress in October 1961, an action that raised the temperature of the simmering Sino-Soviet dispute.[11] The Albanian defection undoubtedly damaged Soviet prestige, but it was the Romanian "deviation" that frustrated Khrushchev's plans and changed history.

Toward the end of the 1950s Khrushchev became preoccupied with turning Comecon from the stillborn organism inherited from Stalin into a viable structure promoting socialist integration and hastening the millennium. The key was to be bloc-wide planning by a central body with supranational authority—essentially Soviet authority. The economic policy of the Stalin years had been a senseless waste of resources. Every state in Comecon, no matter how unsuited or unendowed for it, was laying the basis for full-scale, all-round heavy industry. It was high time for some rationality. The less-developed countries should concentrate on agriculture and light industry.

But Khrushchev's grand design immediately became enmeshed in a tangle of hostility, conflicting ideological interpretations, nationalism, and the dreams of the historically deprived. First, he was trying to explode a carefully nurtured ideological myth: that socialist construction must be predicated on heavy industry; more, that heavy industry was virtually identical with socialism. Second, he failed to understand that, for some countries, heavy industry was a form of national expression. He also ignored the almost mystical significance heavy industry has always had for backward countries. It meant graduation into the higher ranks of nations, with pollution not a mark of shame but a badge of honor. Third, supranationalism, however well intended, meant a Soviet invasion of national sovereignty in an area where a sense of national interest remained strong. And that sense of national interest had been reviving since Stalin. The East European states might still be satellites, but they were no longer lackeys.

Some members of Comecon had few objections to Khrushchev's ideas. For the GDR and Czechoslovakia, already heavily industrialized, such ideas actually furthered the national interest. But others, like Poland and Hungary, caught between modernization and backwardness, were equivocal. Romania, rich in resources but still economically backward, was uncompromisingly opposed. And, in its successful campaign against both the principle and the ramifications of Khrushchev's supranationalism, Romania used the Sino-Soviet dispute with nerve and skill, as well as the improvement in East-West relations that began in the early 1960s. It exploited the global opportunities now available.

But Romanian policy could not be solely explained by the three fixations Khrushchev had violated. There was another, more specific, motivation driving it to defy Khrushchev; the need for regime legitimacy. Rejecting Moscow's attempts to keep Romania "backward" was the passport to legitimacy; complying with them would have ruined any chance of legitimacy. In the perspective of thirty years and of the miseries Nicolae Ceauşescu was to inflict on his people, the notion of Romanian regime legitimacy now seems surrealistic. But the fact remains that national communism, as it emerged in Romania under Gheorghe Gheorghiu-Dej and then unfolded under Ceauşescu, did have a large degree of popular support between 1958 and the early 1970s. Its subsequent perversion should not obscure this fact, nor the service it rendered Eastern Europe as a whole.

It was mainly Romanian resistance that forced Khrushchev to shelve his supranational plans for Comecon in 1962.[12] But he had not dropped the principle of supranationalism entirely. He returned to it in April 1964, six months before his overthrow, in a proposal for foreign policy coordination. From a Soviet point of view, supranationalism was simply a logical step in the evolution of the socialist camp. It had two strong attractions, one practical, the other ideological. Despite Soviet dominance, Moscow in the 1960s could not make quick, alliance-binding, decisions, still less enforce them once made. Underlying this practical consideration was the ideological imperative of eventually breaking down national barriers, interests, and loyalties, whatever the temporary concessions to nationalism that might be necessary. The Soviet Union and the East European states were supposed to enter communism "at more or less the same time." This meant a degree of uniformity still far off. In the nationalities policy in the Soviet Union, itself, *Sblizhenie* became the watchword of a process of "coming together." *Sliyanie* was the "merging" of different nations—the ultimate goal. Out of this melting pot "homo Sovieticus" would emerge.

For Eastern Europe *Sliyanie* had never been on any realistic agenda. But *Sblizhenie* was, and Khrushchev believed in it. His much-quoted sentiments in this context, taken from a speech in the GDR in 1959, are worth repeating as illustration:

> With the victory of Communism on a worldwide scale, state borders will disappear, as Marxism-Leninism teaches. In all likelihood only ethnic borders will survive for a time and even these will probably exist only as a convention. Naturally these frontiers, if they can be called frontiers at all, will have no border guards, customs officials, or incidents. They will simply demarcate the historically formed location of a given people or nationality in a given territory. . . . The foundations for Communist relations among peoples have been laid in the Soviet Union and in the entire socialist camp. . . . Extensive cooperation in all spheres of economic, social, political, and cultural life is developing among the sovereign countries of the socialist camp. Speaking of the future, it seems to me that the further development of the socialist countries will in all probability proceed along the lines of consolidation of the single-world socialist economic system. The economic barriers which divided our countries under capitalism will fall one after another. The common economic basis of world socialism will grow stronger, eventually making the question of borders a pointless one.[13]

This was Khrushchev in millennial mood. Most East Europeans preferred his commonsense side.

From the perspective of 1990 it is hard to see how such ideas as those just quoted could ever have been taken seriously, either for Eastern Europe or the Soviet Union. But they were. And the significance of the Romanian role in rejecting them should not be underrated. It helped the East European countries to preserve their national sovereignty in the 1960s when it was under strong pressure. Had Moscow made a breakthrough on economic supranationalism in the early 1960s, on foreign policy planning in 1964, or on strengthening the Warsaw Pact in the second half of the 1960s and during the 1970s, the whole course of East European history could have been different. Some of the countries could have been on their way to becoming Soviet republics, and 1989, had it ever been possible, would have been indefinitely postponed. The knee-jerk naysaying of the Romanian leadership did much for the cause of East European freedoms.

Just over a year after Khrushchev's fall, Brezhnev called for a greater political unity within the Warsaw Pact which strongly suggested supranationalism. In early 1966 the Soviet regime circulated proposals for a tightening of military integration. In less than five years, therefore, Moscow had broached supranationalism in three key areas: economic, foreign policy, and military. Thanks largely to Romanian resistance, these initiatives came to nothing.

Romania not only resisted but also counterattacked. In response to the Soviet proposals for strengthening the Warsaw Pact, it suggested watering the Pact down. In response to Soviet insistence on a solid front of rejection against West German diplomatic overtures at the beginning of 1967, Romania established full diplomatic relations with Bonn. But its most defiant, significant, and courageous resistance of all was to the Soviet-led invasion of Czechoslovakia in August 1968—supranationalism at its ultimate. Ceauşescu not only refused to join the invasion, but roundly condemned it, risking, for all he knew, a Soviet invasion of his own country. Only Tito in 1948 showed more courage. Ten years later, with his domestic policy already grounds for deserved condemnation, Ceauşescu rendered his last service to the cause of East European sovereignty by rejecting Soviet attempts to get an allied commitment to send troops to the Far East in the case of conflict with China.[14]

Romania, of course, could not have done it all alone. Poland and Hungary also resisted Soviet pressure on certain issues at different times. But the Romanians kept up the sustained resistance for about seventeen years. Nobody thanked them for it; few were prepared to recognize it; but everybody gained from it.

One irony of the whole supranationalism episode was that, had Khrushchev got his way at least in the economic sphere, had Romania lost the

Comecon battles in 1961–62, the Romanian economy, and the material condition of the Romanian people, would have been much the better for it. Romania would have been spared the lunacies of heavy industrialization, the subsequent environmental disasters, and probably the massive human deprivations. And what applied to Romania would have applied to Bulgaria, even to Hungary and Poland. But had Khrushchev won the Comecon battle, he and his successors would not have stopped there. The price of defeat—more sensible economic growth—would, given Soviet domination, have been prohibitively high. Romania's tragedy was that the results of victory were catastrophic.

The Khrushchev Sixties

Khrushchev's defeat on economic supranationalism was the result of precisely that viability he had already been able to inject into the system in Eastern Europe. After 1956 his legacy was indeed impressive: a growing viability, vitality, and spontaneity in Eastern Europe that pointed to progress—economic, political, cultural. And in the course of this improvement, some of the regimes started to acquire a certain legitimacy—the Romanian, for example, even the Hungarian under Kádár, certainly the Czechoslovak in 1968 during the Prague Spring.

For most East Europeans life was perceptibly better than it had been before 1958. The crushing of the Hungarian Revolution had denied the hope of self-determination, but, within the framework of communist governance and of Soviet domination to which many East Europeans were now resigned, there was hope of a better life—materially and, to some extent, personally.[15]

Economic progress was satisfactory during these years. The differences in the levels of economic achievement continued, but all the East European economies made progress, and personal consumption rose. The average citizen was better-fed and better-clothed. Visitors noticed how many had shed the deprived, often numbed, look of only a few years before. Their situation was still difficult, but it was not without hope. The Czechoslovak economy, it is true, ran into serious difficulties in the early 1960s, but most Czechoslovak citizens were protected from the effects of the downturn. Elsewhere, the statistics painted a rosier picture. (They were usually unreliable, but generally reflected an approximate trend.) Considerable progress was made in the development of the social services, encompassing those "human rights" communist propagandists had always argued were more important than "bourgeois" human rights. Free and equal health and social welfare benefits—these, along with full employment, cheap housing, and public services, were the "human rights" socialism could, it was claimed, both guarantee and deepen. Without them, the "bourgeois" human rights of free speech, free association, free press, etc., were alleged to be meaningless, a cheap exercise in deception by the exploiting classes. The East European welfare state facilities also varied widely in the early 1960s. They were good in Czechoslovakia and the GDR, in some cases equal to what was available up to that time in countries like Austria and Belgium, considerably better than in Southern Europe. In Romania and Poland the welfare state facilities were still often very poor. But even there they were improving. And they were vastly better than anything that had existed before.

So was social and professional mobility throughout Eastern Europe. The communist revolution had totally destroyed the old social foundations in all the East European countries. (These had varied greatly, from the highly differentiated in Hungary, to the relatively egalitarian in Bulgaria.) Peasants poured into the developing cities and into the rapidly growing heavy industrial sector. In the region as a whole, millions of new jobs were created in the economy and the swelling bureaucracy. And not just jobs were to be had, but advancement, too. One of the undoubted appeals of the new order was the creation of equality in education and opportunity for the mass of the population—and the opportunity was abundant. Social and professional mobility, intense during the Stalinist years, continued until about the mid-1960s. Prospects of advancement, which to most East Europeans had earlier seemed beyond their wildest dreams, now became a reality. And not many who were scaling up the ladder stopped to ponder the price they were paying.

During this period the term "convergence" began to acquire coinage among some Western observers. Some socioeconomic elements in East and West were, it was argued, beginning to equate or approximate.[16] Capitalism and socialism were moving gingerly toward each other. Reformed political and economic practice in Eastern Europe was beginning to look more liberal and Western, and the rapid development of the welfare state in many Western countries was giving them some similarities with the social system in the other half of Europe. Today, after a quarter a century of progress in the West and decline in the East, the notion seems absurd. But, then, it was taken seriously. It was partly due to the exuberant self-confidence in Moscow. No one radiated it more than the ebullient Khrushchev himself. The Program of the CPSU, approved at the Twenty-second Party Congress in 1961, incorporated all his millenarian fervor. Catching up with the United States in two decades was the most shining example of its fantasies.[17] But some of this exuberance rubbed off on the ruling elites of Eastern Europe. Despite previous and present difficulties, socialism was reforming itself and seemed to be getting somewhere.

In the sixties Eastern Europe also returned again to "domesticism." But now domesticism had freer rein than before. Khrushchev himself, at the apex of the whole Soviet and East European system, was of an inquiring, receptive, empirical turn of mind, and, again, the example rubbed off. The ruling elites in the new "socialist commonwealth" now had considerable latitude (just how much was never again tested during Khrushchev's time) to face and solve their problems. True, the answers must be socialist, but there were now "different roads to socialism." And this latitude revealed the contours and the characteristics of each East European polity more clearly than ever. They had never lost their individuality, even in Stalin's time, but now they had the chance to reassert it. Eastern Europe once again laid out its "patchwork quilt." Each patch was different and was to remain so.

Much of the political tone for the 1960s was set by Khrushchev's second onslaught against Stalin at the Twenty-second CPSU Congress. Reformers in several countries took heart. It proved that de-Stalinization was now the norm, not an aberration. More, there was a license to reform.

The Prague Spring

It was in Czechoslovakia that Khrushchev's second de-Stalinization really took hold. It was the key that unlocked several doors previously barring reform. The Novotný leadership's past refusal to conduct anything but the most halfhearted examination into the crimes of the Stalinist past now caused a restlessness that refused to subside. Many writers and journalists seized the chance to enlarge their freedoms. Perhaps most significant for the future was the resurfacing of Slovak nationalism, its champions demanding, indirectly at first but then more openly, home rule for Slovakia. Slovak nationalism began stirring again. A few years later it would become one of the most important catalysts for change.

Most important, though, for the immediate future was the birth of economic reform in Czechoslovakia. Some economic changes providing for a limited degree of decentralization had been introduced in 1958, but with little effect. The economic situation continued to worsen, and it was this, and the new permissiveness, that led to the rebirth of economic reform. An able group of economists in Prague, of whom Dr. Ota Šik became the best-known, set about updating and adapting the "market socialism" precepts popularized during the Polish October. The program published in 1964 was not nearly as bold as what they wanted or what was needed, but it was a start. Economic reform also became the mode elsewhere. The Bulgarians worked on a model similar to the Czechoslovak. In East Germany the Ulbricht leadership also prepared a blueprint containing some pretentious social and ideological aspects as well. Meanwhile, in Hungary the ground was being laid for a distinctive economic reform which, under the name of New Economic Mechanism (NEM), was to be only one that survived 1968.

In the context of today, over a quarter of a century later, when all the East European states are moving away from state socialism toward free market capitalism, the programs of the 1960s, including the Hungarian, look almost pathetic. What they did was merely tack bits of capitalism onto socialism and hope for the best. But in their own time and context they were sincere and not unimportant. Had they been implemented and allowed to develop in a supportive political climate and a stable economic situation, they might have moved gradually toward market socialism and then beyond to a mixed economy. But the opportunity was lost. Later, only capitalism, rigorously applied, could salvage anything from the wreckage.

The Brezhnev Reaction

But whatever chance even these timid attempts had was doomed by the coup that unseated Khrushchev in October 1964. The Khrushchev ethos was smothered, first in the Soviet Union and later in Eastern Europe. It survived longer in Eastern Europe thanks partly to the early domestic and international preoccupations of the new Brezhnev-Kosygin leadership. In Hungary the quiet preparations for the future NEM continued, and in Czechoslovakia the different strands of change were quietly interweaving into a complex texture. It was in the Prague Spring that the Khrushchev era actually came to its climax.

The Prague Spring was the highpoint of reform socialism in Eastern Europe. It was not a popular movement, but a party reform movement that subsequently acquired popular support. Worker support was conspicuously lacking until very late. The liberal spirit which undoubtedly came to permeate the events was largely Czech. Slovaks gave the movement its nationalist element, aimed not so much at democratization but at Slovak "home rule," at federal status for Slovakia and against "Czechoslovakism."[18]

The Prague Spring was a noble venture whose aim was to humanize socialism.[19] The Soviet-led invasion of August 1968 ensured that this would not happen. What it also ensured was a quicker demise for socialism of any kind than might otherwise have been the case. Apart from the total collapse of 1989 to which it inevitably led, the Soviet-led invasion of 1968 was the

most significant event in the history of East European communism. It sig-
naled Moscow's refusal to allow any East European regime to try to regene-
rate itself. After 1968 pressure for change would not originate from within
the system but from outside it, in the streets and the factories, in the circles
of disaffected intellectuals.[20] This was the case in Poland, first in 1970, and
then, more significantly, with the establishment of Solidarity ten years later.
Brezhnev's action against reform in Czechoslovakia in 1968 was the *second*
step in the Soviet-bloc bureaucratic counterrevolution: the first had been the
coup against Khrushchev in 1964.

What Brezhnev succeeded in doing in 1968 was to make the system
moribund. He destroyed whatever attractions communism as an ideology
still retained; communists from now on were career communists, not convinced ones. (Most had always been career communists, but from now on
there was no doubt.) All illusion was spent. It was the youth who came to
nurse the most implacable and uncompromising grudge against communism and those ruling in its name. After Czechoslovakia, the communist
system in Eastern Europe slid into a decay that was terminal. Whatever
millennial idealism had existed was now reduced to day-to-day opportunism.

A caveat may be entered to this generalization. The Hungarian party in
the second half of the 1980s showed strong reformist tendencies. But the
radical reformers in the Hungarian Socialist Workers' Party took a path not
leading to socialism but away from it, toward social democracy—*and con-
sciously so.* They were trying to have it both ways: transform the party's
philosophy and values system, and at the same time retain its power and
material base. It was a valiant if not wholly ingenuous effort to keep up with
the times. But as the Hungarian elections in March 1990 showed, it carried
little conviction or credibility.

Détente's Corrosive Effects

A subsidiary reason for the Soviets wanting to destroy reform in Czechoslovakia was to insulate its dependencies against the dangers of détente. In
the Warsaw Pact declaration of March 1969, only seven months after the
invasion of Czechoslovakia, the Soviet Union renewed its campaign for
relaxation in Europe and, specifically, for the convening of a conference on
European security. This had been interrupted by the Prague Spring. Both the
Soviet and the East European regime leaders knew that the *very existence* of
Western Europe was a destabilizing factor in Eastern Europe and that any
real interaction between the two halves of Europe could lead to a new and
more dangerous instability.

Détente therefore—the perception, prospects, fear of it—was a strong additional motive for driving for "safe" conformity in Eastern Europe. The assumption, held by some Westerners, as well as many East Europeans, that détente presented few dangers to the Soviet-dominated East, while exposing the West to siren songs it was too feeble to resist, was fallacious from the start. Détente always weakened, not strengthened, communism in Eastern Europe. The first thaw—such as it was—in East-West relations in 1955 obviously did not *cause* the ferment in Hungary and Poland, but it added to it. Similarly, the international relaxation in the middle of the 1960s helped facilitate the stirrings which culminated in the Prague Spring. The "decade of détente" in the 1970s tended to make some East European regimes beholden to the West, especially in the economic sense, and hence more tolerant of societal dissent than they would otherwise have been.[21]

This argument is best borne out in the case of the CSCE process. The Conference on Security and Cooperation in Europe, with its "Final Act" signed in Helsinki in 1975, was spurned by many as the West's ultimate "sellout," the sealing of Yalta. The American government, for its part, was suspicious of the idea from the start, participating in it only because not to have done so would have been construed as self-exclusion from Europe. Subsequently, the United States often seemed content to use Helsinki mainly as a battering ram against Moscow on the human rights issue. But Helsinki turned out to be a crushing blow at regime stability in Eastern Europe. The Soviets, who had touted a security conference in Europe since the mid-1960s, saw it whisked from their hands once it took place. The West European strategy of "accepting the status quo in order to change it" worked triumphantly. All that was needed was persistence and patience. East European dissidents, like their Soviet counterparts, may have at first been discouraged, even dismayed, by Helsinki. But they soon took heart when they realized that it could be turned to their advantage. The liberalism of the Final Act of 1975 may have been intended as just so much rhetoric by their regimes, but for the dissidents it became the writ justifying their existence and activity, as well as the public yardstick by which official behavior could be judged. And they knew, and the regimes knew, that Helsinki was being monitored in the West. CSCE, designed to protect communism in Eastern Europe, exposed and weakened it.

The Third, and Last, Act

The invasion of Czechoslovakia ushered in the third, last, and longest act in Eastern Europe's communist history. The first act, Stalinism, lasted from 1948 to 1956, three years after its eponym died, despite the improvements after his death. The second, associated with Khrushchev, lasted not till 1964, but 1968 with the Soviet-led invasion of Czechoslovakia. The third, typified by Brezhnev, lasted from 1968 to Gorbachev's accession in 1985. This third act neatly divides into two parts: the "years of organization," up to about 1975, and the subsequent "years of stagnation." (Gorbachev's dismissal of the whole Brezhnev period as the "years of stagnation" is not quite accurate—at least for Eastern Europe.) But despite the organizational flurry in the early years, little or nothing was ever *constructed* during Brezhnev's rule. The Stalin period was, after all, one of frantic construction, however perverse and inhuman. The Khrushchev period was not only constructive but even had its *creative* aspects. But Brezhnev's rule was essentially negative, mainly dedicated to the preservation and the prolongation of power.

It began with a burst of activity. Up to the mid-seventies it was all bustle and vigor. Those who remember Brezhnev only in decay should cast their minds back to the turn of the 1970s. Then he was still the robust reactionary, powering an ideological counterreformation against the heresies that had invaded the communist body politic during the previous decade. But, however active he was, he did nothing positive. His aim was to prevent anything like the Prague Spring from happening again and the consequent necessity of Soviet coercion. His policies were predicated on conformity; the spontaneity that had sprung up during Khrushchev's time he attempted to extinguish. The days of experiment were over; those of caution had begun.[22]

It was not a return to Stalinism, as many were fearing at the time. It was an effort to rebuild cohesion through integration. But, first, the Soviet action against Czechoslovakia had to be given some legalistic underpinning. This was provided by the "Brezhnev Doctrine," one of great statements of dogma in the entire history of communism. What happened to socialism in one country was the business of the other socialist countries (notably the Soviet Union). Moscow's position as Grand Inquisitor was restated and "legalized."

The Soviet integrationist policy principally focused on economics (though the underlying motive was always political), and the main instrument for economic integration was again Comecon. The Comprehensive Program for all-round economic cooperation, formally approved in 1971, was meant as both centerpiece and showpiece of integration in the new era of "real existing socialism." It did not entail supranationalism, but it did lay down guidelines for coordination in both planning and production. At the same time the Soviet Union tightened its grip on Eastern Europe by increasing its dependency for supplies of energy, oil and natural gas, and a range of other raw materials. The East Europeans gained economically but lost politically. They received a relatively abundant supply of cheap raw materials for their burgeoning (if useless) industries—much cheaper than anything on the world markets. But the more they received, the more political and diplomatic freedom they were in danger of surrendering. Moscow, of course, was paying an economic price for its political gains. It could have earned much more for its raw materials on the world market. But it was a price worth paying. As for the political price the East European states were paying, many articulate citizens were worried by it, including many members of their ruling elites.

The integration concept went further and deeper than just economics. The accent was also heavily on political, cultural, ideological, and military integration—"all-round integration," as the saying went. The Brezhnev leadership went much further than Khrushchev, for example, in exploiting the unifying potential of the Warsaw Pact. The regular summit meetings of party leaders represented only the apex of a pyramid of "togetherness." Much publicity accompanied this flood of meetings at different levels of the hierarchy. Some Westerners even saw them as forming a "conciliar movement." At times the Soviets did, indeed, appear to show unwonted deference to East European sensitivities. Consultation there certainly was, but it was not joint consultation. Though never admitted, the inequality of the participants was accepted. The Soviets' "leading role" was no longer proclaimed; it was, in fact, loudly denied; but it was still assumed. And the consensus that was reached—except when the Romanians, and, occasionally others, balked—was *directed*, not democratic, consensus.

Sometimes, though rarely, direct consensus did not work, and Moscow had to resort to old-fashioned interference. In 1971 Walter Ulbricht, the East German leader, had to be removed because of his opposition to détente. More damaging was the interference in Hungary a year later. Moscow, suspicious of the Hungarian economic reform from the start, intervened behind the scenes in 1972 to freeze it, a shock from which it never recovered.

The "Consumerism" Dynamic

Reactionary though the Brezhnev system was, it was not unmindful of the lingering legitimacy problem in Eastern Europe, or of the need to infuse some viability into its economies. The expedient adopted, or stumbled on, was "consumerism," the political opium and the economic energizer, the antidote to the spontaneous eccentricities that had swarmed into the Prague

Spring. Raise the living standards, put consumer goods within reach. Enforce peace and quiet but be prepared to pay for it. Dull their wits but quicken their energies. If East Europeans could hope for a Trabant or a Polski-Fiat, and not just dream about them, then they might respond, producing without protesting. "Consumerism" now became the master gimmick on which the whole new policy would turn.[23]

The urgent need for some such gimmick was underlined by the riots in Poland in December 1970 that toppled Gomułka. Coming so soon after the Czechoslovak debacle, it was a jolting experience for Moscow, not to mention the East European ruling elites. Polish workers took to the streets and overturned a leader who had become one of the pillars of communist stability in Eastern Europe. Nothing like it had happened since 1956. Brezhnev knew better than to intervene in the Polish imbroglio. As it turned out, he had luck (short-term) in the new Polish leader's (Edward Gierek) ability to calm the situation and restore some kind of normality.

The significance of the Polish riots and the toppling of Gomułka was not lost on the other regimes. They must not only raise living standards but make it obvious that they were doing so. In the GDR this lesson had been more or less accepted before December 1970; the Polish riots just brought it home. It had also been implicit in the NEM in Hungary. In Czechoslovakia improving the living standard became a basic and, for a long time successful, part of Husák's whole "normalization" policy after 1968. In 1972 it was also embraced in Bulgaria in the massive, meaningless way associated with the rule of Todor Zhivkov. Only in Romania where Ceauşescu's messianism had just taken the road to perdition, did the consumerist lesson fail to become part of official policy. But even there, real incomes showed some signs of improvement for a short time.

In Poland itself the material improvement looked quite stunning for several years, while Gierek basked in the limelight of his spurious success. Living standards rose perceptibly, and, in Poland of all places, it seemed for a time that the communist regime might have discovered the Holy Grail of legitimacy. But it was simply a case of the bubble getting bigger before it burst. Gierek was to pay later for his flamboyance; so were the Polish economy, the Polish people, and Polish communism.

The life of "consumerism," in fact, turned out to be unexpectedly short. The factors that made it possible—cheap energy from the Soviet Union, a favorable global economic climate—soon disappeared. Later, it was sustained for a while by diverting for consumer use the flood of Western credits that swelled into Eastern Europe, ostensibly to promote long-term economic modernization. By the middle of the decade the party was over. Eastern

Europe was plunged into an economic depression. By 1980 it could not get out of the pit it had dug for itself. The engulfing economic disaster would have tested even the most flexible and well-managed economies. But since August 1968 all the East European economies, except the Hungarian, had returned to the essentially Stalinist command structure. Even the Hungarian economy, increasingly badly managed, could not cope. "Consumerism" by 1978 had become the fancy of a bygone era. The new reality was the hopeless struggle to make ends meet. The Soviet response to this crisis was quite different from the concern and energy shown earlier over Czechoslovakia and subsequent reorganizational spasms at the turn of the 1970s. It was lethargic, slow to see the danger signals or, at least, to understand their significance. Even renewed Polish disturbances in 1976, marking the end of the Gierek boom, did not alert Brezhnev sufficiently.

He was always a bad judge of crises. He cocooned himself against awareness of them. In Czechoslovakia his record was particularly poor. In December 1967, on a visit to Prague, he failed to notice that spring was coming, and later he was slow in realizing that it had arrived. Now, with Poland, he was ready to close his eyes and listen to Gierek's bland reassurances. But even allowing for Brezhnev's personal obtuseness, the best explanation for Soviet inactivity was complacency bred of apparent success. The early gains of the normalization process in Czechoslovakia after 1968 and Poland after 1970 had been impressive. They produced a calm, apparent stability, deceptive to Soviet leaders, Western observers, and many East Europeans alike. This induced a tendency to which no Soviet leader should ever have succumbed: that of taking Eastern Europe for granted. Moscow evidently concluded that, after years of trial and error, it had at last hit upon the magic formula for stability, cohesion, and viability. This was consumerism, plus integration, with ultimate order enshrined in the Brezhnev Doctrine. For Moscow, Eastern Europe was now passing from pacification, through normalization, onto the consummation of socialism, Soviet-style. Now the Soviet leaders could turn to the more global initiatives and ambitions that were adding a new dimension to their policies in the 1970s.

Toward the end of the decade a more elemental reason may have played a role in the Soviet passivity: the sheer physical enfeeblement of the leadership's hard core, Brezhnev himself the most conspicuous and painful example. It is hard to see how a fit and energetic leader, however blunted his sensitivities or numerous his distractions, could have failed to see how the dangers were multiplying. This was especially true in Poland. From a Soviet point of view, therefore, Brezhnev must take most of the blame for the rise of Solidarity as well as for the Prague Spring—indeed, for the total collapse of communism throughout the region at the end of the 1980s. When one adds the state of decay in which he left the Soviet Union itself, his becomes a record of failure that has few historical parallels. Those apparatchiks who had backed him in October 1964 reaped the whirlwind just a quarter of a century later.

The failure of consumerism itself had two deleterious effects—the one short-term, the other longer. First, as the economic situation turned sour, failing to fulfill the promises it had kindled, the rising expectations of the public were dashed, creating an ominous political situation. Second, since consumerism was the only gimmick the Brezhnev mentality had at its disposal, when it failed there was neither flexibility nor fallback. The command economic structure had nothing to offer except more failure. Economic reform had been anathematized after 1968, and Eastern Europe was locked into a self-defeating orthodoxy with no escape hatch. In a more permissive, less dogmatic climate, with regimes confident enough to be resourceful, there could have been recourse to a healthy dose of pragmatism before it was too late. But nothing was worse for themselves or their subjects than wallowing in doctrinal impotence while the walls fell in around them. The fleeting, enervating success of consumerism, therefore, might at first have postponed the end of communism, but in the end only succeeded in hastening it.

The Environmental Disaster

At this point it is necessary to register another crisis that was already looming large in the 1970s, easily observed but still overlooked. This was the environmental disaster, to which the communist response was belated, inadequate, and hypocritical. From the beginning there was an ideological block about the environment: capitalism, by definition, was destructive of the environment; socialism, by definition, was protective. This paralyzing dictum was being propagated while, for ideological reasons, heavy smoke-stack industries were being unleashed on the region. Moreover, with the Stalinist mania for quantity—volume rather than value—industrial managers had no option but to concentrate on material production, with scant regard for natural surroundings. The problem was also bedeviled, to some extent even in the more advanced East European countries, by the "pollution means progress" fallacy. Czechoslovakia, where some civic awareness survived the onslaught of socialism, was the first to take effective steps to mitigate the damage, prescribing preventive measures and penalties. But harassed managers, helpless in the face of production imperatives, often preferred to pay the fines rather than comply. In the GDR the regime often seemed preoccupied, not with tackling the problem, but with exonerating itself from blame. On environmental issues, Poland exposed itself as a thoroughly backward country, with rulers and ruled heedless of the mounting destruction. The effects of this neglect became evident: a large, transnational stretch of territory, from northern Bohemia up into the southern parts of the GDR and then across and down into Silesia in Poland, became the most ravaged stretch of land on earth. Many other smaller parts of Eastern Europe were no better.[24]

Nor was it just the natural environment that was ravaged. The population was beginning to be seriously affected. Respiratory ailments were the most common, but a wide range of other diseases were attributed to the environment. Infant mortality rates were markedly higher in badly polluted areas, and by the beginning of the 1990s it was widely accepted that life had become practically unlivable in many areas. In brief, the situation was such that if the downward ecological trend were not reversed within the next twenty-five years, then the rest of Eastern Europe's problems would have become insignificant, even irrelevant, by comparison. It was no longer simply the quality of life that was endangered: it was life itself.

Solidarity

If proof were needed that the communist system was moribund by the end of the 1970s, the rise of Solidarity in Poland furnished it. Born as a trade union in the summer of 1980, Solidarity within just a few weeks had become a surging national movement. And, despite its disclaimers and even its intentions, throughout 1981 it steadily encroached on the prerogatives of communist power in Poland.[25]

Solidarity was a distinctively Polish phenomenon with its roots and causes in recent Polish history. But, as mentioned earlier, it was also a logical consequence of the crushing of the Czechoslovak reform in 1968. Reform now had to come from outside the system because it could no longer come from inside—from society, not from the ruling elites. In the course of the 1970s Polish intellectuals who later cooperated with the workers to set up, and then advise, Solidarity, made it clear that this was how they interpreted 1968. (At that time they still talked in terms of reforming the system, not replacing it. December 1981 and the suppression of Solidarity decisively changed that.) Solidarity was, therefore, the outcome of a historical lesson that the Poles learnt. It was also historically notable in that it marked the revival of the intellectual-worker link that had been such a strong characteristic a generation before in the Hungarian Revolution and the Polish October, but which had subsequently broken. This link was to remain vital during Solidarity's years underground and then, for a short time, in the establishment of Poland's first democratic government in 1989.

The circumstances of Solidarity's birth and early development showed the extent to which communist power and authority had crumbled in Poland. For the third time in ten years Polish workers revolted against the inefficiency of the regime's economic management. The Gierek regime, always more a confidence trick than "serious government," had now lost the swashbuckling confidence of just a few years before. It lamely knuckled under to the workers' demands and signed an agreement for a free trade union that struck at the very heart of the Leninist governing system. From then on the regime betrayed its weakness almost daily. Relief came only with the declaration of martial law in December 1981, a demonstration of military efficiency but the ultimate confession of political bankruptcy. And the military only had the mettle to act because it knew the power of the Soviet Union was behind it. Eight years later it was a different story. Moscow was no longer in the business of propping up tottering regimes. Hence, neither was the Polish military.

For several years in the 1980s Poland looked like the exception. Other regimes, though plagued by difficulties, looked durable by comparison. It was easy to rationalize Poland's uniqueness. Communist rule had always been thinner there than anywhere else, with the least claim of all to be totalitarian. Institutions like the Catholic Church and the free peasantry were permanent reminders of the limits of communist power. A combination of tribal indomitability and communist incapability had kept the body politic in a state of neurosis, punctured by upheaval, throughout its communist history. And the Polish spirit was immeasurably strengthened by the election in 1978 of a Polish Pope, itself a reflection of the invincibility of the Polish spirit. But, in the end, Poland, though special, was not all that much different. Other regimes might have looked more stable and efficient, but the main difference was that they could better conceal the rents that were tearing them apart. Many Western observers (including myself) had tended to mistake for stability the muddling, malfunctioning endurance that characterized these regimes, underestimating the degree of corrosion from within. All the regimes were now brittle, with diminishing depth and substance. Even the Hungarian and the East German, the two regimes, each in its different way, that were considered relatively stable, were palpably vulnerable. Come 1989, the year of revolution, and even such a dark fortress as the Romanian regime quickly collapsed.

The Collapse of Support

The decline and fall of each regime is discussed in the chapters dealing with particular countries. Here it is worth generalizing on the layers of support, active and passive, the East European regimes once enjoyed and why these layers came to peel away.

First, though, a capsule distinction between three relevant concepts: legitimacy, authority, and power.[26] None of the regimes enjoyed *legitimacy* for any sustained period of time, though some leaders enjoyed it for longer. For example, in the special case of Yugoslavia Tito became an institution that unquestionably enjoyed legitimacy. Gomułka did for a short time after October 1956 and then squandered it. In Hungary Imre Nagy was carried forward on a veritable surge of legitimacy in the 1956 revolution. Kádár enjoyed a quasi-legitimacy for a considerable period during the 1960s and 1970s. Alexander Dubček enjoyed legitimacy during the Prague Spring. So, ironically, did Ceauşescu in those few nervous days in August 1968 when he defied the Soviet Union over the invasion of Czechoslovakia.

Authority flows from legitimacy. When the leaders mentioned above enjoyed legitimacy they also commanded authority. But the two need not always be identical. Kádár, for example, retained some authority when his legitimacy level had lowered. Honecker, never enjoying legitimacy, for a time commanded a certain personal authority. Furthermore, neither legitimacy nor authority need be indivisible. Even the regime could enjoy legitimacy *among certain sections of society*, while a leader could enjoy legitimacy or authority, or both, among wider sections of the population. But authority is quite different from *power*. Power entails the capacity to ensure obedience, which all the regimes were able to do for long stretches, simply because of the coercive means at their disposal. Authority induces obedience based on legitimacy, or on a certain respect that need not imply legitimacy but, at the same time, is far from being obedience compelled by power.

The regime-leader-societal relationship, therefore, was more complicated than it might have appeared. For long periods, there existed between support for, and opposition to, the regimes a large gray area of acceptance, compliance, toleration based on sincerity, necessity, opportunism, or a mixture of all three. It is against this background that the apparent solidity of regimes and their subsequent dissolution can best be understood.

The ruling elites were obviously the pillar of the governing system in Eastern Europe.[27] They could roughly be divided into five separate sub-elites: political; economic; cultural; professional; and military.

The political sub-elite was, with the possible exception of the military, the strongest single pillar, with its base in the party bureaucracy in the provinces and at the center. It was from this elite that the party leadership was drawn. It had the strongest stake in the system and was the most dependent on it. Indeed, with very few exceptions, its members had nowhere to go without, or outside, the party.

The economic sub-elites grew in importance with industrialization and modernization. By the turn of the 1970s most of the older generation of managers, some colorful, many incompetent, were giving way to a new type of technocrat-manager, well trained and generally loyal to the system as long as it functioned. But when the economic difficulties mounted and the regimes failed to respond, loyalties wavered. By the end of the 1980s many were offering their services to the new order. Some displayed entrepreneurial talents that might blend in well with the new capitalist landscape.

The cultural sub-elite covered a wide spectrum of different pursuits: teachers of all grades; men and women in the creative and performing arts; journalists. Many of them were party members. These were the high priests of the system, not usually taking their sacerdotal duties very seriously, but not too remonstrant of the life they led or the orders they obeyed. It was the numerous honorable exceptions who helped inspire the 1989 revolutions— Václav Havel, for instance, Adam Michnik, Doina Cornea, and Christa Wolf, the best German writer on either side of the Wall who remained a loyal GDR citizen and lost no respect worth having because of it. It is invidious, though, to name just a few, for there were more than these. They, not their more ambivalent colleagues who waited long enough to be sure but too long to be trusted, deserve admiration.

The professional elites were composed of doctors, dentists, lawyers, accountants, engineers, etc.—not to mention the battalion of men and women athletes, cradled and cosseted like no other section of society. They provided rare and essential services and were usually well-rewarded, in many cases through the bribes they levied in what were becoming increasing corrupt societies. But many in the "free professions" opposed the system, at first carefully but later candidly. Some became pivots of resistance and were drawn in, without controversy, to the service of the successor governments.

Finally, the military, the officer class. The question of their potential loyalty in war was the subject of much, well-financed Western speculation, and presumably much Soviet worry. Their loyalty in peace was to the regimes. The officer corps was materially privileged and responded with obedience. The behavior of the Polish officers in December 1981 was a telling case in point. If a generalization can be made, it is that senior officers were "safer," more loyal, to the regime, and the Soviet Union. Junior officers tended to be less certain. In Czechoslovakia, for example, in 1968 many supported the Prague Spring and were rooted out afterward by the Husák regime. Many Polish junior officers appeared to have voted for Solidarity in the June 1989 elections in which the communists were routed. In the Romanian uprising many senior and junior officers went over to the people rather than murder them. By the late 1980s, with loyalty to the Soviet Union much less of a relevant issue, and with their own regimes on the brink of collapse, most of the officers abandoned their former allegiance and made the revolutions possible. Bulgaria was a clear case in point here, with the veteran Defense Minister, General Dobri Dzhurov, turning against Zhivkov. So was Romania. But in two countries, the GDR and Czechoslovakia, ambiguous, even ominous, pronouncements (as well as alarming rumors) about the military being ready to defend "the achievements of socialism" contributed to the nail-biting uncertainty of the times.

A pithy description of how the ruling system was maintained was given by the Czechoslovak economist Valtr Komárek, at first a vice-premier in the new democratic government, in an interview with the West German magazine, *Der Spiegel,* in December 1989:[28]

> Komárek: This system was based on a clear division which worked for almost half a century: on the one side there was a power mafia consisting of 200,000 to 500,000 members of the party apparatus, the State Security Service, the officers, and the leading people in the enterprise and local administrations; on the other side there were 15 million citizens, the people, who were kept at bay by the power mafia, but otherwise largely led normal lives.
> *Der Spiegel:* This was possible?
> Komárek: Yes. We did our research, the actors played their parts on the stages, the doctors treated the people, who slept with each other, had children, and died. . . .
> *Der Spiegel:* And what about ideology?
> Komárek: There was something like an unwritten social contract between the regime and the people. The people were prepared for cheers at official events, while the regime did not further intervene in their lives—of course, only as long as they did not openly oppose the system. It went without saying that the people were kept under surveillance by the State Security Service, but this was also part of this contract, as well as the fact that the regime did not demand too much of them.
> *Der Spiegel:* But why did it break down so quickly in the end?
> Komárek: The power mafia only worked as long as it was able to use the

Brezhnev system as its basis. When it broke down and Gorbachev introduced perestroyka, the abnormality of the system became apparent. The
people took a breath, started to walk more upright again, the power
mafia was forced onto the defensive, became nervous, and started to
make mistakes.

The members of these different elites—most, though not all communist
party members—constituted what in Anglo-Saxon terminology had long
been, not so much the Mafia, as the establishment. Many were, continually
or periodically, critical of the regimes employing them, particularly its
leaderships, and many were active in efforts to improve the system. But they
had all had a strong vested interest in its survival. Even the most critical
would have preferred a bad system to a different one. It was often not so
much a question of loyalty, still less of conviction, as of needing to be
convinced that the system's overthrow would not endanger the niches they
had carved out for themselves. Two factors in the course of the 1980s upset
this behavioral code. The first was the accelerating decay of the system. The
second was the unnerving effect of Moscow's behavior under Gorbachev.
The message was coming from Moscow loud and clear that the system had
become rotten and needed radical change. Yet this message the leaderships
in four out of six East European members of the Soviet alliance—the GDR,
Czechoslovakia, Bulgaria, and Romania—were choosing to ignore. After the
beginning of 1987 there was no perceptible effort by the Soviet leadership to
influence the leaderships one way or the other. Charles Gati entitled a canny
essay on this subject: "Eastern Europe on its Own."[29] Some members of the
ruling elites may have welcomed the lack of pressure for reform. But the
official evidence suggests that many (except in the special case of Romania)
were worried by the unhinging of the traditional relationship with Moscow.
This was particularly true in Czechoslovakia and the GDR. Many were also
worried by the corollary of Moscow's new hands-off approach: that the
Soviet Union would not intervene to save them. The tanks would no longer
roll. Thus, the ultimate reassurance no longer existed. It was not surprising
that by early 1988, if not sooner, that classic characteristic of a prerevolutionary situation—the ruling elites' loss of confidence in themselves—
became recognizable.

The Annealing of Society

What about the rest of the citizens who, in Komárek's words, were "kept
at bay by the power mafia"? There were many who despised the system but
who, like many in the establishment itself, would hesitate to see it replaced

while it operated in a way not totally injurious to themselves. This included many technical workers, factory foremen, well-off collective farmers (of whom there were many in Hungary, Czechoslovakia, and the GDR), technical personnel, social service employees, and even some latter-day entrepreneurs who darted nimbly through the loopholes of egalitarian legislation. This large number of people had varying degrees of "vested interest" in their regimes' survival. For a long time it was their involvement with the system rather than their alienation from it that dictated their conscience and actions. But by the end of the 1980s this diverse societal group was coming to the conclusion that it was time to distance themselves. The system they had tolerated had now become the failure many of them feared it would. Some of them now actively helped in its downfall; others connived in it; nobody lifted a finger to save it.

The attitude of the workers, by now the largest section of East European society, toward the oncoming ruin deserves special attention. They were, after all, the theoretical centerpiece of socialist construction. In whatever version of "social contract" the regimes countenanced, the workers were unquestionably held to be the main beneficiaries of it. In some countries, most notably Czechoslovakia, workers, especially in heavy industries, were treated very preferentially. For many years the nominal income of Czechoslovak coal miners was equal to, or even higher than that, for doctors. In Hungary, from the middle of the 1970s, energetic workers could earn very good money, provided they could keep on the treadmill, damaging their health, their nerves, often their family life, and sometimes their mental balance. At the opposite end of the spectrum from Czechoslovakia was Poland, where the workers had frequently rebelled against, and almost always distrusted, the regime. But throughout Eastern Europe the system was such, and the labor shortage generally so tight, that workers could often make their own rules at their place of work. This was the real "social contract" in Eastern Europe: "They pretend to pay us and we pretend to work" was the folksy saw. Some preferred the sublimity of a Prague construction worker just halfway through the morning and already onto his third beer and sausage break: "There's one thing you must say for communism: it's a damn sight better than working."

An ethos like this tended to make many East European workers rather shy of systemic change. Many also tended to distrust the stereotype of the metropolitan intellectual: clean fingernails, glib tongues, huge pretensions, no guts. As in 1968, the Czechoslovak workers, though mainly supportive, were not nearly as enthusiastic for the November revolution in 1989 as were the urban youth and intellectuals. (The Civic Forum was wise to restrict its call for worker support to a two-hour strike in the lunch hour. See chapter 6.) Similarly, neither the Hungarian nor the Bulgarian workers were as ready to bring the system down in its entirety as their better educated countrymen wanted. But, in the end, that did not matter: The majority of the workers everywhere had become so contemptuous of their regimes, and so disaffected from them, that they would do nothing to support them. This finally sealed communism's fate.

No section of society was, and still is, less susceptible to generalization than the youth. Nowhere is the danger of distortion greater. One of the few safe generalizations is that the years of effort Eastern Europe's rulers put into the attempts to ideologize their youth were largely wasted. For many youth, the short-cut to a better future that had once beckoned had become a dead-end of broken promises. The brutalities that some had once excused as a means to a better end had become an end in themselves. And the socialist "achievement," such as it was, was a travesty of the original socialist promise. Many youth, therefore, quick to detect hypocrisy and inconsistency, turned angrily against the ideology, the leaders, and the system. Many, when younger, had accepted everything. Now, a little older, they rejected everything.

Some, though, unconverted or disillusioned though they may have become, had simply taken to outward conformism. Especially after the disenchantment following August 1968 many settled into conventional career patterns. It would be glib automatically to compare their behavior with that of the post-sixties' generation in the United States but, mutatis mutandis, there were similarities. Another large group turned inward, spurning both regime and many aspects of society itself. Members of this group looked to "alternative" politics and culture like many youth in Western Europe, particularly the Federal Republic.[30] They became, therefore, part of the large transnational segment of youth on the fringe of both system and society.

The many-faceted *Western* orientation of Eastern Europe's youth struck most visitors to the region immediately. One of the few achievements of Soviet domination in Eastern Europe was to make its citizens feel more western than ever they felt before. But many youth were not just Western-influenced, they were *American*-influenced. Their elders may have been drawn mainly to Western Europe; the better-educated among them may have aspired to, harked back to, or simply imagined, a central European identity. But the youth looked, not to Vienna or Paris, but to New York or Los Angeles. The impact of American youth culture, subculture, or counterculture on East European youth became important, not only culturally, but socially and politically. Anybody who ignores this point may miss an important trend in the future Eastern Europe. Western Europe may elicit respect; America exercises fascination. And it is not always rock, pop, and the rest of it. Riding the Jefferson Starship is sometimes Jefferson himself.

The pop obsession (with or without Jefferson) and its milder confrere, jazz devotion, were big parts of the transnational ethos. Nowhere was fascination with America more evident, or audible, than in these diversions. But, for many they were not so much diversions as a whole way of life. To some regimes, however, especially the Czechoslovak, which made itself ludicrous as well as repressive in its victimization, they reflected a mockingly destructive value system. And the louder officials railed, the higher the decibels rose. Much more dangerous—and subversive—was the link between this musical passion and the audio- and videocassette phenomenon. Cassettes could obviously be used—and increasingly were—for more direct political propagation. By the time the collapse came in 1989 they were already more than a nuisance: they were an arm of revolution.

Another section of youth, burgeoning during the 1970s, was caught in "single issue" politics—the environment more than any other. Nothing galvanized concern on this issue more than Chernobyl in 1986. Throughout Eastern Europe, even in Bulgaria with its less permissive rule, there was anger and concern. Only in Romania, by now terror-ridden, was the silence rarely broken. It was no coincidence that immediately after the collapse of communism, "green" parties sprouted in every country of the region.

In this growing youthful restlessness and spontaneity, religion, by the end of the 1970s, was playing an increasingly important part, drawing growing numbers to its different forms. In Poland Catholicism had historically been interwoven with nationalism, as it had, though less honorably, in Slovakia and Croatia. The election of John Paul II, of the "Polish Pope," not only immeasurably strengthened the self-confidence of the Poles (a characteristic they had never noticeably lacked anyway) but stiffened the faith in other lands, too. František Cardinal Tomášek, for example, long considered a typically pliant Czech prelate, took heart and by 1989, when he was ninety, had taken on a new lease of life as a defender of the faith. This won him much admiration, even from many Czech youth who, unlike their Slovak counterparts, had never taken religion too seriously. But throughout Eastern Europe, the less dialectical materialism appealed, the more youth turned to creeds teaching other things in life than those contained in communism's holy writs.

Many youth still hewed to organized religion—the established churches like the Roman Catholic, or, as in the case of Hungary or the GDR, the Lutheran or Reformed. But many continued to be drawn to the individualistic (do-it-yourself) type of religiosity, without prayer book, rule book, or offertory. This was especially true in Hungary from the late 1970s, but there were strong signs of it in the Czech Lands, too. As to be expected, this religiosity was fervently ecumenical. It worried the regimes and the religious hierarchies to about the same degree. It was likely, though, to persist after liberation, enlivening, enriching, and troubling the societies that emerged.

The Strands Draw Together

As long as dissent remained fragmented and inchoate, the communist regimes could feel relatively safe. But in the second half of the 1980s, dissent acquired form, purpose, even some order. As the following "country" chapters describe, the separate strands were drawn together, and it was the "Gorbachev factor" that largely did it. Poland, as usual, was different. Opposition there was already strong. In Hungary it existed but was much less consequential. In both these countries Gorbachev's emergence as a radical, systemic reformer strengthened and reinspired the forces of change. In the other countries, where opposition had been slight, it was activated, given purpose and hope by Gorbachev. In Czechoslovakia and the GDR opposition had existed for years, but its interaction with the population had been slight. The entrance of Gorbachev, his force of personality, the miracle of Moscow espousing change rather than repressing it brought opposition and society together.[31] In Bulgaria and, especially, Romania, where public awareness was less and the regimes more repressive—terroristic by now in Romania—active opposition had barely existed. But in 1988 it began to grow rapidly in Bulgaria. Through 1988 and 1989 the opposition multiplied, became active, and swept away the old regimes. The sheer speed of it has been well described by Ron Linden:

> Our jaws cannot drop any lower. Our predictions could not be more confounded: By the end of 1989 the face of Europe was totally different from what it had been at the beginning, even from what it was half way through the year. Nothing that had happened before, not even the breaking of the ground that had occurred in Poland and Hungary, pointed to this.[32]

The analysis attempted in this chapter may partly explain why it happened, but nothing could have predicted its suddenness, the speed, and conclusion.

The 1989 revolutions indeed took the form of a huge avalanche. The strikes in Poland in the spring and summer of 1988, and then the Polish regime's surprising offer to negotiate with Solidarity, were early warnings. So was Kádár's fall in May. The ground was beginning to give, but in eighteen months communist rule was swept away. Although some parts remained, the landscape was profoundly and permanently altered. What took a year in Poland and in Hungary, took a few weeks in the GDR, a few bloodless days in Czechoslovakia, and a few bloody days in Romania. In Bulgaria communist tyranny was gone, but reform communism, clinging, ingratiating, even sincere, remained. For how long? It was facing its day of reckoning.

Linden mentions that the rapid shrinking of the role of the party, once the alpha and omega of public life, was one of the most remarkable aspects of the whole process:

> In some cases, as in Czechoslovakia and East Germany, this change was accompanied by the formal repudiation of constitutional provisions guaranteeing the party its "leading role." In almost all countries, but especially in Bulgaria, East Germany and Romania, the process was facilitated by a relentless stream of criticism directed against former leaders by new authorities, whether communist or not. For some new leaders, such as Egon Krenz in East Germany and Peter Mladenov in Bulgaria, these attacks served as a means of separating themselves from the old guard. In Krenz's case the attempt was unsuccessful; Mladenov is still trying.[33]

As the parties weakened and then succumbed, public life became pluralistic and institutionalized to an astonishing degree. In Hungary, for example, fifty-one parties were expected to contest the parliamentary elections in March 1990. Millions of people who had been excluded before or had excluded themselves were drawn into the political process. They and the parties to which they (perhaps temporarily) gave their allegiance were reveling in the new experience, as if trying to make up for so much lost time. Glasnost triggered this proliferation and exhilaration. The media opened new horizons and exposed old evils.

Historical and emotional symbols assumed a new importance: Katyn for the Poles; the vindication and reburial of Imre Nagy in Hungary; the names and flags of countries reverting to their precommunist form. Living symbols and inspirations assumed high office, like Václav Havel, president of Czechoslovakia, Tadeusz Mazowiecki, premier of Poland. Old patriots, exiled for decades and branded as traitors by the communists, returned to be feted by their compatriots and to offer their services. The world was suddenly turned upside down—or right side up—after forty years. Communist history had ended, as had Soviet domination. East European history was beginning again.

And the communist epitaph? Alexandur Lilov, Bulgaria's struggling communist leader, put it well in early 1990. After saying he wanted to change his party's name to Bulgarian Socialist Party, he was asked why the system had failed. He replied: it "proved to be unable to implement the ideas of and values of . . . freedom, democracy, justice, human rights, equality before the law, equal opportunities for every member of society, and freedom of thought and opinion."[34] The list, though long, was not complete, but it was credible. Communism had failed in precisely those areas where its founders said it could best succeed.

2 Gorbachev's Policy Revolution

▬▬▬▬▬▬▬▬▬▬▬▬▬ It could not have happened without Gorbachev. Yet it was more by his example, even his neglect, than his exertions. The 1989 revolutions in Eastern Europe could not have occurred without the beginnings of a revolution in the Soviet Union itself and, above all, without what amounted to a revolution in Soviet policy toward Eastern Europe.

This was the revolution that was the most impossible to predict and for many (including myself) the most difficult to detect when it was actually under way. To put it in perspective, to give some idea of its scale, it is necessary to outline the premises and the purpose of Soviet policy toward Eastern Europe before Gorbachev.[1]

The Soviet Union saw Eastern Europe as (1) A defensive glacis. Obviously, this perception mainly applied in the military sphere, but it also acquired an ideological aspect in that Eastern Europe was partly seen as a protection for the Soviet Union against Western liberalism—especially by ideological conservatives. In the event, Eastern Europe proved less of an ideological moat than a conveyor belt—of both Western sedition and its own.

(2) A basis for an offensive strategy. This "springboard" function of Eastern Europe had three aspects: (a) Ideological. Here, Eastern Europe was seen as both the vanguard and the first fruits of the world communist movement—an example for the rest of the world to follow. (b) Military. Either for purposes of intimidation or aggression, Eastern Europe was seen as an essential forward base. (c) Political. Eastern Europe was seen as a suitable base for initiatives designed to manipulate Western Europe, especially the Federal Republic of Germany.

(3) The nucleus of an international bloc of political and diplomatic support in world politics. The building and expansion of an ostensibly

allied grouping of states was considered essential if the Soviets were to be viewed by world opinion in the same light as the United States.

(4) A source of Soviet political and ideological legitimization. This closely interacted with some of the preceding perceptions. But there was evidently a Soviet conviction that the continuing allegiance of Eastern Europe and the preservation there of a system basically similar to its own was essential, not only for the Soviet system's domestic legitimacy, but for its overall standing and reputation. Thus the ignominy incurred from periodic repression in Eastern Europe was seen as less damaging than basic changes in the system that could make such repression unnecessary. This is the factor that made ideas about the Soviets' tolerating any Finlandization of Eastern Europe seem unrealistic.

(5) A source, originally, of economic exploitation. This was soon part of history. Eastern Europe ceased to be the bounteous source of loot it had been in Stalin's time. But up to about 1954 it played a considerable role in the Soviet Union's postwar recovery.

(6) A part of the Soviet heroic mythology. Eastern Europe was the base from which Hitler attacked the Soviet Union. But, much more important, it was the last region to be "liberated" before the final defeat of Nazi Germany. As reflected in Brezhnev's emotional outburst to the Czechoslovak leaders in August 1968,[2] many Russians regarded the blood spilled in those last weeks of world war as giving them a proprietary interest in Eastern Europe. It was an emotional Russian factor not to be taken lightly.

These, then, for forty years were the main Soviet perceptions of the importance of Eastern Europe. Obviously, they did not carry the same weight. Nor did all maintain the same level of importance over four decades. And they were far from mutually exclusive; in fact, they constantly interacted.

The GDR and the "Northern Tier"

All six originally—with Yugoslavia and Albania, all eight—East European countries were important to Moscow, but some were more important. None more so than East Germany or, as it became in 1949, the German Democratic Republic. It was the division of Germany after World War II, and then (almost literally after the building of the Berlin Wall in 1961) the cementing of that division by the creation of the GDR, that constituted Russia's greatest single historical gain from World War II: the emasculation of German power.[3] Thus one of Russia's most basic historical security ambitions had been satisfied. The GDR emerged in the course of forty years as an apparently strong economic power, a remarkable achievement in view of its unpropitious beginnings. Its importance, however, was not so much in what it was, or in what it became, as in the strengthening of Russian power that its mere existence signified. This distinction between existence and significance led to much international ambivalence about the GDR. The GDR was often viewed with disdain as an artificial creation with rulers sometimes inhumanly repressive. But for what it signified in terms of European and even world stability, it was largely viewed, if not with satisfaction, then at least with relief. And only when the prospects of its early demise burst on the scene on November 9, 1989, with East Germans in the scores of thousands pouring through the Berlin Wall, did the European states, East and West, not to mention the United States, realize how comforting its existence had been. Nor were they then slow to realize just how precarious the stability of the post-World War II order had also been, resting on an artificial creation like the GDR that turned out to be even weaker in some respects than the rest of the Soviet Union's satellites.

The GDR, along with Poland and Czechoslovakia, formed a triangle of countries that for purposes of convenience was sometimes called the Northern Tier. Economically, strategically, geopolitically, these countries were a much more important asset to the Soviets than the countries to the South. Hungary, neither north nor south, was hard to situate, but, from any Soviet consideration of importance, could not be grouped with the Northern Tier. Of the others, the real Southern Tier, Yugoslavia bolted in 1948 and Albania had broken away by the early 1960s. Romania, after 1964, was not reliable; it had never been important except as a milch cow for Stalin in the first few years after the war. This left Bulgaria, unimportant in itself, but strategically valuable, bordering on Greece and Turkey, two unstable and mutually antagonistic Western allies. And Bulgaria's relative importance obviously increased as Moscow's three other Balkan satellites left, or partially left, the fold. By 1965 Bulgaria was the only loyal Soviet dependency in the Balkans, a region Moscow had totally dominated twenty years before. Had Greece fallen to the Soviet Union after World War II, which at one time looked likely, the Soviets would have become a Mediterranean power.

The difference, therefore, between the two tiers, Northern and Southern, could not have been more striking; nor could Moscow's perception of them. None of the three Northern Tier states would have been allowed the leeway permitted to Romania. Czechoslovakia's domestic deviations in 1968 were in themselves considerably less serious than those of Romania in intrabloc and international affairs, but they were far more threatening to the Soviet Union. The GDR, Poland, and Czechoslovakia, separately and as a unit, were vital to the Soviet Union's perception of itself as a great power.

The Soviet Aim in Eastern Europe

Soviet relations with the European countries operated on two levels: the national (direct) and the domestic (indirect). The national level involved relations between the Soviet Union and any given East European country, through whatever channel—party, state, intelligence services, military, personal groupings, etc. The domestic level involved relations between the ruling elites of each East European country and society in that country. The two levels were obviously far from mutually exclusive.

The Soviet arm in Eastern Europe, from Stalin onward, was to strike the right balance between cohesion and viability.[4] Cohesion meant a situation where—allowing for some degree of diversity caused by differing local conditions—there was a general conformity of both domestic and foreign policies as well as an identity of the institutions implementing these policies in both the Soviet Union and its East European dependencies. Viability meant a degree of confidence, credibility, and efficiency in the East European states that would increasingly legitimize communist rule there and consequently reduce the Soviet need for a preemptive preoccupation with the region.

The Soviet Union was never able to find the right balance between the two. From Moscow's point of view the postulates of cohesion and viability were complementary and interacting, not subject to separation. East European communist history, however, constantly showed cohesion predominating over viability—with the cohesion being produced by actual or threatened coercion. This was due to a general popular disdain for Soviet hegemony and the system and values associated with it, a disdain that necessitated various degrees of repression either directly by the Soviet Union or by the local governing elites, whose rule was guaranteed by the Soviets. With the perspective of hindsight it is now clear that real viability, with stability, was never attainable. It would have involved three types of basic change in (1) the economic system, (2) the political system, (3) relations with the Soviet Union. The closest these changes came to occurring was in the 1960s under, or because of, Khrushchev. But, reformer though he was, gambler even, Khrushchev would never have tolerated the degree to which change of all three types was necessary. It needed a gambler on the scale of Gorbachev to venture that—and then Gorbachev never saw his boldness as being so dangerous. As explained in the preceding chapter, Brezhnev in the early 1970s seemed to have stumbled onto a kind of viability with consumerism. But this depended on an economic prosperity that did not last. Even had prosperity persisted, this spurious viability would have been no substitute for the real thing. East Europeans would not have been lulled into an eternal slumber by better living standards. For one thing, rising material expectations would soon have exceeded the capacity to satisfy them; for another, economic satisfaction would have eventually led, not to political apathy, but to political activism, and all Brezhnev's organizational energy of the early 1970s would have eventually come to nothing.

East European Leverage

Any discussion of the history of the Soviet-East European relationship risks conveying the impression of a relationship so unequal that there was little or no real interaction. Nothing was further from the truth. Unequal though the relationship was, the East European regimes were by no means without leverage, bargaining power—if ever they cared to use it.[5] There were several sources of leverage, depending on the type of relationship involved:

1. Economic value. This applied to the GDR and Czechoslovakia and depended to a considerable degree on the machinery, consumer durables, and sheer knowhow that these countries exported.

2. The ability to turn elsewhere, diplomatically and economically. The GDR had this leverage through its unique relationship with the Federal Republic. The Soviet Union itself derived indirect benefit from this East German-West German link, thereby strengthening even further this East German source of leverage.

3. The performance of extraneous tasks furthering the cause of Soviet foreign policy. Obviously, the GDR with its burgeoning military, political, and economic activity in Africa was again the most noteworthy case. Czechoslovakia, through its own foreign aid, also had leverage of this kind.

4. A domestic weakness threatening collapse. This is a classic source of leverage and a major recourse of many small and weak countries. In Eastern Europe it was evident immediately after violent upheavals that shook communist rule and Soviet domination. Examples were Kádár's Hungary after 1956, Gierek's Poland after 1970, Husák's Czechoslovakia after 1968, and Jaruzelski's Poland after 1981.

5. Soviet indebtedness to a leadership that restored order after chaos or to one on which Moscow gambled in the hope that it could restore order. Again, all the examples cited would be applicable, and the Soviets almost always chose soundly in such crisis situations. The last striking example of this potential for leverage was Jaruzelski.

6. A new, weak, or indecisive leadership in Moscow. Andropov was simply new. All three adjectives applied to the Chernenko leadership.

7. A strong East European leadership firmly in control of a viable economy and body politic. No East European state since World War II was in such an enviable position—at least for a sufficient length of time. The Kádár leadership in Hungary came closest to it in the late 1960s.

But such a listing as the above gives little idea of the complex set of relationships every East European country had with the Soviet Union. It might, however, convey one aspect of these relationships that was vitally important: unequal though the alliance was, the East European states could not be treated as inanimate objects within it. The Soviet Union may have been dominant, but after Stalin it never was a case of *Moscow locuta causa finita*. For the Soviets the East European problem had always been there, and it grew rather than diminished.

It would have been a much bigger problem had the East European leverage been concerted rather than single and disunited. Soviet rule in Eastern Europe was always difficult, but it was made easier by the national enmities, jealousies, and rivalries that have dominated so much of the region's history. They persisted strongly under communism, and one of the few senses in which Soviet rule was stabilizing was that it prevented them from boiling over into conflict. The nationalism of most East Europeans often seemed as much internally directed as externally against the Soviet Union. And immediately after liberation in 1989, it was these traditional animosities that quickly reemerged, casting a cloud over Eastern Europe's future in freedom.

But that was for the future. Soviet-East European relations under Gorbachev quickly moved into a phase where leverage would matter less, where the changes became so revolutionary as to make the very notion of it partly obsolete.

Gorbachev's Inheritance

When Gorbachev succeeded Konstantin Chernenko in March 1985, Soviet-East European relations must have seemed in as much need of repair as the Soviet Union itself. The economic condition of most states in the region appeared worse than that of the Soviet Union (although a closer look by Gorbachev was to show that was not necessarily the case). The state of Comecon was perilous and leading to ever-growing recriminations. Moscow was increasingly bitter about the perceived disadvantages to itself of the existing trade structure: the Soviet Union exporting valuable raw materials and importing East European junk. "Make the East Europeans pay" was the general Soviet view. Some East Europeans—the Hungarians and the Poles, particularly—complained that as a commercial organization Comecon, still almost totally run on the barter system, was unworthy of the second half of the twentieth century—or of the twentieth century at all. As for political relations within the alliance, these had just been through one of their most turbulent periods since 1968, a period whose main features are worth recounting.

The turbulence arose because of the change in Soviet policy toward the Federal Republic of Germany as a result of Bonn's Intermediate Nuclear Force (INF) decision accepting American cruise and Pershing II missiles on its territory in late 1983. The GDR, for many years considered one of the most obedient of Moscow's satellites, refused to accept that the freeze with Bonn should apply to itself. It was obviously mindful of the profitably improving relations it was developing with the Federal Republic. The GDR was joined by Hungary and Romania in its objections to turning its back on Bonn. Even Bulgaria showed inferential signs of sympathy with their approach. Czechoslovakia rigidly supported the Soviet position. After a few weeks of defiance, easily detectable in the official media of the states concerned, the "rebellion" petered out, and a Honecker visit to West Germany, scheduled for September 1984, was put off, obviously at Soviet insistence.[6]

This unseemly disarray occurred just a few months before Gorbachev took power. It typified the decay into which the alliance had fallen, and Gorbachev's early behavior appeared to indicate a desire to take the alliance by the scruff of the neck and shake it into a sense of unity, purpose, and responsibility.

His accession to power in March 1985 was greeted in Eastern Europe with curiosity mixed with hope, and some apprehensiveness. He had been a member of the top Soviet leadership too long for him to be unknown, but not long enough for his profile to have clearly emerged. He was known for his relative youth and vigor, and all the East European leaderships expected these attributes to be reflected in his attitudes toward them. After the stagnation in Soviet rule which, by then, had lasted over a decade, even the more conservative East Europeans may have welcomed the prospect of firmness and movement. But what some East European leaders probably feared was a new broom being wielded with personal as well as policy implications. In fact, except in the special case of Jaruzelski in Poland, they all had good grounds for fearing that their advancing age and close identification with Brezhnev would disqualify them in the eyes of this impatient young man in the Kremlin.

In the event, they need not have worried. Gorbachev appears to have decided, or been persuaded, that leadership changes could dangerously rock an already precarious boat. Abrupt changes of top leaders could, after all, mean the overturning of a whole leadership pyramid, causing a profound instability nobody wanted. Besides, longevity itself was soon likely to solve most of the East European leadership problems. In the meantime there was much to be done, modernizing and reorganizing the alliance, strengthening Comecon and the Warsaw Pact, pooling inventiveness and resources for the world scientific and technological challenge, and making joint preparations for the resumption and expansion of relations with the West.

Once the threat to them personally appeared to have passed, each East European leader, in some way or in some degree, could find satisfaction, or at least consolation, in this new dispensation. Honecker was pleased that Gorbachev's ideas on tighter bloc coordination did not mean disturbing a relationship with the Federal Republic of Germany, whose economic advantages were obvious and whose political dangers he was still confident he could contain. And in 1985 the GDR leadership was claiming economic and even political success, the type of modernization and efficiency to which Gorbachev himself at that time seemed to be aspiring. Poland was a special case after the apparent crushing of Solidarity in 1981. When Gorbachev came to power in 1985 Jaruzelski appeared not only to be slowly mastering the situation, but was also bent on a Gorbachev-type modernizing reform. At any rate, there soon developed a unique relationship between the two men which was to survive the upheavals ahead.

In some ways it was the Husák leadership in Czechoslovakia that looked the most vulnerable. Installed as part of the post-1968 "normalization," this regime had more than any other been identified with the Brezhnev era. Still, the "normalization" seemed to be working, or lasting, and Moscow realized that the consequences could be incalculable if it were disturbed. In Hungary, though political dissent and economic dissatisfaction were growing, and Kádár was obviously showing signs of physical and mental strain, few suspected that he was on the brink of losing his credibility and authority. A new wave of economic reform was in motion, and, once the early misgiving over Moscow's new attitude to reform in Hungary had been dispelled, Kádár seemed likely to negotiate the transition to Gorbachev as well as he had the Khrushchev-Brezhnev transition back in 1964. In Bulgaria the veteran Todor Zhivkov at first seemed the East bloc leader personally singled out for Gorbachev's immediate displeasure. But he survived, and in his timeworn posture of calculating obeisance to Moscow seemed set for a few more years of power. As for Ceauşescu, he made it clear from the start that, if any adapting were necessary, it should be by Moscow, not Bucharest. Gorbachev, for his part, seemed content to go on doing what his predecessors had done—wait while Romania rotted.

Gorbachev's Second Phase

This "activist" phase of Gorbachev's policy in Eastern Europe lasted roughly between March 1985 and the beginning of 1987. For convenience it can be designated as Gorbachev Mark I.[7] In this phase he appeared the organizer (or reorganizer), coordinator, modernizer—a reformer, certainly, but in the "in-system" sense. It was the East European extension of his domestic policy. In the Soviet Union itself he was giving little indication of the radical reformism that emerged by the end of 1986. In retrospect, this first phase was one of "education," in which he realized the dimensions and the nature of the problems facing him. And he learned that all efforts to "modernize" a ramshackle Soviet Union would be self-defeating. By the end of 1986, his education completed, Gorbachev the "radical reformer" emerged, as reflected in his famous Central Committee speech in January 1987.

The East European reflection, or extension, of this change can be characterized as Gorbachev Mark II. It was one of laissez-faire, or hands-off and was in its way just as revolutionary as his change in domestic policy. For the first time since the end of World War II the Soviet Union was, if not cutting the leash tying Eastern Europe to itself, then extending it to the point where the connection steadily lost virtually all its former significance. The basic reform the Kremlin now sought to apply at home was obviously "recommended" for Eastern Europe. But it was not obligatory. There was no overt pressure. In fact, the clearest signal coming from Moscow to the East European states was that they should fend for themselves. The sheer novelty of it was too much for some of them.

This revolution in Moscow's policy appears to have been heralded by a series of top-level Soviet and alliance leadership meetings in the autumn of 1986 and to have been implemented gradually in Eastern Europe during the following year.[8] The result was that, in their response to the developments in the Soviet Union, to the challenge of reform, the differences among the East European states became more pronounced than ever. Poland and Hungary, each in its own way and in quite different circumstances, unwittingly embarked on reforms that were to lead to the overthrow of the communist system. The GDR, loudly proclaiming freedom of choice, denied the need to imitate Soviet reforms on the grounds of its own success. The Czechoslovak regime was ready for a fairly comprehensive, but "orthodox," economic reform, but, with the trauma of the Prague Spring still fresh after twenty years, recoiled from the notion of political change. The Zhivkov leadership made grandiloquent gestures threatening much, but meaning little. The Ceauşescu regime did nothing, except get worse.

The East European patchwork quilt, therefore, was very much evident as far as regime response to Gorbachev was concerned. But in terms of societal response—the response of the East European people to Gorbachev—there was a marked similarity. This was one of curiosity, hope, even enthusiasm, all three reactions tending to overcome an initial skepticism about anything good coming out of Soviet Russia. In particular, Gorbachev became the inspiration for reform movements in Eastern Europe and for growing societal dissent. He was also used as a handy and powerful weapon against the entrenched forces of conservativism and reaction. Hence, a crucial paradox emerged in all the East European countries. The more Eastern Europe was left to itself by the Soviet Union, the greater the Soviet Union's impact became. Whether his policies or preferences were being implemented or ignored, Gorbachev dominated the political agenda in a way no Soviet leader had done since Stalin.

Moscow was now regarded not as an impediment to change but as a catalyst for it. Gorbachev's criticism of conditions in the USSR and his call for radical reform automatically legitimized criticism of existing regimes and policies in Eastern Europe. Even if the Soviet Union were not directly pressing recalcitrant regimes to change, the indirect effect of his example was to unleash significant pressures inside most East European countries. The limits of Soviet tolerance remained undefined, but the previous deterrent factor inherent in Soviet attitudes was now removed.

Though Gorbachev calculated on change in Eastern Europe, he cannot have anticipated its speed and character, certainly not the revolutions it caused, striking successive countries like an avalanche. He was ready for change in Eastern Europe to be different from that in the Soviet Union, more radical and taking into account national characteristics, but still change within the socialist system. But he obviously could not have expected that the reforms he encouraged could result, not in the strengthening of socialism in Eastern Europe, but in its demolition. The regenerated socialism he sought was too little, too late for most East Europeans. They wanted not socialism but democracy, not the East but the West, not a new relationship with the Soviet Union but their own independence, with as little of the Soviet connection as geopolitical realities would permit.

This point needs to be stressed, especially to counter arguments about a Gorbachev "secret" or "hidden agenda." According to this theory, the Soviet leader not only expected, but actually desired, a basic transformation of the kind that occurred in Eastern Europe in the hope that these changes would then rebound into the Soviet Union itself.

The fallacy in theorizing like this lies not so much in the assessment of Gorbachev's policy toward Eastern Europe as of Gorbachev, himself, as leader. He was an improviser, not a planner. But even to describe him as the "great improviser" failed to convey the immensity of his struggle with the storm he unleashed. The waves he made, drawing on their own chemistry and intensity, became a tidal surge. Tossing perilously, he tried to ride them, never in real control, always precarious, visibility almost nil, destination undetermined. The fact was that, throughout, Gorbachev tried to insist on the preservation of socialism. Obviously, his definition of socialism broadened immensely as time went on, but it was certainly too narrow for what happened in Eastern Europe. In perestroika, for example, a veritable gold mine of political ruminations, he writes:

> I want to note here that it was not socialism that was to blame for the difficulties and complexities of the socialist countries' development, but, chiefly, miscalculations by the ruling parties. And, of course, the West can also be "credited" with helping, through its constant and stubborn attempts to undermine the development of the socialist states, to trip them up.[9]

Similarly, speaking in Prague in April 1987, the Soviet leader argued there was nothing wrong with the socialist system as such:

> Of course it is not the socialist system that is to blame, as our ideological opponents claim, but miscalculations among the leadership in the running of the country about which we have openly told the party and the people.[10]

Speaking to Polish intellectuals in Warsaw during his visit in July 1988 Gorbachev ruminated about socialist cooperation:

> We have noticed in Poland that you have the same concerns. I feel that we are following the same road even more confidently, taking into consideration the specific differences, which is obvious and clear. It was a great error to ignore specific differences; at last the dispute about the model of socialism is at an end. It is scientific socialism, and it must be realized in concrete conditions of every state, taking into consideration tradition, level of development, political culture, and the potential of each country. This is my view of the model of socialism.
>
> Nevertheless, acting independently, following the chosen road, we feel how much we need each other, perhaps as never before. . . .[11]

The progress in his thinking was evident. But the model was still very much socialist.

As late as July 1989, during his visit to France, in both Paris and at the Council of Europe in Strasbourg, Gorbachev repudiated any ideas about rejecting socialism. In Strasbourg he warned that any Western attempt to tear down socialism in Eastern Europe could lead to "confrontation."[12]

But Gorbachev's policy led to precisely what he did not want: socialism became not transformed or redefined, but simply rejected. Leading communist reformers had all along stressed that a basically new type of socialism was needed. They also became more and more convinced that Eastern Europe was indeed on its own, that Moscow was no longer willing or able to provide substantive political and economic assistance and could no longer be counted on to rescue any of these regimes in a future crisis. The Soviet withdrawal from Afghanistan, the announced troop reductions in Eastern Europe itself, along with statements by Soviet officials that the Soviet's long-term goal was the eventual elimination of Soviet troops in Eastern Europe, all underlined a single message: that changes in Soviet policy were not only encouraging but indirectly compelling basic change in Eastern Europe, too. And this change was to mean the unintended end of socialism.

As for the noncommunist opposition now taking over or sharing power in Poland and Hungary during 1989, its members had developed new theories and strategies for political renewal increasingly modeled along Western lines. Polish trade union leader Lech Wałęsa captured this ambivalent combination of sympathy for Gorbachev, along with deep skepticism concerning the reformability of communism, in an interview with a Western newspaper when he stated:

> I wish Gorbachev and his reforms all the best. But we still don't know what communism in its final form will look like. In contrast, we know very well which political and economic models in Europe and in the world have passed the test of time, and it is to these models that we must turn as opposed to attempting to "reform" failed ideologies and concepts.[13]

Such statements reflected two crucial differences between the USSR and Eastern Europe that came to the fore. First, whereas Gorbachev could hark back to, and try to pin his legitimacy on, an ostensibly "healthy" pre-Stalinist communism in Soviet history (however much disputed this "healthiness" was now becoming), this option did not exist for East European regimes where communism's ascent to power was intertwined with the evils of Stalinism. Second, the countries of Eastern Europe, some more than others, were historically far more integrated into Western political, economic, and cultural traditions. Despite forty years of Europe's division, the yearning to be reintegrated into the West was kept alive. And as the push for reform became stronger in the late 1980s, this yearning only increased, reinforced by the obvious failure of the Soviet system.

A Third Phase for Gorbachev?

Breakneck at the end, the element of speed, the almost blinding pace of the changes in Eastern Europe in 1989, must again be emphasized. The pace of change was almost as important as the change itself. Lech Wałęsa's statement in August 1989 after the formation of the Solidarity government—that what they had hoped to be able to do in four years (i.e., from a democratic government) they had been forced to do in less than four weeks—illustrates the acceleration of events.[14] In the Hungarian situation, which moved sedately by comparison, Rezsö Nyers, to become leader of the Hungarian socialist (former communist) party, when asked whether the party had ever anticipated having to give up its leading role, replied: "Frankly we were not prepared for the appearance [of this question]. In 1986, for example, we had no inkling at all that the question was going to be raised."[15] Subsequently, in the GDR, and then Czechoslovakia, it was not so much an avalanche that destroyed the ruling system, as a stroke of lightning. About the same time, ending a rule that seemed to have become permanent, Todor Zhivkov was forced out as Bulgarian leader after thirty-five years and Bulgaria was on the brink of basic change. In December 1989 came the Romanian Uprising, the spectacular, nerve-racking finale.

The sudden collapse of communist rule in the GDR and Czechoslovakia, and of the old regimes in Bulgaria and Romania, countries that had looked so stable, was partly the result of internal decay, partly external contamination, and partly the "domino effect." But Gorbachev who, despite himself, had originally sparked off the whole revolutionary process appeared now to play a last-minute role in warning some of these long-established leaderships of the perils of their policies. Seeing the growing discontent on the streets of the East German cities in October, he is reported to have warned Erich Honecker, the East German leader, of the dangers of clinging to power and of refusing to make major concessions. He almost certainly indicated that there would be no Soviet assistance to prop him up.[16] Similarly, unofficial reports of his warnings to Miloš Jakeš, the Czechoslovak leader, as popular pressure mounted, sounded plausible. There were even plausible reports later of a KGB attempt at a preemptive coup against Jakeš designed to put in a communist reformist regime and avert total collapse. Gorbachev must have known about such an attempt.[17] In Zhivkov's case, he seems to have been content to let him fall. There are some indications, even, of his connivance in it. Zhivkov's successor, Petur Mladenov, and his supporters were reported in contact with Moscow before staging their coup.[18] As for Romania, theories of Soviet involvement in the revolution remain unconvincing.[19] But there was no doubt about Soviet approval. In the fall of 1989, therefore, there could well have been a third Gorbachev phase—or Mark III—in relation to Eastern Europe. As surprised as anyone on seeing the system on the verge of collapse, he first warned and then let drop those leaders whose refusal to change had not saved socialism but destroyed it. In retrospect, he might wish he had introduced Mark III earlier.

Subsequently, in the face of attacks from conservative forces for having "lost Eastern Europe," the Gorbachev leadership insisted that it was not its fault. The situation could have been saved if only the East European regimes, above all the GDR, Czechoslovakia, and Romania, had stirred themselves sooner. A passage from an interview given by Shevardnadze to *Izvestia* on February 20, 1990, is worth quoting at length:

> There was a lag but not on our part. I am convinced that if the leaders of the GDR had embarked on reforms say two years ago, the situation today would be different. But they doggedly stuck to their viewpoint: We have built socialism, we do not need any amendments, we are proceeding on the correct path, we have solved the social problems in our country. . . . Honecker was not aware of the sentiments of his people. As a result, the time for reform was lost, never to return.
>
> But what should we have done? After all, we could not impose our position on Honecker. One of the basic principles of our new thinking is the rejections of *diktat*, of interference in the internal affairs of others . . . even though we realized that sooner or later the leaders of that country would encounter serious difficulties. Just like the Czechoslovak leaders. It was impossible not to see that. It is sufficient to recall how people greeted Gorbachev in Prague and Berlin. They hailed him as a savior and asked him to help, to exert influence. . . . If Jakeš, on coming to power, had started with serious reforms of the economic and political system, then I believe that many questions would not be so acute today in Czechoslovakia, too. . . . As for Ceaușescu, things were far more complex, of course. He was convinced that he was building precisely the society that accorded with the interests of every Romanian. But as it turned out. . . .

The Soviet leadership continued, then, to cling to the illusion that, even toward the end of the 1980s, socialism in Eastern Europe might still have been redeemable, just as, up to the very end of 1989, even after the Berlin Wall had been breached, it was still clinging to the illusion that the GDR, suitably reformed, could still survive.

In a variation on the "hidden agenda" speculation, some of Gorbachev's supporters in the Soviet Union have argued that he deliberately let the conservative East German and Czechoslovak regimes collapse because this would further discredit opponents of reform inside the Soviet Union itself, who by the autumn of 1989 were again pressing him hard.[20] Pointing to Eastern Europe, whose dramatic developments were having an increasing impact on the Soviet reform debate, the conservatives claimed a link between reform and ruin as exemplified by Poland and Hungary. (They were claiming the same for the Soviet Union.) In the conservative states, by contrast, the GDR and Czechoslovakia (Romania being excluded, for obvious reasons) the situation was held to be stable, and, while dissidents might fret and frown, the *real* people were alleged to be satisfied. There could be little doubt that many conservatives were, indeed, making that argument. Where there is doubt, though, is whether Gorbachev would have wanted to counter it by aiding and abetting the overthrow of the East German and Czechoslovak regimes, thereby ensuring the collapse of the system throughout Eastern Europe. The whole argument, in fact, sounds too "Russo-centric."

It would, in any case, have been a dangerous game to project East European developments more broadly onto the Soviet scene than they already were. One of the ironies of 1989 and after was the way reform in Eastern Europe, made possible by Gorbachev, interacted with Soviet developments much to his embarrassment and political disadvantage. Would the East European revolution devour its own patron? Reform in Eastern Europe had raced ahead while perestroika was dangerously stalled in the Soviet Union. For example, change everywhere in Eastern Europe by the end of 1989 had already involved accepting the multiparty system, replacing one-party rule. Gorbachev first resisted this, then hedged hopefully, and finally in February 1990 was forced to concede it. Economic change in Eastern Europe was embracing capitalism or many key aspects of it. Gorbachev resisted this, too, at first, only later partly giving way. Whether his resistance was due to conviction or political maneuvering was not clear— nor was it particularly relevant. What was to the point was that Gorbachev's opponents on the "left" of the Soviet political spectrum—the reformers— were now finding Eastern Europe a strong card to use against him. And conservatives were hoping they could still use it against him in the event of disaster in the region.

Even worse for Gorbachev was the "nationalist interaction" between Eastern Europe and the Soviet Union. By the end of 1989 the East European countries had all become virtually independent of Moscow. All that remained to be cleared up were the residuals, the forms, and the formalities of empire. This was certainly not lost on the restless nationalities within the Soviet Union itself. Thus Eastern Europe was impinging on the most vulnerable part of the Soviet body politic, indirectly contributing to the unraveling of the Union of Soviet Socialist Republics.

The different roads from socialism in Eastern Europe were noted by many Soviet citizens with either hope or foreboding, according to political taste. Would their country take the road of Poland, and, particularly, of Hungary, toward the civil society by constitutional steps? Would change have to come by bloodless revolution in the streets as in the GDR and, particularly, Czechoslovakia? Would the Soviet leaders continue to do what the new Mladenov leadership in Bulgaria was trying to do: stop halfway at the same reform socialism attempted during the Prague Spring more than twenty years before? Or—and this was a scenario haunting many—would it come to the "Timişoara [the Romanian] syndrome?"[21] Some Soviet citizens, keeping the impact of Eastern Europe in mind but looking to China for both a warning and a distinct possibility, saw Tiananmen Squares erupting, not just in Moscow, but up and down the land. Whichever way, Eastern Europe, which for forty years the Soviet Union had sought to saturate with its influence, was now retaliating. It was the Soviet Union that was susceptible and being made more vulnerable to *its* influence.

The Break with the Past

Obviously, it was the Gorbachev Mark II, from early 1987 to late 1989, that was the revolutionary. In this period Soviet policy switched from interventionist to laissez-faire in Eastern Europe. Gorbachev Mark I had been clearly interventionist. So, desperately, was the apparent Gorbachev Mark III right at the end. Mark II was quite different.

But Mark II turned out to be the huge miscalculation Gorbachev had to live with and, typically, try to make the best of. Judging from his pronouncements quoted above, Gorbachev could not think of any East European changes, however radical, on any basis other than socialism. This was the first big gamble he took—and it failed. The sensational defeat of the Polish communists in the elections in June 1989 and the formation of the

Solidarity-led government in August was proof of that, as was the ominous but less devastating process of dismantling socialism in Hungary.

This was a very serious blow but not a mortal one: a socialist residual and a safeguard for Soviet interests might still have been retained. As late as mid-1989 there was undoubtedly a sense in East European reform circles that caution was still necessary. In August the new Polish Solidarity government was still worrying about the "red line" of Soviet permissiveness and took care to give the defense and the interior ministries to communists, with Jaruzelski, communist leader through most of the 1980s, already installed as president.[22] Poland was a special case, perhaps, vital to the Soviets' link with the GDR. But for a brief period the Polish compromise appeared to serve as a guide for those other East European states in the process of reform. So much so that participants in Eastern Europe as well as observers in Western Europe saw a new "Gorbachev Doctrine" for the region emerging from the ashes of the old Brezhnev Doctrine.

The inferred Gorbachev Doctrine was seen as embodying three main provisions:[23]

(1) The East European states should abide by their existing bilateral and multilateral treaty obligations—Comecon, and especially the Warsaw Pact.
(2) Though within the framework of the multiparty system a noncommunist government could emerge, the "decisive" ministries, defense and interior, should remain with the communists or their trusted allies.
(3) However much "bourgeois-democratic" any East European state became in form, its "nature," "character," or "content" should remain "socialist."

Before dealing with the fate of this imputed doctrine (if indeed it existed at all), we need to deal briefly with the inexorable, keenly observed demise of that erstwhile pillar of Soviet domination, the Brezhnev Doctrine. Always dismissed by Moscow as a figment of malicious Western imagination, the Brezhnev Doctrine's main principle of "limited sovereignty" and "limited right of self-determination" in the region had been the chief assumption on which Soviet-East European relations were based after the invasion of Czechoslovakia in August 1968. It was also assumed during Gorbachev Mark I.

But during Gorbachev Mark II the assumption markedly weakened. After the beginning of 1987 Soviet statements on the subject emphasized the themes of autonomy, plurality, and diversity. Still, the Brezhnev Doctrine was not repudiated by any Soviet leader. Such a repudiation could be inferred from many statements, including Gorbachev's. But there was an obvious reluctance by the Soviet leader to go that extra step, or make that extra statement, that would have removed all doubt. And it was this reluctance that prompted many Western observers, slow to realize that a revolution was in the making (or actually being consummated), to assume that Moscow still reserved for itself the ultimate right to intervene. Actually, it seems likely that the reluctance was prompted by a general desire not to risk further destabilizing an already precarious situation in Eastern Europe and a particular reluctance to weaken further the post-1968 regime in Czechoslovakia. In the event, in a most appropriate linkage the Czechoslovak regime and the Brezhnev Doctrine disappeared together in November 1989. When the one expired, the other had lost its own raison d'être.

No sooner, however, had that happened when the Brezhnev Doctrine's pale shadow, the putative "Gorbachev Doctrine," seemed to lose whatever relevance it may ever have had. In September the eminently trendy Gennadi Gerasimov, the Soviet foreign ministry spokesmen, when challenged on the degree of Moscow's permissiveness, blithely rejected the premise on which such questions were being put by expounding what he dubbed the "Sinatra Doctrine." This was apparently based on the illustrious Frank Sinatra's famous song, "(I Did It) My Way," and was meant to indicate that the East European states could do the same thing.[24] Certainly by the end of 1989 a formal membership in the Warsaw Pact, as well as honoring bilateral treaties, seemed to be the only condition on which the Soviet Union still insisted. And the other East Europeans now took a more relaxed view of their obligations to Moscow than the Poles had. Most Hungarians, for example, looked forward to a new democratic government after the free, unconditional parliamentary elections of March 1990 in which the communists (now the "socialists" after their reincarnation congress in November 1989) would not be represented at all. In the new Czechoslovak government formed in December 1989, however, in which the communists were in a minority, the ministry of defense did go to a communist. The interior ministry, in a typical fudge, was to be run by a committee, but the responsible minister was not a communist. The new government also promised to respect Czechoslovakia's existing alliances. As to the "socialist content" of the state, Hungary for example, in a constitutional amendment described itself as being anchored in the principle of social justice; but it did not describe itself as a "socialist state."

And it was Moscow's passivity in the face of the collapse of communist power in the GDR that seemed to remove the last doubt about Soviet policy. The Soviet Union was not willing to intervene to prevent the loss of its greatest historic gain from World War II and the front position of its security system in Central Europe. Through this inactivity it was—and it knew it— bringing to the fore the issue of German reunification.

Before this happened, the Soviet leader had already accepted that the multiple importance of Eastern Europe to the Soviet Union—security, political, ideological, diplomatic, emotional, psychological—had now been trimmed to one dimension—security. But the permissiveness over the GDR, and over Czechoslovakia, indicated that Gorbachev was now resorting to yet another gamble. He was banking on East-West relations in Europe improving to the point where even the security dimension could be marginalized. He had reached yet another stage in improvisation. But he was dangerously running out of options, or fallback positions.

The Soviet Debate on Eastern Europe

The revolution in East European policy, therefore, came about not through planning but through improvisation, making the best of a situation that increasingly got out of hand. Systemic change became system overthrow; increased autonomy became virtual independence.

Obviously, the policy that led to this revolution could not go unchallenged in Soviet ruling circles. But it was difficult for Gorbachev's opponents to mount an effective attack on it at any one time because of its ad hoc and improvised nature. Clearly, once its results were becoming evident, the criticism became more focused. But in the course of his East European policy, as in most aspects of his domestic policy, Gorbachev was a moving target, easy to oppose but difficult to pin down.

Still, the general principles of his "new thinking" in Eastern Europe (though not their results) must have become known to a large number in the Soviet apparat by the end of 1986. Though they must have been viewed with suspicion even then, it is instructive to note that Yegor Ligachev, later to become the most vocal of Gorbachev top-level opponents, is on record as approving some of the early important changes in Hungary.[25] But the evolution of Ligachev's views is also instructive. His support for Hungarian reform stopped with Károly Grósz, János Kádár's conservative successor; Grósz, in fact, became known in Budapest as the "Hungarian Ligachev." It certainly did not go beyond Grósz to the coterie that pushed him aside and lowered the curtain on even reform communism. When it came the turn of the GDR and Czechoslovakia, Ligachev was solidly for the status quo.[26] His views must have been very common—initially tolerant, even approving, of extensive economic, with some political, reform, but then appalled at the breadth, depth, and speed of the change and at the degree of repudiation involved. Others, though, mindful of 1968, and suspicious of change from the start, must have felt totally vindicated by events.

But as the Soviet system there crumbled, Eastern Europe became one of the (many) issues on which even Gorbachev's group of supporters divided. The differences on Eastern Europe reflected the differences, first, on the quality and degree of reform considered necessary in the Soviet Union, and later on the consequences of the failure of that domestic reform. Gorbachev's political and intellectual support could roughly be divided into "Leninist reformists" and "social democrats"; the former subscribing to extensive political reform and often radical economic reform but within the limits of one-party rule and a "socialistic" economic structure. The "social democrats" leaned toward breaking the one-party monopoly of power, introducing private property and capitalist mechanisms and practices.[27]

Generally, the "Leninist reformers" were more conservative in their views about the East European relationship. Politburo member and Central Committee Secretary for ideology Vadim Medvedev was reliably reported in 1989 as an exponent of these views, with considerable support in the Central Committee apparatus, a body whose steady loss of power under Gorbachev only strengthened its opposition to reformist opinion.[28] On the other hand, it was the "social democrats" who favored, and in some cases forcefully advocated revisionist, almost revolutionary, thinking. Politburo member and Central Committee Secretary Alexander Yakovlev, believed to be Gorbachev's closest adherent and confidant in the party apparatus, emerged as a champion of the permissive school, as did Foreign Minister Eduard Shevardnadze.

In this spectrum Gorbachev's own position seemed somewhat anomalous. On Eastern Europe the course of events forced him into the revisionist (social democratic) school; not to have supported this line, at least tacitly, would have been an obvious and damaging confession of failure. Domestically in early 1990 he seemed to be following a zigzag course, first leaning to conservatism on the nationalities' issue and to reformism on economic and political issues. On Eastern Europe itself he was to say little in public.

The debate on Eastern Europe was taking place while a profound *institutional* shift was underway in the formation of East European policy and foreign policy generally. The shift reflected the growing supremacy of the Soviet foreign ministry in policy formation at the expense of the party (Central Committee) apparatus and the military, a development personified in the rise of Eduard Shevardnadze,[29] and the consolidation of power by Gorbachev. The party apparatus embodied the ideological dimension of the

Soviet interest in Eastern Europe that had remained constant for forty years through all the vicissitudes of Soviet history. The military embodied the strategic/security interest; this also had remained constant. Gromyko as foreign minister for twenty-eight years unimaginatively represented the combined orthodoxy of these two Soviet imperatives. But under Gorbachev and Shevardnadze the "new thinking" that steadily emerged on a global basis also involved the revolution in thinking on Eastern Europe, with ideological and military considerations having to give way to a more sober concept of the Soviet Union's capabilities and priorities.

To facilitate and then consolidate the new preeminence of the foreign ministry, Shevardnadze established a loosely organized body of unofficial consultants, most of them academics or quasi-academics, who formulated much of the deideologed concepts behind the "new thinking."[30] For example, Academician Oleg Bogomolov and Professor Vyacheslav Dashichev, director and deputy director, respectively, of the Institution for the Study of the World Socialist Economies, both urged sweeping revisions in policy toward Eastern Europe before it was fashionable to do so. But they quickly had the satisfaction of seeing their heresies become respectable—almost, indeed, the new orthodoxy.

The Residuals of Empire

Gorbachev began as if wanting to breathe new life into the Soviet alliance's multilateral organizations. This was particularly true in the case of Comecon. In December 1985, still in his Mark I modernizing phase, he got the Comecon member countries to approve the "Comprehensive Program for Scientific and Technical Progress" for the year 2000. Such a program, he said, was necessary to ensure "technological independence from, and vulnerability to, pressure and blackmail on the part of the imperialists."[31] (Note the language in the Mark I phase!) Once he had taken a good look at his Soviet inheritance, not to mention his East European dependencies, such bravado disappeared. He soon realized that there could be no scientific and technological revolution without the West. In fact, there could be no talk of "revolution," even with the West. The only hope was to slow the widening gap between East and West.

In the new Gorbachev that was evolving, there was little role for the old Comecon. Any attention now given to it centered on how to revolutionize it. The problems of Comecon cooperation had long been endemic and had now become exacerbated by the different and conflicting needs and wishes of countries in various stages of economic reform. The emergence of a defacto two-tier Comecon, with Hungary, Poland, and the USSR wanting to move toward new market-oriented mechanisms for trade, and a more orthodox group of countries including Bulgaria, Czechoslovakia, the GDR, and Romania, expressing varying degrees of skepticism, if not opposition, had led only to an increasing paralysis.[32] By the end of 1989, with all the countries on a new path, it might have been easier to agree on the steps to take. But the minds of the new East European leaders were now on cooperation with the West, not consolidation with the East.

The old Comecon died in 1989, aged forty. The Comecon council meeting in Sofia in January 1990 was its funeral service. There were no eulogies, just debate over whether any new Comecon would be compatible with what had happened the previous year. Most of its East European members would have liked to say no. They wanted nothing more than to feel strong enough to go their own way in the world and win the competition for investment, assistance, technology, expertise, and markets that only the advanced industrial countries (including, of course, Japan) could provide. But they knew they were not strong enough for that—not yet, at least. As an editorial in the *Financial Times* put it at the time: "But they cannot simply walk out. They may have hated being tied together, but they still need the bonds: in particular, they need cheap Soviet energy and, in the short term, the undemanding Comecon markets for their substandard goods."[33]

It was agreed, therefore, that a special commission should be established to review the future of Comecon. The deliberations of this commission were dogged by a serious dispute. The East Europeans agreed to the Soviet proposal that Comecon should move to prices based on hard currency from the beginning of 1991. But, led by the Czechoslovaks, they argued that this would benefit the Soviets because of their energy exports and penalize the kinds of goods, at least in the short run, the East Europeans would be able to export. The Soviets, therefore, should help subsidize the East Europeans' difficult transition to global competition.

This argument had some justice and merit. But it hardly received a sympathetic ear in Moscow. The Soviets, for their part, could argue that they had been subsidizing East European imports of their energy and raw materials for years, taking in return the shoddy offerings of their partners. The dispute promised to be drawn out and difficult. In the meantime, the *Financial Times* penned a fitting epitaph for the old Comecon:

> Comecon was an instrument of the Stalinist model of development. At its best, it assisted the industrialization of poor peasant countries like Bulgaria, even if that industrialization has left a technically-backward infrastructure within a polluted environment. At its worst, it was an

economic absurdity, ruining industrial and commercial cultures—Czechoslovakia being the extreme case, hence the Czechoslovaks' present vehemence—and enforcing a technical backwardness. That backwardness only became more pronounced as the advanced industrial countries adapted to computers and microelectronics, while the Communist countries did not.[34]

If a new Comecon emerged, and if it were to be successful, it would have to be as little like the old as possible.

However complex the questions regarding Comecon's future may have seemed, they were simpler and less consequential than those affecting the Warsaw Pact.[35] The sea change sweeping Eastern Europe would inevitably prompt questions about the Pact's future and the relationship of individual countries to it. If the communist system were being dismantled at home, how long, or in what form, could the international communist system survive?

Responding to a growing debate over neutrality in Hungary which developed in the course of 1989, two Hungarian Central Committee officials responsible for international affairs openly raised the question whether the de-Stalinization of Hungarian domestic politics required a similar reorientation of Hungarian foreign policy. The answer they provided can be best described as "yes but." The authors warned of illusions about trying to leave either Comecon or the Warsaw Pact unilaterally. But they favored a looser and more autonomous Hungarian participation in the Eastern alliance like that of France or Greece in NATO.[36] Another plan touted in Budapest went farther and outlined five concrete steps toward neutralization, each stage labeled with a West European parallel: "Danish" (in the alliance but not allowing nuclear weapons on its soil); "Greek" (in the alliance but scaled-down participation); "French" (left the military command of the alliance and no foreign troops on its soil); "Finnish" (totally out of the alliance but with bilateral security ties with the USSR); and "Austrian" (true neutrality).[37]

Neutrality had a special significance for Hungary because of its common border with Austria and the legacy of the 1956 Revolution. Moreover, in geostrategic terms what happened in Hungary was of little significance for the Warsaw Pact generally, giving Budapest greater leeway in debating its role. Leading Hungarian communist reformers sought to defuse the issue by embracing neutrality as a long-term goal, simultaneously making it clear that unilateral Hungarian moves toward a neutral state would be counterproductive. The strongly reformist communist leader Imre Pozsgay argued that Hungary was becoming sovereign enough, that Warsaw Pact membership was, therefore, not an immediate issue, and warned against any pre-cipitate action.[38] Issues of alliance membership should be resolved when the process of international détente had progressed to the point where the blocs could be abolished.

But the attempts of Pozsgay and others to defuse the issue were not entirely successful. Among the Hungarian opposition, leaving the Warsaw Pact became good politics as the popular tide of anticommunism swelled and the degree of Soviet permissiveness became more evident. Some regime leaders responded to the growing public pressure, sometimes awakening suspicions of opportunism. Mátyás Szürös, for example, former Central Committee secretary, speaker of the Hungarian parliament and interim head of state, who had been in the fore in channeling popular indignation over the condition of the Hungarian minority in Transylvania, spoke of neutrality in September 1989 as if it were a matter of urgency.[39] The issue became an important one in the parliamentary election campaign in early 1990 with the Association of Free Democrats, the League of Young Democrats (FIDESZ), and the Independent Smallholders gaining some electoral capital out of it.

Similar pressures for the "depoliticization" of the Warsaw Pact also arose in Poland. Whereas the significance of the neutrality debate in Hun-gary was largely symbolic, Poland was quite different. Among the East European Warsaw Pact countries, Poland had by far the largest armed forces and nearly as big a population as the GDR, Czechoslovakia, and Hungary together. Moreover, its central location made it the linchpin of Soviet influ-ence over Eastern Europe, especially with regard to logistics and communi-cations with Soviet troops stationed in the GDR.

Foreign policy was not much of a priority for Solidarity and the Polish opposition prior to the dramatic events which brought them to power in August 1989. During the roundtable talks between the communist regime and the opposition which led to the elections in June, foreign and security policy was deliberately excluded—a topic to be left to the future. Solidarity, though, while recognizing Polish membership in the Warsaw Pact, stood for the establishment of equal relations between the USSR and Poland. Still, after they were invited to form a government in July 1989, Solidarity offi-cials went out of their way to not offend Soviet sensitivities.

In their initial policy statements Prime Minister Tadeusz Mazowiecki and Foreign Minister Krzysztof Skubiszewski were at pains to make clear that the new Polish government did not intend to leave the Warsaw Pact and that it would fulfill the country's obligations under the treaties. Both pointed to the country's sensitive geopolitical position and the need to maintain stability in the region. At the same time, both insisted that Poland's sensitive location could not be used as an excuse for interference in its internal affairs. And like their Hungarian counterparts, they called for the deideologization of foreign policy and the depoliticization of the Warsaw Pact. In the long term, they made it clear that their goal was military neutrality and closer political and economic ties with Western Europe.[40]

But, whatever problems the question of Hungarian and Polish Pact membership and possible neutrality presented to the Soviet Union, they were nothing compared with what was fast becoming "the German Question." After the East German revolution in October 1989, and particularly after the failure of Honecker's successor, Egon Krenz, to stabilize the situation, the GDR began collapsing into the arms of the Federal Republic. Reunification, which only a few months earlier had been dismissed as a matter of generations—and even immediately after the collapse of communist authority in the GDR had been considered at least several years away— now took on a destabilizing immediacy. For Moscow this presented the most serious East European challenge of all. The threatened loss of suzerainty over East Germany was serious enough. But the looming certainty of a reunited Germany was not just a huge strategic loss but an emotional catastrophe. Coming on top of the other catastrophes which many Russians thought Gorbachev had brought on their country, some considered it a fatal blow even to his chances of survival. Most urgent of all, but just one aspect of this complex problem, was the question of 380,000 Soviet troops stationed in the GDR. Nearly everyone in Europe, on both sides of the former dividing line, wanted some of them to stay at least temporarily, in the interests of stability. Those who did not want them, however, constituted the clear majority of the East German population, on whom the final decision about reunification would rest. To postpone resolution of the dilemma, Gorbachev had proposed a new Helsinki (CSCE) conference composed of the thirty-five signatories of the original Helsinki Final Act in 1975. What he wanted was a breathing space. But events were conspiring to deny even this to him.

The Soviet side had been aware for some time that, as in the case of Comecon, there was a pressing need to give the Warsaw Pact a new rationale. With the onset of détente, the West in general, including the United States and the Federal Republic of Germany, was no longer the mortal threat it had for so long been made out to be. Hence the Pact's military raison d'être had diminished, and its internal cohesion was fast corroding anyway, for totally different reasons.

At the Pact summit in Bucharest in July of 1989 Gorbachev almost wistfully acknowledged that "life changes and no doubt this organization will change, too." As East-West confrontation was reduced, the Soviet leader continued:

> probably this alliance will be transformed first of all from a military-political alliance to a political-military one. And then probably we shall approach resolving the final task and achieving the goal that we have talked about, namely that this [i.e., the alliance structures] are not forever. The time will come when the need for these will pass. But I think this is a matter for the future.[41]

Just how the Warsaw Pact could evolve into a political alliance without the cohesiveness of an official common ideology and with most of the East European countries making clear their preference for more Western, and less Eastern, contacts was not clear. (This question will be discussed further in the last chapter.) But one thing was certain. Whatever became of the Warsaw Pact, assuming it survived at all, it would have to take the national interests of what were once its junior members very seriously. They were likely to become highly sensitive on this point. Each country now had the ultimate leverage: the ability to pack its bags and leave.[42]

3   Poland: The Crowning of Solidarity

Poland's democratic revolution in 1989 can be traced directly to the Polish "October" thirty-three years before. The frustrations associated with the aftermath of that apparent "victory," the rapid demolition of its gains, the way Poles felt insultingly deceived, cut deep into the national consciousness. The coalition of reform communists with a militant society seemed to have won a stable victory in October 1956. United under Władysław Gomułka, restored to the leadership by popular demand and with (reluctant and nervous) Soviet acquiescence, Poland seemed set to evolve toward a status that, if still undetermined, held the promise of both national dignity and domestic progress.

Polish hope soon lapsed into despair. Gomułka lost little time demolishing the liberal pedestal on which most Poles had placed him. Within two years he had "closed down" the Polish October by rescinding all the reforms to which it had given rise. Poland then settled into a continuum of disappointment and decline, punctuated by upheavals in 1968, 1970, 1976, 1980, and 1981. The bloodiest of these, in December 1970, cost up to fifty lives by the official count. It also cost Gomułka his party leadership, which was now assumed by Edward Gierek. Gierek brought with him from Silesia a modernizing, managerial reputation which, however deserved it may have been at the provincial level, was rapidly belied on the national scene. After a deceptive flurry of reforming energy, Gierek's leadership became complacent, self-deluding, and corrupt. A rash of workers' strikes in 1976 against food price increases, the cause of Gomułka's fall in 1970, marked the beginning of the end of his regime. This collapse eventually occurred in September 1980, just weeks after his delegates had been forced to sign into existence the first free trade union in the history of communist rule: Solidarity.[1]

Gomułka and "Polish Distinctiveness"

Gomułka's disservice to his country and to the prospects for reform socialism have been discussed in chapter 1. By dismantling "October" he effectively ruined any chance communism (of whatever variation) had of being grafted onto the Polish political tradition. He therefore helped make 1989 inevitable. In the shorter term he also hastened the birth of Solidarity, not only by his political vices but also by his virtues. These virtues not only took the edge off some of his reactionary policies, but helped preserve a societal cohesion and institutional basis essential for the eventual recovery of Polish liberties.

Gomułka's relations with the Kremlim disappointed the initial hopes Poles placed in them after October 1956. He had been swept back to power on a wave of national feeling. It was hoped that, as far as geopolitical considerations allowed, he would adopt the model set by Tito's Yugoslavia. In the event, he followed a course, not of "national communism," but of "national distinctiveness." It was less heroic, more realistic, and more suited to his own personal inclinations. (It was quite different, at any rate, from the conformism of contemporaries like Novotný, Zhivkov, and even Ulbricht.) For example, throughout 1957 he openly resisted the suffix "headed by the Soviet Union" which became almost obligatory when referring to the "socialist camp." He refused to join in the Soviet-orchestrated denunciations of the Hungarian Revolution, Imre Nagy, and the "revisionist" Yugoslav party program of 1958 as enthusiastically as Moscow would have liked. In a domestic affairs, too, by preserving (although hardly protecting) those two unique Polish institutions, the Roman Catholic Church and the private peasantry, he retained this sense of "national distinctiveness." He did his best to suppress the "spontaneity" which was the essence of the Polish October, but he did not systematically persecute those who had embodied it. Polish cultural life remained relatively free and quite dynamic; there was much private freedom of speech; and the Polish media remained the liveliest in Eastern Europe, with the spasmodic exception of the Yugoslav.[2]

Gomułka was able to keep Poland's national distinctiveness for four reasons:

1. His own stubbornness and determination, though often a negative, destructive characteristic, helped repel recurring pressures for conformity from Moscow, Poland's other East European allies, and from within his own party.
2. If faced with sufficient determination, Khrushchev was ready to tolerate

limited diversity in the interests of legitimacy and viability. As for Brezhnev, he paid little attention to domestic East European matters until the onset of the Prague Spring. By that time Gomułka himself had become alarmist about developments in Czechoslovakia, and a Soviet ally against the Czechoslovak reform.

3. The emerging Sino-Soviet dispute unleashed centrifugal forces which the Soviets considered far more dangerous than any Polish unorthodoxies.

4. Gomułka never claimed any universal application for his Polish unorthodoxies. The contrast here was with Tito, whose Yugoslav revisionism was considered a threat by Moscow precisely because of its ecumenical pretensions.

Gomułka's grip on Polish politics began to weaken in the second half of the 1960s. His personal dogmatism became more evident as his political pragmatism waned. In March 1968 during mass repressions against students and liberal intellectuals, many of whom were Jewish, he virtually lost control to the party's national-populist faction. It was probably only the overriding need for bloc stability after the Czechoslovak trauma in 1968 that saved him from removal after the "March events." But his final, most disastrous political mistake—the imposition of steep price increases on basic foodstuffs just before Christmas 1970—led to riots along the Baltic seacoast, then to his quick deposition and replacement by Edward Gierek.

But just before Gomułka's final act of folly, Poland had signed its historic treaty with the Federal Republic of Germany "normalizing" relations between the two countries and involving de facto West German recognition of Poland's postwar Western frontier on the Oder-Neisse. This was preceded by an eighteen-month period of busy European diplomacy in which Poland had achieved international prominence and respect. It acted, of course, with both the approval and support of the Soviet Union, but, for all that, very much in its own national interests. The agreement with West Germany, therefore, was in some ways the crowning achievement of the policy of "national distinctiveness" which now acquired a truly international dimension. Poland was communist. Poland was a Soviet satellite. But Poland was different.[3]

Though these retrospective considerations in no way rehabilitate Gomułka, they could make the total assessment of his legacy less negative. His suppression of the October reforms relegated Poland to a backwardness from which it might never recover, and it is for this that he must mainly be judged. Still, he left institutions, practices, and principles intact that provided the backdrop for Poland's two-stage revolution in the 1980s. He may have deliberately destroyed the Polish "October," but (totally unawares) he helped facilitate the rise of Solidarity.

Gierek, Solidarity, Jaruzelski

Between 1956 and 1968 the so-called Iron Triangle, or Northern Tier of socialist states in Eastern Europe, experienced a period of strong leadership stability. Walter Ulbricht had been East German party leader since the foundation of the GDR in 1949, Antonín Novotný had been Czechoslovak party leader since 1953, and Gomułka Polish party leader since 1956. But in less than three years, between January 1968 and May 1971, all three had been pushed from power. (In Czechoslovakia there were two changes of party leader during that period.) Novotný went in January 1968, Gomułka in December 1970, and Ulbricht in May 1981. The first two were dismissed for solely domestic reasons, Ulbricht because he stood in the way of Soviet détente with the Federal Republic of Germany. Novotný was succeeded by Alexander Dubček, who himself was succeeded by Gustáv Husák in April 1969 following an eight-month void after the Soviet-led invasion in August 1968. Gierek succeeded Gomułka, and Erich Honecker succeeded Ulbricht.

Gierek bounced into power on promises of reform and revitalization. During the first four years of his rule he seemed to be not just adopting Kádárism from Hungary but broadening and deepening it. In fact, whereas the early 1970s in Hungary witnessed retrenchment and even retreat, Poland fermented with activity and promise. The trailblazing, however, was largely confined to rhetoric. The second half of the 1970s saw Poland slip into stagnation and then slide toward collapse. At the same time, the goodwill with which many Poles had greeted Gierek evaporated. His regime will probably be remembered for two things: (1) It signed the agreement that brought Solidarity into being. (2) It was the first communist regime to have the immensity of its corruption publicly exposed. Not that it was the first corrupt communist regime, just the first to have some of its books opened— during the Solidarity period in 1980–81. In the event, this turned out to be only a curtain raiser to the much bigger exposé of the Brezhnev regime that followed after 1985 in the Soviet Union.

Gierek's regime did not just fall in discredit; it ended with the party's morale, authority, and organization shattered. The party limped on after Gierek's removal in September 1980 under Stanisław Kania. His hapless rule was at least partly vindicated by his honesty: he seemed ready to try to work with Solidarity. (Later, he was frank in his disclosures about Soviet pressure and threats to invade.)[4] Kania's replacement in October 1981 by Jaruzelski, already prime minister, was in retrospect one of the final preparations for the declaration of martial law the following December. Solidarity already appeared to be superseding the party in some aspects of its public role. Now the military, backed by the police and those sections of the technocracy prepared to cooperate with the new order, superseded the party in everything except the rituals of power.

The party, in short, was being replaced. This, again, was unprecedented. Right from the beginning of military rule, after the declaration of emergency in December 1981, Jaruzelski emphasized that his main aim was to bring the party back to center stage, with the army retiring first to the wings and then to the barracks. But whatever appearances of revival the party may have shown were fraudulent. The Polish United Workers' Party (PUWP)—the official title of the Communist Party—was basically no stronger at the end of 1988 than it was at the end of 1981. With hindsight it would probably have been wiser for the PUWP to have been dissolved when the military took over and a new, leaner party established. (The Hungarian case after the revolution in 1956 could have served as an example.) Jaruzelski did throw overboard some of the accumulated ballast of inefficiency and corruption. But the party remained a body without coherence or profile, with most of its members unconvinced of the need for basic change.

Yet, again, this degeneration was unprecedented. No other communist party has remained so impotent for so long, a factor that must be taken into account when explaining the initial Polish response to Gorbachev's perestroika. The contrast with, for example, Hungary is clear. There, the party, despite the steady loss of reputation and confidence caused by its failures of the 1980s, did remain the *only* institutional entity with any coherence until the end of 1988, when new political movements emerged. In Poland there were actually *three* such entities: the military, Solidarity, and the Roman Catholic Church—but *not* the party. The party in Poland remained an inchoate force with no real strength. There were many party members who saw the need for reform. Some of them were to emerge strongly at the roundtable talks in early 1989 when they made some common ground with the Solidarity representatives. But they never cohered into a wing or group, with a platform agreed on in the Hungarian sense. In this regard these members were both a reflection and a product of the decimation of the Polish party over the previous decade.

When Gorbachev first praised Jaruzelski publicly at the Tenth PUWP Congress in July 1986, he was endorsing the leader of a most unorthodox, controversial regime, a leader in effect with no real party, with no popular following, whose position rested directly and blatantly on military strength.[5]

Any Soviet leader would have had to recognize the service Jaruzelski had rendered the Soviet Union. He averted, with remarkable ease, potentially the worst crisis in East European communist history. He saved communism in Poland from extinction. But, relieved though the Soviets were, they also had reservations at least until Gorbachev took power in March 1985. In saving communism Jaruzelski had not restored communist rule, but imposed military rule. His coup was directed against Solidarity, but it was not aimed at restoring the system that had preceded it—the Brezhnevite system. This was the reason why Gorbachev liked him, and it was what they had in common. In his own way Jaruzelski was a radical, like Gorbachev.

As soon as he became prime minister in February 1981, Jaruzelski strongly supported the concept of *odnowa* (renewal) which a few reformers, particularly at the lower level, saw as the only means of avoiding collapse. For most party officials, though, *odnowa* was at best a handy pose till the situation changed. After December 1981, therefore, when catastrophe had been avoided, they considered it high time to return to apparat rule. The Soviet leadership believed this too—from Brezhnev to Chernenko. But Jaruzelski disappointed them. His aim was to revive the party, but it would be a changed party, with a different attitude toward power and those that it ruled. This alone made him a radical in terms of the ethos personified by Brezhnev and Gierek.[6] What he cared about most strongly was clean government, with power seen not as a mark of superiority but as a pledge of service. He also insisted, much as Gomułka had done, that, though Soviet hegemony was not to be questioned, Poland's special character and situation must be taken into account.

This kind of radicalism in no way made Jaruzelski a "liberal," an overturner of institutions or systems. He was a military communist, a special breed whose East European variety might need deeper analysis, inclining toward centralization and strict procedures. Not for several years did he accept the need for systemic reforms in politics and the economy. Then he tried to promote them with the same austere single-mindedness he had shown throughout his career. But during the 1980s his regime was not dissimilar—ideology apart—from traditional military dictatorships of the South European or Latin American variety—bent on regulation, modernization, centralization, efficiency, and the fight against corruption. Much closer to home, there were similarities with the prewar Polish dictatorship of Marshal Józef Piłsudski, of whom Jaruzelski (like Lech Wałęsa) had always been a strong admirer.

Immediately after 1981 the Polish situation seemed suited to central-
ized prescription. It was not dissimilar from that in the Soviet Union when
Gorbachev took over in March 1985; initially, Gorbachev also seemed to be
the reorganizer, the modernizer, the efficient manager.

It took Jaruzelski longer than Gorbachev before he realized the inevitability of systemic change. But he totally lacked Gorbachev's flair, even
genius, for embracing the political imperative of the moment. Jaruzelski, the
soldier, could never shed his unbending rigidity. He never embraced systemic reform, but dutifully submitted to it. Nor did he ever really understand its nature and ramifications; he was thus unprepared for its consequences. He totally lacked the political touch that not only Gorbachev
showed in plenty, but also Tito and Kádár, even Gierek for a few tawdry
years. In the end he became the military commander blundering with his
company into a minefield. At the close of the 1980s Poland, despite Jaruzelski's best intentions, was even worse off than at the start.

Once physical order had been restored after December 1981 Jaruzelski
single-mindedly attempted to neutralize Solidarity. Organizationally this
was done in a few weeks. But he was never able to break the popular
identification with it, although in 1986 and 1987 outsiders assumed that he
was fairly close to doing so. He first tried to appease a sullenly hostile
society by offering it *participation* in public life, a typical military-in-
politics gesture. When this offer was rejected, he indicated he would settle
for an *acceptance* of his power, however grudging. The spirit of this policy
was reflected in a passage in a speech to the party Central Committee in May
1983: "We must carefully study views that differ from ours but are characterized by a sense of responsibility for Poland. . . . We have enough real foes
who are passionate and stubborn. That is why we do not want to regard as
adversaries those who are not adversaries in fact."[7]

There was similarity of sentiment here—although, typically, it was less
felicitously expressed—with Kádár's clarion call of reconciliation of 1962:
"He who is not against us is with us."[8] But the Poles rejected any social
compact, especially when Jaruzelski could offer them nothing like the material inducements Kádár could offer the Hungarians. And the Poles never
were won around.

The implacability of the Polish population was ultimately responsible
for Jaruzelski's failure to achieve reconciliation. But some elements in his
regime were lukewarm, others downright hostile, to the attempt being
made. His regime, in fact, was a model of disunity. Though his success in
1981 made his leadership unchallenged, it did not necessarily make him all-
powerful in policy formulation, especially in implementation. He still had

to contend with those who opposed his whole policy approach and looked askance at the basis of his power.

First, it was the military dimension that many party officials opposed. Though it was precisely the military which had saved them, they feared the threat of Bonapartism and its attendant dangers. But many were carryovers from the Gierek regime and beyond, and they feared something more immediate than any Bonapartist specter: for their privileges, even their jobs. And not without reason, as it turned out. Martial law did not mean automatic security of tenure. While not questioning the principle of the *nomenklatura* system, Jaruzelski was intent on purifying it. One observer estimated that, between 1981 and 1986, 80 percent of the posts in the party apparatus were filled by new cadres.[9] Many of those purged were, of course, deemed unreliable because of ties or sympathies with Solidarity. But many others were the incompetent, corrupt, and primitive ballast which Jaruzelski despised as much as Solidarity had done. These time-servers were soon to find that the present savior could be just as dangerous as the previous threat.

Within the party leadership under Jaruzelski serious factionalism persisted from the imposition of martial law until at least the Tenth PUWP Congress in July 1986. It centered on both personalities and policies. There were two main discernible groups: one of "hard-liners"; another that looked "liberal" by comparison. In between were floaters, mostly opportunists uncommitted to either side until one of them appeared to be winning.[10]

For several years the hard-liners seemed to have the initiative. There were differences among them, but they were united by a hatred and fear of the Polish public for having supported Solidarity and a vague desire to return to what they called "orthodox Leninism." For several years the generally recognized leader of this group was Stefan Olszowski, an able political figure with good connections in Moscow who had come to the fore in the late years of Gomułka.

The liberals around Jaruzelski were mainly well-educated communist officials. They regarded economic reform as a prime necessity, with the creation of markets and independent enterprise as its main ingredients. Politically, they favored some concessions to former Solidarity supporters and the appeasement of society generally. Some also accepted the notion of political pluralism, but they insisted, at least for several years, that it be safely tucked under the party umbrella. Mieczysław F. Rakowski steadily emerged as their leader. But Rakowski had become a highly controversial figure since his acrimonious negotiations with Solidarity representatives in 1981 when a mutual antipathy developed that persisted throughout his public career. Rakowski also became the Polish intellectuals' best-hated figure. Still, within the definitions in Poland for most of the 1980s, Rakowski was a liberal. In fact, his fortunes and those of Olszowski roughly served as weather vanes that indicated the political climate of the period. When Olszowski was in, Rakowski was out; when Rakowski came back, Olszowski left. It was to be Rakowski and his reform group which steered the regime toward the overture with Solidarity in the summer of 1988 and took part in the roundtable talks in the first half of 1989.

The security apparatus also must be considered in this review of the elements in Jaruzelski's regime. The security apparatus was beyond politics, yet pervaded them. Many of its members were totally unreconciled to the aftermath of December 1981. What they wanted was repression; Stalinist-type terror held few fears for them, because they would administer it. They were bewildered by Jaruzelski's course, especially by his mildness toward his opponents. This was not the kind of normalcy they had looked forward to. Many particularly resented his correctness shown toward the Church, for which some of them always sustained a violent animosity. In view of this attitude and their freedom from legal restraint, something like the murder of Father Jerzy Popiełuszko, the militant pro-Solidarity priest, in October 1984 was bound to happen. In killing him they were both venting their hatred against the Church and their spleen on Jaruzelski. And there are grounds for thinking that their selective murders of some popular priests—much more cleverly carried out—continued through the 1980s.[11] Many of the old security apparatus continued in place, perhaps chastened but not changed, presenting a serious problem for the new democratic government after August 1989.

Very briefly, then, this was the Jaruzelski regime, its situation, components, and divisions. But to try to explain Poland in the 1980s through its ruling elite and institutions would be even more misleading than it would be at other periods of its history. The fact is that, except for about a year between September 1986 and November 1987, when it appeared it might be taking the initiative, the Jaruzelski regime was not directing Polish society but responding to it. Though Western observers recognized this, they failed to understand the situation because they continued to misjudge the tenacity and resilience of Solidarity and its ability to survive as a political force.[12] Many observers began to discount Solidarity, but it stubbornly refused to become yet another monument in the Polish pantheon of lost causes.

There were several reasons why Solidarity did not become a historical relic: (1) its ability to form an underground network soon after it was suppressed; (2) Wałęsa's charisma and realism—a legend, leader, and symbol all in one; (3) the ability of Solidarity's advisers; (4) the militancy of the younger workers; (5) the deteriorating economic situation; (6) the regime's own political ineptitude; (7) the Gorbachev factor. These factors allowed Solidarity to endure, revive, and then come back to center stage (they will be discussed later). But they do not totally explain what happened.

Ultimately, the explanation lies in the Polish temper. A catastrophe such as martial law can turn the public against, not the oppressors, but against the leaders of the cause that has been repressed. Yesterday's heroes become today's scapegoats. Czechoslovakia after 1968 was a case in point. For nearly twenty years afterward most Czechoslovaks in their despondency turned their backs on the leaders of the Prague Spring. But Poland was different. The nation did not reject Solidarity or its leaders. Its level of *active* support fell off noticeably. Workers became less impressed by underground Solidarity's occasional calls for militancy (always nonviolent), were selective about taking its advice, often niggardly in their financial contributions toward it. Other opposition groups began to proliferate that rather dimmed Solidarity's appeal. Many Poles, too, settled into "organic work," the Jaruzelski era having some similarity to that of foreign occupation in the nineteenth century when the practice of "working for tomorrow" began. Some members of the older generation, weary of a lifetime of turmoil, just settled for peace and quiet.

These signs were unmistakable and they accounted for the widespread view that, except as a symbol, Solidarity might be passé. But for a nation with a history like the Poles, those symbols that are identified with national aspirations are not just supportive, but inspirational. After martial law, Solidarity did not become the casket of Poland's defeat but the vessel of its hopes. What had begun as a trade union became a national cause, with strong intellectual support, tempered by struggle and betrayal. It was more than something to hold unto; it was something not to let go.

Without the Roman Catholic Church, however, Solidarity still might have gone under. The Church's relationship with it had not been without a shadow. Cardinal Wyszyński had hardly greeted its foundation with enthusiasm. As for Cardinal Glemp, though he later strongly defended its members, he initially appeared to greet its suppression with relief. Nor did he bother to hide his reservations about some of Solidarity's (nonbelieving and Jewish) intellectual advisers. But most of the bishops and the mass of the priesthood supported Solidarity, a few with rather more valor than discretion. It was the blessing of Pope John Paul II that made the final difference. His election in 1978 stirred the wave of national assurance that gave birth to Solidarity and then sustained it. And it was his third visit to his native land, in June 1987, during which he called openly for the return to legal status of Solidarity, that hastened its full return to public life.[13]

Jaruzelski's Failure

By the time of the Pope's third visit another factor was beginning to weigh heavily against Jaruzelski: approaching economic destitution. In 1987, some six years after the imposition of martial law, one observer described the situation as follows:

> Poland has one of the lowest growth rates in Eastern Europe, about 3 percent. Spare parts for industrial machines, as well as cars, trucks, and freight trains, are virtually unobtainable, and they stand idly rusting away. Sixty-two percent of industrial capacity is not being used. Ryszard Bugaj, the economist, . . . puts the rate of inflation at nearly 20 percent. State investment is growing at 4.5 percent annually, but since consumption increases at little more than 2 percent a year, the average Pole's living standard hasn't improved at all. Housing construction is practically at a standstill—which means that young couples, even those with children, are forced to live in cramped quarters with their parents, a situation breeding domestic tension and divorce. Polish products, once fairly common on the industrial market, are now so shoddy that no one wants to buy them.[14]

After 1983 the gross social product and the balance of trade improved considerably, but in 1985 national income per head was 20 percent lower than in 1979.[15] In the first year after martial law the Polish people had experienced shortages of consumer goods more crippling than anything since Stalin's time. Goods did become somewhat less scarce and the shopping queues shorter. But this was due to the series of large price increases which eventually, in 1988, shattered the social calm. The regime did, however, have one stroke of luck: agriculture, overwhelmingly private, produced well for a number of years because of a rational policy and kindly weather.

Looming over the economic situation and all attempts to better it has been Poland's massive hard currency debt. In 1989 it stood at over $38 billion. (In 1970 it had stood at $1 billion.) About 40 percent of the debt was owed to West Germany and the United States, and 40 percent to four other main creditors—France, Britain, Austria, and Italy.[16] Relatively, the debt may always have been low in per capita terms, compared, for example, with that of Israel, several Latin American countries, and even Hungary.[17] But that was cold comfort for both the Polish economy and the Polish population. Polish hard currency exports recovered gradually during the 1980s, but they could not cover interest payments, let alone capital repayments. In addition, the Soviet Union, an unexacting economic partner for thirty years, was now showing signs of business rigor.[18]

As if all this were not enough, two ominous new factors had emerged. The *first* undermined one of communism's basic claims to legitimacy: that it could, far better than capitalism, ensure its citizens, not just the basic material essentials of life, but also, however modestly, necessary social services like medical attendance, job security, child care, and education. (Housing, once on the list, was quietly dropped long ago as the years of waiting went into double figures.) These were among the human rights on which the "socialist system" was originally predicated. But it was now obvious that in Poland, as well as in other parts of Eastern Europe, the assumptions were no longer valid, the promises could not be kept. The *second* was the ecological threat. In some parts of Poland, especially in Silesia, this threat had already become disastrous before either the regime or many citizens could bring themselves to recognize it even existed.[19] Now it was feared that while time might be needed for other problems, it was running out for the environment. Yet the resources needed to begin to rectify the situation would be immense. Where could they be found, and from what other pressing priorities should they be diverted?

Urgent measures for reform were needed. All sides—official, semiofficial, and opposition—agreed. The martial law regime had inherited, and rejected, a model of reform—the Reformed Economic System (RES)—worked out by Solidarity's economic advisers. Its characteristics:[20]

(1) Enterprise independence, based on the "3 S's" principles; self-administration, self-management, and self-financing.
(2) Greater flexibility in pricing and the encouragement of competition, even to the point of allowing for bankruptcies.
(3) Central planning to be indicative, not directional. Financial instruments to be used to steer enterprises toward required performance levels.
(4) The introduction of "economic glasnost"—widespread use of the media, trade unions, professional bodies, the Sejm (parliament), and other institutions to publicize and debate economic questions and influence the planning center in its choice of economic decisions.

The RES would have gone into operation at the beginning of 1982 if martial law had not intervened. It could have put Poland in the forefront of economic reform, had it been implemented. At the end of the 1980s, however, though it would have still been revolutionary in, say, Romania, it had a mildewed look by the side of reform models in Hungary, Poland itself, and even the Soviet Union. However much capitalism was being added, the socialist frame of the RES was still intact.

But in 1982 the RES was too progressive for the Jaruzelski regime. (The

"3 Ss," fortunately, were retained and at least kept alive the principle of enterprise autonomy and internal democracy.) Whatever his common sense might have dictated, Jaruzelski was by instinct and by training a centralizer, and Poland's anarchic condition at the beginning of the 1980s must only have strengthened his inclinations. Yet even as late as the Tenth Party Congress in July 1986 he outlined an economic program—the so-called "attestation" proposals—that involved more centralization and government control than ever. Had these proposals been implemented, the "3 Ss" probably would have been scrapped. In the event, the intention was less important than the widespread resentment it aroused. Nor was the resentment just from opposition circles. It came from elements inside the ruling establishment—from members of the Sejm, in meetings of the usually predictable PRON (Patriotic Movement for National Rebirth) set up by Jaruzelski as a "popular" front organization, workers' self-management groups (an institutionalized expression of the "3 Ss"), from the media, and from the official trade unions that had officially replaced Solidarity and hence occasionally had to show some backbone. In fact, the opposition became so strong that Jaruzelski withdrew his proposals and ordered his advisers to come up with new ones.[21]

This episode did not receive the attention it deserved. It was notable on two counts: (1) The vigor shown even by regime bodies in opposing Jaruzelski. Official political life, itself, was beginning to respond to the resilience of the opposition and the popular defiance on which it was based. (2) Jaruzelski's combination of rigidity, uncertainty, and then readiness to change. This explains the inconsistency in his political behavior much more convincingly than the interpretation often given: sheer bad faith and duplicity. It accounts for his sudden conversion in the second half of 1988 to "socialist liberalism"; to the roundtable talks; to partly free elections in June 1989 and to acceptance of their results. His single-minded dedication to centralism was replaced by what seemed an equally single-minded dedication to liberalism.

Jaruzelski's retreat on the "attestation" proposals was the first, and least, of the three retreats he made between 1986 and 1988, each more consequential than the previous one. The second was in November 1987 immediately after the referendum rejecting his political and economic reform proposal. The third was the decision in the summer of 1988 to talk with Solidarity.

The period between the first retreat and the second—July 1986 to November 1987—was the watershed for the Jaruzelski regime. It covered his eventually unsuccessful effort to build a national consensus through his own reform program. When it was defeated—and this became clear only in the summer of 1988—the reform initiative passed to the opposition. Then Jaruzelski's retreat turned into the rout of communism in Poland.

The effort he mounted was serious, and most Poles were unprepared for it. It followed on a period of repression in the first half of 1986 when, for a time, it seemed that even Wałęsa might be arrested. Then, at the Tenth Party Congress in June came the "attestation" proposals, very much in tune with the prevailing rigidity. But after the congress the strategy changed toward conciliation. There were two reasons for the change. First, the opposition had obviously not been intimidated by the repression during the first half of the year, and (as already mentioned) several components of the regime's own support system had rebelled against attestation. But more important was the Gorbachev factor.

The Soviet leader attended the Tenth Party Congress. He had been in power for more than fifteen months and was already well along in his evolution from reorganizer to radical reformer, now understanding more fully the extent of the Soviet Union's own problems. He also must have realized that Jaruzelski was backing Poland further into the dead end in which it had been since the beginning of the decade. But he also was convinced that Jaruzelski was the only man to lead Poland out of the dead end and on toward revitalization. Poland without Jaruzelski would still be in more danger than Poland with him; Gorbachev continued to hold firmly to this view. Hence, the Soviet leader played a dual role at the Polish party congress: as demonstrative supporter of Jaruzelski and, at the same time, as strong counselor for change.

Jaruzelski lost no time warming to his task. The total amnesty he announced in September 1986 was a political and psychological master stroke which, for the first time since December 1981, gained him the national initiative. There had been partial amnesties in 1983 and 1986 which satisfied nobody. There was also an amnesty before the Tenth Party Congress, but this was hedged around with tantalizingly vague conditions. The September 1986 decree was what it said it was: a full amnesty. And it was plainly successful. It caused some shift in public opinion toward participating in public activities and was favorably received by the Church leadership, removing previous obstacles to negotiation. It also was a serious blow to an already divided opposition, which now became even more divided over how to respond. Finally, it refurbished the regime's tarnished image in the West, paving the way for the American decision in February 1987 to lift the economic sanctions imposed five years earlier. Most important, it softened the attitude of the Vatican. Pope John Paul II received Jaruzelski during his state visit to Italy in January 1987.[22]

The papal audience, however, turned out to be a mixed blessing for Poland's communist regime. Whatever its immediate advantages, it served to hasten the demise of Polish communism because it led to the pope's third visit to Poland in June 1987. Just as in 1979, on his first visit, he had given Poles the confidence to stand up to a faltering regime, so he now renewed that confidence and helped channel it toward a specific national goal.

But, for the moment, it seemed to be Jaruzelski who was confident. Toward the end of 1986 he established the Social-Consultative Council, designed to be a body of notables to advise on the broader issues of public life. Most of Poland's notables remained chary, but some respected figures did join, and the Church made no objection to lay Catholics cooperating.

As the regime gained ground, the opposition seemed to be in disarray. The issue of the amnesty only illustrated the organizational, political, and generational divisions that were now dividing it. Solidarity was contending with several other groups that were recruiting support and attracting publicity.[23] It was still the largest group and its reputation was unchallenged, but it had steadily been losing active support, and nobody saw it regaining its old powers. Some observers were already writing it off, even those still aware that a bedrock of popular opposition to the Jaruzelski regime persisted. What no one could foresee was the chance confluence of events that, within a year, would restore Solidarity to its national mandate. The pope's visit was probably the most crucial, certainly the most spectacular, of these events.

Its momentous impact was not immediate, and for the moment it was the regime that tried to exploit its apparent advantage. The regime hoped that the goodwill arising from the September amnesty and the momentum it was gaining would ease acceptance of the basic economic reform it was now contemplating. Everybody knew that if the reform were to be effective, it would be painful. The regime's task was to acquire the minimum popular legitimacy necessary for the acceptance of the sacrifices. Then, if reform worked, the economic upturn would broaden that legitimacy into unassailable support. That was the strategy.

For much of 1987 the regime's economic and political planners worked on new blueprints. The plans that resulted showed signs of both inner and outer direction. The economic reforms were influenced by the old RES, shelved in 1982, and the political proposals, vague as some were, reflected the thinking of the more liberal members of Jaruzelski's entourage and went some way to meeting the opposition's proposals. But, again, the Gorbachev factor was evident. The new Soviet leader had begun his domestic reform offensive at the beginning of 1987, and in both Poland and Hungary the impulse for change consequently quickened. The difference between the two countries was that, whereas the Kádár leadership was complacent about its achievement and did not grasp the significance, or realize the dangers, of the new situation, the Jaruzelski leadership, with no achievements to be complacent about, was desperately anxious to follow and adapt. The Polish leadership was at least responsive to the new zeitgeist, while the Hungarian was not.

The binding public referendum on the new proposals, held at the end of November 1987, demonstrated Jaruzelski's willingness to experiment. In retrospect, it can be considered the prelude to the much bolder move the following summer when the regime offered talks to Solidarity. The aims were basically the same: to seek the public's support and get it to commit itself to change on regime terms. The regime's failure lay in the fact that, as much as the public might want change, it did not want it on regime terms.

In the referendum the voters were asked to decide on two propositions: (1) a "full government program for economic recovery"; (2) a "Polish model" for "democratizing political life aimed at strengthening self-government, extending the rights of citizens and increasing their participation" in public life. In the event, the operation took on the aspect of fiasco. Both propositions were rejected—but mainly on a technicality. A majority of all *eligible* voters had to approve, and, though about two-thirds of those who voted did say yes, this amounted to only about 45 percent of the eligible electorate. About one-third of the voters stayed home. To complicate matters, many voters had been baffled by an unnecessarily complicated balloting procedure that somehow symbolized the doom-laden destiny of the whole venture.[24]

Many Poles, inclined by history to a conspiratorial view of the "my (us)–*oni* (them)" dichotomy, concluded that the regime actually wanted rejection so that it could now claim popular backing for a policy of *non movere*. But it remains highly doubtful whether Jaruzelski would have engineered a deception that also involved such humiliation. His mistake lay in exposing himself to a judgment that transcended the specific issues in question and covered the broader issue of public confidence in, and identification with, his leadership. These issues could not be isolated from public sentiment at the time of the referendum. Taking an economic cure was one thing; giving Jaruzelski a blank check was quite another.

The referendum illustrated not only the weakness of the regime's broader political conception, but of its managerial and procedural skills— the same combination that was to bring on the electoral disaster some eighteen months later in June 1989. The vote in November 1987 was not just poorly conceived, it was badly handled. Yet Solidarity, which had called for a boycott of the referendum, had little cause for satisfaction. Over two-thirds of the electorate defied that call (which was taken then as a further sign of Solidarity's diminishing pull), and two-fifths actually supported the regime's proposals. If nothing else, the referendum confirmed the divisions then existing in Polish society. Unofficial opinion polls in 1987 indicated that about 25 percent of the population supported the regime to some degree, with the same percentage actively supporting the opposition. The remaining 50 percent tended to float between the two viewpoints. Only later did a decisive part of this 50 percent tip toward the opposition.[25]

After the referendum, the regime announced that, regardless of the result, it would have to introduce steep price increases on basic commodities at the beginning of 1988. These were the price increases that started the chain of events leading to the rout, not only of the regime, but of the whole communist system, in the middle of 1989. Strikes for higher pay followed the increases within a month. With no clear instructions from the center, and acting autonomously under the rubric of the "3 Ss," many factory managers opted for social peace at any price and gave the workers what they wanted. Dangerous precedents were set. Preserving social peace meant encouraging social unrest.

The social unrest that began in April 1988 marked the beginning of the next historic round between state and society in Poland.[26] The strikes, which affected only a few of the major industrial concerns throughout the country, were both economic and political, for higher pay but also for Solidarity's return to legality. The strikes petered out in early May amid disappointment and recriminations. They did not spread and, though some strikers went back to work with bigger pay packets (though not much bigger purchasing power), their demands on Solidarity were rejected out of hand. These strikes, though, were important. They set off a process that eventually changed the country's political face.

But, again, Solidarity seemed to come out of this episode with its reputation hardly enhanced. Its internal generational conflicts had surfaced again, vitiating the effectiveness of strikes which had been badly organized anyway. They were mainly started by young militants who, like some of their forerunners in 1981, chafed under Wałęsa's caution. Wałęsa himself thought the strikes premature, supporting them only for the sake of a unity that did not really exist. Some observers were yet again writing off Solidarity. Others, not prepared to go that far, argued that its whole existence, purpose, and strategy needed redefining. Actually, the divisions that affected Solidarity, though serious, were endemic to any organization of its kind. What was remarkable was Solidarity's resilience in surviving them, this due in no small part to Wałęsa himself. He rode the rapids with skill and nerve, though every new ride seemed more hazardous than the last one.

The Offer to Negotiate

In response to a new wave of strikes beginning in August, the Jaruzelski leadership made its offer of talks with Wałęsa with a view to legalizing Solidarity. It was a sensational reversal of policy and marked the real breakthrough for the historic developments to come. Four interacting reasons can best explain it:

(1) The regime realized that, though it might defeat the strikes, the victory would be costly and tenuous. The strikes were always in danger of spreading and becoming an unsustainable national disaster.

(2) The regime sought to deepen the division among the opposition by a dramatic conciliatory offer, the actual substance of which could be scaled up or down as circumstances dictated.

(3) The regime's own divisions resulted in a decisive victory for the liberals, who convinced Jaruzelski that the impasse stretching back to 1981 was now degenerating into simmering civil war. The process might be halted by a sweeping gesture which would at the same time return the political initiative to the regime.

(4) Gorbachev. The Soviet leader visited Poland again in July 1988, between, as it happened, the two strike waves. Jaruzelski must have discussed the advisability of such a move with the Soviet leader, who must have concurred. In doing so, Gorbachev was adding his own unwitting twist to the unraveling of communist rule in Poland.

The regime's offer, and its acceptance by Solidarity, began the last stage in the process. It caused a minor upheaval inside the regime's leadership, resulting in the withdrawal of those who could not adapt to defeat. Zbigniew Messner, prime minister since October 1985, resigned, as did Zbigniew Szalajda, one of the acknowledged leaders of the hard-line faction. The ascendancy was now with those "liberals" who had long favored contacts with the "moderate" elements of the opposition. The liberals also supported some degree of institutionalized political and trade union pluralism. This group included the Politburo members Józef Czyrek, Władysław Baka, the regime's most respected economic official, Stanisław Ciosek, president of the ill-fated PRON, Kazimierz Barcikowski, Czesław Kiszczak, and, of course, Rakowski. Typically, Jaruzelski apparently took some convincing of the wisdom of this course but, once won over, single-mindedly pursued it.

Similarly, among the opposition, support had grown since the general amnesty of September 1986 for contacts with what were considered the "moderate" elements on the regime side. Since the beginning of 1988 the lead had been given by Bronisław Geremek, a medieval historian turned Wałęsa's intellectual equerry, later one of the giants of Poland's democratic revival. Geremek insisted that Solidarity be legalized as a precondition for talks; hence, his overtures up to now had been rejected by the regime.[27] But times were changing, and the dividing line between the moderates on both sides was softening, even blurring. This process eventually made the round-table possible. And it was the roundtable that agreed on the historic elections of June 1989.

Wałęsa's role during this period once again confirmed the importance of personality in politics. In 1980–81 he was the principal founder and leader of Solidarity. During the period of repression and illegality his real importance became that of a national, even international, symbol. But in the second half of 1988 he reemerged as popular leader and hero, vindicated, wiser, and politically mellow. (His personal arrogance was already suspected, but it had not become a political problem.) But the regime's dramatic offer to negotiate in August 1988 had actually pulled him back from the edge of what could have been a steep decline. Solidarity's divided, ineffectual showing during the spring strikes, coming on top of a long period of stagnation in the movement's fortunes, cast doubt on its relevance. But history gave Wałęsa a second chance, and, in taking it, he showed not just resilience but a touch of greatness.

Nothing secured his triumphant return more than his *mano a mano* debate on television with the leader of the regime trade unions, Alfred Miodowicz, a self-anointed tribune of the plebs, telegenic, and no mean performer in the medium. Wałęsa ran all over him, and on that one night in November 1988 more than made up for the ground lost in the years before.[28] He followed this triumph with a celebrity visit to Paris.

Wałęsa's return testified not just to his abilities, or to the power of television; it illustrated yet again the regime's political ineptitude. Offering to negotiate with Wałęsa was one thing, making him a star before the negotiations had even started, quite another. The television debate was probably a brainstorm of Rakowski, who succeeded Messner as prime minister in September 1988. His appointment was greeted with dismay by Solidarity and practically the entire Polish intelligentsia. His hubris of 1981 could not be expiated in their eyes. Now, the TV debate idea was probably a case—not the first—of Rakowski being too clever by half. Allowing Wałęsa to go on television (as well as to Paris) would, he probably thought, demonstrate his own no-hard-feelings magnanimity, as well as attesting to his oft-disputed liberalism. But once on the small screen, Wałęsa, whom Rakowski always despised, would be bested by Miodowicz. Wałęsa, would, therefore, die of overexposure. In the event, Wałęsa was not the one who died.

The Peaceful Revolution

The roundtable was the result of a basic change in politics, habits, and psychology in Poland, so basic as in itself to be revolutionary. The leaders of both sides—regime and Solidarity—had been under great pressure from many of their supporters not to negotiate at all. For the party apparatus, for example, with its many representatives in the Central Committee, the nego- tiations were more than a reversal of the policy of the last seven years: they were a betrayal of the whole principle of communist rule. For their part, many members and supporters of Solidarity regarded negotiation with "communists" as immoral and a betrayal of Poland. Many workers bridled at the thought of Solidarity negotiating with the people who had suppressed and persecuted them since 1981. They were led by some of Solidarity's leaders from that time, household names and heroes, like Andrzej Gwiazda, Wałęsa's old deputy; Marian Jurczyk from Szczecin; Jan Rulewski from Bydgoszcz; and Seweryn Jaworski from Warsaw. Many young people, too, well educated and less so, opposed negotiations, their implacability often alarming their seniors who had been through 1981, 1970, 1956, the commu- nist takeover, and even World War II. With opposition so fierce, the Soli- darity leaders, both trade unionists and their intellectual advisers, more than ever needed the support of the Church, not just from their own bishops but from the bishop of Rome. Without it Solidarity might never have ad- vanced to the roundtable, or might never have taken its historic opportunity.

But, however difficult it was for Solidarity to come to the negotiating table, it was more difficult for the regime. No matter how important the moral objections were for many of Solidarity's followers, the political reality was that the movement had already won a big victory by being offered talks. For the first time in communist history, for the first time since well before World War II in Poland, there was the prospect of a *legal* opposition. And, beyond that, the prospect of a democratic government. Democracy seemed only a faint hope at the end of 1988, but Wałęsa and those around him realized that an underlying shift was taking place in the communist system. What looked impossible today might be possible tomorrow, all the more so because the shift this time began at the system's center—the Soviet Union— not on its periphery.

But politics in Poland was still a zero-sum game. If Solidarity were gaining, the regime must be losing. This simple fact was not lost on many communists. And, in terms of both Leninist political theory and established political practice, what the regime was losing was nothing less than its right to rule. What was perhaps surprising, therefore, was that the regime's decision to negotiate came to be accepted at all, however grudgingly. It did, however, lead to two of the most turbulent Central Committee sessions, in December 1988 and January 1989, since Gomułka fell in December 1970, sessions that heard threats to resign from Jaruzelski, Rakowski, and others. But after weighing up the apocalyptic alternative, the opponents settled for trying to save something rather than risk losing everything. In doing so, the Polish Central Committee at least showed a certain realism. Many of its members had always mistrusted Jaruzelski, but they stuck by him now. In 1989 Jaruzelski was as indispensable in failure as he had been in success eight years earlier.

The roundtable talks in the first quarter of 1989 made history. They demonstrated that Poles *could* negotiate, and they revealed fascinating glimpses into the Polish national character. But the Polish public, unlike foreign observers, maintained no sustained interest in them, in spite of the publicity on television. After the initial excitement, many Poles found them too long, drawn out, and sometimes even irrelevant. What was most relevant to them was the deteriorating economic situation. The seriousness of this brooked no diversion.

The significance of this public attitude was not lost on the clearer-sighted members of either the regime or the opposition. For them it could be the harbinger of public impatience at both the law's delay and the complexities of democratic procedure, particularly when the solution of the basic problems of physical existence seemed further off than ever. Of these the most crippling of all was likely to be inflation. (Yugoslavia's case was already worrying many thoughtful Poles.) Inflation could destroy not only existing democracies; it could prevent new ones from being formed.[29] It was already emerging as the single greatest danger to a new society in Eastern Europe. The public, therefore, expected important and speedy results from the roundtable, and its impatience no doubt spurred the participants to come up with compromise and eventual agreement.

The roundtable's most important result was the agreement to hold Sejm (parliamentary) elections the following June under a *Proporz* arrangement for the distribution of seats. Sixty-five percent of the seats in the Sejm were allotted to the "ruling coalition"—Communist party, Peasant party, Democratic party, and pro-regime Catholic groups—while 35 percent could be contested by Solidarity. In the newly created Senate (re-created, if precom-

munist history were considered) the hundred seats were to be freely contested. The newly created (re-created) presidency was to have broad powers,
especially over defense and foreign policy.[30]

The roundtable, however difficult, marked the highpoint of political
consensus in Poland for many years to come. The discussions, though often
lapsing into seemingly interminable bickering, could be seen as part of the
energetic striving toward a civil society—the same process, mutatis mutandis, as that taking place in Hungary,[31] Slovenia, and, very slowly, in the
Soviet Union. As the discussions continued, the growing common interests
over means, if not ends, dulled the sharp edges separating the two sides and
made compromise possible. General Czesław Kiszczak and Wałęsa, the
leaders of the two delegations, set the example of moderation and revealed
themselves as effective negotiators. Wałęsa, in particular, lionized by the
world press, only enhanced his already towering reputation. Kiszczak, the
epitome of the "civilized" Chekist, interior minister, police chief, and erstwhile stalker of Solidarity, emerged as receptive and moderate, contributing
much to the eventual success of the talks.

But the regime side would certainly not have been so ready for compromise had it had even the faintest inkling of what would happen at the
elections. No one had such an inkling, certainly not Solidarity. At the June
balloting the Polish regime's claims to govern were annihilated, despite the
65 percent advantage in the lower parliamentary house.[32] This electoral
manipulation had been designed to ensure gradualism in the pace of reform,
a breathing space for the regime, and a period of preparation for the opposition, as well as to give Moscow the assurance that reform did not mean revolution. But what happened *was* a revolution—peaceful and parliamentary.
It went much further, though, than anybody expected, or wanted. Wałęsa
and his Solidarity advisers had all along been thinking that, all being well, a
Solidarity-led government could be formed in the early 1990s, say in four
years. But what was expected to take four years took less than four weeks. By
August, Poland had a Solidarity-led government with one of its chief advisers, Tadeusz Mazowiecki (Catholic intellectual, friend of the pope, "old-
fashioned" Pole), as prime minister.[33]

In retrospect, perhaps the regime's humiliation in the elections made
both the decisiveness and the speed of what happened inevitable. Only one
of the fifty regime candidates, a total nonentity, who ran unopposed on the
"national" ticket, got the required 50 percent of votes to be elected. The rest
were simply crossed off by an electorate intoxicated with the exuberance of
their freedom to say "No." In the newly created 100-member Senate, to
which the elections were totally free and without conditions, the regime

coalition got one seat. In the lower house (Sejm) it got only the 65 percent of seats agreed on. (It had contested all of them, but where opposed its candidates had failed miserably.)

It was the continuing obtuseness even after this colossal defeat that shattered everybody's schedule and calculations. Still assuming that its lead in any new government was assured, because of the accepted certainty that Jaruzelski would be the new president and of its built-in 65 percent advantage, the communist leadership tried to salvage as much as it could. But its crudeness in doing so only hastened the revolution. It should have been chastened by the fact that Jaruzelski was, in fact, elected president by only one vote in parliament. And it was not Solidarity that nearly upset him, but a revolt among members of the communists' satellite parties and groupings—the United Peasant Party, the Democratic Party, and a small traditionally pro-regime grouping of Catholics. Joined together, these took 27 percent of the coalition's built-in majority, leaving the Communist Party only 38 percent of the Sejm's 460 seats. The satellite parties, having so recently felt the winds of change at the elections and seeing Communist domination gravely shattered, now decided to think, act, and juggle for themselves. Hence Jaruzelski's demeaning one-vote majority.

Still, the regime leadership, without sensitivity itself, insisted on affronting everybody else's sensitivities. Jaruzelski, elected president, had to give up his Communist Party leadership. But this went to Rakowski, recently prime minister, the intellectuals' bête noire and the workers' old enemy. Jaruzelski then asked General Kiszczak to form a government, the same Kiszczak who, despite the good impression he had recently made, had been, as the minister of interior and police chief, one of the main props of martial law. It was too much for almost everybody. It was certainly too much for many United Peasant and the Democratic party members. Also too much for Wałęsa, who, much against his better inclinations, began negotiations with the numerous rebels in both these parties.[34] The result was Poland's first democratic government since well before World War II—a government dedicated to democracy, market capitalism, social welfare, and a foreign policy that took into account both the Polish raison d'état and geopolitical considerations.

The New Order

One of the most striking aspects of the new order after August 1989 was the speed with which communism became politically irrelevant. The old order which had dominated political, economic, and cultural life for more than forty years melted away, not without trace, it is true, but without impact, influence, or effect. Jaruzelski, still a communist, as he readily admitted, but adapting to the new situation with dignity, even honor, may have been important in the initial stages of the new democracy as a guarantee of stability and a reassurance to Moscow.[35] But, as it became evident that the reassurance to Moscow was not as important as was once thought (or feared), his value diminished and voices urging his resignation were to become louder.[36] As for Generals Kiszczak and Florian Siwicki—interior and defense ministers, respectively, also held over because of the "red line" that many now claimed had never existed—they cooperated, like Jaruzelski, with the new order, not only in the letter, but apparently also in the spirit, of Poland's democratic decision. Their value lay in creating no difficulties and, much to the surprise (and chagrin) of those who had seen a *laager* complex forming among the police and the military, they were remarkably cooperative. (Some suspicious Poles thought ostentatiously so.)

As for the Communist Party—the Polish United Workers' Party—within six months it had disappeared. At its last congress in January 1990, with public support dropping to an estimated 6 percent, it voted to go into liquidation and reemerge as the Social Democracy of the Polish Republic. Actually, it split into two: a smaller group calling itself the Social Democratic Union formed, even more to the center than the main new party.[37] There was also a possibility that a third grouping would soon emerge, this time composed of hard-liners, insistent that the swing toward the center was opportunist and not in the interests of the party's main constituency: the working class. It was not just the "last-stand" mentality that prompted this third group, but the political calculation that (the hoped-for) widespread discontent with the new government's economic reforms would redound to their benefit.

The leaders of both Social Democracy and the Social Democratic Union were mostly a "modern," attractive bunch—the kind to make Edward Gierek stare at his television set in stupefaction and Władysław Gomułka turn over in his grave. They thought, talked, spoke, behaved—and almost looked—like Italian communist leaders. Aleksander Kwaśniewski, Social Democracy's new leader, was liked and respected, a friend, incidentally, of Adam Michnik, a fact speaking well for both of them. Many Poles thought he was in the wrong company. They thought the same way about Leszek Miller and Sławomir Wiatr, two of Kwaśniewski's lieutenants. The leader of the Social Democratic Union, Tadeusz Fischbach, was no newcomer to the political scene. Though party leader in Gdansk when Solidarity was formed, he always had a reputation for "liberalism" and enjoyed the respect of most

Solidarity leaders. Though now appearing more progressive than Social Democracy leaders, Fischbach looked sadly like "yesterday's man" in comparison with them; still a necessary reminder that, bad as the PUWP had been, it also had a share of decency and political sense.

But if Kwaśniewski, Miller, Wiatr, and company were "today's men" in the erstwhile communist context, did they have a tomorrow? In 1990 it hardly looked so. Rakowski was quoted as saying it would be ten years before the communists could think about getting back to power.[38] As yet they had formulated no long-term strategy, but the more perceptive of them were hoping for an eventual "neo-socialist" comeback. They rationalized as follows. Give the massive antisocialist, procapitalism mood a chance to spend itself. Whatever early successes capitalism might achieve, it would be accompanied by failures—and these failures would eventually predominate. Then a more caring, compassionate view of society would prevail and that would be the chance for a new party like Social Democracy, now thoroughly divested of its communist past. Then would be the time to cooperate with the strong social-democratic element within Solidarity (if, indeed, Solidarity itself had not by that time split along capitalist-social democratic lines) and with the many Polish citizens who subscribed to Catholic social doctrine, so forcefully expressed by the Polish Pope John Paul II.[39] How realistic these hopes were remained to be seen, but they reflected the only type of thinking that might eventually get the new Social Democracy back into the mainstream of Polish public life.

In the meantime, the new democratic government began its work of reconstruction. The key to its future, and to Poland's, was what a British observer called "one of the most remarkable experiments ever carried out, anywhere." "The country has been turned," he went on, "into an economic laboratory in which a packet of measures—which might normally be implemented over a decade or more, is being distributed over a few months."[40]

The government's immediate aim was to bring inflation, soaring to 1,000 percent at the beginning of 1990, down to single figures (on a monthly basis) in just a few months. State subsidies, which took up 31 percent of all budget spending in 1989, were abolished. An independent banking system was established and a nationwide policy of privatization inaugurated. The zloty was made convertible with the dollar at one stroke of the pen. As a result of the abolition of subsidies, the price of coal increased 700 percent at the beginning of 1990, train, bus, and train fares by 250 percent, and postal services by 300 percent. Staple foods like bread, milk, sugar, and most kinds of meat more than doubled. As if this were not enough punishment for the consumer, a strict program of holding down wages was initiated.[41] This was an essential measure because for several years under the Jaruzelski-Messner-Rakowski-led governments workers had responded to price increases by demanding huge wage increases, and getting them.

It was a draconian program, and many observers doubted whether the Poles would put up with it. Its social consequences soon showed. Some 56,000 workers had registered as unemployed by the end of January 1990—hardly an alarming figure by Western standards but a grave shock in a society led to believe that full employment was one of the basic human rights. And there was a lot more to come—with unemployment insurance quite inadequate. (By the end of March 1990 the figure was 267,000, and it was rising rapidly.)[42] Warsovians were likely to be the least hit by unemployment because of the relatively big labor market there and the chance of moving from one factory to another without having to move their homes. But outside Warsaw a new job, if any could be found, usually meant changing residence. And that was when the acute housing shortage began to bite. Polish citizens lucky to have their own apartments found their rents rising considerably (to help meet costs) as a consequence of economic reform. Moreover, in the process of laying workers off, there were growing complaints of unfairness, the settling of old personal and political scores. Weaker members of society—handicapped workers, pregnant women—sometimes had to go first.[43] There also was much anger among workers over communist directors taking care of themselves (often by becoming Milton Friedman converts overnight) and of their old comrades of the lost cause. In this respect, much was similar to the situation in Hungary. The rapidity with which numerous communists were converted to capitalism led to the joke—heard in both Warsaw and Budapest—that there was "a traffic jam on the road to Damascus."

Finally, many workers of condemned factories could not understand the grounds on which the decision had been made or the speed with which it was being implemented. Meanwhile, on the land, many farmers had a different kind of worry. Despite the huge increases in food prices they were convinced that either: (1) they were still not getting adequate return; (2) if they withheld their produce from the market, food prices would go even higher. Either way it hardly improved relations between town and country.

Still, popular loyalty to the government continued into 1990. There was much grumbling—ominous at times—and a rash of strikes in the Silesian coal-mining area. Certainly the old official unions under Miodowicz were waiting to exploit any difficulties. But the Solidarity government started off with probably more legitimacy than any other government in Poland's entire history, and Poles seemed prepared to sacrifice much in supporting it.

It was not only a popular government; it was a good one.[44] Its key figure was undoubtedly Mazowiecki, quiet, dignified with a suggestion of physically frailty yet strong in moral authority, a gentleman of the highest order, yet by no means unaware of the pitfalls of political life. Among members of the government he led the popularity polls along with Jacek Kuroń, the labor and social affairs minister. It would be difficult to imagine anybody less like Mazowiecki than Kuroń. Kuroń brought to office a communist past (including, a Trotskyist flirtation), intellectual brilliance, personal and political dynamism, a suggestion of irresponsibility, an honorable jail record beginning in 1965, and an abundance of human compassion. It was too early to say what kind of a minister he would make. But as a publicist for the government explaining its policies and the need for sacrifice he was unparalleled. Kuroń's skill in articulating government policy was all the more noteworthy because he had been leader of the "social-democratic" group in Solidarity that had wanted a more gradual, less "capitalistic" economic reform.

The minister whose policies were adopted was Leszek Balcerowicz, finance minister and architect of the economic reform. Aloof, dedicated, and without public emotion, Balcerowicz did not appeal to his compatriots the way most of his colleagues did. But he had principles, and believed in what he was doing, and this elicited a certain respect.[45] He was ably supported by the highly personable Marcin Święcicki, a quintessentially Polish amalgam of two diametrically opposed characteristics: communist and admirer of Professor Friedman. As minister of foreign trade, seeking to balance Poland's ties with the East with its gravitation westward, there might have been a certain logic in the combination. Krzysztof Skubiszewski, foreign minister, formerly professor of international relations at Poznań, and expert on Germany, had the totally unexpected problem of German reunification thrown in his lap. It was a gigantic issue that the new government, with its domestic agenda and the task of disentangling from the Soviet alliance, could well have done without. Skubiszewski suddenly became one of the most important and probably the most visible member of the government. He needed to establish a firm Polish relationship with the European Community and the United States and, most vital of all, a balanced relationship between the new Germany and what would probably be the new Russia. Poland had recovered its independence, but also its old historical dilemma.

Outside government, but crucial to it, was Adam Michnik, now editor of *Gazeta Wyborcza*, the Solidarity newspaper, who along with Kuroń had been the most watched and often wanted enemy of the former Jaruzelski regime. Now in articles and speeches and by personal example, he was urging Poles to reconciliation, to reconstruction rather than revenge. His was the voice of a better Poland urging fellowship with, and understanding of, neighbors and other nations. So also was the voice of Bronisław Geremek, the old Solidarity adviser, now leader of the Solidarity group in the Sejm. Geremek's contribution to Poland's rebirth would one day be realized by everybody. He put not just Poles in his debt, but the rest of humanity, too.

Finally, *stupor mundi,* Lech Wałęsa had gone from out-of-work shipyard electrician to uncrowned king of Poland in ten years. His contribution to Poland was almost unimaginable, and his place in the Polish pantheon of heroes already assured. But his country still needed the qualities he showed over the previous decade. In early 1990, many were beginning to worry. Would he still bring those attributes to bear, or would his arrogance and overweening vanity supersede them? Such was his power and stature that Poland's future seemed to depend on the answer. Wałęsa's virtues had made him a savior. His vices could make him a spoiler.

By mid-1990 Wałęsa had deliberately broken the political consensus he had helped to create and which had seemed likely to steer the economic reform through the social tensions it was unavoidably creating. He claimed he was doing this to hasten the introduction of real democratic reform. But his repeated attacks on his old colleagues in the Mazowiecki government, including Mazowiecki himself, his unabashed determination to become president of Poland, and the increasingly megalomaniac nature of his behavior threatened to sink the country in a morass of controversy and disunity.

4   Hungary: Toward the Civil Society

▬▬▬▬▬▬▬▬▬▬▬▬▬ Hungary's march toward constitutional government could retrace its steps to 1956. Just as Poland's democratic revolution had its origins in the Polish "October," so could Hungary's be dated back to the revolution—a revolution that, though defeated, continued to cast its long shadow over Hungarian life and wielded a powerful symbolism during the dismantling of communism and the building of democracy. In November 1956 the defeat looked decisive and permanent, but it was the revolution's apparent victors who became the vanquished more than thirty years later.

Paradoxically, it was János Kádár, the victor of 1956, who effectively prepared the ground for his, and for communism's, eventual defeat. In chapter 3 it is argued that Gomułka unwittingly helped prepare for Solidarity in Poland. Kádár much more demonstrably and directly helped prepare for Hungary's turn to democracy.

János Kádár began his rule with the stigma of having betrayed the revolution, and until the end of the 1960s his policy was generally one of repression. But he was soon to reveal a political dexterity, flexibility, and receptiveness, allied to an attractive public persona, that helped bring a remarkable change in Hungarian life. His success in conciliation was dramatically shown in 1964, eight years after the revolution and only four years after repression ended and revival began. When Khrushchev was ousted in October of that year, many Hungarians obviously feared that the same thing might happen to Kádár.[1]

The "Social Compact"

Kádár's policies were based on what some observers have called the "unwritten social compact" between his regime—above all himself—and the majority of Hungarians.[2] In 1956 the Hungarian nation, though defeated, again asserted itself and its historic right to be reckoned with. Once its active resistance was put down by Soviet military power, it was Kádár's task to induce Hungarians through the phases of passive resistance and noncooperation that followed, then toward those of acceptance, of cooperation, and eventually, of support. Even if the support were not active, it was enough for Kádár. "He who is not against us is with us," became the motto of the Kádár years.[3] What he offered was a system of rule which, while thoroughly Leninist, was tempered by humanity. While not respecting the individual, it at least left him alone. What Kádár promised was a perceptible, continuing increase in the material standard of living, and this promise he kept. The Hungarian people accepted their part of the bargain—1956 never again—at first with resignation but then more readily, some even willingly. Theirs was hardly a noble role—as some of their intellectuals, keepers of the nation's conscience, kept telling them. But after the trauma of the revolution, it was not without dignity. Kádár's policy was not only much better than they had expected; as it developed, many Hungarians even began to feel that at least some of the goals of 1956 were being recovered.

But just as important as Kádár's political leadership skills within Hungary was his ability to "manage" the Kremlin.[4] With Khrushchev this task was relatively easy once the Soviet leader's erratic ebullience ceased to disconcert or intimidate. Khrushchev was as eager for Kádár to succeed as Kádár was himself. The Hungarian Revolution might well have cost Khrushchev his position. He was then still only primus inter pares, and many of his peers resented not only his grab for power but what they considered his reckless reformism, typified by his onslaught against Stalin at the Twentieth CPSU Congress in March 1956.[5] The upheavals in Poland and Hungary the following autumn could in part be traced back to Khrushchev's secret speech—many Soviet communists and East European hard-liners considered it *totally* responsible for them—and it was clearly in Khrushchev's interests to see the postrevolutionary reconstruction in Hungary proceed quickly and smoothly. The choice of the new Hungarian leadership was, therefore, crucial not only for Hungary, but for Khrushchev's political survival, as well as for the Soviet Union's international credibility.

The situation made Kádár much more than the Soviet puppet he was at first dismissed as being. It gave him considerable leverage with his Soviet protectors, and, while his relationship to Khrushchev was one of dependence, it was not one of total subjection. A good working relationship developed, eased by a growing mutual respect and even friendship. What was most important for Hungary's future was the conviction of both that the wounds of the revolution must be healed quickly and that the country that had so nearly been communism's East European graveyard should now become its showcase. The ensuing policy became known as "Kádárism," and in the climate of the 1960s it stood out for its boldness and its success. This gave the Kádár leadership increasing self-confidence as its East European, and even its international, standing grew.

Kádár safely negotiated the transition from Khrushchev to Brezhnev. By October 1964 he was a pillar of stability in Eastern Europe, safe and successful, thoroughly compatible therefore with the new Soviet leadership's predilections. He was left to deepen and expand his policies of domestic conciliation and to prepare for the introduction of the New Economic Mechanism (NEM) in January 1968, designed to hasten the prosperity he had promised.

The smoothness of Kádár's relations with Brezhnev, however, was to be disturbed by the consequences of the Prague Spring, one of the catalysts of East European communist history, measuring in importance with the Hungarian Revolution itself. Kádár's own reaction to the reforms in Czechoslovakia was one of caution, but also understanding, perhaps some sympathy. But in August 1968, however reluctant he was, his loyalty to bloc unity came first. He joined in the Soviet-orchestrated warnings against the Prague Spring and then in the Soviet-led invasion that ended it.[6]

But his support for the invasion, and for the Brezhnev Doctrine justifying it, was not given unconditionally. When, after August 1968, even the very use of the word "reform" was inhibited in the Soviet bloc, the NEM proceeded. Hungary became the only country in the entire Soviet bloc where reform was tolerated and sustained. It brought the Kádár regime much notice and growing prestige.

Success Turns to Failure

Despite having joined in the invasion of Czechoslovakia, Kádár's international reputation stood high at the beginning of the 1970s. The NEM had made what looked like an auspicious beginning, and in a generally gloomy Soviet and East European setting Hungary stood out as both reformist and relaxed. Its compliance with Moscow on the invasion was excused on the grounds of *force majeure* and the memories of 1956.

Kádár's reputation continued to grow for at least another ten years. Despite the difficulties into which both the Hungarian economy and the attempts to reform it were to run during the 1970s, Hungary continued to be the only East European country that was reforming at all, not to mention its climate of political and psychological relaxation. Above all, the general standard of living kept rising, a fact to which the increasing flow of Western visitors readily attested.

But, despite its early success, the NEM revealed, not only its own inconsistencies, but a basic weakness of the Leninist system. As early as 1972, just four years after the NEM's introduction, the regime began restricting even the limited application of the market mechanism originally envisaged, making it clear that the huge industrial combines, always more ideological than economic, would generally continue to enjoy the same state protection as in the past. At the same time three forces converged (or colluded) to check further progress of the reform.

The first was the conservative faction inside the Hungarian party. Kádár had been successful in neutralizing the small neo-Stalinist grouping that had entered the newly constituted Hungarian Socialist Workers' Party after the revolution. But the NEM roused more widespread opposition as many party members who had genuinely supported the strategy of reconciliation could not make their peace with the implications of the NEM.

The second force consisted of a large number of industrial workers who nursed a grievance and harbored a fear. At the turn of the 1970s Hungary benefited from the global economic boom. This was more responsible for domestic prosperity than the NEM, but it was to the latter that the regime's propaganda attributed its success. But whatever their source, the fruits of success mainly went to the official and managerial classes, and to the farmers. Little of it went to the workers, most of whom, despite their views on socialism, were not averse to being considered the vanguard of the revolution when any benefits accruing from it were being distributed.

Some workers saw not just present injustices but future dangers: the insecurity inherent in economic reform; the deeper the reform, the greater the danger. Thus, at an early stage in the implementation of economic reform in Eastern Europe, the conservative case against it was already taking shape. One of the great propaganda successes of the Soviet and East European rulers was in inducing so many workers to identify socialism with job security and social welfare—and capitalism with their opposites.

Obviously, this proletarian restlessness was grist to the party conservatives' mill. But the third force now opposing reform provided yet more grist: the Soviet Union itself. Kádár may have deflected Soviet opposition when the reform was introduced in 1968, but he had not disarmed it. It was only to be expected that the Brezhnev leadership, bent on ideological counterreformation, would revise its original permissiveness toward the NEM. Beginning in 1972, pressure was exerted on Budapest to slow down and modify the reform.[7] The regime at the same time became less tolerant of political and cultural dissent. Conspicuous champions of reform were dropped, not only Premier Jenö Fock, but Rezsö Nyers, the "father of the NEM." Nyers, however, remained close to the surface of public life and was to reemerge in the late 1980s as one of the leaders of Hungary's second (peaceful) revolution.

Just as the NEM was being shelved, an economic disaster was looming that helped radically change the whole course of East European development. The first OPEC oil price explosion of 1973, though it affected the Western industrialized states almost immediately, took well over a year before it began to affect Eastern Europe, partly insulated by its protective economic ties with the Soviet Union.[8] But the Soviets could not be expected to continue their liberal pricing policy for energy exports to Eastern Europe when world oil prices were rocketing. In 1975 they made their fixed price scale more flexible to more quickly reflect the movement of world prices. As a result, the price of Soviet oil to Eastern Europe doubled between 1974 and 1976 and quadrupled between 1976 and 1983. Even with these increases, though, it still remained well below the world price and, except for a period in the mid-1980s when the world price rapidly dropped, continued to do so.[9]

But favorable comparisons with world prices held little relevance and no comfort for Hungary, or any other East European country, all of which (except Romania) were almost totally dependent on Soviet oil. They were now faced with a massive readjustment of which none was capable. For several years Hungary seemed to be coping better than most, better certainly than Poland, whose economy, after a spuriously brilliant showing in the first half of the 1970s, went into a rapid decline with momentous social and political repercussions. Hungary's success was partly due to the relative flexibility of its economic system, but mainly to the regime's ability to maintain the political consensus that had been forming since the early 1960s. This consensus stemmed from Kádár's own political skills and his ability to project continuing economic success for a long time after the serious weaknesses of the economy had been realized by those in the know, or by the few interested in finding out. Thus Eastern Europe's "consumerism," conceived by the Kremlim as a strategy of divertissement after the trauma of Czechoslovakia, and artificially kept going by the increasing— and eventually ruinous—resort to Western credits, held up better and longer in Hungary than anywhere else.[10] In fact consumerism for Hungarians, the need and the reason for it, went back not to the Czechoslovak reforms but to their own revolution. Consumerism in the 1970s was an expansion of the material concessions Kádár had started to make in the 1960s, a codicil to the postrevolution social compact.

But the maintenance of the political consensus was not just due to well-filled shops and what they signified. It derived from the still strong memory of 1956 itself. This made not only for a prudent calm, but even for a national eagerness, amounting often to neurosis, to enjoy the good days while they lasted because Hungarian history, recent and bygone, taught that they might not last long. It was this buoyancy that helped keep Kádárism afloat. But when, in the early 1980s, the good days did come to an end, the euphoric high sank to a correspondingly bitter low, and the hunt for scapegoats was on. Kádár was the obvious choice. As Kádárism failed, its eponym fell from grace. His reputation could not survive the unraveling of the social compact. Once he failed to deliver, he was vulnerable.

Opposition began to grow at a time when Kádár was losing his political touch. His physical health was deteriorating and his mental grasp weakening. But even more significant was his inability to adapt to, or even understand, the new complexities and demands of the situation. By the 1980s economic reform, as many Hungarian economists were now telling him, no longer meant deciding which bits of capitalism to tack onto socialism but which bits of socialism to keep after the introduction of capitalism.[11] He had come to accept that economic and political reforms were a tandem, even that political reform might have to go in front. But he could not face the political imperative of the 1980s: the dismantling of Leninism. Pluralism was to be accepted, even encouraged. But only within the framework of party supremacy. He had always believed in inner-party democracy, but even more in democratic centralism. He simply could not countenance the party genuinely *sharing* power. Parliamentary democracy and the multiparty system were for the other side.

Kádár had outlived his usefulness and his relevance. He was the pilot waiting to be dropped. It is true that a good ten years before his dismissal, Hungary resumed the economic reform that had been shelved in 1972, and introduced bold departures toward enhancing the market and capitalist practices. But he really understood none of these, and even they could not cope with the seriousness of Hungary's crisis. Now pressure mounted for what must have sounded to him like the "counterrevolution" of more than thirty years before. Thus it was more than the ghost of Imre Nagy that finally returned to break Kádár's health and spirit. It was the heresies that had caused him to desert, disown, and betray Imre Nagy in 1956.

From Failure to Collapse

But appearances, as they often did in Hungary, continued to deceive. Certainly, compared with any other East European country, Hungary looked prosperous for well into the 1980s. In retrospect, the great Hungarian decline, leading to Kádár's fall in May 1988, had already begun by the turn of the 1980s; ironically, it took place about the same time that Gierek in Poland, whose early successes had led to spurious comparisons with Kádár, was forced from power in September 1980. The beginnings of the decline were quietly noted by many regime officials, by none more so than Imre Pozsgay. A former minister of culture, whose growing rebelliousness led to his "rustication" as leader of the politically harmless Patriotic People's Front, Pozsgay used this unpromising position as a base to build the reform wing of the Hungarian Socialist Workers' Party.[12] The decline could also be measured by the growing number of extra-establishment dissidents who were to be the basis of the eventual opposition.[13] But it was the mid-1980s before the *public* mood changed. It took even longer for outsiders to grasp that a historic epoch was ending.

The catalyst for the change was inflation. In the 1970s price hikes became as familiar in Hungary as they were in Poland. But the finesse with which Kádár handled them was taken as an example of his adroitness, unlike the calamitous blundering with which Gomułka and Gierek treated the issue.[14] Kádár could also bank on his continuing political credibility; the social compact was still holding. Higher prices were explained as the down payment to the NEM for the good times coming. But by 1985 the good times for most Hungarians were farther away, not closer. Slowly, at first, but then torrentially, the grievances poured out.

Charles Gati has summed up the six interrelated factors that led to the public's disenchantment.[15]

The economic factor. Inflation became intolerable, and this quickly discredited the reform process as a whole. The response to inflation—spending, borrowing, panic-buying—further jeopardized the reform's chances of success. The fears of unemployment and about social benefits, poor as they were, compounded the malaise. The confidence necessary for the reform to work was undermined: confidence in Kádár eroded with astonishing swiftness.

The social factor. A chasm had been developing between rich and poor in a society still mostly attached to the principle of equality, or at least to the appearance of equality. The NEM brought conspicuous consumption back to Hungary—for the very few. Private entrepreneurs started flaunting their wealth. (The *nomenklatura* nobility were modest by comparison.) At the other end of the social scale there was a huge, glaring increase in poverty. Gati reports that, as early as 1982, 30 percent of the people at the bottom of the social scale received 18.6 percent of the population's total recorded income, while 30 percent at the top got 44.2 percent. In 1987 the average monthly wage was about 6,000 forints ($130 at the—low—official exchange rate). The official poverty line was set at 4,800 forints, only 20 percent less. Many workers had to take one or two extra jobs to keep up. Most pensioners were in a pitiable condition with practically no one taking effective pity on them. This situation exacerbated social problems like suicide (always alarmingly high even in precommunist Hungary), divorce, and alcoholism. Drugs were making inroads on the younger generation. NEM, and behind it the regime, were getting the blame.

The generational factor. By the 1980s the post-1956 generation began setting the pace of public life. Its criteria were not set by the revolution and its aftermath; anyway, it did not think so. It was unaffected by the social compact of 1956. Many rejected it openly. For many young Hungarians it was simply the cover for inertia, double-think, double-talk, and corruption. Kádár personified for them a foul compromise that had worsened with time.

The oppositional factor. Opposition flourished on the disillusionment of the young. Hungary's dissidents began to surface after 1968. At the start the most vocal of them were left-wing sociologists and philosophers who accused the regime of perverting Marxist ideals. The most prominent were András Hegedüs, an erstwhile Rákosi "whiz kid," prime minister of Hungary at thirty-three, when the revolution started, now recycled into a scholar and reform sociologist; and György Konrád and Miklós Harasti, both able writers who came to reject socialism and helped inspire the reform movement of the 1980s. Subsequently, the nucleus of dissent enlarged, with several samizdat publications to give it expression. As it developed, the movement could be divided into (1) the "urbanist" group, (2) "the populist" group, (3) a "liberal" group, and (4) an "economist" group, urging far-reaching political as well as economic reform. All four drew on honorable Hungarian traditions. The liberals and the economists often collaborated and were sometimes indistinguishable. The urbanists and the populists, on the other hand, were quite distinctive, sometimes hostile, rarely collaborating. They provided the cutting edge of the opposition in the 1980s. Roughly speaking, the urbanists, some of whom were Jewish, were international in outlook and favored quick, radical change. The populists were very Hungarian (some even spoke nothing but). They stressed the minorities abroad issue, but domestically they stood for a gradualist, incremental approach toward liberal Christian democracy. The Kádár regime at first shrugged off the dissidents, taking them seriously only when it was too late. Dissent grew as the situation worsened. Disaffection among the young became particularly evident. Eventually the dissidents, now graduated to the status of "opposition," developed a mutuality of interest with party reformers, and the road toward change was open.

The Gorbachev factor. Gorbachev did not initiate reform in Hungary. He may even have cribbed some ideas from the Hungarian experience. By the end of 1989, in terms of what was on or near the statute book, reform in Hungary—economic, political, social, cultural—already went some way beyond what was only being contemplated in the Soviet Union. Still, Gorbachev did make an impact on Hungary, on the public at large, as well as on the governing process. By identifying with reform itself, he broke through many of the inhibitions that still clouded and slowed its course in Hungary.[16] He also helped undermine the continuing opposition to reform. In doing so, he broke Kádár's grip on power. For the first time in thirty years Kádár could not manage the man in the Kremlim. He was more than out of touch with Gorbachev: he was incompatible with him. When this was realized in Hungary itself—and it did not take long—Kádár's last line of political defense—his line to Moscow—was breached. But Gorbachev went out of his way, not to cause, but to hasten Kádár's fall, with protocol slights, diplomatic snubs, and other signals by which communist elites communicate disdain for one another. Kádár must have known the game was up, but he did not realize just when.

The Romanian factor. The steady policy of assimilation of the Hungarian minority of 2 million people in Romania pursued by Ceaușescu's regime became a crucial public issue in Hungary in the 1980s.[17] It grew not only as the pressure in Romania grew, but as the domestic situation in Hungary itself worsened. The lowering mood caused by the latter served to raise indignation over the former. To disinterested observers the indignation, which was justified, often became a fixation about a "Romanian threat," which was not.[18] But what counted was that Romania became another potent political issue in Hungary in the 1980s as it had been in the 1920s and 1930s, regularly fueled by the provocative truculence of the Bucharest regime. This unrest was politically exploited by both sides in Budapest. The opposition first argued that the regime's reticence on the subject showed a communist lack of patriotism. Then the regime, increasingly beset by difficulties at home, soon realized that Romania was good politics. Transylvania was back on the Hungarian agenda.

One more point might be added to Charles Gati's list of six. *The Austrian factor.* While Romania was resuming its status of inveterate enemy, Austria was becoming the irresistible attraction. Through travel and television Austria became the yardstick by which the Hungarian condition was measured, and this only added to the rising dissatisfaction. But the Austrian impact was not solely materialistic. It was nostalgic, emotional, political, and intellectual, with a touch of snobbery thrown in. It encompassed respect, admiration, envy, and plain wishful thinking. Its appeal was both historical and current. The Vienna link, not much liked by many Hungarians before 1918, now seemed like paradise compared with the Moscow link since 1948. (Otto von Habsburg was feted during a visit to Budapest in the spring of 1989; some Hungarians later wanted him to run for president.) More to the point, modern Austria was free, neutral, democratic, economically prosperous, and socially caring.[19] By one of the miracles of East-West relations it secured independence in 1955. One year later, when it tried the same, Hungary was crushed by Soviet troops. This was the key to the Hungarian preoccupation with Austria. Austria was the great "might-have-been" for the Hungarians, a nation always wistful about its past, morbid about its present. *Tu, felix Austria!*

These, then, were the main reasons that the Kádárite consensus collapsed. The consensus had been built between 1960 and 1970 and firmly maintained between 1970 and 1980. Then it began to weaken, and between 1985 and May 1988 it shattered. Now there was the need to build a new consensus, built not on the public's acquiescence, but on its active participation. In both Hungary and Poland, whatever regime/society consensus had previously existed depended on the economic situation. With prosperity there was passive, depoliticized consensus. But when prosperity waned, as it did in Poland in the second half of the 1970s and in Hungary a few years later, the consensus fell apart. What reformers in both countries now aimed for was an active consensus, on the Western example, based on a notion of a civil society, not predicated on material prosperity alone.

The Democratic Triumph

By the beginning of 1988 the situation in Hungary was becoming tense and expectant. An era that had lasted thirty-two years was felt to be coming to an end. Even so, few people expected the fall of Kádár at the party conference in May 1988, least of all himself. He was expected to hold on till the regular party congress due in 1990 when he would retire of his own free will. But he was outmaneuvered and bundled out, much to his obvious chagrin—registered mercilessly by television—two years earlier.

But though Kádár's ousting was a historic event, it was only a partial breakthrough. It led to democratization, Eastern-style. There was a delay, a period of transition, before the real breakthrough occurred toward democracy, Western-style. This period of transition is associated with the name of

Károly Grósz, who had become Hungarian prime minister in June 1987. Grósz was never a reformer, although with reform becoming more de rigueur every day, he tried hard to look like one.[20] He was more the Gorbachev Mark I type of modern political manager (see chapter 2) with a touch of populism and more than a touch of opportunism. He could make a good impression on both Margaret Thatcher and Erich Honecker.

When Grósz replaced Kádár, after a carefully planned conspiracy among allies who later became adversaries,[21] he seemed very much Hungary's man of the moment. He combined for a time both the party leadership and the premiership, a fashion that went out with Khrushchev but had been revived by Jaruzelski during Poland's crisis in 1981. The fact that it was now revived in Hungary was a reflection of anxiety over the country's condition. It also tended to impute almost salvational properties to Grósz himself.

But Grósz had no recipe for salvation. The surge for reform following Kádár's downfall soon made him irrelevant and isolated. As a politician he was ready for both the market and for pluralism. But he remained at heart a party official—county Borsód and the city of Budapest—and balked at capitalism and Western-style parliamentarianism. As the reform gathered pace, he tried to slow it. He stood for party supremacy, modified but still basic. But, in the words of one eminent Hungarian, the party was like the man being chased by the wolf, shedding his clothes step by step to avoid being caught, until he was stark naked.[22] Most Hungarians, of course, relished the sight. But not Grósz, especially when it became clear that the man most immediately concerned was himself, and that he was not going to get his clothes back. As Imre Pozsgay, Rezsö Nyers, and Miklós Németh (the new prime minister and once considered Grósz's minion) moved further toward dismantling the old system, Grósz became an embarrassing obstacle. The reburial and rehabilitation of Imre Nagy in June 1989 and the immense national sentiment it evoked[23] accelerated his decline. In June 1989, thirteen months after he gained the party leadership, he was effectively deprived of it.

The changes in the party leadership in June 1989 involved the creation of a four-man presidium composed of Pozsgay, Nyers, Németh, and Grósz. (The changes also involved the creation of a new Political-Executive Committee of twenty-one members,[24] and the abolition of the Central Committee was announced.) Nyers was named party chairman, a post that had been created for Kádár when he was ousted in May 1988. Then the position was honorary, but there was nothing honorary about the post Nyers assumed. He was now the real leader of the party and was recognized as senior in the new quadrumvirate. An erstwhile social democrat who "merged" with the communists in 1948, Nyers in the 1980s had capitalized on his intimate association with the NEM in the 1960s and then his eclipse in the 1970s when reform was shelved. His reputation, therefore, was vindicated now that comprehensive reform was seen as the only alternative to disaster. At sixty-five he had returned to the Politburo in May 1988, some thirteen years after his dismissal from it.[25]

Németh at forty-one was a promising politician who had ditched his patron, Grósz, and embraced reform with all the zeal of the converted. His inclusion in the four-man presidium derived from his post of prime minister. But the leading spirit of reform was still Pozsgay. Out of his position with the Patriotic People's Front, Pozsgay had created a veritable power base. As the party as well as Kádár lost credit in the 1980s, the search began for both institutional and personal alternatives. Pozsgay's answer was that Hungary need look no further for either. By 1980 he became basically a social democrat and was almost ready to admit as much. The Hungarian Socialist Workers' Party, he argued, should and could evolve toward social democracy: the multiparty system; parliamentary democracy; a constitutional state; a mix of public and private property; capitalist practice tempered by the welfare state.[26] Capable, canny under his ingenuousness, personable, and courageous, he was well-liked and admired by intellectuals and reformers.

But among much of the party apparatus, where the conservative strength lay, Pozsgay was considered public enemy number one, much more feared and hated than Nyers, for example. By 1989 the authority of the apparatus had lost much of its credibility because it had lost control of many of the levers and channels of power. But it was not impotent. Like the Polish apparatus, it still retained, through the *nomenklatura* and its control over provincial administration, large reserves of power. In both countries the apparatus would remain in control until there were free local elections and a determined assault on the *nomenklatura*. In the present circumstances, although the apparatus could not endanger reform outright in either country, it could delay it, even partially block its implementation, and exploit the many ways of discrediting its viability. In Hungary the apparatus, therefore, remained a threat which any reformer with political sense and responsibility took into account. That was why Grósz, irrelevant, reduced, even humiliated, was still not totally disabled. As long as the apparatus could obstruct, and as long as it identified with Grósz—which it now did, even if *faute de mieux*—then Grósz could not be discarded. Hence, he retained the post of party secretary-general, though with the near certainty (subsequently borne out) that he would lose it at the next party congress in October 1989. (He was already intimating his retirement in August.) Grósz also could not be discarded as long as there was some hope of maintaining party unity. But as the acrimony increased, there was a growing expectation of a split. Many on both sides of the ideological fence regarded it as inevitable.

As the reforms edged toward democratization, a band-wagon effect was created. It made its way even in some sections of the party grass roots, among the "reform circles," which were at the most distant end of the spectrum from the conservative apparatus. The reform circles began as a youthful "ginger group" but were now a serious political movement.[27] (Observers compared them with the reform groups in the Polish party in 1981 which demanded internal party democracy, based on a horizontal instead of vertical organizational structure, and rejecting democratic centralism.) Most members of the reform circles liked Pozsgay, but they wanted to go even further than he—and faster. The HSWP, they agreed, must become a new, grass-roots party with a new name (suggesting socialism but not communism), controlled by the rank and file and not by the apparatus. Where they mainly differed from Pozsgay and most reformers in positions of authority was over methods. They rejected the need for tactical caution, insisting that the party conservatives were no longer a threat; hence, patience was no virtue, but a self-defeating vice, and discretion just an excuse for faintheartedness. These so-called reform circles were being regarded by many Hungarians, and not just opponents of reform, as latter-day Jacobins, embarrassing, not assisting, the cause they espoused.

There was much in common between many members of the "reform circles," party members though they nominally were, and intellectuals in some of the main oppositional groupings, such as the Alliance of Free Democrats, led mainly by "urbanist" intellectuals, and particularly the youthful and radical Federation of Young Democrats (FIDESZ).[28] But the chief oppositional grouping at this time, in terms of ascertainable membership and following, continued to be the populist Hungarian Democratic Forum, with its "Hungarian-ness" reflected, inter alia, in its militancy on the question of Hungarian minorities abroad, and, above all, in its robust provincialism. Newest on the scene was the Democratic League of Independent Trade Unions, composed of several branch unions which separated from the official trade union organization.

Adding to both the profusion and confusion of the Hungarian political landscape was the reappearance of former parties which had disappeared under Rákosi in the late 1940s. Most notable were the Smallholders, the strongest party before the communist repression; the Peasant Party, the Social Democrats; and the Independence Party. It remained to be seen what impact they would have. At least one of them, the Social Democrats, was gravely weakened by generational conflicts among its leaders. It was becoming evident that some of the oppositional groups just mentioned would become real, formal, political parties and gain most of the oppositional support. The Hungarian Democratic Forum, for example, competed against the communist party in four parliamentary by-elections in July 1989 and won three of them.

There was one largely unknown factor remaining on the Hungarian scene, clearly distinguishing it from that in Poland and lending a quite different character to its reform politics. This factor was the attitude of the working class. Whereas in Poland since 1956 worker militancy usually became the main driving political force, in Hungary the workers had been largely quiescent since the revolution of that year. True, toward the end of the 1970s when inflation began to bite, scattered strikes became a very common occurrence, but the Kádár regime managed to contain them. Many workers were becoming increasingly dissatisfied, but as long as a second or even a third job could put the prizes of consumerism within their reach, they stayed on the treadmill. And as late as the second half of 1989, when the conditions of most workers had seriously deteriorated and their prospects looked even worse, they still hesitated over the reform option. Not that they necessarily opposed it. In fact, many had, in one way or another, been initiated into the capitalist ethos through their second or third jobs. But how much they supported systemic economic reform, especially when it began to bite, was still a matter of conjecture and debate.

This absence of worker commitment to Hungarian reform for some observers gave the whole process an air of inconsequentiality, a lack of knuckle that could be fatal if opposition to it stiffened. For the moment, reform in Hungary did, indeed, recall 1848, "the revolution of the intellectuals." But, however intellectually exciting this may be, reform would not go far without worker support. Conversely, the main danger to reform in Hungary in the future could lie in this lack of commitment among the workers turning to antagonism as the pains of economic reform became more acute for the many, while its rewards became more conspicuous for the few. In this respect, Poland was already becoming a deterrent for some Hungarians rather than an inspiration. If anything, Czechoslovakia in 1968 offered the best analogy to the situation in Hungary. The Prague Spring blossomed from the same combination of regime reformers and opposition intellectuals. The Czech working class was slow to respond. Only when the invaders were already there did the working class realize what it might have lost. The Hungarian workers had never been as content as their Czech counterparts, but they might think they still would have something to lose. Neither had they ever been as numerous, solid, or prickly as the Poles. But they could still eventually make or break reform in Hungary. Reformers could not afford to assume they were bound to be on their side. Most of the tens of thousands who lined the streets for János Kádár's funeral in July 1989 were workers, a gesture not without political significance.[29] Some reform intellectuals scarcely hid their belief that life would be much simpler without the workers and its improvement much easier to achieve. It was a safe enough notion in the universities, and the cafés. On the streets it could be risky.

Some Hungarian intellectuals had, in fact, tried earlier to contact and cultivate the workers, mindful of the revolution in 1956, and of their belief in the common fate binding all Hungarians. Intellectuals who later formed the Hungarian Democratic Forum were especially notable in these efforts. They made the attempt during the 1970s, but it was part of the Kádár regime's divide-and-rule strategy to prevent it. During the 1980s, however, it became easier to establish contacts but some of the Democratic Forum's leaders were the first to admit that more could have been done and that many intellectuals could find neither the time nor the inclination to approach the workers.[30] The Democratic Forum felt that if it could develop its worker contacts, this, combined with its stand on the minority issue, could put them in good stead for the general elections in 1990. The Forum hoped it would finally breach the dwindling communist working-class strongholds.

On the Threshold of the Constitutional State

While Poland from the end of 1988 was approaching the goal of a civil society more directly through the legalizing of an independent opposition and eventual elections, in Hungary the reformers were taking the more roundabout way of trying to "constitutionalize" public life. It was reformers within the regime itself who took the lead in changing certain basic laws. In August 1988 the minister of justice, Kálmán Kulcsár, an internationally known sociologist, called for a complete revision of the country's constitution.[31] His aim, and that of others who saw this as the crux of the whole issue, was to make Hungary's new constitution a "*real* document genuinely transcending and enfolding" the political power of the Communist Party, which should now accept the superior power of the constitution. Basic civil rights such as the presumption of innocence and the ban on retroactive legal regulation, should also be anchored in the constitution. The new constitution should abolish the "discretionary quality of Hungarian life in which fine-sounding . . . principles are undermined by ad hoc powers given to administrative organs in excess of their proper competence."

In politics the constitutional state meant parliamentary supremacy over state power. Parliament, therefore, should become a vigorous, even troublesome, actor, in session for much longer periods than before. The powers of the presidential council to enact legislation were to be curtailed. Above all, the principle of competitive politics should replace that of one-party rule. The Communist Party would take its place in the new multiparty system, but any future ascendancy it might enjoy would be through the ballot box and not by right or "scientific laws." Other parties, legally recognized and independent, would now have no less, and no more, right to compete for power than the Communist Party.

The goals for both Poland and Hungary were the same. But they had come via different routes, through different stages. Poland formed first its free trade union, Solidarity, in 1980, which quickly burgeoned into an independent national movement in 1981. Suppressed in December of that year it reverted to an underground opposition, becoming a national symbol. In April 1989 it reemerged as a recognized opposition, legalized by the same regime that had originally suppressed it. It then competed in the elections of June 1989 which, despite their restrictions, put Solidarity in power. This was the Polish way, from socialism to the civil society.

By contrast, the Hungarian way was more like "the long march through the institutions," the strategy Enrico Berlinguer designed for the Italian communists. The Hungarian and the Italian environments, of course, were quite different, but the framework in Hungary that had been provided by Kádár was spacious enough for incipient political expression, and it increased rapidly after his downfall. Reformers in Hungary could therefore hope to transform the system from the inside, despite the constant danger of splitting the party, whereas in Poland the only recourse had been to confront it from the outside.

On their way to future equity both societies also had to repair past iniquities, and the very act of doing this—its emotionalism—lent strength and conviction to their efforts. With the Poles it was their recognition of Solidarity. In Hungary it was even bigger and more poignant: the rehabilitation and the reburial of Imre Nagy, symbolizing the vindication of the revolution in 1956. In both countries these were issues that transcended present politics. They concerned that indefinable but, to East Europeans, unmistakable entity: the soul of the nation.

A German commentator has best described what the reburial of Imre Nagy meant to Hungarians:

> For the Hungarian nation which, for three decades, had to live with the trauma of this lie (i.e., regarding Nagy's treason) his reinterment means not just the moral rehabilitation of Nagy and his political associates: It is the rehabilitation of a humiliated nation, as well as the precondition for the success and the credibility of the heralded reforms.[32]

After the reburial of Imre Nagy on June 16, 1989, Hungary's roundtable conference, which had opened just two days before, could begin in earnest. Designed to further the whole reform process, it was obviously modeled on the Polish example, but it was altogether a more complex affair than that which had ended successfully in Warsaw. The opposition delegation, which became known as the "opposition roundtable" (ORT), was a veritable mosaic of groupings united only by a general desire for change. A roll call of its nine-member composition gives some idea of a variety that made meaningful coherence almost impossible: (1) Social Democratic Party; (2) Federation of Young Democrats (FIDESZ); (3) Independent Smallholders Party; (4) Democratic League of Independent Trade Unions; (5) Hungarian Democratic Forum; (6) Christian Democratic People's Party; (7) Alliance of Free Democrats; (8) Hungarian People's Party; (9) the Endre Bajcsi-Zsilinsky Friendship Society, a progressive environmentalist organization. These groups covered a very wide range of Hungarian aspirations for a better life, while not necessarily all giving the most businesslike impression round the conference table.[33]

Actually, the conference also included a third grouping—delegates from a number of vaguely pro-regime or conservative organizations ranging from old classic conveyor belts like the official council of trade unions (SZOT), and the Patriotic People's Front organization, through mildly Stalinist holdouts, unrepentant Kádárites, to the National Council of Women. There were seven groups in all, united at least in the cover name they chose for themselves: "The Silent Majority." They were sometimes derisively dismissed as "Leninism's Last Line of Defense," but some of them claimed that outside Budapest they were a force to be reckoned with.[34]

As a demonstration of the pluralistic profusion that had swept over Hungarian public life, the roundtable was certainly impressive. But it was there to fashion a modus operandi to bring democracy to Hungary, a practical task for which it did not seem ideally equipped. Neither the regime (party) side nor the opposition was well-led; neither had its Kiszczak or its Wałęsa. Grósz opened the conference for the regime, and the position of main spokesman was then taken by György Fejti, a Central Committee secretary. But just over a month after the talks opened, both men were demoted, and, though this reflected a victory for the more progressive faction in the party, it did little to improve the showing of the regime in the negotiations as a whole. The opposition's main spokesman was Imre Kónya, one of the leaders of the Hungarian Democratic Forum but chosen mainly on the strength of his membership in the Independent Lawyers' Forum. Kónya was much respected but still had his reputation to make as a public figure. The occasional inability of the Social Democratic Party to field a delegation because of divisions within its ranks was the most extreme example of the opposition's incoherence, but for many Hungarians it was not atypical. There was a common element of purpose but too little unity on how to achieve it.

The regime's strategy was to try to confine the discussion to economic topics. For one thing, such subjects presented a better chance for agreement. Both sides (though not most of "the Silent Majority") accepted a market economy and private businesses. But there was disagreement not only between the two sides, but in the ranks of each, on the extent to which these principles should be taken. For example, two important sets of proposals submitted to the HSWP Central Committee by one team headed by Iván T. Berend, president of the Academy of Sciences, and another headed by Csaba Csáki, a well-respected economist, differed considerably in boldness and on several specific recommendations.[35] On the opposition side there were throughgoing capitalist converts as well as Austrian-type social democrats. But if some of the differences were quite sharp, they were not totally incompatible. At least, they need not hold up the proceedings.

But the regime did not prefer economics simply because it provided a better chance of agreement. It was watching the public, too. The economic situation was still deteriorating. Remedy was getting more urgent than ever. And like its Polish counterpart, the Hungarian regime did not want to be seen by the public as the sole prescriber and purveyor of whatever bitter medicine was necessary. The opposition must also share the odium. At the very beginning of the conference Grósz put it nicely: "Even if it was not so in the past, the responsibility for the future is joint."[36]

But, however pressing the economic necessity, the opposition rightly insisted on the primacy, or at least the equality, of politics. Hence, political matters should be fully discussed and the solutions fully agreed on. But, for the regime, the primacy of politics meant the reality of the power it had enjoyed for over forty years and the degree to which it was prepared to give up that power; this was a painful, as well as divisive, issue. That was the real reason the regime wanted to avoid politics as much as possible; the less said about such questions, or the less they were debated, the better. The opposition, therefore, was finding itself confronted by an agenda which it could not approve. In substance, procedure, and atmosphere the Hungarian roundtable was soon in deep water, as the Polish had been in the early part of its course.

At the beginning of August 1989 the talks temporarily broke down amid a welter of mutual recriminations. The opposition accused the regime of not allowing full enough discussion on vital issues, while the regime accused the opposition of assuming that the present organs of government, now mainly staffed by officials who genuinely supported change, had no legitimacy and therefore no right to initiate change without their advice and consent.

Roughly, the contentious issues fell into five interconnected categories: ideological, institutional, personal, administrative, and political/military. The ideological wrangle, as the opposition insisted, had serious implications. It centered on the regime's wanting to insert into the new constitution a formulation affirming the leading role of the working class in society. This would replace the old shibboleth about the leading role of the Communist Party which both sides agreed had to be dropped. The opposition saw the new formulation as an attempt to retain a communist essence in the new constitution.[37]

One of the most complex issues concerned the presidency. Both sides agreed on investing it with strong powers, like the new Polish presidency. But where they disagreed sharply, and where the opposition was concerned about being outmaneuvered, was over how and when the new incumbent should be chosen. The regime wanted it done by popular vote before the parliamentary election. The opposition saw this as a ruse to get Imre Pozsgay elected. Despite the growing anticommunist mood, he was probably still the most popular politician in Hungary—certainly the best known. And he wanted the job. The opposition was well aware of this. For them, he was a respected figure whose own striving for reform made their own efforts that much easier. But as long as he remained a member of the Hungarian Socialist Workers' Party, no matter how penitent it was becoming or whatever it might evolve into, he stood for an interest many considered alien to the Hungarian nation and inimical to themselves. They wanted the new president to be elected *after* the election by the newly elected parliament, which would certainly contain an anticommunist majority. The regime side, for its part, thought it was sitting pretty on this issue—probably the only one that it was. In electoral terms, Pozsgay was running miles ahead of his party, and, once installed in the presidency, the reasoning went, much as he might relish the role of *tribune of the plebs*, he would be in a position to do something for his old comrades, either collectively or even individually. Besides, looking at the cliff-hanging suspense attendant on Jaruzelski's election as president of Poland, would it not be fitting for a more orderly nation like the Hungarian to do things somewhat differently?[38]

As for Pozsgay, he was desperately anxious to avoid becoming the center of this kind of controversy. It could only hurt his chances of election and his own image as being above the battle. To be detested (as he was) by many of his fellow communists was a huge electoral asset these days, but to be suspected by the population of being used by the party to further its own political ends was a liability even he might not survive. His position was difficult. He was very anxious for the roundtable talks to succeed, so much so that he sometimes made the lives of the regime negotiators more difficult by sounding too conciliatory. He seemed rather slow in learning that time can run out on a man for all seasons.

The nitty-gritty of reform lay in the fourth category: the administrative. The Poles had been able to put off many acts of administrative change because of the halfway character of their parliamentary election in June 1989. But the Hungarians, set for multiparty elections without conditions, could not do the same thing. Access to the media was one important question here; it caused opposition indignation, but turned out to be solvable. Ultimately, the most difficult group would be the *nomenklatura*, which all communist systems in dissolution would have to shed. In both Hungary and Poland the *nomenklatura* had been pared down over the years. The Hungarian regime, for example, for some time had been claiming that its "list of cadres" was being reduced.[39] The *nomenklatura* had always presented problems of definition and composition. Statistics on them were often misleading, although in recent years the behemoth had been shrinking. But this did not mean that the *nomenklatura* was destined to disappear without a struggle. It was the hard core that would fight most tenaciously.

But that was for the future. One pressing problem now was what the opposition considered the ill-gotten gains—wealth, assets—the party had accumulated over the last forty years. Now the party, once the standard-bearer of collectivism, stood on the principle of what's mine's my own. The opposition, on the other hand, took time off from hailing the advent of capitalism and adopted classic socialist slogans about sharing the wealth. They felt most strongly about the assets of the old "bourgeois" parties that had now revived and wanted restitution. The communists argued that these assets had been acquired lawfully. Their opponents pointed to the difference between lawful and legalistic, observing that, if the party was not willing to share its wealth, how could anyone believe it would ever share its power? So the quarrel went on, and the Hungarian public looked on, with admiration withheld. Admiration was withheld even further when the opposition gleefully revealed that the party had been salting away many of its assets in a company imaginatively called "Next 2000."[40] The comrades-turned-capitalists had to desist, but Next 2000's future would at least be assured in Budapest's political cabarets.

Another pressing problem concerned the continuance of party organizations (cells) in the factories. The ubiquity of these organizations not only in industry but in every facet of public life had been an essential feature of communist rule everywhere. It was one of the essential underpinnings of the party's existence, part of the quintessence of Leninism. To challenge the communists' presence was, in its way, just as serious a threat to communist rule (or survival) as to challenge communist predominance in the ruling institutions at the center. Both sides realized this fact, and the issue looked as if it would become intractable.

Finally, one category cast its shadow over the whole compass of reform in Hungary, and in Eastern Europe as a whole: the civil-military-Soviet interaction. There was a whole cluster of issues here on which the regime would have liked to remain as tight-lipped as possible. Ostensibly, this was because of the regime's extreme sensitivity, but in reality the Soviet connection was the communists' ultimate hope, and Soviet fears about the connection constituted the best chance of containing the advances of reform. Specifically, the regime insisted, and quoted the backing of the Soviet military, that no depolitization of the armed forces could occur, that whatever changes the multiparty system might bring, the party's leading role in the military must be preserved.[41] The opposition was not united on this issue. Some groups accepted the issue's sensitive nature and wanted it dropped from the conference agenda. Others insisted that Hungary could neither be free nor democratic until this question was resolved. It was another case of Hungary's opposition being divided between the strategies of the shortcut and of gradualism.

Toward Democracy

As most Hungarians and foreign observers expected, the Hungarian roundtable talks eventually ended in compromise. They began in mid-June and ended in mid-September. The agreement[42] included:

1. The election of president. This most controversial issue apparently resulted in a regime victory. The new president, invested with strong, but as yet unspecified powers, was to be elected by a direct, nationwide vote, and *before* the free parliamentary elections.
2. Parliamentary elections were to be held not later than ninety days after the presidential election.
3. A new electoral law which was closely based on the West German system involving both direct election and proportional representation.
4. An overhaul of the legal system, including the criminal code, to conform with the "accepted norms of human and political rights."

5. The total depolitization of the armed forces, meaning the disbanding of (communist) party committees and the end of political (communist) training. The Workers' Guard, the armed detachment of the party which many reformers feared as potential regime "shock troops," was to be brought under the army's direct control.[43]

On this last issue, the opposition clearly won its point because the regime, as mentioned, strongly insisted on retaining party influence in the military. But the regime, for the moment, won its point on the retention of political activity in the factories. It clearly had to give up its monopoly here—their political parties and groups could also now begin activities in the factories—but it was ready to do so because it still believed its strongest support rested in the large industrial concerns.

But while the regime and the opposition were hammering out these broad but obviously vulnerable agreements on the country's future, both Hungary's government and its party were each in the process of making history. In September the Hungarian government permitted several thousand East German citizens, who had been vacationing in Eastern Europe and refused to return to the GDR, to cross over into Austria on their way to the Federal Republic of Germany. It was the most significant foreign policy decision any Hungarian communist government had made since Imre Nagy's fateful declaration of neutrality in 1956 (the vital difference, of course, being that this decision presumably had Soviet approval). By permitting this massive exodus of East Germans, the Hungarians not only were spurning their alliance obligations—even going beyond an assertion of neutrality—but they were declaring their preference for the West over their ties to the East in a crisis situation involving a frontline ally. This made their action truly unprecedented. Its effect on the whole course of European history was momentous. As the future Czechoslovak foreign minister, Jiří Dienstbier, put it: "The [Berlin Wall] was leveled by [Foreign Minister] Gyula Horn, who opened the Hungarian border with Austria."[44]

In early October it was the party's turn. The Hungarian Socialist Workers' (communist) Party dissolved itself and became the Hungarian Socialist Party. After the revolution in 1956, János Kádár formed the new Hungarian Socialist Workers' Party to replace the old Communist Party that had disintegrated during the revolution; it was the symbolic and organizational shift from Stalinism to Leninism. Now, thirty-three years later, the Hungarian party, by an overwhelming majority of the delegates represented, was disavowing Leninism and acclaiming democratic socialism on the West European model. For some the move was too drastic. Károly Grósz, for example, declared his unwillingness to belong to the new creation, and a new Leninist party was being formed. But the momentum was with the name-changing reformers. Eyes were now on the forthcoming free election. The new party, as the Hungarian Socialist Party, led by Rezsö Nyers, considered it now stood a better chance of not being totally humiliated like the Polish United Workers' Party the previous June.[45] The more optimistic were even still hoping for a large enough vote to have a role in the future government.

But the optimism sounded more and more forced. By the end of 1989 the popular mood in Hungary had turned sharply against communism, whatever its form, however human and purified it may have become. This mood seriously threatened the assumptions and calculations on which Hungarian political life had been based only a few months before: that reform communism, as well as some of its leaders, had considerable public support; that an orderly transition to democracy required this reform communist participation; that, however permissive the Soviet Union may have become in Eastern Europe, there still seemed to be, as the democratization process in Poland apparently indicated, lines that should not be crossed. But anticommunism only increased as the inhibitions about Soviet permissiveness diminished. Anyone associated with the past regime became suspect, as did those democratic forces prepared to deal and cooperate with them.

The principal victim of this change of mood was Pozsgay. He was partly paying the price of trying to please everybody, and it was proving politically suicidal to try to appease members of the old Hungarian Socialist Workers' Party in the effort to hold it together. Therefore, though Pozsgay would almost certainly have wanted to abolish party organizations in the factory and in the armed forces, to dispense with the party's great wealth, and to abolish the Workers' Militia, he found himself hedging on these issues to try to preserve a party unity that was collapsing anyway. In the event, what seemed to him to be good politics turned into a serious political defeat when the Hungarian parliament, correctly sensing the political mood, voted to abolish the party presence in the economy and to completely disband the Workers' Guard.

The roundtable agreement, therefore, which Pozsgay had worked so hard to bring about, began to unravel almost as soon as it was signed. Three of the more uncompromising groups had refused to sign the agreement anyway. They were the Free Democrats, the Young Democrats (FIDESZ), and the independent trade union organization. And it was the Free Democrats and FIDESZ that went on to inflict on Pozsgay a decisive political defeat. They had refused to sign the roundtable agreement specifically because they objected to the provision on the election of the new president—that the office should be invested with strong powers, and the incumbent be elected on a direct, nationwide vote *before* the parliamentary elections. Their argument was that, in the present context, this system of election would be undemocratic because it would heavily favor Pozsgay. The parliamentary elections would be a more accurate reflection of the general popular will, and it would therefore be more democratic if the president were elected by the new parliament.

Thus, the Free Democrats and FIDESZ were not prepared to see a partially stage-managed transition to democracy, as had been attempted in Poland. They went so far as to take advantage of a constitutional provision allowing a referendum to be held on the method of the presidential election, provided that a petition with the required number of signatures be presented. About 200,000 signatures, twice the number required, were obtained with surprising ease. The petition asked for the nationwide presidential election system to be set aside. The readiness of 200,000 people to sign the petitions already looked ominous for Pozsgay. But the result of the referendum appeared decidedly more threatening. The communist-turned-socialist party, as well as the Hungarian Democratic Forum, had advocated a boycott of the referendum, a move tending to strengthen the public suspicion of collusion between the two. But about 58 percent of eligible voters did vote, and the Free Democrats and FIDESZ won the point, if only by the narrowest of margins. The presidential vote would take place *after* the parliamentary elections.

Pozsgay's star, therefore, was almost extinguished, and the political situation looked more uncertain than ever. This uncertainty was compounded by the fact that scores of parties and groups were now in political contention and would contest the general election, set for March 1990. But practically none of these parties or groups spoke with a unified voice. Different members were saying different and conflicting things in the heady political free-for-all. Different factions also emerged in the main political groupings like the Socialists, the Hungarian Democratic Forum, and the Alliance of Free Democrats. But it seemed fairly sure that two closely related issues would figure prominently in the election: anticommunism and Hungarian independence.

The election campaign was fiercely contested and not always characterized by sportsmanlike behavior. The Free Democrats complained, with some justice, about anti-Semitic slurs against some of their Jewish members. The Democratic Forum had to counter charges that some of its leaders were too friendly with prominent communists. But no free elections had ever been governed by Marquess of Queensbury rules—now less than ever.

In the event, the Hungarian Democratic Forum won the March 1990 elections quite decisively. But the main thing about the result was that democratic Hungary could now get a *stable government*. This was the first necessity. Now it would be policies that counted.

As a footnote not only to the first free Hungarian election in forty-five years, but to the history of communist rule in Hungary, it is worth recording that, standing in his constituency of Sopron, Imre Pozsgay got 17 percent of the total vote. This was the same percentage that the Communist Party received nation-wide in the last free Hungarian election in 1945 before communist rule began.

5 The German Democratic Republic: The State Without a Nation

While Poland and Hungary were predestined to be the trailblazers for reform in Eastern Europe, the ruling communist elites in both the GDR and Czechoslovakia each had their own specific reasons for rejecting any experimentation. Not only were both regimes led by men who were clearly a product of the Brezhnev era, but each had its own dilemma and fear of reform. In the Czechoslovak case the Husák–Jakeš leadership was dominated by orthodox and conservative forces installed with Moscow's support after the 1968 Soviet-led invasion. In the GDR the Socialist Unity Party (SED) leadership faced its own unique dilemma resulting from national partition after World War II. From the outset, the SED regime's very legitimacy was intertwined with its efforts to inculcate a sense of national identity based on socialist ideology. Whereas other East European regimes could experiment with elements of capitalist economics or Western notions of political pluralism, such moves were seen by the SED as dangerously diluting the differences between East Germany and West Germany and eroding the justification for the very existence of a second German state.

The basic East German response to perestroika, therefore, was generated by considerations having to do with the way the GDR saw itself in the perspective of German history and in relation to that other Germany, the Federal Republic. This reason for East Berlin's glacial response to Gorbachev had been diagnosed right at the beginning by Western observers, but it took until August 1989, not long before the East German people took matters into their own hands, before this was officially admitted. As Otto Reinhold, rector of the party's Academy of Social Sciences, candidly put it in an interview, socialism was the GDR's raison d'être: "What right to exist would a capitalist GDR have alongside a capitalist Federal Republic? In other words, what justification would there be for two German states once ideology no longer separated them?"[1]

Reinhold was thus admitting to the basic reason for East German reluctance. Previous official propaganda had maintained that the GDR had no need for systemic reform. Its leaders argued that its economy, give or take a few faults here or there, was doing very well, and they could point with some justice to how badly the economic situation was in reforming countries like Poland and Hungary. (For several years now the faltering New Economic Mechanism in Hungary had drawn a hale of patronizing comments from both the East German and Czechoslovak media.)[2] East German complacence, even hubris, on the subject was clearly demonstrated as early as May 1986 when at the Eleventh SED Party Congress head of state and party leader Erich Honecker, in the presence of Gorbachev himself, politely but firmly rejected the Soviet leader's reform policies. The GDR was doing well enough without them was his unmistakable message.[3]

There were many examples of official East German "formulations of rejection" regarding Gorbachev's perestroika, but the best known was that of the regime's longtime top ideologist, Politburo member, and Central Committee secretary, Kurt Hager. Asked early in 1987 about the relevance of Soviet reforms for the GDR, Hager dismissed their significance by saying that the fact that your neighbor wallpapered his house did not mean you had to do the same.[4] (Hager's riposte, it might be added, was not just a classic piece of nose-thumbing at perestroika; it was a case of the GDR following the letter—if not the spirit—of Gorbachev's policy of more independence for the East European states.)

To give its defiance an ideological and nationalist coating, the East German leadership launched a concentrated campaign to develop and justify its past policies as a national communist strategy, reviving the old slogan of "socialism in the colors of the GDR." While tolerating a budding reform debate among party intellectuals, the SED's main efforts were directed at explaining to the mass of the population why the type of dramatic change taking place elsewhere in the region was inappropriate for the GDR. Officials claimed that the SED had avoided the serious mistakes committed by ruling communist parties elsewhere and pointed to the GDR's past superior economic performance as proof of the correctness of its policies. In addition, party ideologues never lost the opportunity to ask what reforms had done for the USSR, Hungary, and Poland.

Last but certainly not least, SED officials repeatedly pointed out that the GDR's sensitive geostrategic position, bordering the Federal Republic, and the allegedly incessant propaganda waged against it by Bonn, made the margin of error for reform in the GDR extremely narrow. Calls for reform in the GDR were increasingly deflected with the argument that they would jeopardize stability and were therefore in no one's interest. Speaking at the Seventh CC plenum in November 1988, Honecker criticized the West German media for insisting that the GDR introduce reforms, noting the irony of those "for whom our policies were always 'too Russian' were now recommending that we follow the Soviet example." To follow this advice, Honecker continued, would be "equivalent to demanding that we deviate from our course and march into anarchy."[5] Moscow understood, according to Otto Reinhold, that the key foreign policy task of the GDR was to ensure "stability and to make sure that a second Tbilisi does not erupt in Rostock."[6]

This mixture of defiance, complacence, and fear continued right up to the fall of Honecker in October 1989. It put the GDR in the same unenviable bracket as Romania as the two East European Warsaw Pact states least responsive to perestroika. The GDR's attitude was soon to prove massively counterproductive, antagonizing the population to the point of open, peaceful rebellion. It was not so much reform as it was the regime's refusal to reform that led to a situation where the very existence of the GDR came to be challenged.

The International Importance of the GDR

Because of its apparent stability for nearly thirty years—from the building of the Berlin Wall in August 1961 to its collapse in 1989—it was easy to overlook the unique role the German Democratic Republic played in the post-World War II European security system. The GDR appeared so stable that both its existence and its permanence were taken for granted. Only when its extinction became first possible and then certain did international attention concentrate on the role that the GDR's existence had played and on what the situation might be like in Europe without it.[7]

After the Wall was built in 1961, the GDR was to emerge as the strongest East European economic power and even made (spurious) claims to be a world economic power. But the GDR's international importance lay not so much in what it was but in the reinforcing of Soviet power that its very existence signified.

The benefits deriving from the GDR's existence, however, were never considered as solely accruing to the Soviet Union. As already mentioned in chapter 2, the rest of Europe—East and West—and many people in the

United States and Canada saw the German Democratic Republic as an unattractive but effective means of preserving a status quo that, if disturbed, could have serious international repercussions. On several occasions throughout the 1950s the Soviets may have toyed with the idea of a reunited, neutral Germany, but as it became obvious that neither the Federal Republic nor the post-Wall German Democratic Republic (August 1961), not to mention the Western powers, were receptive, these ideas steadily receded.

The GDR, therefore, continued as the great paradox of modern international relations. As the creation and protectorate of the Soviet Union and on account of its sheer unbending grimness, it was viewed with general scorn and even horror. Yet, not for what it was but for what it meant, its crimes against humanity were sometimes overlooked. For over forty years it enabled the world to avoid thinking about German reunification. The world was grateful for this, including the West Germans. The vast majority of the Federal Republic's citizens, despite their paying lip service to reunification, and despite the fact that the goal of German unity was enshrined in their constitution, were content to relegate this issue to the dim, distant future. No one suspected that in 1989 the dim, distant future would become tomorrow, or the day after tomorrow.

Economic "Miracle" and Reality

The shock of the GDR's collapse was all the greater because for many years—at least since the middle of the 1970s—it really did seem to be the emerging, prosperous socialist state claimed by its leaders. After the demise of the Honecker regime, though, it began to be revealed what many had suspected: the success was not nearly as great as was claimed, and, in any case, it always had its darker and potentially fatal aspects. Guenter Mittag, for many years the "overlord" of the East German economy, who had been given much of the credit for the regime's economic "successes," now became the object of almost as much public opprobrium as Honecker himself. Once credited with everything, he was now blamed for everything.[8]

Still, whatever the reservations and deceptions, East German economic progress after the building of the Wall in 1961 was impressive, especially if one remembers the blight of World War II and the Soviet demands for war reparations, plus the loss of between 2.5 and 3 million of its citizens by migration to West Germany before the Wall was built in 1961.

Already by the end of the 1960s the GDR had replaced Czechoslovakia and Poland as the Soviet Union's most important economic partner, and during the 1970s, the East German general standard of living equaled and then probably surpassed that of Czechoslovakia. This was largely due to a deliberate policy of "consumerism" initiated by Erich Honecker after he replaced Walter Ulbricht as party leader in 1971, Ulbricht having been removed because he opposed détente with the Federal Republic, the cornerstone of Brezhnev's new Westpolitik. Honecker's "consumerism" was in keeping with general policy in Eastern Europe at the time (see chapter 1). But it also had a specific East German context. Honecker accepted Brezhnev's Westpolitik and the "normalization" of relations with the Federal Republic it entailed. But he immediately initiated a policy toward the FRG that became known as *Abgrenzung* (demarcation) designed to ensure that, despite the new technical relations between the two Germanies, the GDR would more than ever go its own way, delineate its own socialist separateness, and have as little to do with West German capitalist contamination as possible. However, to strengthen whatever specifically East German socialist sentiment existed among the population (there was always precious little), and to further help ward off capitalist dangers, it was necessary to raise living standards.

The attempt to raise living standards and improve all-around economic performance was made unexpectedly difficult by the international economic crisis of the 1970s originated by the two OPEC oil price explosions in 1973 and then 1979. The GDR, about 93 percent of whose oil supply came from the Soviet Union, was paying $25 a ton for Soviet oil at the beginning of the 1980s. Honecker himself complained in 1979 that the GDR was having to export three times more produce to pay the Soviet Union for a ton of its oil than it had before 1973.[9]

The most serious consequence of the crisis was the international hard currency debt the GDR began to accumulate. This debt, facilitated by the glut of petrodollars on the world market, was partly caused by the need for protection against the rigors of the new international economic climate and partly by the new overall policy of "import-led growth" on which the East European states, except Czechoslovakia, had embarked with more enthusiasm than discretion. In 1971 the GDR's gross hard currency debt was $1.4 billion; by 1975 it was $5.9 billion; in 1981 it was $14.2 billion.[10]

In the early 1980s the difficulties of repayment were one of the GDR's most serious economic problems and this caused it more than ever to lean on the West German "crutch." Honecker's *Abgrenzung* policy toward the

Federal Republic had never extended to refusing West German financial payments and subsidies to the GDR, relating to a whole series of transactions between the two states but centered mainly on commercial relations and on the location of West Berlin in the heart of GDR territory. By the middle of the 1970s these payments amounted to about 2.5 billion West German marks a year.[11] The East German government was able to manipulate the West German connection in its commercial relations. Taking advantage of the European Community provision giving it unhindered access to the West German market, the GDR began shifting its pattern of Western trade even more toward West Germany. Because of special standing provisions— the so-called "Swing Credit" factor—this enabled the East Germans to avoid paying hard currency for West German imports, thereby considerably easing their foreign trade burden.[12]

This long-standing West German "crutch," prompted mainly by Bonn's determination, despite almost constant provocations over the years, to keep the hand extended to the other part of the German nation, was sometimes given sole credit for whatever aspects of the East German economic "miracle" that were genuine. But crucial though this connection was, its importance need not detract from the success, however temporary, of some of the GDR's own economic efforts.

These efforts were seen at their best at the end of the seventies and the turn of the eighties. The East European economies were all affected by the downturn of the world economy in the second half of the 1970s, the East German economy being no exception. Relative to the rest of Eastern Europe and the Soviet Union, its performance was still good, but in no single year could it meet its Net Material Product target. The Honecker leadership met this challenge with what, in East German terms, was a major economic reform, dubbed, "the Economic Strategy for the Eighties." Essentially it was a major reorganization project with strong emphasis on economizing and rationalizing. Its principal organizational innovation was to attract world attention, and its early successes enabled the East German regime to claim that it had reformed long before Gorbachev burst on the scene. This was the *Kombinaten*, some 130 large combines formed by grouping together numbers of existing enterprises. Each *Kombinat* had between twenty and forty factories and employed an average of 25,000 employees.[13] It had wide powers and responsibilities and incorporated research as well as spare part manufactures for the main product. Many *Kombinaten* managers were competent, and many of its workers could still draw on the historic German reservoir of discipline and skill.[14]

The *Kombinaten*, the impact of the new economic strategy as a whole, the reorientation of Western trade even more toward the Federal Republic, the continuing West German crutch, plus the minor inundation of the GDR with West German marks as a result of increased travel between the two Germanies, led to a better East German economic showing in the first half of the 1980s than many had expected. And, though the increase in living standards did not keep pace with the overall satisfactory economic performance (or the general smugness with which the GDR's leadership contemplated its own performance), it continued to compare well with the general East European standard.

But, as later became evident, the GDR was never nearly as successful as it made itself out to be. In February 1990, with the fate of his country already decided, Gerd Koenig, the GDR's ambassador in Moscow, was interviewed by representatives of the West German weekly *Der Spiegel*. At one point the conversation went as follows:

> [Der Spiegel] The GDR was a world expert in deception.
> [Koenig] I agree with you. It was perhaps one of our biggest "achievements" that we knew how to give the impression that we were a political and economically stable state. Of course, for the Soviet citizen the view of the GDR was approximately like the one for the GDR citizen in the FRG. Thus, no one became aware of the fact that, in reality, the GDR was the weakest link in the chain of the East European states.[15]

Koenig might have added that one of the reasons it became the weakest link was that the GDR's leaders deceived not only the world, but eventually themselves as well.

The Long Passivity

The history of Eastern Europe under communist rule, a period that lasted forty years—between 1948 and 1989—was punctuated by upheavals caused by popular dissatisfaction. These began with the Berlin Uprising in 1953, continued through the Hungarian Revolution and Polish October of 1956, the Prague Spring and the December 1970 riots in Poland, Solidarity 1980–81, and finally to the events of 1988–89 in Poland, Hungary, the GDR, Bulgaria, Czechoslovakia, and Romania that effectively saw the end of communist rule.

The East German population's contribution to this steady erosion and final collapse of communist dominance occurred at the very beginning and the very end of the process—1953 and 1989. Why the long passivity in between? Several reasons present themselves, all of them interacting but some of obviously greater importance than others:

1. The sobering memory of the 1953 riots themselves.
2. The resignation induced by the building of the Berlin Wall in 1961.
3. The fact that the approximately 3 million East Germans who defected before the Wall was built probably embodied the most active oppositional spirit among the population.
4. The presence in the GDR of between 300,000 and 400,000 Soviet troops.
5. The efficiency of the East German security apparatus (*Staatssicherheitspolizei*—Stasis).
6. The relative success of, first, the regime of Walter Ulbricht and, then, of Erich Honecker in neutralizing and then even co-opting crucial strata of society.
7. The steady increase in the standard of living due to a combination of domestic policy and Soviet, and particularly West German, assistance.
8. A conviction, once strong but steadily eroding, on the part of some in East German society that, whatever the faults and deficiencies of the GDR, the socialist bases on which it was purported to be built were superior to those of capitalist societies, most notably the Federal Republic.[16]

These factors helped keep the East German population relatively quiet for so long. This quiescence simplified the task of the East German regime and emboldened Honecker to take risks on solidifying the GDR's future which, though apparently successful in the short term, eventually helped bring on the final disaster.

The biggest initial risk Honecker ran was the one from which his predecessor, Ulbricht, shrank: the normalization of relations between the two Germanies in the Basic Agreement (*Grundvertrag*) of December 1972. Honecker's own nervousness over the situation, shared to various degrees not only by the regime but by the total party membership of about 2 million, was betrayed by the *Abgrenzung* strategy. But the risk appeared to have paid off. Almost immediately the GDR was recognized internationally by well over a hundred states around the world; it entered the United Nations simultaneously with the Federal Republic; it was soon counting itself, as mentioned, among the ten most economically developed countries in the world. All this without the societal instability caused by the opening to the West that Ulbricht had dreaded and Honecker sought to head off through *Abgrenzung*. Again, the East German population was not totally passive, but it was never so prickly as to warrant either the *Abgrenzung* measures or some of the more hysterically brutal actions of the police authorities, particularly at the border with West Germany or internally in parts of the GDR itself.

Indeed, as it seemed that international détente was working to the GDR's advantage rather than to its detriment, the regime tended to become more confident and relaxed. But it never lost its basic nervousness. In fact, Honecker's eighteen-year rule in the GDR can only be understood in terms of the interaction (or the dialectic) between boldness and nervousness, between gambling and playing safe. Nonchalance about the dangers West German television's saturation coverage of East German territory went along with neuroses about the possible consequences of the Helsinki Final Act of the CSCE process in 1975.

But into the second half of the 1970s confidence seemed to be prevailing over fear. Helsinki certainly left its marks on the GDR. It moved many in its cultural milieu to be more active and demanding, which in turn provoked both severity and pettiness on the regime's part. Several of East Germany's best writers, for example, found their way, with various degrees of persuasion, into the Federal Republic.[17] But Helsinki's bark, at least in the short term, seemed worse than its bite, and after a while it seemed no more dangerous than the *Grundvertrag* had been. Honecker could breathe more freely and concentrate more intensely on what had always been the main problem of any East German leadership: acquiring legitimacy.

The Struggle for Legitimacy

The initial hopes of the founders of the GDR, not to mention their Soviet protectors, had been that ideology alone would provide the main legitimizing factor for the new state—the ideal of, quest for, the first German socialist state. Walter Ulbricht, though in other respects a pragmatic politician, always retained this ideal, and despite all the rebuffs of subsequent experience, many older East German communists, schooled in the struggles for communism and against Nazism, also clung to the belief that socialism meant legitimacy. Ideology certainly met a slower death in the GDR than in any other East European country.

But Honecker saw that ideology alone was not enough. He was aware of what Stalin had known all along, what Yugoslavia in 1948 had reinforced, and of what the satellites realized after Stalin's death: that when communism became national communism, it must pretend to a national coloration if it was to have any chance of survival. Khrushchev had soon understood this point and had promoted "home" communists in Eastern Europe to replace "Muscovites" in the leadership. But this was Honecker's dilemma: to promote nationalism in a state that was unique in its lack of any national foundation. The GDR was indeed the exception to the rule that all communism becomes national communism. As the Finnish diplomat Max Jacobson put it:

> The GDR is fundamentally different from all other Warsaw Pact members. It is not a nation, but a state built on an ideological concept. Poland will remain Poland, and Hungary will always be Hungary, whatever their social system. But for East Germany, maintaining its socialist system is the reason for its existence.[18]

History has been full of nations seeking statehood, but the GDR was a state searching for nationhood, a state in which almost 400,000 foreign troops were stationed, troops whom most East Germans considered to be a foreign occupier.

Honecker was helped by a few factors in his quest for legitimacy. There was a strong historical tradition of regionalism in German history. Some sense of East German "distinctiveness," on which it was hoped a sense of nationhood could be based, also had developed. More recently there had been the extraordinary, though meticulously prepared, successes of the GDR's athletes. But all these things fell far short of a sense of nationhood. No one after all could achieve legitimacy through anabolic steroids alone. Honecker, realizing that it was history that molded the consciousness of nations, decided to summon the past to try to stabilize the present and secure the future. He thus began the famous historical "rehabilitation campaign," searching into German history for figures to fit into the mold of a progressive German nationalist outlook. Thus, notables who had previously been vilified as the epitome of reaction, like Frederick the Great, Bismarck, even Wagner (or parts of him), and several other cultural luminaries, were solemnly deposited into the GDR pantheon. The high point of this historical rehabilitation campaign was the commemoration of the five hundredth anniversary of Martin Luther's birth, a gala event lasting months.[19]

The vast majority of East Germans greeted these displays with a mixture of cynicism and bewilderment. They were somewhat more impressed, though, by a genuine display of GDR nationalism in the summer of 1984, a display all the more genuine because it was directed against the Soviet Union. It arose from Honecker's determination not to let the GDR's improving relations with the Federal Republic be disturbed by the East-West imbroglio over INF and the subsequent Soviet freeze on relations with Bonn at the end of 1983 (see chapter 2). The dispute came to focus on a long-planned visit to the Federal Republic by Honecker, due to take place in September. Eventually, at Soviet insistence, Honecker dropped the visit, as everyone expected he would. This show of independence, however, in the summer of 1984, was the real high point of the GDR's nationalism and seemed to have elicited considerable sympathy from many East Germans.[20]

Much of the sympathy, though, stemmed from the Federal Republic's involvement. Therefore, even when he was earning some popular respect, Honecker was partly beholden to the other Germany. Indeed, the "summer of '84" only illustrated all the more clearly the GDR's ultimate dual dependence—on the Soviet Union and on the Federal Republic. Regarding dependence on the Soviet Union, that was not only implicit in the GDR's very existence but in its multifaceted role as a prime Soviet satellite. With regard to the Federal Republic, not only did the GDR increasingly become its economic satellite, but it became its psychological satellite, too. Much of what the GDR did, said, even thought was predicated on its need to feel superior to, or separate, from the FRG, to anticipate, preempt, equal, better, improve on, or denigrate what it was doing. It was not so much a policy as a complex of *moi aussi*—anything you can do we can do better (or, at least, we can do, too). It was one of the ironies of the European postwar arrangement—and eventually its basic weakness—that the linchpin of its stability, the GDR, should be penetrated and dominated by the Soviet Union and the FRG. One was the leader of the Warsaw Pact, the other the most powerful continental member of NATO the two adversarial alliances that maintained this precarious stability for so long.

A Penetrated Society

The GDR, in fact, furnished a unique example of the penetrated society.[21] At first the penetration came largely from the Soviet side. It was comprehensive, but it had remarkably little effect on the essence of society. East Germany, for example, became much less Russified than West Germany became Americanized.[22] But the penetration from the West German side began in earnest only after the *Grundvertrag* of 1972, i.e., after the onset of détente. As mentioned, its dangers, though recognized by the GDR leadership, seemed manageable. Eventually, of course, this turned out to be the fatal miscalculation. Penetration helped bring about the regime's final destruction—sooner than anyone had anticipated.

The three main instruments of West German penetration after the onset of détente were (1) the West German mark, (2) West German travelers, (3) West German television.[23]

The West German mark quickly became the currency that mattered in the GDR, and the regime made every effort to get its hands on as many as possible. It was impossible to tell how many Deutsche Marks there were in the GDR at any particular time—they were usually converted into goods and services very quickly or simply hoarded—but they became an essential mechanism for large areas of social and economic life. Against their short-term convenience, however, they had a gravely deleterious impact. Deutsche Marks undermined the regime's legitimacy further by debilitating what should have been one of its pillars of credibility: its own coinage. The Ostmark became further debased. But Deutsche Marks also undermined social trust and cohesion. Those with access to D-Marks, either dubiously or fairly—often from relatives in the Federal Republic—not only could bribe their way to good service, but they had access to the special shops, with good-quality Western merchandise, set up by the regime to soak up Western currency. Many East Germans automatically became second-class citizens because they did not have access to D-Marks. This led to outbursts of individual and sectional anger—workers, for example, demanding part of their wages in D-Marks—and it created a deeper frustration just waiting to be unleashed.

West German visitors to the GDR had become a flood by the end of the seventies. In 1979 alone, they numbered over 8 million, bringing both their money and their mores. On balance, these visitors did help subvert Honecker's ongoing attempts at legitimation. But some of them were far from being the best advertisement for the Western way of life. There were numerous complaints about their arrogance, ostentation, and insensitivity. Many of them did, in fact, tend to make East Germans feel a race apart, becoming Honecker's unwitting agents in his legitimation drive.

Much more effective in the subversion of the GDR was the growing traffic the other way—the number of East Germans visiting the Federal Republic. For many years, as a general rule, only East German pensioners were allowed to travel to West Germany. They would be no loss if they did not return; the GDR would even gain somewhat financially. But the Helsinki Agreements demanded more liberalization in this regard for everybody. The pressure for emigration to the West increased sharply, and the regime had to respond. In 1984 emigration touched about 40,000, and the applications grew insatiably. Between 1 million to 1.5 million were believed to have applied for emigration by 1989, and in that year some 200,000 were expected to leave legally. Beginning in 1986, however, restrictions on ordinary visits to the Federal Republic began to be noticeably relaxed. In that year 587,000 East Germans traveled to West Germany, many of them below retirement age. In 1987 it was estimated that over a million East Germans *below* retirement age made the trip. At the time these concessions were seen as a basic change of official policy as well as a sign of the regime's increasing self-confidence, which was boosted further by the remarkably low percentage of travelers who failed to return: 0.025 percent in 1987. The liberalized travel policy also appeared to be paying off by temporarily reducing the number of applications for permanent emigration. In the first quarter of 1987 emigration was down almost two-thirds on the same quarter for the previous year.[24]

Liberalized travel seemed to be a Honecker gamble that was paying off. But, again, whatever the immediate benefits, in the longer term it proved to be another gigantic miscalculation. It induced a fatal self-confidence, a false sense of security leading to a distorted view of reality. This illusion that the regime could be more and more sure of the population was also a big factor in the leadership's refusal to follow Gorbachev in reform. And it was that refusal that led to the final popular repudiation of the German Democratic Republic. Honecker and company might have taken note of the rising numbers of emigration applications *after* the first quarter of 1987. They were a reliable barometer they chose to ignore.

The most intriguing form of penetration into the GDR was by means of West German television. All the communist states of Eastern Europe, including the Soviet Union, had been bombarded with Western radio programs for many years; Austrian television also could be picked up by residents of adjacent parts of both Hungary and Czechoslovakia. But the East German situation was unique. From the beginning of the 1970s, 80 percent of the East German population could tune in West German television and in the course of the 1980s this was extended to 100 percent. Practically the whole of the East German population, therefore, could clamber into the Federal Republic through their television screens every night, stay there for a few hours, and then clamber back.

In his political apprenticeship as SED youth leader, Erich Honecker used to mobilize large numbers of East German young people in raids designed precisely to thwart the growing number of watchers of "subversive" television. Once in full power, though, he gave up the costly, practically impossible struggle. Sociological and psychological evidence was apparently adduced suggesting that watching West German television might actually sublimate popular dissatisfaction and diminish yearnings for reunification. Certainly, the seamier sides of capitalism that West German television showed in abundance would, it was hoped, make the East German citizenry thankful for their socialist egality and order. Finally, any massive attempt to block off West German television, whether over the airwaves or in the homes of millions of East Germans, would have involved the kind of humiliating loss of international and domestic prestige the Honecker regime just could not afford to incur. On the other hand, allowing West German television to come in unimpeded and then actually facilitating its extension, would suggest, it was hoped, an enviable sangfroid, a cool indifference to any kind of propaganda the other Germany could throw at the GDR.

It was another of Honecker's gambles, a big one, and a far-cry from the *Abgrenzung* mentality of the early 1970s. And, for a time, it worked—at least in the sense that it seemed to do no harm. There was little serious political dissension that could safely be attributed to the seductions of West German television. The difficulties resulting from the Helsinki (CSCE) agreements of 1975 could hardly be blamed on West German "propaganda." (In any case, the East German official press was forced, under the terms of the agreements, to print the text of Helsinki in full.) The considerable increase in crime and lowering standards of social behavior in the GDR might, with some plausibility, be blamed on contacts with the capitalist west, and the authorities spared no effort to do so. But this was only grist to their propaganda mill—further "proof" of just how lucky the citizens of the GDR were.

The lack of obvious harm in the short run (or of evidence thereof) was a further case of regime complacency. Constant exposure to the West German political, popular, and consumer culture did, however, undoubtedly have an insidious effect on East German life, an effect unmeasurable but probably substantial, countering the communist ideology and undermining the regime's legitimacy. No one could predict when and how its effects would be felt. But few outside the East German leadership doubted they eventually would.

The Alternative Authority

But the various forms of West German penetration, however ruinous they might turn out to be, were in themselves too diffuse to make a concentrated impact. What was needed was a *domestic* institution to channel and focus discontent. The institution that took on this role, very unwillingly at first, was the Evangelical (Lutheran) Church. It never aspired to a political role and for many years had a difficult job maintaining its religious role among a population, the majority of which, although nominally Protestant, contained ever fewer practicing Christians. But in a state that aspired to totalitarianism it was steadily pushed into the situation of being an alternative point of loyalty for the community, especially for the growing number of young East Germans ready to take a stand on important public issues. As a French commentator observed:

> These Germans have found their area of freedom in the Protestant churches. The comparison with Poland is tempting, but quite misleading. The Polish church was a refuge for the Poles' faith and a bastion of the resistance to communist ideology. The Protestant churches in the GDR have rediscovered their Reformation calling. They have taught the East Germans, by no means all of whom have a religious faith, to assert their individual freedom and their free judgment in the face of the state; they have given them the courage not to be afraid of either the authorities or their prohibitions.[25]

The Evangelical Church grew in strength by taking firm stands on issues of political and social significance. It strongly opposed the increasing militarization of East German life and pressed for arms reductions, nuclear disarmament, the right of conscientious objection and alternative service. It also became a focal point for pressure on environmental issues, as the ecological situation in the GDR worsened and the regime showed itself unable or unwilling to face up to it. These were just two of a whole series of issues in which the Protestant churches became involved.[26] Already by the 1980s the Evangelical Church had moved from the margin of East German society to the center. It never directly challenged the regime. In fact, it was continually offering its cooperation. Sometimes it seemed rather pliable and some of its leaders and local clergy were often quite ready to please the authorities. Honecker, as his confidence grew during the 1970s, was ready for his own kind of cooperation with it. It could be useful to him as a safety valve, perhaps even a transmission belt. But the Evangelical Church steadily generated a spontaneity fatal to the totalitarian concepts on which the GDR was built. The final clash came after 1985 in the response to Gorbachev. While the regime resisted the new Soviet leader, the Evangelical Church welcomed him. In doing so it inevitably moved into opposition along with the growing number of East Germans who were demanding change. In November 1987 the increasingly nervous Honecker leadership raided an East Berlin church which was housing an unofficial environmental library. It was a declaration of open hostilities that had been coming for years.[27]

Failing the Final Test

The popular image of the GDR throughout most of its history was that of a pliant Soviet satellite. But, like all Moscow's East European allies, it was not without leverage in intra-bloc relations, leverage stemming from both its strengths and its vulnerabilities. The Soviet-East European relationship was often punctuated by issues over which unanimity was conspicuously absent and in which the East European states resorted to the leverage at their disposal.

Since its foundation the GDR had been involved in three major disputes with the Soviet Union. The *first* involved Ulbricht's objections to the role envisaged for the GDR in Brezhnev's Westpolitik at the turn of the seventies. Ulbricht, who had irritated the Soviet leadership on several counts before this, was forced out of office as a result. The *second* dispute was the "summer of '84" episode, already referred to. Honecker, though defeated was able to make his state visit to West Germany in September 1987, as Moscow's policy reverted to courtship of Bonn.[28]

These two disputes clearly centered on what the East German leadership believed to be the national interests of the GDR.[29] So, in its own way, did the *third*, involving the rejection of perestroika. Honecker and the rest of the leadership were again acting in the GDR's national interests as they saw them. For the GDR to move toward marketization and democratization would mean losing its raison d'être, as Otto Reinhold argued in the passage quoted earlier. Its very survival as a socialist state would also be threatened if Poland reformed to the point of shedding its own socialist system. This was truer now than it had been in 1981 when East Berlin got so disturbed about Solidarity. The matter was indeed of vital concern to the GDR, but the concern of the leadership was in no way shared by the vast majority of the East German people. Whatever they may have thought about the existence of the GDR and its social system—and some were not initially averse to either—they were not willing to be left out of the growing surge toward reform because of what their leaders told them would be its consequences. For them, better no GDR at all than the GDR of "real existing socialism." Finally and comprehensively, the first German socialist state had failed its legitimacy test.

The Last Phase

Like the Czechoslovak and Bulgarian leaderships, as well as the Romanian, East Germany's leaders must have hoped initially that Gorbachev would be either removed from power or would himself slow down the impetus for reform in the Soviet Union. If this were to happen, a corresponding slowdown in Eastern Europe would be inevitable, and everybody could breathe more freely. But this was not taking place. On the contrary, the political upheavals continued in 1988 in Poland, Hungary, and the Soviet

Union itself. The East German attitude, therefore, soon hardened into a clear anti-Gorbachev position. In April 1988 the SED leadership obviously took sides against Gorbachev in the famous Nina Andreeva affair, the clearest dispute so far in the Soviet leadership. *Neues Deutschland* was the only East European party daily to print Andreeva's attack on Gorbachev and her defense of "Bolshevik principles."[30] It eventually did publish *Pravda's* counterblast to Andreeva's attack but only along with an article alluding to Gorbachev's alleged similarities with the Prague Spring "revisionists."[31]

By the end of 1989 the East German leaders openly criticized the course of developments in the Soviet Union and Eastern Europe. In December, Honecker referred to the Soviet reforms as a "march into anarchy," and the hyperactive Otto Reinhold was lashing out at reformers in general and Hungarian reformers in particular.[32] East German spokesmen now constantly hammered on how lucky East Germans were compared with the benighted citizens of the Soviet Union, Poland, and Hungary—all victims of the new disease of perestroika.

But the more their official spokesmen railed, the less notice the East German people took. Western visitors to the GDR from the end of 1988 to early 1989 reported a growing restlessness, even militancy, on the part of many East Germans. The population was convinced that the reform in Eastern Europe was taking root and that Gorbachev represented something genuinely new. This gave them the spirit to question, to demand, even to resist the actions of leadership which no longer looked as impregnable as it had even a few months ago. Regime and population were already on a collision course.

One of the striking and ironic symptoms of the SED's nervousness and isolation was its reintroduction of *Abgrenzung*. This time the portcullis was not lowered to keep out baleful influences from the Federal Republic, but from the Soviet Union. The danger from the East was judged greater than that from the West. The GDR's first attempt to insulate itself from the new threat came in the fall of 1988 with the almost hysterical rejection of the Soviet anti-Stalin film, *Repentance*, made by the Georgian director, Tengiz Abuladze, and eventually shown in the Soviet Union through the good offices of Abuladze's compatriot, Eduard Shevardnadze. Its showing was forbidden in the GDR, but it was carried on West German television. Enough East Germans saw it and were impressed enough for the SED leaders to lash out fiercely at what must have seemed to some of them a clear case of Soviet-West German ideological collusion. Critical reappraisals of communist history, it was argued, could be misused by "anti-communist forces" both at home and abroad. Abuladze's film, made by the Soviets, carried by the West

Germans, delivered into "the enemies' hands new material for demagogic tricks."[33]

The Abuladze film episode led to a continuing dispute between East German and Soviet ideologues and historians on the critical reassessment of history going on in the Soviet Union. But this was noticed by a relative few. What brought the SED-Soviet dispute to the forefront of national, and even world, attention was the announcement in November 1988 that the Soviet monthly press digest *Sputnik* had been effectively banned in the GDR, apparently for carrying "distorted" versions of history. What particularly angered the East German regime were articles in *Sputnik* that allegedly discredited German communists of past eras and contained interpretations that "violated" the GDR's constitution.[34] This may have been the nub of the whole issue and again showed the acute sensitivity of the East German leaders on the legitimacy question. Flaws in German communist history could not be admitted, particularly when suggested in the new spirit of spontaneity that was sweeping parts of the communist world.

This, then, was the new *Abgrenzung*, reflecting the current realities of Soviet-East German relations and the quickening erosion of alliance unity. But the East German regime did not settle for isolation; it looked around for soul mates. It tried to form a latter-day "little entente," this time comprising the GDR, Czechoslovakia, and Romania, like-minded states in their aversion to the reformist spirit. Particularly strong efforts were made to strengthen links with neighboring Czechoslovakia. These were, after all, the two "front-line" states in Europe, the first line of defense against the capitalist West. The Czechoslovaks were apparently not too happy about this East German hug of desperation, preferring to keep their options more open. But both leaderships realized that, if one of them began to give way to the reform surge, the other must succumb before long.

The GDR's most bizarre *mariage de convenance*, however, was with Romania, regarded since the mid-1980s as Europe's pariah state. In a perverse sense the two states were simply continuing their alliance of the summer of 1984. Again, perceived national interest, with the Soviet Union as the adversary, was the nexus. But now the context had changed completely. What had gained respect in 1984 aroused only disdain four years later. Honecker did himself no good, least of all among the East German population, by linking himself with Ceauşescu. But by now he seemed prompted by nothing but dogma and insecurity. *Neues Deutschland* went so far as to praise Ceauşescu's much abhorred "systematization" program for transforming the Romanian countryside.[35]

What was unnerving Honecker, though, was not the mounting opprobrium abroad, but the growing restiveness at home. The party rank and file was asking more questions than it used to, and many were obviously not happy with the answers they got. The *agitprop* apparatus simply could not cope. The banning of *Sputnik* caused special perplexity and indignation. Hundreds of local party organizations lodged official protests. A prominent East German writer (also a party member) told a West German magazine that the "unrest in the party" showed that "communists were becoming more mature." He continued:

> People are becoming more aware of what they actually are; of what role they should be playing in a socialist state. [They are aware] that they are not here to follow orders and to stand around with their hands in their pockets; but that they are free people and that important goals cannot be reached without broad discussion or without taking the risk of making mistakes.[36]

What statements like this also reflected was a growing mood of rebellion among some party intellectuals—not just writers and other creative artists, but social scientists and economists. The first example of a well-established member of the ruling elite breaking ranks and giving full support to perestroika was Markus Wolf, the GDR's long-standing "chief spy" who for many years was considered second in the security apparatus behind the veteran minister for state security, Erich Mielke. In his autobiographical novel, *The Troika*, published both in East and West Germany in 1989, Wolf enthusiastically backed both perestroika and glasnost. He was one of many East German communists trained in Moscow with a real loyalty to the Soviet Union and what it happened to be doing at any particular time. Many communists of this kind must have been puzzled by Honecker's line. After the fall of Honecker and the collapse of the system, an old "Muscovite" veteran explained what went wrong by saying that the SED did not do what the Soviet Union was doing.[37]

Wolf was the only top political establishment figure to speak up like this. No Politburo members, for example, were suspected of fully sharing his views. Guenter Schabowski, the party leader in East Berlin, seemed inclined toward reform and played a leading role in the ousting of Honecker. But the man in the top party ranks viewed as most sympathetic toward reform was Hans Modrow, SED first secretary in Dresden, who had been kept out of the Politburo because of his less than conformist views and had also become the target for considerable vindictiveness on the part of the Honecker coterie.[38]

Domestic restlessness increased with speculation over Honecker's physical condition. In the summer of 1989 his robust health at last showed signs of failing. In July he was hospitalized amid rumors that he was dying of cancer. The succession question, therefore, became urgent. Schabowski was being mentioned, but so was the longtime "crown prince," Egon Krenz. It was, in fact, Krenz who would take over from Honecker and try to salvage something from the collapse. Krenz at forty-nine had not only followed in Honecker's career footsteps—first as communist youth organization chief, then Central Committee secretary for security—but was an uncompromising supporter and articulate proponent of the hard line. Most recently he had endorsed the Chinese regime's bloody repressions in Tiananmen Square.[39] Many East Germans disliked him even more than they despised his master.

Background to the Collapse

In view of the massive popular demonstrations in October 1989 protesting and then rejecting communist rule, it seems extraordinary that only a few weeks before there had been little hint of such massive and rapid repudiation. From the beginning of the 1980s there was a marked rise in open dissatisfaction over economic conditions, especially consumer shortages, rising prices, and the housing shortage. And the public was increasingly irritated when the regime belabored the point that things were still better than in the rest of the Soviet bloc. The East Germans' yardstick was not, say, Poland, but West Germany, which all of them knew through television, and many of them were getting to know at first hand through the regimes' more liberal travel policy.

This growing dissatisfaction over economic conditions reflected one of the rising expectations many East German citizens had been entertaining for several years. Objectively, conditions in the GDR had been improving, and not just economically. Politically, as well as in the sphere of human rights and personal freedoms, life, in spite of all the irritations, had been getting easier. As mentioned, this was due to the increasing confidence of the Honecker regime, from about 1978 and 1985, and to the regime's need to live up to the Helsinki prescriptions. Living up to Helsinki became the passport to greater international respectability, something for which Honecker personally seems to have developed a craving.

Expectations, therefore, were already growing when Gorbachev appeared on the scene. His appearance gave the East German reformists a powerful boost, and for the Honecker regime this was a most threatening development. Without Gorbachev and against a background of relative international calm, Honecker would probably have continued his policy of gradual relaxation. But now the Gorbachev phenomenon was threatening not just the pace of this relaxation (turning it in a wrong direction, subverting the system and the whole principle of rule on which the GDR was based), but Gorbachev was unquestionably the catalyst in this mounting conflict that quickly led to the system's downfall. Honecker raised expectations; Gorbachev hijacked them. Now these expectations threatened Honecker, and the only recourse he knew was suppression. This explained the new *Abgrenzung* against Soviet "subversion." More seriously it explained punitive actions, already mentioned, against the Evangelical Church, the increased nervousness and erratic behavior of the police, and the regime's inconsistency. In short, the SED was losing control. The people knew it. They became bolder, more critical, less resigned to accepting a situation dictated solely by their ruling oligarchy. The GDR was slipping into a prerevolutionary situation.

The event that set the erosion on an accelerating, irreversible course was the local elections of May 7, 1989. The official results—the usual massive victory for the SED—were achieved only by the most fraudulent manipulation. Everybody knew there had been a considerable anti-SED vote that was in no way reflected in the official results. Besides, the regime's falsification campaign was unusually blatant.[40] Its director was Egon Krenz.

But, important though that episode was in arousing and concentrating popular indignation, the regime still had the strength to survive through suppression. Then came the mass defections to the Federal Republic through Hungary in the late summer of 1989, followed by those through Czechoslovakia. The defections through Hungary were a fatal blow for the Honecker regime—both the defections themselves and the action of the Hungarian government in permitting them, with the collusion of Moscow. Honecker could hardly have expected much from Gorbachev, but he might have hoped the Soviet leader would have avoided complicity in an action that so clearly undermined the GDR. He was now too weak and unnerved to withstand any more.

The beginning of the end came with the mass demonstrations in Leipzig in October that spread throughout the country. These had nothing to do with emigration or defections. They were conducted by East Germans intending to stay but repudiating the communist system. At the macabre forty-year celebrations at the beginning of October of the founding of the GDR, the self-congratulations sounded almost hysterical. Honecker himself, back on view after his severe illness, looked a shadow of his old self. The principal guest, Gorbachev, himself, was noncommittal in public about the crisis, but in private he is believed to have urged concessions, ruling out any interference from Soviet troops stationed in the GDR.[41] The celebrations, as a whole, only spurred the public anger that hastened the end.

There was still the possibility of a Tiananmen Square "solution," and Honecker and others appear to have considered it. This was apparently when Egon Krenz finally realized that the GDR's turning point in history had arrived. On October 9 in Leipzig he is reported to have been finally persuaded by local dignitaries to prevent the use of armed force against demonstrators, thereby avoiding a bloodbath.[42]

He succeeded Honecker very soon afterward and set about trying to shed the ballast of forty years of communist rule in the German Democratic Republic. In doing so he made the historic concession of November 9, 1989, the opening of the frontiers. The turning point in East German history had now become the turning point in European history.[43] As for Krenz, shedding the ballast, with the huge concessions this involved, was the necessary prelude to salvaging what could be saved. He set about his job with extraordinary energy and apparent self-confidence, seeking continually to stay ahead of the situation, meeting change by provoking more change. But his situation again recalled the jibe made much earlier in Hungary about the Hungarian Communist Party behaving, in its policy of concessions, like the man being chased by a wolf and shedding his clothes to stay ahead.[44] More than any Hungarian, Krenz was very much in that situation—running faster, shedding more. And the chances were that the wolf would get him.

The wolf did get him. On December 3, 1989, after forty-four days of trying to keep up with the galloping pace of events, Krenz was unseated when the whole SED Politburo and Central Committee resigned. The more Krenz tried to disown the past, the clearer his own intimate association with it became. And the more the whole SED tried to disown the past, the more it disowned itself.

Actually, December 3, 1989, was a crucial day not just for Egon Krenz, but for Germany and Europe. If November 9, the day the frontiers were opened, was the decisive day in German and European history, December 3 was the day when its full significance became obvious. It was the failure and fall of Krenz that put aside all hopes and illusions about the viability of the GDR.[45] Clearly, East German opinion was not only massively in favor of reform but was becoming massively in favor of reunification. From then on, it was just a question of time, and the time was running out.

Hans Modrow, the reformer from Dresden, now took over as prime minister. It was too late, though, for him to do anything but make the demise of his country as orderly and dignified as possible. But even that was impossible. Between two thousand and three thousand East Germans a day were moving to West Germany, and on the unofficial level reunification was in full swing by the end of 1989. In the new year the economy and civil authority in the GDR began to come apart. East Germany was almost literally collapsing into the arms of West Germany. Fears were expressed about a total breakdown of order. The worst-case scenario depicted the Soviet troops stationed on East German territory themselves being involved in violence and bloodshed. But with the early elections and their decisive result, and Gorbachev's acquiescence (albeit with qualifications) in German reunification, the nightmare scenario did not materialize. The rest would be history, no longer East German, but German, and European.

6 Czechoslovakia: The Kinder, Gentler Revolution

In January 1983 Antonín Dolejší, by no means one of the most obtuse of Czechoslovak conservatives, wrote an article in *Nová Mysl*, a party theoretical journal, entitled "The Revolutionary Epoch Can Last Centuries." The key to the article was his flat statement that "the present and the future already belong to communism."[1] It was an orthodox, thoroughly dogmatic article, strongly against private farming, small-scale industry, whether private or public, and any concession to the growing East European fad for small private holdings in any field. The communist party was the exclusive leader of society and must constantly be on its guard against infiltration and subversion. The Soviet experience was of paramount importance, as was the concept of the dictatorship of the proletariat, "whose fundamental features have a general international validity." Dolejší acknowledged the current difficulties through which the movement and his own country were passing and the opportunities all this was giving to the "counter-revolutionaries." But socialism would survive, because socialism was right, and it would all work out in the end.

Dolejší's article was intended as a counterblast to the doubts about the future that the deteriorating economic situation in Czechoslovakia was raising and to the calls for reform, usually along Hungarian lines, that were timidly being raised. Premier Lubomír Štrougal, for example, was speaking about socialist entrepreneurship, and Jaromír Šedlák, a senior member of his staff, was writing the following:

> No really fundamental turning-point in the economy can be reached in Czechoslovakia unless qualitative transformations are brought about in the overall social climate, at all levels and in all social groups. . . . The social climate that prevails at the moment is characterized by increased feelings of hopelessness. Many people are losing hope in the future.[2]

The conservative constituency represented by Dolejší was strong in 1983. It had considerably weakened by the end of 1989 but was still a political force to be reckoned with. In this respect there was a strong similarity between it and the German Democratic Republic (GDR), at least until the Honecker regime's dramatic collapse in October 1989. Dolejší and his counterparts in East Berlin spoke for strong left-socialist and communist political tradition. The East German tradition is often cited, but the Czechoslovak (here "Czech" is more correct) is often ignored amid the acclamation of the democratic character of the interwar republic.

The point is that the large communist movement, breaking off from the former socialist mainstream after the establishment of the Comintern, prospered in the democratic tolerance of the first Czechoslovak republic. Even during the 1920s when it obediently followed the Comintern's line against the newly founded Czechoslovak republic as an instrument of Western imperialism, the Communist Party of Czechoslovakia got solid electoral backing.[3] After the popular disillusionment with the West resulting from the Munich Agreement of 1938, and then with the Soviet victories in World War II, the communists' fortunes rose further, and in 1946 they were clearly the strongest political party in the Czech Lands (though not nearly so strong in Slovakia). In the Czech Lands, immediately after World War II, the leftist trend politically and the Pan-Slavic trend culturally were both very strong. The democratic, pro-Western trends, once personified and so ably led by Tomáš Masaryk, were on the defensive, poorly led and disorganized. The liberal-democratic structure, reinstated in 1945, fell an easy victim to the brilliantly led communist coup in February 1948.

The subsequent record of communist Czechoslovakia was a failure by any yardstick, and the communist and Pan-Slavic tradition had been shattered. But in the 1980s, as represented by people like Dolejší, it still had its hard core of adherents whose defense of it seemed only to get more shrill as its credibility grew weaker. This hard core now existed only in Czechoslovakia, the GDR, and probably in Bulgaria—the three East European countries which had a communist tradition.

In Czechoslovakia, since the crushing of reform by Soviet-led troops in 1968, this hard core had been supported by a large careerist bureaucracy put in place by the "normalization" process after the Prague Spring. It amounted to a new governing class bent on preserving the status quo, only marginally for ideological reasons and mainly for reasons of power, place, and privilege. To preserve the status quo, the Czechoslovak leaders, under Gustáv Husák, were not averse to reforms which, at any other time before the late 1980s, might have seemed considerable, even extensive. But reform had come to mean *systemic* change, and, in relation to that, what the Czechoslovak leaders would countenance was marginal, even irrelevant. In any case, the essential precondition for systemic reform in Czechoslovakia today would be the repudiation not only of the August 1968 invasion and the subsequent normalization, but also of those who had ruled it for the last twenty years. For Czechoslovakia's governing class, therefore, the question was one of survival. It amounted to the same for their counterparts in the rest of Eastern Europe. But nowhere else was the matter quite as poignant or momentous.

These mixed but converging motives made Czechoslovakia's leaders so resistant to change. But this resistance would not have been as effective for so long had there been persistent, concerted pressure from below. Pressure from below there certainly was, beginning in the late seventies and mounting during the eighties. But for many years this pressure, involving intellectuals, large numbers of young people, and increasingly confident religious believers, lacked any component of working-class support. The same, of course, was true for Hungary. But in Hungary there was an effective combination of regime reformers and opposition intellectuals. This brought the country toward parliamentary democracy and the constitutional state. But the absence of strong worker commitment still left open the question of how firm the Hungarian progress would be in the long run.

In Czechoslovakia it was to be very late in the day before worker dissatisfaction was strong enough to tip the scales away from the ruling leadership. What this signified in historical terms was the patient proletarian acceptance—as distinct from support—of the communist regime. Throughout its more than forty-year history the Czechoslovak communist regime had made a point of appeasing the working class, especially in the heavy industrial sectors. Since the beginning of the 1960s, this had been one of the main reasons for the decline of the economy. But until it declined to the point where the workers' material interests were seriously affected, their attitudes were not likely to change in favor of systemic reform. Nor could they have been impressed by the economic performance of Eastern Europe's two reform pioneers, Hungary and Poland—a performance that only served to fortify traditional Czech smugness about the backwardness of their neighbors. As to political reform, most of them had always been for it; very few of them had any affection for their communist rulers. But the liberal tradition of Masaryk was never so strong among Czechoslovakia's workers (not to speak of the collectivized peasantry) that they would rashly risk the material benefits of the present for the promise of future political freedoms.

Even toward the end of 1989, therefore, Czechoslovakia seemed some way from the traditional "prerevolutionary situation." Those who espoused reform were growing in numbers and were losing their previous fears and inhibitions. They also were affected by the spirit of reform sweeping parts of Eastern Europe and the Soviet Union. But their best hope of support in the shorter run seemed to lay not so much with the workers as with the increasing number of defections to their cause from the ranks of the ruling elite. Because of 1968 and after, the ruling elite did seem locked into the conservatism of self-preservation. Still, the numbers of those apparently ready to make the leap were growing. And, once they did, others would follow. Then, when self-preservation begins to look like self-destruction, the trickle would become a flow, then a flood.

Movement Without Purpose

There had been serious, specific obstacles to systemic reform in Czechoslovakia. But the lack of systemic change had not meant total immobility. During the 1980s, especially after the emergence of Gorbachev as a radical reformer, there was considerable movement. Some of this was the result of economic necessity, some of popular pressure. Together, they brought changes to Czechoslovakia, even if these still fell far short of any systemic reform. But the fact that any changes were attempted made the regime uneasy lest they begin to threaten the system they were designed to protect.

It was economic reform with which the Husák regime was almost exclusively preoccupied. During the first half of the 1980s the leadership's favorite expression with regard to the economy was *intensification*. This was not only because the Czechoslovak economy urgently needed intensification but because some political leaders (although very few real economists) believed this could be done without basic reform. Intensification in Czechoslovakia had been discussed ever since the mid-1960s and had been very much on the minds of the Prague Spring reformers. They, however, knew that real intensification meant real reform. But after the August 1968 invasion, even the word "reform" disappeared from all but the most specialized journals throughout Eastern Europe. This was especially the case in Czechoslovakia where the trauma of the Prague Spring had a local and immediate relevance.

Both the economists and the more perceptive political leaders, like premier Lubomír Štrougal, realized how self-defeating it was for the economy to keep prolonging its extensive phase. Modernization had been slow and patchy. The manufacturing base was too broad, producing too many items. The employment rate was very high—many women were in the work force—but there was still a labor shortage. Absenteeism and loafing on the job were standard operational procedure. After all, "in an economy short on labor, laxity at work is a kind of fringe benefit the management is forced to concede."[4] Extensive economic development also led to priority being given to primary processing of manufactures at the expense of more sophisticated forms. There was plenty of crude steel, but far too few fine washing machines. There also was a huge waste of energy as well as manpower.

In retrospect, in view of all the blunders and procrastination, what was remarkable about the Czechoslovak economy was its capacity to survive, its ability to stumble along without the comprehensive breakdown many predicted. (This ability, of course, had long played into the hands of political conservatives.) This resilience enabled Husák to achieve one of the essentials of his "normalization" policy: promotion of the standard of living through "consumerism." Between 1971 and 1975, although real wages rose only by about 5 percent, personal consumption in Czechoslovakia rose by 27 percent. In 1971 one in seventeen people had an automobile; in 1975 one in ten; in 1979 one in eight.[5] Figures like these did much to explain why "normalization" worked for as long as it did—and without the massive Western credits to which all the other East European countries resorted.[6]

But this politically motivated determination to keep up living standards could not last indefinitely. It distorted the overall economic situation and eventually made economic reform all the more necessary. Even by the mid-1970s the outlook was much less promising. The OPEC price explosion of the early seventies and the Soviets' response in sharply raising their own oil prices for Eastern Europe, then the second OPEC price explosion at the end of the decade, brought on a crisis in which Czechoslovakia and the GDR, as the region's two most industrialized countries, tended to suffer the most. By 1980 Czechoslovakia was paying nearly five times as much for a ton of Soviet oil as it had in 1971—and was importing about twice as much. Nor did the situation improve. In 1980 Czechoslovakia's Soviet oil bill was 8,600 million crowns (fifteen crowns to the dollar at the official rate of exchange). In 1986 it was 23,500 million crowns.[7]

This was a crippling disability which helped produce, and partly coincided with, the economic depression many had predicted. The economy experienced negative economic growth in 1981 and 1982 and overall negative national income in 1981. It all recalled the situation at the beginning of the 1960s, the situation that had helped set off the chain of events leading to the Prague Spring. Indeed, in some key respects it was now worse. At the beginning of the 1960s both industry and important elements of the infrastructure were twenty years younger, and the price of Soviet raw materials was cheap and expected to stay cheap. The deterioration since then, in both the external and internal economic situation, was both cumulative and accelerating. But the biggest single problem was domestic: the huge numbers of unfinished investment projects. At the end of 1981, about 30,000 industrial building sites stood unfinished—tied-up capital representing just over 20 percent of all capital funds in the Czechoslovak economy for that year.[8]

It was an alarming economic situation, emboldening an increasing number of economists to urge that basic reform could no longer be delayed. Even the regime leadership was prompted to do something. But its response was very disappointing, even for some relative conservatives. The so-called "Set of Measures," which through allowing for some degree of decision-making decentralization in both industry and agriculture, merely recalled the remedial steps that had been taken twenty-three years before, in 1958, which even then were considered inadequate to the need.[9]

But some regime leaders and apologists were to claim that the "Set of Measures" was by no means the only part of their early eighties strategy. In this context the "intensification" came into its own. An economic official defended the allegedly "do nothing" policy of those years as follows: "If the word stagnation is to be used, then it must be said that we gave preference to stagnation over growth, or to be more precise, to internal and external balance over excessive growth."[10] Hungary "was not for us," said the same official, echoing a widespread Czechoslovak opinion.[11] The decision to stagnate, or to let stagnation take its course, should really be seen as a decision to intensify.

Leaving aside the complacency of remarks like these, it remained a moot question just how much calculating guidance the regime did exercise over the course of economic development in the first half of the 1980s. The Czechoslovak economy's slow performance during that period was probably due more to accumulated past mistakes than to any deliberately planned reorientation. All the same, some of the desired effects of intensification did become apparent by 1985. The cutbacks made earlier in the decade in the imports of energy and raw materials (some of them made necessary by a 10 percent cut in Soviet oil exports) and the reduction of investments and of the already small imports of Western technology undoubtedly contributed to the depressed growth which regime spokesmen said was deliberate. And when from 1983 to 1985 the economy began to pick up again, it showed signs of intensive growth, i.e., growth sustained by the mobilization of reserves and the better processing of available inputs.

The year 1985 was considered crucial in the whole intensification process. Domestic net material output was scheduled to grow faster than the volume of output, i.e., value added was more important than growth in quantitative terms. Increases in national income were to be achieved mainly through increased productivity and continuing reductions in the use of energy. More automation, electronic innovations, and whatever modern technology was available were to be introduced into the economy as quickly as possible.

Reform Options

Whatever the motives, or the exaggerated claims made for it, "intensification" did have some effect. But it only scratched the surface of Czechoslovakia's economic problems and made the debate about further reform all the more acute and urgent. Broadly speaking, there were three options: (1) basic reform, (2) the "halfway house" approach, (3) doing nothing.

Although much militant conservatism, and probably even more inertia, favored the "do-nothing" option, the serious, practical, debate tended to center on basic reform and the halfway approach. Thus, the third important debate began on the economic structure since the invasion of Czechoslovakia in 1968. The first had been at the beginning of the seventies and resulted in a complete victory for the reactionaries and the return to the command structure. It was this structure, with a few subsequent modifications, that the "do-nothing" school was defending now. The second debate had been at the turn of the eighties and had brought forth the "Set of Measures." Now, as the Czechoslovak economy deteriorated and reform was gathering pace in the Soviet Union and parts of Eastern Europe, the advocates of basic reform were more numerous, more courageous, and with a palpably stronger case than ever before. What they appeared to have in mind were some of the proposals being implemented in Hungary and those contained in the Polish Reformed Economic System (RES) prepared during the Solidarity period and then shelved after martial law. (Compared with the Hungarian, Polish, and even Soviet reforms of the late eighties, such proposals barely qualified, of course, as basic or systemic reform, being much closer to the "halfway house" variety.)

The principal political champion of this first option was Premier Štrougal, although, typically, he never specifically committed himself.[12] The boldest reform champion in the governmental ranks, however, was Leopold Lér, the finance minister. Lér had been closely associated with the 1981 "Set of Measures" but had since realized their inadequacy and apparently wanted to go much further. He was forced to retire in October 1985, not apparently for political reasons but for genuine reasons of poor health. Lower down the hierarchy was a whole bevy of professional economists who became more audacious as the decade wore on and as the economy wore out. The most notable of them was probably Valtr Komárek of the Institute for Economic Forecasting in Prague, the main stronghold of the economic reformers. Komárek had almost certainly been an advocate of basic reform long before he considered the political climate ripe enough to declare himself one.[13] (At the end of the decade he was briefly first deputy prime minister of Czechoslovakia.)

The pressure for at least some basic reform was obviously strong enough in 1985 for President and party leader Husák to step in with one of his ex cathedra declamations. It showed both his awareness of the political implications involved and the continuing impact of the trauma of the Prague Spring. "We will not take the road of any of the market-oriented concepts that would weaken [the system of] socialist collective property and the party's leading role in the economy. We have had bad experience of that kind of thing."[14]

Husák in 1985 was not nearly as powerful as he had been even five years earlier, but he certainly had strong enough apparatchik backing when he disparaged anything that smacked of the Prague Spring. In such remarks, however, Husák was not explicitly ruling out reform. He was warning any actual or potential "wild men" not to go too far. In practical terms he was conniving at the "halfway house" option. In typical fashion he was not saying what should, but what should not, be done.

A Yugoslav correspondent, Lazar Martinović, summed up the situation well, revealing a keen insight into Czechoslovak political mores. The problem, he said, in an article entitled "Subtle Indications of Change," was how to introduce a certain amount of decentralization "without basically disturbing central planning as the key regulator of the country's economic life." But "even the most responsible personalities do not have a clear-cut idea of what should be done." "Market socialism" was being generally criticized, but, continued Martinović, "such criticism is generally accepted more as a theoretical point of departure than a categorical negative precept for practical economic policy." Martinović added that when the official press was recommending neither "exaggerated centralization" nor "absolute decentralization," that was a reliable indication that some changes were being prepared. The sense of expectancy had aroused considerable public interest in the subject, according to Martinović. "This is why the public has recently been agitated by such a development and everybody wants to speak his mind."[15]

What had happened over the previous two years was that the official mood of opposition to basic reform had changed to one of ambivalence, even resignation. And with the change of mood many Czechoslovaks who were engaged in the economic process began evading or ignoring the restrictions applying. Again, Martinović captures perfectly the Czechoslovak way of doing things:

> You can see in Czechoslovak towns stalls from which the owners of gardens sell their fruit and vegetables. Gradually, private services are also being allowed, especially for people working after normal hours in the socialist sector of the economy. True, there is not much talk about the full-fledged revival of the private sector, but there are signs that this will be done gradually and cautiously.[16]

Subsequently, in 1986 minor reforms were introduced in agriculture, as a result of which only procuring grain and slaughtering animals was left obligatory. At the same time general state subsidies for agriculture were reduced. The idea behind the new changes was that some of the money saved by reduced subsidies should be used to increase procurement prices for high-quality products.

There also had been some movement in trade policy toward the West. By mid-1986 eight joint ventures were being conducted with Western partners, and the permitted foreign share of the equity had been raised from 40 percent to 49 percent. (Again, to keep such progress in perspective, it might be mentioned that in a matter of two years the Hungarian government was permitting 100 percent foreign ownership of equity.) But joint *production* ventures with Western companies now numbered more than a hundred. Such ventures had the advantage of giving the Czechoslovak companies increased access to Western technology without them having to pay for it. Not surprisingly, the Federal Republic of Germany was the biggest Western operator in this field, participating in 46 percent of Czechoslovakia's Western joint-production ventures.[17]

As the seventeenth Czechoslovak Party Congress in March 1986 approached, there was an air of expectancy about economic reform. Some anticipated that far-reaching reforms would be announced at the congress; others warned of the enormous dislocation such reform would entail. In late 1985 *Nová Mysl* wrote that "the reconstruction of the economic mechanism represents a task comparable in its complexity with the reconstruction of the economy in the period of industrialization and the collectivization of agriculture."[18] Many were prepared to settle for "intensification" and give it a chance to work. For them, basic reform was a risky leap.

The Impact of Gorbachev

The lines being drawn in the economic debate generally reflected the main political alignments in public life, in which the Gorbachev factor was now beginning to play an important and unsettling role. Gorbachev had been elected Soviet party leader in March 1985 and quickly became a disturbing element for the long-established Czechoslovak leaders. Though he did not emerge as a radical systemic reformer till about two years later, right from the beginning he stood for change and modernization and was considered to have little sympathy or patience with several of the East European leaderships, of which the Czechoslovak was, unsurprisingly, assumed to be one.

For many Czechoslovaks the question of reform—economic reform in the first instance—became closely linked with that of the reaction to Gorbachev. Responding to Gorbachev would break up the established pattern of Czechoslovak politics, sharpen existing divisions, and let some much-needed fresh air into a stifling atmosphere. But it would be wrong to conclude that Gorbachev began the reform process in Czechoslovakia. What he did was to give a political edge to the economic process already under way. He also dramatized it and gave it a note of urgency, raising at the same time the question of how long one or more of the current Czechoslovak leaders would politically survive.

The Czechoslovak leaders divided on Gorbachev the way they had divided over economic reform. Štrougal and his followers lower down the ladder (he was virtually isolated in the Politburo itself) saw Gorbachev as both an ally and an opportunity. At the other end of the ruling spectrum Vasíl Bilak, with several supporters in the highest leadership, instinctively rejected Gorbachev's perestroika. Bilak himself at first sounded almost East German in his tone of rejection.[19] In between was a group of senior leaders who, whatever they may have thought initially about the necessity for change, had come to regard it as unavoidable. The question was what kind of change and how much? At the center of this group was Husák, standing before yet another new phase in his variegated and turbulent career.

At the Seventeenth Party Congress in March 1986 Štrougal's speech reflected the differences over reform inside the leadership. He complained that the question of "perfecting the economic mechanism" had been on the agenda for the last five years, i.e., since the introduction of the "Set of Measures," but that precious little had been done about it. "Intensification" had not been carried far enough, nor had the federal agencies of government "seen to the necessary systemic requisites." Czechoslovakia and its economy were not keeping up with the needs of the time.[20]

Though, characteristically, the congress reelected the same old leadership virtually intact, the divisions between the supporters of reform and those expressing caution were evident throughout. (The degree of caution expressed was a generally accurate measure of the actual *opposition* the speaker felt toward reform.) Husák, steadily becoming persuaded of their inevitability, argued that the country "must not be afraid of reforms."[21] He was voicing the conclusion of the reluctant majority that there was little point in resisting the irresistible. Even Bilak concurred, although in his resourceful and tactically astute way he began a delaying action aimed partly at diluting whatever reforms might be enacted and partly in the hope that Gorbachev, perestroika, and glasnost would turn out to be yet another ephemeral aberration—like the Prague Spring.

Actually, Bilak and the many like him were not averse to a considerable degree of "socialist" economic reform, one that preserved the command structure and safeguarded the leading role of the party. Nor did he believe that a socialist state should resort to "administrative measures"—that is, unless absolutely necessary. Despite his severity toward the enemies of socialism he did not advocate anything like a return to the terror of the fifties. He was fond of describing himself as a "man of January," i.e., he had heartily welcomed the downfall at the beginning of 1968 of Antonín Novotný, the veteran communist leader (against whom he bore a strong personal animus), and favored federal status for Slovakia. But he was adamantly opposed to the way the 1968 reform developed into the Prague Spring.

Bilak and most of his supporters drew a sharp line at *political* reform. This, they felt, could lead to that weakening of party rule which they associated with the Prague Spring. It would also begin to undermine the whole post-1968 "normalization" regime. On this score they abhorred the very notion of glasnost. Just as glasnost in the Soviet Union had unavoidably led to yet another inquest on the Stalinist period, so in Czechoslovakia it would lead to a reexamination of every aspect of the Prague Spring, especially the invasion, and subsequent normalization. And, in their vehement opposition to this, the Bilak conservatives were joined by the moderates around Husák, as well as many, if not most, of the supporters of economic reform itself. This was the factor that inhibited Štrougal, for example, from emerging as a full-fledged reformer. (There were also enough old skeletons in his closet.) This fear of the past was still the nexus in Czechoslovak public life binding the ruling elite together. But as the 1980s progressed, more and more members of that elite broke away and embraced reform. Their numbers would multiply but, until almost to the end of 1989, it still seemed they were not strong enough to become a determining factor on the political scene.

In the course of their delaying action Bilak and his followers also resorted to another stratagem, one that involved a seeming repudiation of a deeply held principle regarding the Soviet Union. During the Brezhnev era none had been stronger than they in holding up the Soviet Union as the universal paragon and model. This, of course, had been a Czechoslovak communist tradition since Klement Gottwald, carried on by Novotný and by the post-1968 Husák. Bilak, personally, had elevated it to a canon of "normalized" behavior. Now, however, to the derision of many of his opponents, Bilak became an ardent upholder of the principle of "own roads to socialism." While ostensibly, if only occasionally, praising Gorbachev, and even perestroika in its Soviet setting, he became almost "Romanian" in his insistence on national solutions. What was good for the Soviet Union was no longer automatically good for Czechoslovakia. Bilak actually went further. The Czechoslovak experience, he argued, might even be useful for the Soviet Union. Having gone through 1968, the Czechoslovak comrades might act as a moderating influence on the "impulses" of their Soviet colleagues, as well as on others similarly tempted.[22]

Gorbachev's disturbing impact reached a peak in Czechoslovak politics during the first half of 1987. In January at a CPSU Central Committee plenum, Gorbachev made the first of the great speeches that stamped him as a radical systemic reformer. It was also announced that in April he would make a state visit to Czechoslovakia. To prepare for his arrival, Soviet foreign minister Shevardnadze and Politburo member Lev Zaikov paid separate visits to Prague amid great speculation about how far the Czechoslovak leadership would follow Gorbachev's initiative. The Soviets, for their part, were anxious for their East European allies to follow but were also at pains to stress both state and party independence within the alliance. Valentin Falin, for example, the deputy head of the Soviet Central Committee's international department, told the West German daily Die Welt that they were not "writing prescriptions." "Our friends will decide themselves," he continued, "what they consider appropriate. I am sure that whatever happens in Czechoslovakia will not happen in a Soviet way."[23]

But no matter how different the two approaches were, the Czechoslovak leadership was anxious to see the forthcoming visit of Gorbachev pass off without serious signs of division. Moreover, whatever the Czechoslovak leaders, collectively or severally, may have thought about the new Soviet leader and his policies, they had to take into account the increasingly important factor of public opinion. And this was solidly behind Gorbachev. True, there was some popular skepticism about the Soviet leader; however impressive his reform credentials might be in Moscow, many Czechoslovaks would judge him mainly in reference to the Prague Spring. Indeed, the Prague Spring and the Soviet-led invasion cast their shadow over the entire visit, much as the Czechoslovak leaders tried to behave as if neither had ever happened. But, overall, the public's view of Gorbachev was one of positive curiosity, and this was enough to make their leaders nervous.

They showed their nervousness, as they usually did on occasions of tension, by both concessions and repression. At the beginning of 1987 a long-term economic reform program was announced amid considerable publicity. Its main aspects will be discussed later, but its character and timing were at least partly designed to appease any impatience in Moscow. On the eve of Gorbachev's visit Husák, at a Central Committee plenum in March, almost sounded like a genuine reformer—at least more like Štrougal than ever before. He not only referred to economic reform but, however vaguely, to some aspects of political reform. For example, he promised that the possibility of conducting party elections by secret ballot was being examined. (This change was subsequently introduced and kept.) Social organizations, he said, should be "activated." Finally, in an obvious reference to reform in the Soviet Union, he said the Czechoslovak regime was "studying the experience of the fraternal countries" and "looking for optimal forms suitable to our condition."[24]

Actually, the period immediately prior to Gorbachev's arrival was in some ways more exciting than the visit itself. The public rumors and the signs of official nervousness demonstrated the Soviet leader's impact. But both the hopes and the fears surrounding the visit turned out to be exaggerated. Gorbachev did not, as many officials worried, try to enforce a reformist policy or a top-level purge. On the other hand, the "wishful thinking" rumors that he would meet Alexander Dubček, rehabilitate the Prague Spring, and condemn the Soviet-led invasion turned out to be totally groundless. (The three-day delay in his arrival, ostensibly due to influenza, only served to stoke the wildest conflicting rumors.)

In relation to these hopes, fears, and expectations, the visit itself could not have avoided being an anticlimax. Neither the best hopes nor the worst fears were fulfilled. Gorbachev's clearest reference to the Prague Spring certainly disappointed many hopes that had been kindled:

> It did not grow out of nothing. Problems had been allowed to pile up in society. Some people declared that the working class was a conservative force. See what kind of revolutionaries and zealots of renewal surfaced at that time! According to them the revolutionary force included artists and journalists, while the communist party was a party of the working

class, and useless. They also made all manner of other claims such as that the economy had to be returned to private hands.[25]

To most observers at the time, Gorbachev's remark still seemed to reject the Prague Spring. Not once during his visit, however, did he endorse the Soviet-led invasion of August 1968. But neither did he reject the Brezhnev Doctrine. In brief, on all the neuralgic issues, Gorbachev was deliberately ambivalent. The regime must have been relieved; it could not have expected better. The public, on the other hand, had hoped for more.

On the more immediate issue of following his own example of reform Gorbachev was also equivocal:

> One can say that the most reliable yardstick by which to measure the seriousness of a ruling communist party today is its attitude not only to its own experience but also to the experience of its friends. As regards the value of this experience, we consider that the following is the only criterion: social practice and the results of socio-economic development, the strengthening of socialism in practice.[26]

That was the kind of formulation even a Bilak could live with. There was no pressure here—at least in public—for the regime basically to change course—perhaps just accelerate it somewhat. And that it could say it was already doing with its major economic reform program.

The Question of Reform

"The Concretization of the Principles of the Restructuring of the Economic Mechanism of the CSSR" ("Principles of Reconstruction"), had been announced in January 1987.[27] But the program as a whole was due to begin only with the start of the next Five Year Plan (1991–95). Prior to this, some important preparatory experiments were to be carried out. Among them were decentralization as applied in selected enterprises, a reform of wholesale prices to be prepared by January 1989, and more flexible forms of "socialist enterprise" involving the greater use of indirect indicators and exchange rates.

In the context of "normalized" Czechoslovakia since 1968, the "Principles of Reconstruction" did represent a real step forward. A significant shift was envisaged toward enterprise autonomy away from the central and intermediate agencies. The central agencies were to concentrate on strategic planning and would henceforward issue guidelines rather than directions. There was an element, of course, of déjà vu about much of what was planned. It looked less like systemic reform and more like the old practice of tacking bits of capitalism onto what was still basically socialism. Looked at from the perspective of 1989, with Hungary, Poland, and even the Soviet Union in mind, the "Principles of Reconstruction" look very tame indeed. But, for the Czechoslovak regime, which had virtually avoided reform since "normalization," it was a real effort to adapt both to the domestic needs and the perceived new requirements of Soviet-Czechoslovak relations.

The growing number of basic reformers in Czechoslovakia, not to mention committed members of the opposition, continued to criticize the new plans as inadequate. Štrougal was constantly criticizing the "excessive caution" of the regime. But Gorbachev seemed satisfied with the Czechoslovak situation. In an interview in May 1987, shortly after his visit, he told an Italian correspondent:

> The evaluation of the events of 1968 is primarily up to the Czechoslovak comrades themselves. The leadership of the CPCS, headed by Comrade Husák, has accomplished a great deal since then. Czechoslovakia has made remarkable progress in many fields and I witnessed this personally in my recent visit there.[28]

The Czechoslovak regime's attempts at *economic* reform were, indeed, often underestimated, not only inside the country, but by many Western observers. However, the few who watched Czechoslovakia closely, especially those aware of the formidable obstacles to change, were not unimpressed. A Radio Free Europe analyst, for example, writing in June 1987, thought that "contrary to many Western reports, the Czechoslovak 'normalization' regime's adaptation to the new reformist line has been one of the swiftest. . . ."[29]

In retrospect, the Gorbachev visit was a watershed in the reform process as well as in relations with Moscow. *But it led to quite opposite results from those generally expected.* Rather than further stimulating reform along lines conforming to the Soviet pattern and binding the Czechoslovaks closer to Moscow's policy, it resulted in a slackening of reform urgency and less Soviet direction rather than more.

Actually, the Husák regime had begun to take advantage of one of the great paradoxes of Gorbachev's rule. When Gorbachev, in early 1987, turned to systemic reform at home, he did not insist that Eastern Europe follow suit. On the contrary, the East European leaderships were now left very much to themselves. They could choose systemic reform, partial reform, or no reform. Nothing was mandatory. As for leadership changes, if they occurred, they would mainly be the result of local, not Soviet, initiative.

This Soviet laissez-faire certainly meant relief for a Czechoslovak leadership most of whom had become very nervous. It was now left with a freedom in relations with Moscow that no leadership in the entire history of communist Czechoslovakia had enjoyed. As to how it was to use its unexpected liberty, it was typical that the leadership neither embraced radical reform, like Poland and Hungary, nor rejected virtually any reform, like Romania and the GDR. Its stance was equivocal, neither rejecting nor embracing change. It stuck with its comprehensive, but far from radical, economic reform and avoided political reform.

Husák, for one, seemed content with the results of Gorbachev's visit. There would be change, but it would be defined, and timed, in Prague and not Moscow. "Everywhere," he said in August 1987, "an effort is being made to change deep-rooted notions and habits. Each socialist country is proceeding in this effort in accordance with its own conditions, needs, and experiences."[30]

No one seemed more satisfied with the significance of the Gorbachev visit than Bilak and the conservatives. In an article suggestively entitled "For Our Common European Home," he strongly supported Gorbachev, making an almost fervent plea for the "new thinking," being careful to extol at the same time the right of every country to proceed according to its own conditions.[31] Actually, Gorbachev's new views on the East European relationship vindicated Bilak's line on independence which he had been espousing ever since Gorbachev became Soviet leader. His conversion to "own roads to socialism" had been very timely.

Change at the Top

This new situation must be taken into account when trying to explain Husák's stepping down from the party leadership in December 1987, only eight months after Gorbachev's visit. Many observers assumed, almost automatically, that the Soviet leader was behind the change. But, though one may assume that Gorbachev was consulted, the evidence that exists, direct and circumstantial, points to the change being domestically initiated, partly or largely by Husák himself.

There were important differences between Husák's resignation and that of János Kádár in Hungary the following May. The situation in the two countries was quite different. Hungary was heading toward comprehensive and groundbreaking reform, and Kádár was standing in its way. His political demise, though the result of a carefully laid plan, took place openly, and much to his surprise, at a Central Committee plenum. Husák was certainly not standing in the way of any groundbreaking reform in Czechoslovakia, and his departure was less "democratically" arrived at than Kádár's. It was, in fact, initially intimated by the classic ploy of "nonappearance," beloved of all Kremlinologists. It was his failure to appear on the reviewing rostrum in Red Square in Moscow at the October Revolutionary celebrations in November 1987 that prompted the expectancy of his departure.

But, however different the two resignations, they were basically similar in being initiated and engineered domestically, not in the Kremlin. Neither leader was a favorite of Gorbachev's. Husák stood for reaction, or, at best, change with dragging feet, which in the Czechoslovak context was a particular embarrassment for the Soviet leader. For the numerous skeptics about the seriousness and depth of Gorbachev's reform intentions, the Prague Spring, the August 1968 invasion, and the Brezhnev Doctrine together formed a crucial "trinity" testing his real intentions. Yet, as was evident during his visit to Czechoslovakia in May 1987, Gorbachev could not vindicate the one and condemn the other two, without repudiating the whole "normalization" process, as well as the Czechoslovak leadership which had implemented it. It was a problem to be avoided rather than confronted.

Better for Gorbachev, therefore, if Husák and Kádár melted away as a result of essentially domestic processes, with the advanced age and ailing condition of both men an important cause. His approval for their removals was presumably still needed and, in the case of Kádár, there were clear signs of the "withdrawal of Soviet favor." In Husák's case, however, it had to be remembered that his resignation did not mean his complete withdrawal from Czechoslovak politics. He remained president of the Czechoslovak republic and a member of the party Presidium (Politburo). Two years later many observers commented on the considerable role he still played.

One look at Husák's successor should have been enough to dispel any notion that it was Gorbachev who masterminded the change. Miloš Jakeš, aged sixty-four on his accession, was of the postwar communist generation and had a conventional career in the Czechoslovak provincial party apparatus. No one in his right mind would have considered him Gorbachev's beau ideal. Under Novotný, he first served as head of the Czechoslovak Komsomol, was then deputy chairman of the governmental body responsible for the local economy and between 1966 and 1968 was deputy minister of the interior. (There were persistent rumors, believed by reasonable people, about his long-standing links with the KGB.) He supported the Soviet-led invasion of August 1968, and his ascent to the heights began soon afterward. As head of the party control commission, he led the witch hunt which resulted in the expulsion of about 450,000 party members between 1969 and 1971. Jakeš was particularly zealous in rooting from their jobs actual or suspected reformers. He joined the Presidium (Politburo) as a candidate-member in 1977, moving to full membership in 1981.

During the 1980s several Prague "insiders" were reporting that Jakeš had become a supporter of economic reform and was gathering a group of experts around him with a view to implementing it when the political moment was right. But little came of these expectations. Jakeš's was an uninspired reactionary without any of Husák's political ability and stature. Had Gorbachev been set on actively interfering in Czechoslovak leadership politics to promote reform and national reconciliation, the result of his exertions would not have been Miloš Jakeš. And in the event, Jakeš himself proved anxious to dispel any notions about his reincarnation as an economic reformer.[32]

In the case of a change in the party leadership, some Czechoslovaks had been hoping that Štrougal would move over from the premiership and begin to lead a significant reform movement. Speculation on this point increased when Štrougal visited Moscow and conferred with Gorbachev shortly before Husák's resignation was announced. Even after Jakeš's appointment, Štrougal continued in a buoyant mood and was more in the public view than he had been for several months. On the eve of West German Chancellor Helmuth Kohl's visit to Prague in January 1988, he gave an exuberant interview to a West German newspaper urging better relations between East and West and making frank disclosures about differences over reform within the "normalization" regime, projecting himself throughout as the champion of progress.[33]

This may have been his undoing. He seems to have thoroughly alarmed most of those with vested interests in the status quo who now gathered round Jakeš and proceeded to isolate Štrougal. In the late spring there were even rumors about his forthcoming purge, and these coincided with an obvious downplaying of the theme of reform in the media and in statements by regime leaders. The expectation of at least some in the Prague leadership was that Gorbachev's days might be numbered; hence reform might be shelved. There was nothing like the reform publicity that had existed, say, between the Seventeenth Party Congress in March 1986 and Gorbachev's visit in April 1987. This proved detrimental and, in a short time, fatal to Štrougal's position and political career.

The Pressure from Society

As these changes were taking place at the ruling elite level and between Prague and Moscow, an important new element had begun to emerge in Czechoslovak politics: the societal factor and the force of public opinion.

For many it had taken a depressingly long time coming. As Gordon Skilling has written:

For some years after the [1968] occupation, a profound malaise gripped the entire country, and the great majority of people relapsed into what the internationally famous playwright and dissident Vaclav Havel called a state of anomie. Disillusioned by the experience of 1968 and by earlier disasters such as Munich and the Prague coup, most Czechs saw no prospect for early change and were not ready to risk their own futures through any kind of opposition or open criticism.[34]

In this context a distinction must be made between the mood in the Czech Lands and that in Slovakia. For most Slovaks, however much may have been lost by the 1968 invasion, something very important did survive: federal status for Slovakia. This meant the fulfillment of at least part of their national aspirations. It was this, not democracy, that had given the Prague Spring its true meaning in Slovakia. Moreover, it followed that, since the reforms of 1968 had been largely of Czech provenance, the subsequent repression would fall mainly in the Czech Lands. In fact, "normalization" in Slovakia was relatively light. Only against the Catholic Church, with its traditionally strong support in Slovakia, its intimate connection with Slovak nationalism, and historical associations with "clerical fascism," was "normalization" applied severely. Many Slovak Catholics suffered for their faith. But, on the whole, most Slovaks suffered less than did many Czechs, and Slovak home rule was not unwelcome in Slovakia, even for many of its uncompromisingly anticommunist citizens. Moreover, many Slovaks, however much they may have hated Gustáv Husák, did not mind him "lording" it over the Czechs in Prague. Generally, the Slovaks played a relatively small part in the political and cultural currents of opposition in Czechoslovak society in the 1980s. In the growing religious opposition, however, they had an important role which steadily grew.

Husák's "normalization" succeeded rapidly in Czechoslovak society. A simple comparison between Czechoslovakia in the 1970s and the failure of Jaruzelski in Poland in the 1980s only illustrates how successful Husák was. Building on the Czech national mood of despondency, he applied his own combination of compulsion and incentive. Vladimir Kusin has seen this combination as consisting of the "3Cs"—coercion, circuses, and consumerism. The *coercion*, in which Miloš Jakeš played a notable part, has already been mentioned. Kusin describes *circuses* as "the toleration of a widened range of individual entertainment [that] formed another factor in the depoliticization scheme." It consisted of "mild" pop (not jazz, which came to be considered politically subversive), Western television features, movies, soap opera sagas, and organized sport. *Consumerism* meant a considerable rise in the standard of living, backed by the availability not only of cheap foodstuffs but of consumer durables such as automobiles, washing machines, and television sets.[35] For many Czechs it meant most importantly a small country cottage, allowing for weekend escape.

The first serious sign of restlessness came in January 1977 with the publication of Charter 77, the famous declaration calling for greater freedoms in the spirit of Czechoslovak democracy, signed by nearly 250 men and women of almost all political persuasions. Václav Havel was the most prominent of these, but they included many of the most notable supporters of the Prague Spring. (All but two or three were Czechs.) Closely connected with Charter 77, but institutionally separate, was VONS (the Committee for the Defense of the Unjustly Persecuted), founded in 1978. VONS issued regular communiqués on cases of persecution of all kinds, and it was not surprising that, even more than Charter 77, it was the object of relentless police curiosity.[36]

Charter 77 and VONS, however, though speaking for society as a whole, had always been elitist in composition and were regarded as such by the population. It was religion—Catholicism—that inspired the first mass movement of opposition. This began with the election in 1978 of Pope John Paul II, the Slavic pope, which inspired and emboldened many Slovak Catholics. It also stiffened the attitudes of some Catholics, especially younger ones, in the Czech Lands where Catholicism had rarely been deeply felt and had often been regarded as an antinational creed. The aging František Cardinal Tomášek, archbishop of Prague, always considered a passive, even compliant, figure, now became a stout defender of the Church's interests.

The most massive demonstration of religious feeling—antiregime by implication—came in 1985 with the 1100th anniversary of the death of St. Methodius, the apostle of the Slavs. In what some observers considered to be a turning point in state-society relations, over 150,000 Czechs and Slovaks gathered to mark this event at the saint's burial place in Velehrad in Moravia.[37] This commemoration created a momentum in religious-inspired civic activity that subsequently gathered pace. In December 1987, for example, a 31-point petition was presented to the regime authorities by Tomášek demanding the rectification of injustices and the independence of the Church from the state. Similar demonstrations of religious strength and determination continued throughout 1988 and 1989. They not only served to strengthen the resolve of society as a whole in all parts of Czechoslovakia, but they pressed the regime into making specific, if minor, concessions. As a result of an agreement in July 1989 between the Czechoslovak state and the Vatican, three of the country's ten vacant bishoprics (out of a total of thirteen) were filled after years of waiting and pointless negotiations. The regime, of course, was under various pressures to soften its image, internationally and internally, but it would not have done this without popular pressure.

In the second half of the 1980s, the number of independent, dissident groups multiplied, particularly in the Czech Lands—social, cultural, religious, and covertly and overtly political. The political groups covered almost every persuasion, from social democratic to nineteenth-century bourgeois-liberal capitalist. All, though, had one common denominator: a demand for self-expression reflecting dissatisfaction with the oppressive stagnation of "normalization." Charter 77 remained the best-known and most prestigious of them all, both at home and abroad. Some of its most prominent members had gone, or been forced, into exile and had continued their activity from the West. Many of the Charter's situation papers on crucial contemporary topics also found their way to the West, and their contents were broadcast back into Czechoslovakia by Western radio stations. They were distinguished by their oppositional sentiments and by their high intellectual quality.

But Charter 77 was now only one of many and, in terms of popularity, was beginning to pay the penalty of simply having been first. It was the younger Czechs who now dominated dissent, and, while paying tribute to Charter 77, some tended to regard it as too elitist, not radical enough, too careful in its methods, even somewhat passé. Some of its members were seen as too much associated with the past, the Prague Spring, and reform socialism. The conviction had rapidly gained ground that socialism anywhere was beyond repair.

The growing militancy among many of these young Czechs and Slovaks was due to the interaction of the domestic situation and the ferment among Czechoslovakia's neighbors. It illustrates the evolving mood to compare Czechoslovak reactions to the changing fortunes of Solidarity in Poland. The birth of Solidarity in 1980 was greeted with skepticism, its demise in December 1981 with *Schadenfreude*. This strongly reflected the continuing post-1968 mood of self-centered dejection, as well as traditional anti-Polish feeling. Seven years later the response to Solidarity's reemergence and then victory was quite different. Here was something to be admired. Perhaps it might not be long before it could be emulated.

Gorbachev did most to break the cloud hanging over Czechoslovak society. In the first place, the very emergence of a reformist Soviet leader weakened the Prague regime. The bedrock of the "normalization" regime in Czechoslovakia, almost its raison d'être, had been the continuance of an orthodox—better still, reactionary—regime in Moscow. This had now been swept away and was being almost totally repudiated by its successors. Though not, perhaps, as dramatic as Khrushchev's de-Stalinization, it was more basic.

The Czechoslovak population was not slow in grasping how its regime was being discomfited. Nor did it fail to see the significance of its resulting decline in confidence. And, as the regime's response to growing societal militancy became less resolute and more erratic, so the awareness of its weakness spread. People, especially the young, were just not intimidated any more.

In the course of 1989, as further cracks appeared in the regime's determination, so the streams of popular discontent poured into them. As the regime became less confident, so many sections of society became bolder. In its response the regime was also inhibited by the various agreements on human rights it had been obliged to sign, especially during 1988 as part of the CSCE process and the increasing international publicity Czechoslovakia was receiving from Western journalists and through interviews given by Havel and others.

Nothing attracted more international publicity than the return to public activity of Alexander Dubček, the Czechoslovak party leader during the Prague Spring. Dubček had lived in obscurity in Slovakia for nearly twenty years and—another reflection of the collapse of popular morale after 1968—enjoyed no great respect for the role he played during that time. But, again, nothing better reflected the recovery of morale than his return to public favor. Young demonstrators in Prague and elsewhere now habitually invoked his name along with that of Masaryk. In January 1988—another sign of the times—the regime did not choose to prevent him from giving an interview to the Italian Communist Party daily L'Unità, in which he drew a parallel between perestroika and the Prague Spring, spoke enthusiastically about the new Soviet leader, and criticized the Czechoslovak regime for paying lip service to reform but then doing nothing about it.[38] Subsequently, Dubček was almost lionized by both the Western press and reformers in Hungary and Poland. A frank, extended interview he gave in the spring of 1989 to the official Hungarian radio in April made the Czechoslovak authorities wonder what the world was coming to and elicited a hefty protest from the Prague foreign ministry.[39]

Nothing illustrates the interaction between increasing societal militancy and growing regime nervousness better than the "Just a Few Sentences" episode in July 1989.[40] "Just a Few Sentences" was the (very Czech) name given to a petition demanding democratic reforms and the opening of a dialogue between the authorities and the population. The appeal had more than 1,800 signatures when it was released to the press at the end of June, and during July the number rose to over 10,000. Not only the petition, but its timing and the publicity it received, embarrassed the Prague regime. The Western press had by now been primed to look for newsworthy material from Czechoslovakia—after a lapse of some twenty years—and gave the event considerable coverage.

Czechoslovakia had also now become the object of much attention from the democratic movements in Poland and Hungary. Over several years a network of consultation and mutual support had operated among Polish, Hungarian, and Czechoslovak dissidents. Clandestine meetings were occasionally held, usually in some of the border areas of the countries concerned. As the political situation eased greatly in Poland and Hungary, and somewhat in Czechoslovakia, the cooperation became more open and widespread. The authorities in Poland and Hungary had long since become resigned to such activity. The Czechoslovak regime still regarded such behavior as outrageous and seditious and looked askance at the tolerance shown in Warsaw and Budapest. But, much as it might rail, it was becoming increasingly powerless to stop it.

The most galling incident of all occurred in July 1989 when an unofficially invited Solidarity delegation, including Jacek Kuroń (soon to become minister of labor in the new Solidarity government), Adam Michnik, and Zbigniew Bujak, the former Warsaw underground leader, came to Czechoslovakia to visit Havel, Dubček, and others. (That they were able to enter Czechoslovakia was itself one of the clearest instances of change.) Inevitably, the public statements issued at the end of the conversations between the Poles and their hosts were deemed impudent and inflammatory by the Czechoslovak authorities. Nor were the regime's feelings softened by remarks made by Bujak on his return to Poland. Helping to put Czechoslovakia onto the reform road was, according to Bujak, crucial for reformers in neighboring countries. Without genuine perestroika in Prague, change in the rest of Eastern Europe would be crippled. He suggested that reform-minded parliamentarians in Poland, Hungary, and the Soviet Union might issue a formal condemnation of the 1968 invasion, and this might force those responsible for the stagnation in Czechoslovakia to begin stirring themselves or to move on.[41]

The Czechoslovak media inveighed against this Solidarity "invasion," the party daily *Rudé Právo* using the kind of charges Prague and East Berlin had always leveled against recent developments in Poland. The Solidarity delegation and its hosts in Prague and Bratislava were trying to force "Polish" reform onto Czechoslovakia and to create "economic anarchy" with the aim of destroying socialism. It was premature for Solidarity members to give advice to Czechoslovakia, for they themselves "had not yet achieved anything positive." Nobody needed lessons from "the Michniks, the Bujaks, and others." *Rudé Právo* continued: "The majority of [the] Czechoslovak population does not pine for the kind of disorders which Solidarity has caused in Poland, does not yearn for economic chaos, empty stores, and inflation."[42]

In the meantime, the authorities stepped up their campaign against "Just a Few Sentences." A criminal investigation was begun to determine its originators with the warning that, when caught, they would be charged with sedition and severely punished. "Countercampaigns" were organized with petitions "voluntarily" signed, denouncing "Just a Few Sentences," a few of whose signatories were pressured into withdrawing their names. It all tended to belie the nonchalance with which the regime tried to pass off the incident to the outside world. Jakeš, for example, in an interview with a Spanish newspaper, dismissed "Just a Few Sentences" as being supported by "barely a couple of thousand people."[43]

The twenty-first anniversary of the Soviet-led invasion turned out to be a still bigger international embarrassment for the regime. It saw the greatest public turbulence in Prague since the previous January, when thousands of young Czechs had taken to the streets on successive nights, and many of them had been brutally beaten by the police. In August similar demonstrations occurred involving an estimated 3,000 to 5,000 people—big turnouts for a Czechoslovak demonstration. Police brutality and, in some cases, clear lack of discipline brought the authorities much unwanted international publicity. But even more embarrassing was the presence of several young Hungarians, all connected with democratic movements back in Budapest, in the thick of the melee. A minor diplomatic incident between two fraternal allies was touched off when two of the Hungarians were arrested, tried, convicted, sentenced, and then expelled, with indignation in Budapest rising with each stage of their highly publicized ordeal.

Incidents like this—and they were increasing in frequency—invariably involved the Prague authorities in a no-win situation. The more they railed, the sillier they looked. The Czechoslovak regime was not losing its capacity to suppress. It could still quell disorder when it wanted to. But it was losing something more important: its credibility and right to be taken seriously. The international situation itself was ensuring that the days of "normalization" were numbered. The regime, by its behavior, was actually hastening its end.

But, having given all due emphasis to the stirrings of Czechoslovak society and to the deepening and broadening of the opposition to the regime, the fact remained that in the fall of 1989 still only a relatively few were fiercely committed to change. The number was small in terms of the Czechoslovak population as a whole, and very small in terms of those who had initiated reform in either Poland or Hungary. On October 28, 1989, in a demonstration marking the seventy-first anniversary of the founding of the first Czechoslovak republic, 10,000 people demonstrated in Prague. It was the biggest demonstration since 1948, but insignificant compared with the hundreds of thousands of East Germans on the streets at the same time. Still, after the fall of Honecker, many Czechoslovaks became convinced that their hour would strike next. It was a question more of how soon than when.

Most heavy industrial workers, however, and most farmers were still some way from feeling the kind of pinch that would elicit a mass, angry response. Many felt little in common with, and less than sympathy for, demonstrating students. This remained the regime's hope for survival. But it was a diminishing hope. What might have saved the regime was *active* worker support. It would not get this. More than forty years had passed since worker militancy had put the communists in power. There was none of that left—only indifference. And indifference at this stage was tending to become the ally, or at least the silent partner, of the forces bent on change. The workers may not have liked the students, but they were showing signs of liking their own leaders even less. This was another cause of the leadership's growing nervousness. After the collapse of the Honecker regime this nervousness grew.

Cracks in the Leadership

The growing restlessness among various sections of the population had two contrasting effects on the ruling elite. A small group under Premier Štrougal considered it more necessary than ever to catch the rising tide and press for change. However, the much stronger groups of conservatives led by Jakeš, alarmed at the example elsewhere in the Eastern bloc, seemed resolved more firmly than ever to resist the tide. For these conservatives the issue, more clearly than ever, was not one of policy but of survival.[44]

In this predicament they drew some comfort from the continued passivity of most of Czechoslovakia's workers and farmers and from the one remaining buttress of orthodoxy in East-Central Europe, the German Democratic Republic. As long as the East German leaders stood firm in their rejection of perestroika and glasnost and kept a tight grip on their own society, then the Czechoslovak leaders had support. And up to the fall of 1989 the GDR appeared to be the bastion it had always been. Indeed, it seemed to many that, after the avalanches in Poland and Hungary, Gorbachev himself was more than happy for the conservative stability in the GDR and Czechoslovakia to continue. These "islands of Brezhnevism," as Zdeněk Mlynář has aptly described them,[45] had their uses. They provided a breathing space—at least as long as they lasted.

The fall of 1988 had seen the most serious power struggle in the Czechoslovak leadership in twenty years, since the cleanout of Dubček and the Prague Spring reforms in the second half of 1968 and the first half of 1969.[46] The struggle began in April 1988 at the Ninth Czechoslovak Communist Party Central Committee Plenum. Rumors circulating for several weeks before had suggested that Husák might retire from active politics, leaving both the Czechoslovak state presidency and the party presidium. It was also expected that Bilak would retire, ostensibly on grounds of age—he was over seventy. If anything, the rumors pointed to a reformers' advantage.

The reality, however, was different. Husák stayed, presumably because he was the only Czechoslovak politician (except Štrougal) with any real international standing, and his departure at this time of uncertainty could have sparked precisely the kind of instability that very few political leaders wanted, either in Prague, or perhaps even in Moscow. But Bilak also stayed, and all in all, it was the conservatives, not the reformers, who did well from the changes. True, several younger and able officials were brought into the top leadership. But neither before nor afterward did they show any reformist inclinations, at least in the political arena. What characterized them was discretion. One long-standing hard-liner, Jan Fojtík, a Central Committee secretary, was actually promoted from candidate to full presidium member. It subsequently turned out, however, that this was in preparation for the time when Bilak did retire. Fojtík took his place as the regime's top ideological official.

The next round of changes immediately followed the changes at the Soviet Central Committee plenum early in October 1988, which resulted in a further strengthening of Gorbachev's personal position. The Moscow changes also meant the departure or weakening of some Soviet leaders who had had a considerable bearing on the Czechoslovak scene. Gromyko, for example, was relieved of the presidency, which was to be assumed by Gorbachev himself. Ligachev, in whom most of the Prague leaders had pinned their hopes, lost his ideology portfolio and went to take charge of agriculture, an obvious demotion. Also transferred was Viktor Chebrikov, head of the KGB, an institution with which several of the top Czechoslovak leaders (including Jakeš) were reputed to have (or have had) connections.

If the Soviet changes were anything to go by, it looked as if a reformist victory would be on its way in Czechoslovakia. But, quite the contrary occurred. The Czechoslovak reformers were hoping that, affected by the Soviet example, enough conservatives would switch or weaken to enable them to win a victory or, more realistically, to make inroads into the conservative majority. This did not happen. The Jakeš leadership refused to be impressed and got enough support, not only to hold its own, but to inflict a decisive defeat on the reformers.

The principal victim was Štrougal, who was forced out of the premiership he had held for eighteen years. He also left the Czechoslovak party presidium. Štrougal had never been a "liberal," not even in the sense that some of János Kádár's followers had been, even Kádár himself. But in the context of Czechoslovak leadership politics during "normalization," at least since the beginning of the 1980s, he had been pragmatic—and that had meant progressive. Whether this was out of conviction or opportunism is difficult to say. Probably, as in most cases, it was a combination of both. From reliable, unofficial reports it would seem that his opponents had been trying for about a year to have him dismissed. If this was true, he was probably helped by two things: (1) the fact that reform had not yet become a crucial issue, one of survival for the conservatives; and (2) Gorbachev's protection, or presumed protection. Štrougal's demise, therefore, came when the question of further reform had become crucial, with the conservatives feeling they had to strike at its champion, and, even more important, when the question of Gorbachev's protection had ceased to be as important as was once thought. Moscow's laissez-faire, in effect, meant that a reformer like Štrougal could lose.

The Collapse

Štrougal's successor as Czechoslovak prime minister, Ladislav Adamec, was a good representative of the economic/technocratic elite that developed under "normalization." Formerly prime minister of the Czech Lands of the Czechoslovak Federation, he had spent most of his career in economic management and administration. His dedication to comprehensive economic reform was sincere; he had certainly had occasion to see the need for it. But with regard to political reform, though by no means a conservative like Jakeš or Fojtík, he had not seemed convinced of its value or its necessity as a concomitant to economic reform. He was an able, circumspect, Czech senior official, more presentable than most of his colleagues but hardly the type to break the conventional mold of normalization politics.[47]

In economic reform there were grounds for believing he would have preferred to be bolder but, unlike Štrougal, he was not ready to fight his colleagues on the issue. He complained about "obsolete and bloated" smokestack industries, Czechoslovakia's lack of competitiveness on world markets, and the huge government subsidies for foodstuffs and public services. He also insisted that the Czechoslovak economy be opened up (within limits) to the West, and that most industries should be drastically "restructured," a term he often used. He admitted that restructuring could mean relocation for many workers and was fairly open in his warnings that the "easy times" were over. But his bolder warnings were usually hedged with cushioning provisions designed to convey reassurance rather than realism. He stressed that administrative means would always be available to monitor market forces and that every worker would ultimately be taken care of.[48] This prudence could, of course, be defended as not only morally estimable but politically necessary considering the sentiments of his colleagues and of many ordinary Czechs and Slovaks. But it conveyed to everybody that, in the last analysis, the regime would flinch from unpopular measures.

Furthermore, on one basic issue—private property—the leadership continued on a dogmatic course. Poland, Hungary, and Yugoslavia substantially eased restrictions on the number of employees in the privately owned sectors of the economy. In Poland and Hungary the number was initially raised to five hundred. But, according to reliable private reports from Prague, a proposal supported by many economists calling for the Czechoslovak ceiling to be raised to two hundred was rejected at the Central Committee level as being "inconsistent with socialism." Similar efforts to increase the amount of privately owned land in agriculture also foundered.

It was small wonder, then, that many Czechoslovak economists became discouraged. Adamec's ideas of radical reform seemed nothing more than radical reorganizations, containing much common sense but nothing like the necessary depth and boldness. "The blueprint of the reform represents only a very small, just a half step," one of them complained.[49] Many Czechoslovak economists during 1989 also joined the dissidents in favoring extensive political reforms.

The "Principles of Reconstruction," the basic program for economic reform, approved (as mentioned earlier) in 1987, were originally to begin operation in 1991, the first year of the next planning cycle; but this was subsequently brought forward to 1990. In preparation, all enterprises were supposed to go over to self-financing (*khoszrachet*) on July 1, 1989, but there were many complaints that this conversion was being done halfheartedly. One of the problems was that many of Czechoslovakia's most famous companies, such as the two automobile firms Škoda in Pilsen and Tatra in

Koprovnice, had been insolvent for many years.[50] In this case, self-financing would have meant instant closure, the kind of social problems the nature and complexity of which—all questions of ideology aside—the regime was not prepared to face.

Even more inhibiting was the fact that this was a question of political influence. The large enterprises had powerful political backers, locally and in Prague and Bratislava, in the party and government bureaucracy. They would not see their political constituencies dissolve and would fight tooth and nail for sufficient subsidies. Thus, it became neither an economic nor an ideological question, but one of bureaucratic politics and established procedures. One critic put it succinctly: "Unless you solve the problem of political unwillingness to close down bankrupt firms, unless we really see it, and the population has the expectation that it will happen, I won't believe in the reform."[51]

It was, indeed, a matter of political will, and, even among most of the regime reformers, it was not there. But the signs demanding change were proliferating. The economic situation was universally expected to worsen. It could not for long keep workers safe in their illusions. Societal dissatisfaction was increasing, as were its manifestations. Junior and middle-level regime officials were speaking up. Some of the satellite political parties, taking their cue from Poland, were no longer as submissive as they once were. Above all, the Czechs as a nation were taking heart. And the pride was returning. The example of Havel and others had taken hold.

Finally, even the conservatives who still dominated the leadership, the "normalization" bloc, were becoming increasingly isolated, not only domestically but internationally. The culminating blow was the deteriorating situation in the GDR. The thousands of East Germans who invaded the West German embassy in Prague in late September and October 1989 were living proof that the Czechoslovak leaders could not count further on East Berlin. The scenes at the West German embassy also symbolized the great change that was coming over East-Central Europe, a change that was going to affect Czechoslovakia, too—sooner rather than later.

The change came sooner. The collapse of the East German regime in October boosted the confidence of the Czechoslovak people and broke that of the regime. Demonstrations began in Prague and in other cities, including—significantly—Bratislava, the capital of Slovakia. At first the demonstrations seemed small—tiny compared with the massive demonstrations going on at the same time in the GDR. But the numbers grew. Havel and others formed the "Civic Forum," a move designed to direct and coordinate the growing popular surge. The severe police brutality on the night of

November 17 angered the whole country and gave a decisive impulse and the necessary element of anger to popular feelings.

On November 25 a demonstration of about three-quarters of a million people took place in Prague. Clearly the whole communist power edifice was shaking uncontrollably, but the final blow to any lingering regime hopes came with the success of the two-hour general strike that the "Civic Forum" called for November 27. The worker response—brief though it was—removed the last plank from under the sinking regime, whose leaders may have been consoling themselves that, however great the disaffection among the youth and the intellectuals, the mass of the workers still remained, if not loyal, then at least passive. The worker response to the strike disabused the regime of this notion. The two main, often opposing, trends in Czechoslovak politics—the intellectual "liberal" and the worker "socialist"—had joined in their disgust with the regime that had ruled for twenty years. Just as important, the demonstrations in Slovakia showed that the Czechs and Slovaks, the two nations of Czechoslovakia, often at odds with one another, had joined in opposition. How long these unities would last was something for the future. The important thing for now was that they had produced the collapse of the communist system in Czechoslovakia.

The Jakeš party leadership resigned on November 24, and a new leadership under the colorless Karel Urbánek was installed. But that was now practically irrelevant. So was the creation of a new federal cabinet under Adamec on December 3. What was important was that the Civic Forum in the Czech Lands and the Public Against Violence movement, its counterpart in Slovakia, were gaining by leaps and bounds. That was where the power now lay. Václav Havel became the unchallenged leader of the Civic Forum and Alexander Dubček, still with his rather touching dignity, reappeared in public life. On December 19 the Adamec government resigned, and a new coalition government was formed under a little-known Slovak, Marián Čalfa. This government contained an almost equal number of communists and noncommunists. Čalfa, a communist, later left the party. But December 10 also saw Husák's resignation from the presidency. It was expected; still, the symbolism of his departure was not lost on Czechs and Slovaks. The leader, the personification of the tyranny called "normalization" was gone.

Now it was only a short time before the Prague Castle at last had a tenant worthy of Tomáš Masaryk. Václav Havel was sworn in just in time to give the customary presidential New Year's (1990) address to the two nations. It was different from what they were used to. It is worth ending this chapter by quoting a passage:

For forty years, on this day, you have heard from my predecessors different versions of the same story: how our country is blossoming, how many more millions of tons of steel we have produced, how happy we all are, how we believe in our government and what beautiful perspectives are being opened to us. I presume, you did not offer me this office to perpetuate these lies.

Our country is not flourishing. . . . We have spoiled the land, rivers and forests given to us by our ancestors. The state of our environment is the worst in Europe. Our people die at an earlier age than in other countries in Europe. . . .

But the worst is that we live in a polluted moral environment. We have became morally ill by not saying what we think. We have learned not to believe in anything, to ignore each other, and to think only of ourselves. . . .

The existing system, armed by a pompous and belligerent ideology, reduced human beings and nature to be the tools of production . . . it turned talented and self sufficient people who wisely cared for their land's economy, into the cogs of a senseless, monstrous, cacophonous and foul smelling machine.[52]

For the first time since Masaryk, not just the Prague Castle, but the whole of Czechoslovakia was back in good hands.

7 Bulgaria: "From Under Another Yoke"

■■■■■■■■■■■■■■■■■■■■■■■ Todor Zhivkov fell from power and whatever grace he may have enjoyed on November 10, 1989. He had been leader of the Bulgarian Communist Party (BCP) for thirty-five years and six months—in effect, ruler of Bulgaria for longer than any other ruler in its entire history, pre- or post-Ottoman. The illustrious Tsar Simeon reigned thirty-four years at the end of the tenth and the beginning of the eleventh centuries; the considerably less illustrious Tsar ("Foxy") Ferdinand ruled for thirty years at the end of the nineteenth century and into the early twentieth century. But Todor, the printer's apprentice from Pravets, outstayed them all. Many Bulgarians in the second half of the twentieth century knew no other ruler. With wry Bulgarian humor, many used to say during the 1980s that conditions in their country were getting so bad that they would like to go into a deep freeze for a hundred years and then thaw out and resume living. But, they acknowledged, it would be pointless because Todor Zhivkov would still be in power.

Zhivkov's rule can be divided into four unequal parts. The two years from March 1954, when he was elected first party secretary, to the April plenum of the BCP in 1956, was really the prelude to power. His election was a gesture to de-Stalinization rather than any sign of its consummation. But the April 1956 plenum, held in the heady atmosphere generated by the Twentieth CPSU Congress two months earlier, was a genuine de-Stalinizaion plenum—not going as far as many wanted but, still, a turning point in Bulgarian communist history. More important for Zhivkov, though, was the fact that it broke the power of the Bulgarian Stalinists, led by Vulko Chervenkov. They were not totally routed and fought a rear-guard action for several years. But the April plenum put Zhivkov in the saddle, and, throughout his career, his main achievement lay in his mastery of the art of staying there.[1]

The key to his longevity in office, apart from his skills in communist

Tammany politics, was his calculating loyalty to Moscow, a self-interested subservience often mistaken for abject groveling. Zhivkov could grovel with the best of them when need be, but he seldom picked himself empty-handed from the floor. Not, perhaps, the most dignified conduct for any ruler, but with a small country in a competitive world, by no means the most unrealistic either.

The real beginning of Zhivkov's rule was, therefore, April 1956. The real end was November 1982, on the death of Leonid Brezhnev. It was during those twenty-six years that Zhivkov worked in harmonious, though obviously unequal, relationship with Brezhnev and with Nikita Khrushchev before him. In this respect the comparison with János Kádár is instructive. The two were almost exactly contemporaneous in power: Kádár from November 1956 to May 1988. Both spanned the Khrushchev and Brezhnev eras and both apparently fitted in well with the personality and policies of each of these Soviet leaders. But, whereas Kádár was united with Khrushchev in a mutual dependence on the success of reconstruction in postrevolutionary Hungary, the relationship with Brezhnev was occasionally clouded by serious differences over policy.

Kádár, therefore, was essentially a Khrushchev man, basically uneasy with Brezhnev's rule, however cordial the relationship appeared on the surface. Zhivkov's ruling "ethos" was more compatible with that of Brezhnev. This may be surprising in view of the huge reorganizations Zhivkov attempted: the "Great Leap Forward" in 1958, for example, or the introduction of Agro-Industrial Complexes in the early 1970s.[2] These seemed hardly the hallmark of the conservative; they even bore signs of the "harebrain scheming" for which Khrushchev was condemned on his overthrow. The crux of the difference was that Zhivkov's scheming, however "harebrained," consisted of reorganizations rather than reforms. They allowed for none of the spontaneity that Khrushchev tolerated and, indeed, personified, a spontaneity that was inherent in the Hungarian New Economic Mechanism. Zhivkov, like Brezhnev, distrusted spontaneity, and, except for one gigantic aberration toward the end of his rule,[3] remained a Leninist of a strongly conservative variety.

The "Unsettling" Period

Brezhnev's death in 1982 ushered in the "unsettling" period for Zhivkov. First, Yuri Andropov, Brezhnev's successor, was considered much less favorably disposed toward him than Brezhnev had been. This may have been due to Zhivkov's reportedly good relations with Konstantin Chernenko, a contender for the leadership and apparently Brezhnev's own anointed. But, apart from any personal incompatibilities, Andropov presumably considered Zhivkov part of the Brezhnevian clutter to be cleared up quickly. His speedy demise and succession by Chernenko provided only interim relief in Sofia, and Chernenko was soon succeeded by a man preordained to be Zhivkov's nemesis. Whether in his Mark I, II, or III phases (see chapter 2), Mikhail Gorbachev stripped from Zhivkov's rule the compatibility with the Moscow center that had anchored it. With this gone, with advancing age, and with the whole change of temper overtaking the socialist camp, Zhivkov lost not only his political understanding but also his political touch.

Before discussing the impact of Gorbachev on what was becoming a sclerotic Bulgarian regime, it is worth looking at several factors during the 1980s that had already disturbed Zhivkov's self-confidence. The downturn by the middle of the 1980s was apparent. A keen observer of Bulgaria over many years visited Sofia in 1982 and then again at the end of 1985. The two visits presented sharply contrasting impressions. In 1982 Bulgaria had appeared to be on the crest of an economic wave. Reform had been comprehensively introduced into an economy that still seemed buoyant enough. The public, in the main, seemed not only satisfied but expectant of further progress. Many young people seemed prepared to give the regime the benefit of their doubts. In the cultural field there was considerable freedom. But by the end of 1985 much of this had changed. Bulgaria was suffering a severe economic downturn, with agriculture and the energy supply the main victims.[4] Sofia and other cities were blacked out at night to ease energy shortages. (Bulgarians used to sneer at Romania for this, but no longer.) The mood of optimism and expectancy had been replaced by sullenness and frustration. Cultural policy had become more restrictive. It appeared that the regime's self-confidence, growing throughout the 1970s, had been severely shaken.

Agriculture, which despite all the heavy industrialization, was still Bulgaria's basic economic activity, was doing particularly badly. In 1985 it was hit by catastrophe. One of the severest winters on record had been preceded and was then followed by a very dry summer.[5] All agricultural and much industrial activity came to a halt. Power cuts and shopping lines became longer, tempers shorter. Apart from the agricultural disasters, the shortages of food and some consumer goods were due to a milder Zhivkov version of "Ceauşescu-ism." As discussed in the chapter on Romania, Ceauşescu eventually paid off the Romanian hard currency debt in 1989 by maximizing exports and throttling imports. Zhivkov tackled Bulgaria's debt problem in a similar though typically less fanatical way. In 1979 the gross hard-currency debt was officially said to stand at $4.4 billion, but by 1983 it was officially down to $2.5 billion.[6] (It was later to grow rapidly.) At the same time the Bulgarian comparative economic growth rate markedly faltered during the 1980s. In short, what some Westerners had dubbed the Bulgarian "economic miracle" in the late 1970s was looking shot through with frailty halfway through the 1980s.[7]

But economic deterioration was not the only reason for the malaise of the early 1980s. The death of Lyudmila Zhivkova and the aftermath of the near-death of Pope John Paul II, both in 1982, were certainly contributing factors.

Lyudmila was Todor Zhivkov's daughter, who put the nepotism from which she benefited to uncommonly good account. She mounted a cultural offensive designed to dispel the classic Bulgarian inferiority complex and replace it with a pride in Bulgaria's historical-cultural achievements. It was a daunting task, but Lyudmila, a European by inclination, showed signs of succeeding, somehow embodying a new and unwonted spirit of national optimism. Her sudden death in 1981 cut that short. A light went out of the kind that had rarely shone in Bulgaria. After Todor Zhivkov's fall, Lyudmila's reputation suffered for a while. She could hardly escape some of the criticism and abuse that rained down on her father. But she still remained a considerable figure. And Bulgarians could not forget (or deny) that her funeral had marked the biggest demonstration of Bulgarian national feeling since the funeral of King Boris in 1943.

The attempt on Pope John Paul's life in May 1981 appeared at first to have nothing to do with Bulgaria. But when, three years later, the would-be assassin, Ali Ağca, incriminated the Bulgarian security service, in general, and Sergei Antonov, a Rome official of the Bulgarian airlines, in particular, Bulgaria yet again attracted the kind of publicity it could have done without. Antonov was arraigned on the testimony of Ağca himself, about whose reliability, not to mention sanity, there was always considerable doubt. Brought to trial in a Roman spectacular that most observers took *cum grano salis*, he was eventually freed in 1986 on a verdict equivalent to the Scottish "not proven." This was obviously of considerable relief to the Sofia regime. But, whatever the verdict, the regime's international reputation took a battering. Despite Antonov's acquittal, the trial brought out some activities of the Bulgarian secret police in Italy that showed just what unwelcome guests they were: gun-running, drug smuggling, murders, and other mayhem. Obviously, such behavior was no Bulgarian monopoly, but that was cold comfort for the Zhivkov leadership. Despite the verdict of the Italian court, some of the suspicion of attempted pontificide was bound to stick. About the other activities that came out in court, there was no doubt. Bulgaria was guilty here, and *all* of that stuck.

Even more incriminating and unsettling were the steps taken against the Turkish minority, believed to number at least 1 million, or over 10 percent of the entire population. In the fall and winter of 1984–85 the Sofia regime ordered the compulsory, assimilative name-changing of the whole Turkish community. They were ordered to shed their Turkish names and assume Bulgarian ones. At the same time they were declared not to be Turkish at all but descendants of ethnic Bulgarians who had been "Turkicized" during the five hundred years of Ottoman rule. So it was now time to "Bulgarize" them back again! Many resisted but were repressed with severity. Nothing could explain this preposterous barbarism except the hankering after a national, unitary state and the determination to use any methods to achieve it. Bulgaria had really put itself in the dock now. But at the time it received considerably less punishment than it deserved. The world reported the action and condemned it. Bulgaria appeared in a bad light. But its leaders had presumably calculated that this would only be temporary. And they were right: the international scandal that the episode warranted did not materialize.[8] But the matter was not to rest there. It returned to haunt Zhivkov in his last months of power.

Finally, a trend gathered strength in the 1980s that had a subtly unsettling effect on parts of Bulgarian society, traditionally the most stable in South-Eastern Europe. For a quarter century, Bulgaria had been the gateway to Europe for more than 1 million Turks. These were not its own Turks but citizens of Turkey who worked and lived in different West European countries. (The Turks were very much back in Europe, but in Western, not Eastern, Europe and at a less exalted status than in days of Ottoman yore.) They used Bulgaria as transit territory. In a single year (1985), about 2.5 million Turks moved in transit to and from Turkey, with some obviously going more than once.[9] The overwhelming majority were on lawful business, and the last thing they wanted to do was loiter in Bulgaria. But a few were less innocent. They were part of a new criminal conspiracy with heroin as its basis, with Sofia as its headquarters, and, presumably, with links to the Bulgarian secret service.[10] Some of the witnesses at the Antonov trial in Rome were denizens of this underworld. Largely thanks to them, Sofia, once a sleepy capital, became a minor center of crime and intrigue.

The Gorbachev Effect

All this and Gorbachev, too! Zhivkov was in trouble with him from the start, or even before it. Still during Chernenko's rule, Gorbachev had paid a hurried visit to Sofia in August 1984 to "dissuade" Zhivkov from making a planned visit to Bonn.[11] (This was when Moscow, at odds with the Federal Republic, was trying to bring its East European allies to order; see chapter 2.) He seems then to have formed an aversion to Zhivkov which showed no signs of abating when he assumed power. His first, and only, official visit to Bulgaria as party leader was an unmitigated disaster for his host, and, had not Gorbachev's East European policy progressed from Mark I to Mark II, a serious effort might well have been made to unseat Zhivkov. Gorbachev's switch from hands-on to hands-off at least gave him a respite, of which, however, he was in no fit state to take advantage. But there were other changes expected in Soviet policy that left Bulgaria unprepared and unsettled. In the context of a tougher attitude in economic relations with Eastern Europe as a whole, Bulgaria seemed to be particularly vulnerable, not because of any victimization, but because its previous treatment had been so favorable. By about mid-1985 the Soviets reportedly began lowering their oil deliveries to Bulgaria, thereby reducing the Bulgarians' opportunities of selling refined oil on world markets. This had been much better business than many had realized. In the late 1970s some 60 percent of Bulgaria's hard-currency earnings came from this source.[12] The role this cutback played also reflected badly on the basic health of the Bulgarian economy, which should have been depending on its manufactures. There were Soviet complaints about the quality of imports from Bulgaria as well, and in the summer of 1985 serious difficulties arose in concluding the new agreements between the two countries on economic cooperation for the next five-year planning period.[13] Since nearly 60 percent of Bulgaria's total foreign trade was with the Soviet Union, the difficulties with Moscow only compounded Sofia's economic troubles.

These alarms coincided with the economic downturn just mentioned. Together, the two brought home again the urgency of reform. And with Gorbachev now at the helm, the time seemed advantageous. For several years before 1985 Bulgarian officials, none more than Zhivkov, complained about basic faults, especially about the twin evils of low productivity and poor quality. The introduction of economic reform into industry in 1982 was both an admission of continuing problems and an effort to solve them. At the Thirteenth Party Congress in April 1986 Zhivkov and other notables dwelt on the need for more economic efficiency and announced considerable extensions of the scope (without changing the basic character) of the existing reform.[14] Just before the congress the prime minister, Grisha Filipov, had been moved to the Central Committee Secretariat and replaced by Georgi Atanasov, a relatively young official who was destined to be Zhivkov's last prime minister.

But the congress gave little indication of the sweeping reforms that were to be announced in the course of 1987. These involved much greater democracy in the election of party and state bodies, a system of self-management perilously close to the Yugoslav, and a massive reorganization of local government and of the central state apparatus, which in effect meant the abolition of the Council of Ministers. All of these changes were to take place in an atmosphere of greater social and individual freedom and were to herald a "new socialism."

Most of the reforms were outlined by Zhivkov himself at a Bulgarian party Central Committee plenum in July 1987.[15] The proposals subsequently became known in official circles as the "July Concept," a title vaguely reminiscent of nineteenth-century Austria (October Diploma; February Patent) and presumably meant to indicate generality rather than precision. They constituted, in fact, a shambling, incoherent document whose amateurish pretentiousness reminded suffering Bulgar-watchers of the Maoist vagaries of the Bulgarian "Great Leap Forward" of thirty years before.

But the sharpest impact the "July Concept" had was apparently in the Soviet Union. In August 1987 Grisha Filipov, no longer prime minister but still a powerful Politburo member, went to Moscow and on his return outlined a proposed reform of the governmental structure quite different from that contained in the "July Concept."[16] But in October, Zhivkov himself paid a one-day visit to Moscow. In an astonishingly frank report about Zhivkov's talks with Gorbachev, the Soviet news agency, Tass, said the Soviet leader had warned his guest about "the need to control the speed and scale of reform and to watch for the leading role of the party."[17] Veterans were reminded of the way Stalin punctured Dimitrov's dream of Balkan federation thirty-eight years before.

The purpose of this warning was to sober Zhivkov, to bring him down from the stratosphere into which, at a ripe old age, he had soared. And it clearly succeeded. Just what Zhivkov's purpose had been in going to such extremes is much less clear. Assuming he was still in possession of those political faculties that had previously served him so well, it is possible that the "July Concept" was an attempt at preemption, at once a deliberate thrust forward in the direction Gorbachev wanted—but further—and an effort to insure that whatever reforms Bulgaria undertook would be of Sofia's and not Moscow's provenance. Or, looking back thirty years to Bulgaria's short-lived flirtation with Mao's China, it could simply have been a similar case of misunderstanding. Whatever, the "July Concept" became not so much a guide to the Bulgarian future as a disturbing reminder of its past.

Even more intriguing was what Gorbachev's sharp response might have indicated in terms of Soviet, and his own, thinking. It was obviously inconsistent with the Mark II hands-off policy begun about the beginning of 1987. What prompted the Soviet leader, then, to break his own rule? His antipathy to Zhivkov may have had something to do with it, but—more important—it more likely indicated the threshold of Gorbachev's political tolerance at the time. Gorbachev's Mark II was *initially* based on the assumption of one-party rule and communist supremacy. More, it was based on the assumption that no regime in Eastern Europe would think of going beyond this point. The framework of reform was certainly being expanded, but what Zhivkov was trying to do with the "July Concept" went far beyond. Hence, he had to be stopped. Gorbachev's rebuke to Zhivkov on October 15, 1987, was not just an important date in Bulgaria's communist history; it was important in the history of Gorbachev's political evolution. During the course of 1988 his assumptions became more relaxed, and in 1989 they became virtually irrelevant. In February 1990 he was advocating, and getting accepted, the end of the one-rule monopoly of the CPSU itself. The improviser's progress—from Leninism to liberalism—could not have been clearer.

The Regime Loses Its Touch

Gorbachev's political evolution, however, was no longer of direct interest for Zhivkov who, like János Kádár, was trying unsuccessfully to come to grips with a world he no longer understood. And his reaction became less rational and more arbitrary as his predicament mounted. Officially, the Bulgarian regime loudly supported the concepts of both perestroika and glasnost, but its efforts to give either concept a real Bulgarian significance were inconsistent in the extreme. They certainly carried little conviction with the Bulgarian public. The "July Concept" was supposed to be perestroika, Bulgarian-style; instead it was a debacle Bulgarian-style. As for glasnost, while declaring his regime to be totally in favor, Zhivkov tried to keep it within limits which, in relation to the outburst of freedom in the Soviet Union, Poland, and Hungary, were ridiculously narrow. True, there was more freedom of expression in Bulgaria than ever before. Reading the Bulgarian press and listening to Radio Sofia was a wholly different experience from what it had been ten years earlier. Television gave a mixed picture. Compared with the Romanian product next door, it was dazzling, but no one in Bulgaria could be impressed by such a comparison. (Soviet television programs, though, began to be shown in large numbers and, as glasnost galloped on in the Soviet Union itself, became the fancied fare of almost all Bulgarian viewers.) By previous Bulgarian standards, though, there was marked improvement. But those standards were no longer enough. Bulgarians now had more of a chance to read and hear what the rest of the world was doing and were demanding more for themselves. Foreign broadcasts ceased being jammed early in 1988 in response to the CSCE agreements in Vienna. Bulgaria was being brought from an obscure corner of Europe closer to the European mainstream. Lyudmila Zhivkova had tried to do this, but only in a limited sense. Now a constellation of circumstances was achieving it more comprehensively.

Zhivkov, on the other hand, was becoming narrow, more tyrannical, and more corrupt. His vanity was something of a grim joke in Sofia. He developed a mania, excessive even for dictators, for getting himself published—collected speeches, articles, and other such utterances, and not just in Bulgaria and in other fraternal countries, where it was customary, even de rigueur, but also in the West. Here he was aided and abetted by paladins like Robert Maxwell, the international publishing and press magnate. (Maxwell, adapting effortlessly to the 1989 revolutions in Eastern Europe, subsequently proceeded to set up shop in the region under the sign of democracy and press freedom.) Zhivkov's insatiable craving to see himself between covers led to the Sofia comment that he was the only man who had ever written more books than he had read.

Zhivkov's attitude toward the publications of his subjects, on the other hand, became more restrictive and vindictive as the Bulgarian media, sensing the spirit of the times, became bolder and more assertive. But official measures that would have achieved their purpose even five years earlier now only seemed to stimulate the opposition they had been designed to obviate. As one observer later put it:

> It seems that the current BCP leadership has been seriously unsettled by a number of developments that together could threaten its political survival. Since early 1988 Todor Zhivkov's tightly knit ruling clique has been confronted by the emergence of reformist currents within the party; the organization of the country's leading intellectuals around a platform of democratization; the formation of Bulgaria's first dissident movements and independent trade union; growing unrest among the ethnic Turkish minority; and the end of the jamming of the Bulgarian services of the BBC, Deutsche Welle, the Voice of America, and Radio Free Europe (RFE).[18]

Zhivkov was beginning to lose control of the situation. Forces within Bulgarian society began to assert themselves in a way that had become commonplace throughout Eastern Europe—except in Romania—but was momentously new for Bulgaria. When Zhivkov doffed his cap to "pluralism" in the spirit of the times, this was not what he had in mind. He seems to have defined pluralism as freer debate within established parameters modifying somewhat, but still preserving, the essential principle of party supremacy and democratic centralism. In other words, in spite of the protestations and the bombast of initiatives like the "July Concept," he was still stuck at the April Plenum in 1956, more than thirty years before. The party initiated, society responded. Now, however, the East European fashion was the other way round. But not if he could help it.

He could no more help it, though, than King Canute could hold back the waves from the shores of England. But when it came to revolt inside the *party*, he was on his home ground and not a man to be trifled with. In striking down presumptive heirs-apparent he was still unrivaled. This he showed once again in July 1988 when Chudomir Alexandrov, Politburo and Central Committee member, with all-round experience in the party and the economy, widely touted as Zhivkov's successor, was stripped of all his offices and later expelled from the party. The same fate befell Stoyan Mihailov, Central Committee secretary for culture and ideology, who was blamed for the "anarchic state" into which the media had allegedly fallen. There is strong evidence, though, that these two tried to mount a palace coup against Zhivkov. Whether they had Soviet blessing is uncertain. But both victims, after their disgrace, continued to enjoy the hospitality of the Soviet embassy—further proof for Zhivkov of the decadence of the times.[19]

Alexandrov and Mihailov and their supporters had doubtlessly been encouraged by the toppling of János Kádár in Hungary the previous May. But Zhivkov was not unmindful of that event, and, yet again, he was more than a match for his challengers. This was nothing really new. But what was new, at least for a quarter of a century, was the use of Stalinist methods to pillory the defeated. Alexandrov and Mihailov were hounded in a manner that recalled the late 1950s.[20]

Bulgarian Dissent

Media viciousness returned as a political instrument. During the course of 1988 it was widely used against Bulgaria's small but increasing number of political dissidents. For several years dissident activity had hardly been troublesome enough for the regime to take much notice. In any case, during his half-hearted flirtation with glasnost and the spirit of CSCE, Zhivkov's threshold of tolerance had not been as low as it subsequently became. In November 1988, however, the first real crackdown on dissident groups began when several members of the "Association for the Defense of Human Rights in Bulgaria" were exiled. Early in 1989 the group's secretary, Petur Manolov, was arrested along with others. This was followed by the kind of attacks on members of the group that had characterized the harassment of

Alexandrov and Mihailov. Slurs of fascism, guilt by association, innuendoes—again harking back to the fifties and early sixties. The hysteria of the media was reflecting the basic reality of a nervous regime.

The year 1989 saw the proliferation of "dissident" groups. One of the most significant was the ecological pressure group, *Ecoglasnost*, which originated in the heavily polluted city of Ruse and was backed by influential establishment figures. Zhivkov tried to suppress it, but it would not stay down.[21] By the end of the year Bulgaria was teeming with dissidents; they were later termed "opposition" groups, then "democratic" groups. By the end of the year there were probably more than forty of them. Eleven were represented at the Bulgarian government-opposition roundtable talks that began in January 1990, two months after Zhivkov's overthrow. It is worth giving their names since, better than any description, the names offer an idea of the flowering and the variety of democratic forms in Bulgaria. (1) Bulgarian Worker's Social Democratic Party (United); (2) The Nikola Petkov Bulgarian Agrarian People's Union (Petkov was a democratic agrarian leader executed by the communists in 1947); (3) Club of Victims of post-1945 Repressions; (4) Independent Association for the Protection of Human Rights; (5) The Ecoglasnost Independent Association; (6) Podkrepa (Support) Independent Labor Federation, a rival to the official trade unions; (7) Glasnost and Democracy Club; (8) Civic Initiative Movement; (9) Committee for the Defense of Religious Rights, Freedom of Conscience, and Spiritual Values; (10) Independent Student Societies; (11) Radical Democratic Party. At the roundtable talks these groups were gathered under the umbrella of the Union of Democratic Forces (SDS) whose chairman and secretary, respectively, were Zhelyu Zhelev and Petur Beron,* two distinguished and courageous advocates of genuine democracy for Bulgaria. The Bulgarian people had been long suppressed, and they had not presented the challenge to communist authority that other East European peoples had. This led to unwarranted, if inevitable, generalizations about their docility or political indifference, even about their alleged compatibility with communist governance. The sprouting of opposition groups like those listed above should have put such misapprehensions to rest. It did not necessarily make Bulgarians democrats, but it showed they were as freedom-loving as any other nation. That, at least, was a beginning.

Before the End

The Bulgarian opposition forced its way through the gap between Zhivkov's repressiveness and the degree of permissiveness enforced on him by the winds of change. Also Zhivkov's ostensible acceptance of, even enthusi-

---

*Beron has since been accused of being a police informer, an event which reinforces the discussion on p. 253 about collaboration with the old regimes.

asm for, perestroika made full-scale repression unfeasible. He was steadily maneuvering himself into an impossible situation: he was witnessing a threat developing that, he knew, if it were not suppressed now, could later sweep him away.

Considering the unfettered powers he had enjoyed under Brezhnev, it was a humbling position to be in—yet another facet of an unsettling situation. The effect on Zhivkov was mildly similar to that which overtook Ceauşescu; he retreated into himself, trusting fewer and fewer subordinates, increasingly losing touch with the population which, with some justice, he had always claimed to understand, and with reality itself. Milko Balev, former chief of his personal staff, whom he had had promoted to Politburo status, moved into a position of close trust and great power—a Bulgarian Martin Bormann, intelligent, arrogant, sycophantic, hated. Dimitur Stoyanov, minister of the interior, responsible for repressive security, was another close confidant.

But to the disgust of many communists, some of them by no means perestroika enthusiasts, and of the population as whole, Zhivkov was now set on furthering his son, Vladimir. If Zhivkov ever thought this worthless scion could become another Lyudmila, it only showed how sentiment—and threatening senility—could obliterate sense. Whereas Lyudmila made nepotism almost respectable, the likes of Vladimir and Nicu Ceauşescu fully lived up to its usual reputation. Vladimir was perhaps not as bad as he was subsequently painted in the vengeful atmosphere after his father's overthrow. But he obviously should have been kept out of public sight. Instead, in July 1989 Zhivkov put him in charge of the Central Committee's commission for culture, evidently seeing him following in his sister's footsteps. But whatever Vladimir's inclinations were, they did not head in a cultural direction. The son, though, was a side issue; it was what the episode told about his father that counted. And Zhivkov père was becoming more than tyrannical: he was becoming absurd. Once he enjoyed a certain grudging respect. He was not difficult for many Bulgarians to identify with. Nor in his earlier days was he without the common touch. Now he was losing touch altogether.

But he was not losing his energy. His physical and mental health never deteriorated the way Kádár's did, for example, or Erich Honecker's. In the very last year of his rule he outlined another series of apparently far-reaching proposals for economic reform, partly as a response to perestroika and partly to the continuing deterioration of the Bulgarian economy itself. The official media made much of "preustrojstvo," the Bulgarian variant of perestroika designed to dispel any doubts about Sofia keeping up with the times.[22]

The document that was supposed to herald a turning point was "Decree No. 56" on economic activity, published in January 1989.[23] In terms of size (126 articles) and scope it was another Zhivkov spectacular. Divided into five sections, Decree No. 56 promised to pull the Bulgarian economy out of the swamp into which it had slid. Some of its provisions were revolutionary—on paper. The economy was now to be restructured on the basis of "firms" or "companies," close to the capitalist sense of the terms. Several types of these would be possible: state firms, joint stock companies, firms with limited liability, firms with unlimited liability, "citizens' " firms (singly or cooperatively owned), and joint ventures with foreign majority participation. Between these types there should be competition, with the possibilities of bankruptcies. All types should have a decisive degree of autonomy.

These were undoubtedly sweeping proposals, bringing Bulgarian reform thinking on paper to the level of that in either Poland or Hungary. But the fine print of Decree No. 56 left doubts, both about the sincerity of the reform proposals and their consistency. Parts of the document bore the same signs of sloppiness and half-baked thinking that had characterized the "July Concept." The state was still to guide the economy through taxes, subsidies, exchange rate manipulation, and wage and price formation. A "state plan" would also continue in existence, and companies were liable to be "guided" by the center in the fulfillment of this plan. These were just a few of the doubts about Decree No. 56 that detracted from its value. Zhivkov issued a further set of proposals in July aimed at facilitating foreign participation in the economy and giving the banks more freedom of action.[24] But by now people, whether abroad or at home, were past taking him seriously. Most important of all, perhaps, was his loss of credibility among Bulgaria's small but competent group of technocrats who had benefited from the Western experience they had gained during the "decade of détente" in the 1970s. It was now clear to them that a real change in the economy depended on a real change in the political leadership.

But apparently unaware of his quickening ineffectiveness, Zhivkov pressed on in his efforts to justify himself. In February 1989 he had made his first ever serious criticism of Stalin. This was in the context of condemning the persecution of Bulgarian communist exiles in the Soviet Union, some six hundred of whom were said to have died between 1917 and 1941.[25] Zhivkov went on to criticize the "period of the personality cult" in the late 1940s and early 1950s, but only in the most general and perfunctory terms. Here, his reference can best be explained, not by any desire to protect himself—he was, after all, a stripling at the time—but by the extreme sensitivity that all but the most radical reformist communists felt regarding Georgi Dimitrov, the "Bulgarian Lenin," Sofia's own "man in the mausoleum." Dimitrov returned to Bulgaria from Moscow in 1946 and died in Moscow three years later. He was obviously not responsible for the trials and executions of 1949. Vulko Chervenkov, Bulgaria's "little Stalin," has been rightly held culpable for that, and for other crimes in the remainder of the Stalin period. But Dimitrov set the tone for the epoch of Bulgarian Stalinism, and it was difficult to see how any objective examination of that period could leave his reputation untouched. Objective examinations of anything were never Todor Zhivkov's strong point, but his reformist successors would be watched to see if they would bring themselves to cut Dimitrov down to size.

Zhivkov's contention had always been that the evils of Stalinism were fully laid to rest by the April Plenum of 1956, in which, of course, he had played a major role. As for pluralism, he had similarly argued that Bulgaria already had it to an optimal degree. His best argument in this regard was the existence and activity of the Bulgarian Agrarian Union, which had an extensive organization and one hundred members in the Bulgarian Subranie (Parliament). But the Agrarian Union, once a great movement in Bulgarian history, had been the classic satellite party ever since its power was broken in the late 1940s. As for the Communist Party, Zhivkov maintained that its leading role was beyond discussion.[26]

Under the party umbrella there could be as much debate and criticism as the party thought fit. But the finger on the regulating trigger must be that of the party. That was Leninism. What was happening in Hungary, where a multiparty system was in the making, was a heresy rejected by Bulgaria—although Sofia continued to maintain cordial relations with Budapest, never remotely supporting Ceauşescu in his suggestions for joint action against Eastern Europe's heretics. But Bulgaria's own heretics were fair game. Throughout 1989 the independent or opposition politicians were subjected to mounting harassment. This did not make the regime "Stalinist," as many Bulgarians were ready to believe and as many Western journalists reported after Zhivkov's fall. Those Bulgarians old enough to remember the late 1940s and early 1950s knew what Stalinism was and found little similarity. Apart from anything else, the regime was constrained by the spirit of the times. Many parts of Eastern Europe, not to mention the Soviet Union itself, were in a state of ferment. Then there was Helsinki, the CSCE process, that kept a watchful eye on human rights violations. And the older Zhivkov got, the more he seemed to hanker after international respectability. He was, after all, doyen of Warsaw Pact leaders and saw himself not only as a Bulgarian leader but as a Balkan statesman.

The official campaign against the Bulgarian opposition drew little foreign attention. But then a disaster occurred that once again put Bulgaria in the dock. Toward the end of May 1989 mass demonstrations took place by members of the Turkish minority against the continued assimilation campaign that had begun in 1984–85. Clashes with the police occurred, and a number of the Turks were killed. The Bulgarian authorities immediately began expelling those it considered the ringleaders of the Turkish discontent. In June, Zhivkov announced that a law passed the previous month giving all Bulgarian citizens the right to travel abroad as from the following September (again Helsinki!) would now apply immediately to the Turkish minority. As many Turks as wanted could leave for Turkey. (Sofia still maintained they were not Turks but "Turkicized" Bulgarians, but it had made a concession on one crucial point. It accepted their emigration to Turkey. In 1985 when some of the Turks asked for permission to emigrate, they were told they could migrate anywhere—*inside* Bulgaria.)

In June 1989, therefore, the exodus of Turks began from Bulgaria to Turkey that became a prime news item for the world's media. Up to late August when the Turkish authorities, overwhelmed by the mass of immigrants, insisted on visa requirements for any further influx, about 315,000 Turks had left Bulgaria, about 30 percent of the total. The harm this did to the Bulgarian economy was considerable; the harm it did to the Bulgarian reputation was incalculable. Some 100,000 Turks subsequently returned, disappointed with their reception in Turkey, and Bulgarian propaganda made the most of them. But the damage was irreparable.[27]

However little sympathy there was for the Turks among many Bulgarians, Zhivkov's elephantine bungling of the whole issue caused his prestige to plummet even further. In August and September 1989 Western diplomats in Sofia were privately predicting his early demise. Bulgarians themselves were more cautious, partly from nature, partly because life without Zhivkov, however desirable, was still barely imaginable. It became more imaginable in October, however, when the Honecker regime in East Berlin, considered by many Bulgarians as a model of stability, was toppled with such ease by street demonstrations in East German cities.

Honecker's fall shook the confidence of the Zhivkov regime further. It was followed by another serious miscalculation on Zhivkov's part. An ecological conference, under CSCE auspices, had been scheduled in Sofia for October, much to the satisfaction of the regime, Zhivkov in particular. This seemed a way to claw back some of the international respectability he had been losing. Zhivkov's record as an ecologist left much to be desired but, for something Helsinki-sponsored, he was ready to become a Green crusader. To enhance Bulgaria's image, he was also ready to allow the country's unofficial opposition groups more latitude than ever before. Here the aim was to impress representatives of the Western media who came to town for the conference. But, again, the strategy went wrong. Bulgaria's oppositional groups, *Ecoglasnost* in particular, took to the streets in large numbers, the police countered with some brutality, and Bulgaria's reputation took yet another much publicized pounding. Bearing the brunt was Foreign Minister Petur Mladenov, in office since 1971 and enjoying considerable respect in the diplomatic community despite the aberrations of the government he represented.

Just a few weeks earlier, Mladenov had had to brazen out the international odium resulting from the Turkish minority debacle. Now he felt constrained to switch to open rebellion against Zhivkov. But the move that overthrew Zhivkov in November was not spontaneous. A palace coup, not a popular revolt, it had apparently been in the making for about three months, the catalyst being the regime decision in May to expel the leaders of the Turkish minority, which had led to the mass exodus. The two other main conspirators were apparently Prime Minister Georgi Atanasov, once a protégé of Zhivkov, and Andrei Lukanov, minister of foreign economic relations, scion of a well-known communist family, who had been kept down by Zhivkov for many years. But the Turkish disaster was not such as to put the majority of the Politburo on their side. It was the unconscionable Vladimir that did that—his promotion to head the department of culture in the Central Committee—and it was testimony to the depths to which the regime had fallen that it was the issue of nepotism that finally tipped the scales against it. The key to the conspiracy now became General Dobri Dzurov, minister of defense since 1964, an old supporter of Zhivkov who might still have been prepared to go along with the father but who could not stomach the son. It was still a close thing in the Politburo, but the conspirators won, and on November 10, 1989, Zhivkov was forced to resign.[28]

Bulgarians had to start getting used to life without him, and in the weeks after his overthrow they seemed to be relishing the effort. Deposed communist leaders anywhere had never been let down lightly, and Zhivkov was now only getting done to him what he had done to many others. Allowing for his tyranny and for the relief of so many at being rid of it, the ocean of denunciation in which he was now engulfed seemed excessive, however, even to some Bulgarians. The recrimination became obsessive, seeming almost to reflect an inverted loyalty to the former leader. A lot of dust would have to settle before Zhivkov could be judged with detachment. But the verdict would not be as severe as that being passed in late 1989 and early 1990.[29]

The conspirators who ousted Zhivkov were clearly favored by the

Soviet Union. Mladenov was credibly reported to have stopped off in Moscow on his way back from China just before the move in the Politburo.[30] The news of the coup and of Bulgaria's new leaders was well-received in Moscow. The Soviet leadership was obviously glad to see the back of Zhivkov, but it was presumably also glad that it had been the party and not the people that brought him down. Much as the Zhivkov leadership may have been shaken by the unprecedented street demonstrations in October and November, it was not they that caused its downfall. It was the Politburo itself, communists against communists; and no matter how reconciled Gorbachev had become to the collapse of the communist system in some parts of Eastern Europe, he must have been consoled to see it surviving in others.

Bulgaria's new leaders were reform communists, rather of the Prague Spring variety. They were without question bent on change, but the degree of change they were ready to countenance at first seemed small in terms of developments in other parts of Eastern Europe and in the Soviet Union. The changes also were small in terms of what most Bulgarians wanted. Pressure from below, therefore, caused the new Mladenov leadership, especially after Lukanov became premier in January 1990, to become more radical. The party's monopoly of power was jettisoned, and promises were made of a gradual move away from socialism toward the market. To symbolize its determination to reform, the Bulgarian Communist Party changed its name to Bulgarian Socialist Party. It won a clear victory in the democratic elections of June 1990. Most of the electorate wanted change but shunned the unknown. This fact, plus the huge organizational advantage the government had (rather than the relatively small degree of electoral fraud which undoubtedly took place) won the election. Now it was up to the socialists to show they had changed more than their name. Mladenov had to resign as president shortly after the election for a remark made the previous December, when he appeared to suggest that demonstrators should be put down by force. The remark indicated that the old ways of thinking would die only slowly—as they were doing in neighboring Romania.

Bulgaria was indeed "out from under another yoke" as a young Sofia student joyfully put it in December 1990, referring to the freedom from the Turkish yoke achieved in 1878. But many young Bulgarians, especially in the towns and cities, wanted full democracy, and they were impatient to get it. The new government seemed incapable of doing anything. The result was that postcommunist Bulgaria seemed to be slipping into anarchy, to which economic deprivation was strongly contributing. The nation seemed more divided than ever. What it would need was leadership, responsibility—and help.

8 *Romania: The Uprising*

"Romania's finest hour in its communist history came on 21 August 1968 when its state and party leader, Nicolae Ceauşescu, denounced the Soviet-led invasion of Czechoslovakia that had just taken place." That was my opinion twenty years later.[1] But within eighteen months this solemn pontification had become triumphantly outdated. It now needed to be amended thus: "Romania's finest hour in its entire history occurred on December 21, 1989, when the nation rose against the tyranny of Nicolae Ceauşescu and overthrew him."

In doing so, Romanians not only defied logic, but expectations. They redeemed their honor and their international reputation. They showed a doubting world that they *did* have courage and fury, that they were prepared to risk everything, whatever the odds. Those who knew Romanian history never doubted this. Romanian troops fought valiantly in World War I, earning the praise of Germans who fought against them, and in World War II, earning the praise of Germans who fought with them.[2] In 1907 the Romanian peasants rose against social injustice in a movement immortalized in Liviu Rebreanu's novel *The Uprising*.[3] They were crushed and thousands of them killed. That was the uprising of the vanquished, but this was the uprising of victors, with the Romanians, townspeople this time, toppling Europe's crudest and most vicious dictatorship.

Mircea Dinescu, the poet-democrat, put it best. He had been persecuted, among other things for a poem the last line of which read: "God has turned his countenance away from Romania." On December 22, 1989, in the midst of the fighting in Bucharest, he went to the television building, which was still under fire, and spoke into the cameras these historic words: "Brothers! God has again turned his countenance on Romania. The Dictator has been put to flight. For decades the Romanian nation was sick with fear, but now, in this December, its courage has prevailed over fear."[4]

The name of Nicolae Ceauşescu figures in both of the affirmations made above, in diametrically opposite connotations. And the recent history of Romania can be written in terms of this difference, of the deterioration reflected in them. On August 21, 1968, Ceauşescu stood at the peak, not only of his own political reputation, but of the legitimacy of communist power in Romania. On December 25, 1989, he and his wife (and coruler) Elena, were hunted down, tried, and executed.

The descent of the Ceauşescu regime into corrupt and inefficient malignancy has been narrated and analyzed many times.[5] No attempt will be made to describe it here—instead, just the outstanding characteristics of Ceauşescu's tyranny, especially in his last years, will be discussed.

One misapprehension should be corrected at the outset. Ceauşescu rule—nearly a quarter of a century of it—cannot be taken as a single whole. The first five years, between his accession in 1965 and 1970, were years of promise, the best half-decade in Romania's communist history. First, there was the major and, from the East European point of view, vital impact Romania was making on intrabloc relations. This has been discussed at some length in chapter 2. It appears there because of its transcending, international importance, but it needs to be restated briefly here. Between 1961 and 1968, first under Gheorghe Gheorghiu-Dej and then under Ceauşescu, Romania turned back supranationalism in Soviet-East European relations. This preserved a crucial leeway and freedom of action for the individual East European states without which their surge to freedom twenty years later might not have been possible. Perhaps the Gheorghiu-Dej leadership, with its successful resistance to Khrushchev's ideas of economic supranationalism, was decisive, but Ceauşescu's subsequent courage and tenacity were also indispensable. The highpoint was August 1968 with his resistance to the invasion of Czechoslovakia. No balanced view of Ceauşescu's role in history will be possible for many years yet. When it is, this contribution must be considered along with all the squalor with which his rule became drenched.[6]

So must his first five years of domestic promise: the relative cultural freedom; the clipping of the *Securitate*'s wings (however incomplete and temporary that exercise turned out to be); de-Stalinization that got close to exposing Gheorghiu-Dej's political criminality; an apparently more benevolent attitude to the national minorities; an improved standard of living; above all, a general atmospheric relaxation in the relations between rulers and ruled. During these years Ceauşescu had sympathy and support. There can be no doubt about this. Where there is doubt (as well as differences) centers on the motives behind the good behavior. Many argue that it was all in the pursuit of consolidating his power; that completed, Ceauşescu took off the gloves as well as the mask. In view of his subsequent malfeasance it is hard to disagree with this judgment. But so precipitate was the decline in Ceauşescu's conduct, as his rule became tyranny, and his once salutary determination became lost in a virulent obsessiveness, that a rational explanation seems altogether inadequate. Political science reveals its limitations with a man like Ceauşescu. So does sociology, however interesting the insights it might give into the peasant mentality of Romania's rulers. Psychology might be more appropriate and rewarding. Ceauşescu's last twenty years can best be explained in terms of obsessional and paranoidal disorder. Quite simply, he became mad, viciously so.[7]

The turning point in Ceauşescu's *domestic* policy—in foreign policy he remained remarkably consistent—is believed to have been his visit to China and North Korea in the Summer of 1971. He certainly returned imbued with the militant fervor characterizing China. But what he saw in North Korea also left a lasting impact. It was much more like Romania in size, population, and official outlook. Both the social engineering and the dynastic pretensions of Kim Il Song appear to have impressed Ceauşescu. So much so that Kim's anointed son and successor, Kim Jong Il, was seen as something of an example and throne model for Ceauşescu's own son, the unspeakable Nicu.

In *Eastern Europe and Communist Rule* I summed up Ceauşescu's complicated personality as follows:

The greatest single factor in Romania's internal debate has been Ceauşescu's capriciousness. No European leader in the second half of the twentieth century has so personified the debilitating effects of power more than he has. An intelligent man, an extraordinarily hard worker, a patriot, not personally cruel (in the sense that, say, Mátyás Rákosi of Hungary or Stalin were); once well intentioned—he has probably remained so in a perverted way—his name has yet become synonymous with many of the iniquities associated with historic tyranny. A willful refusal to take advice; a toleration for nothing but sycophants; a nepotism ever-growing in dimensions; an intolerance visibly hardening as absolute power corrupted absolutely; a self-defeating impatience clamoring for instant success; an inconsistency and unpredictability; a conglomerate of convictions and prejudices; a pretentiousness reflecting little but bad taste; a suspiciousness bordering on paranoia; a wife, Elena, who encouraged the bad and stifled the good in her husband; a self-promoting personality cult the sheer ludicrousness of which insulted, humiliated, angered, or amused most Romanians—it was for these characteristics that Nicolae Ceauşescu would be remembered by most of his countrymen.[8]

Some Romanians have criticized this assessment as being too favorable to Ceauşescu. It was certainly not intended to be. But in the light of his last years it is a description that does miss the demonic obsessiveness of a man possessed and blinded by a crazed sense of himself and his mission, prepared to destroy his country in the pursuit of it. It also misses another important side of Ceauşescu: the sheer banality of the man, of Elena, too— their money-grubbing, macro- and micro-crookedness, her taste for fur coats, their nepotism, gluttony, country bumpkin tastes, nouveau-riche pretentiousness. Everything they touched they reduced to meanness.

The "Homogenization" Madness

In later years Ceauşescu pursued a policy in Romania monstrous and terrifying—far beyond anything his East European counterparts ever contemplated, let alone implemented. And this is where the use of the word "capriciousness" in the first sentence of the above-quoted assessment was ill-chosen—at least in the last decade of Ceauşescu's rule. In those last terrible years his goal was a totalitarianism that went beyond Stalinism and had its only parallel in the North Korea of Kim Il Song. It was as if the experiences he absorbed on his 1971 visit gestated or fermented for several years and then issued forth in their dreadful Romanian variant.

The term totalitarianism does not quite cover what Ceauşescu tried to force on Romania. The most descriptive word, as Gail Kligman suggests, is "homogenization," meaning the "obliteration of differences" through social engineering—between human beings, between villages and towns, between ethnic communities.[9] Not only was there to be no room left for spontaneity, but none for individuality either.

The most far-reaching example of this was in the so-called "systematization" policy, the scheme "to reduce the number of villages radically, from about 13,000 . . . to between 5,000 and 6,000 at most."[10] This represented the maniacal motivation of a plan that began in 1972, when it had some rationality. Many villages were dying and practically deserted. The Romanian communists' national party conference in July of that year issued directives according to which rural settlements were divided into villages with or without prospects for growth. Some of those in the first category were earmarked for urban status, but most were to remain as villages and be "modernized" to some extent. Those villages without any prospects at all would be condemned, eliminated. This plan sputtered along for several years without making much impact or drawing real attention. In 1985, however, it began to be massively reshaped. Ceauşescu ordered the whole plan revised, ostensibly to free even more land for agricultural use. Condemned villages were to be bulldozed and their inhabitants relocated into new concrete housing blocks, with communal facilities and amenities. The scheme became one of Ceauşescu's favorites and ripened into the obsession that achieved worldwide notoriety. It was these intended changes in the social environment that frightened most observers. An underground essay had the following comment:

> Life in apartment blocks is helping to instill a collective consciousness in the people's minds. It means living under the close scrutiny of your neighbors. It is a new way of life in which the behavior and requirements of the collective body are present at every moment. It is a new social environment in which priority is given to the community over the individual.[11]

Mihai Botez, one of Romania's most prominent and courageous dissidents, voiced the opinion of almost every Romanian when he stated that "a private dwelling place preserves a certain way of life." Speaking of small houses that had been destroyed in Bucharest itself, he said that they "represented a European tradition in which the individual is something more than a mere element in an aggregate. That means that a new society is being built: one destroys and tries to replace all traces of the past, a little bit like in Orwell. . . ."[12]

A little bit like Orwell. . . .! There was a lot like Orwell bubbling up in Ceauşescu's mind. Fortunately for Romania, by no means all of it materialized. The "systematization" was a case in point. About 11,300,000 people lived in about 13,000 villages in mid-1980. Nobody knew how many of these would have been affected, but if between 7,000 and 8,000 of these villages were condemned to be destroyed, then the number of displaced residents would have been in the millions.[13] But the plan never got started on anything like the scale Ceauşescu wanted. This was partly because of Western pressure, to which from time to time he was not oblivious.[14] But many suspected that it was partly because the regime simply did not have either the money or the means to get it started on the massive scale required. Some "systematization," however, did take place, just outside the Bucharest metropolitan area, for example. The destruction itself was frightening enough; but also frightening were the inhuman constructions built to house the former villagers. One of the first acts of the new provisional government after the revolution was to discontinue "systematization."

"Systematization" was the excrescence of demented social engineering, and its principal victims would have been the Romanians of Romania. But it was unquestionably aimed also at the distinctiveness, and what remained of the physical compactness, of the country's main national minorities, the German and the Hungarian, most notably the Hungarian. The German minority, numbering under a quarter of a million in the mid-1980s, was steadily decreasing through mortality and through emigration to the Federal Republic.[15] The Hungarians, numbering between 1.7 and over 2.1 million, were a different proposition. Most of them lived in Transylvania, which had been part of Hungary until 1920 when it was given to Romania. Subsequently, it became Hungary's principal irredenta. The northern part was given back to Hungary by Hitler in 1940, only to be returned to Romania after World War II. Then, for well over a decade the Hungarian minority enjoyed considerable self-governing, cultural, and educational privileges. But these began to be seriously eroded in the late 1950s by the Gheorghiu-Dej regime. It was one of the early manifestations of the nationalism of Romania's communist regime but, in a broader context, should be seen as part of the drive toward the unitary state, one of the main features of nationalism in Europe in the late nineteenth and twentieth centuries. The Hungarian minority, its diminishing rights and privileges constantly under pressure, constituted the thickest layer of passive, and potentially active, resistance to the Ceauşescu regime. Maintaining its dignity, it warded off all attempts to assimilate it and remained a constant challenge to the policies of the central government.

Ceauşescu's "systematization" marked a new phase in the drive for integration and assimilation, now being pursued at the micro-level—in the villages, the homes, the families, of Hungarians in Romania. Ceauşescu's goal was to obliterate differences, to make people the same, and there was no more effective way of doing it than by "systematization." The Hungarian authorities in Budapest (not to mention exile circles in the West) were aware of this and did much to draw world attention to it. One of "systematization's" welcome by-products was the temporary uniting of ethnic Hungarians and Romanians in their opposition to Ceauşescu. His rule, therefore, was not without its miracles. Hungarian-Romanian enmity ran deep. But hatred of Ceauşescu was running deeper.[16]

Even more ominous than "systematization," and striking at the very heart of civilized ethics, was Ceauşescu's "gender" policy. Women were not just denied the status of masters of themselves—they had never been this in any society, least of all in the Balkans. Official policy now considered their bodies to be in the service of the state, as a means of enhancing the population, which Ceauşescu believed could rise from 23 million to about 30 million by the end of the century. It was not just that abortions were illegal and severely punishable; other means of contraception, though not illegal, were deliberately made unobtainable. Women were pressured to produce four children. This was the most inhuman aspect of all Ceauşescu's policies. It was more than tyrannical: it went beyond evil into horror.[17]

"Homogenization" at the level of the intensity attempted by Ceauşescu was unique. It was enforced by the type of terror that had originated with Stalin but had been unknown in Eastern Europe since Stalin's death. In Romania itself there had been savage reprisals straight after the Hungarian Revolution, particularly in Transylvania. But what Ceauşescu began to reimpose at the turn of the 1980s, after an interval of so many years, was a systematic terror that permeated both public and private life. If the 1989 revolution had not occurred, Ceauşescu, with his mixture of madness and terror, would have made Romania not just unique, but unrecognizable.

Ceauşescu Worship

How was he able to do this? How could a leader, no matter how strong-willed, terrorize a nation of 23 million people, when terror in the entire communist system, except possibly for Albania, had largely become a thing of the past? Many non-Romanians have asked this question and have usually come up with unsatisfactory answers relating to history, alleged national character, or lack of political culture, Romanians being depicted as more susceptible to oppression than other, "sturdier" nations. Since the revolution in December 1989 many thoughtful Romanians have asked the same question and have urged their countrymen to do the same. Nor is it enough simply to find the explanation in the formidable strength and efficiency of the *Securitate*, for which, at the height of the terror before the revolution, a large number of Romanians were believed to have worked, if only in the role of occasional informers.[18] How did the *Securitate* get to a pinnacle of power which none of its counterparts had reached since the days of the Soviet NKVD? An explanation would need fuller and more expert treatment than is possible here. But it surely lies in the demoralization of Romanian society, pressed down by poverty, war, oppression, then Stalinist communism, and without the benefit of any supportive institution like the Church (which was such a buttress in a country like Poland). An important contributory factor was the sheer physical isolation of Romania, tucked away in a corner of southeastern Europe, bordering only on other communist countries. Another was the fact that the most coherent sections of society allowed themselves to be seduced by nationalism. However much nationalism might raise morale, it is dangerously incomplete without a complementary development of domestic reform and democratization. Without the latter, the former became, not the patrimony of the whole people, but the instrument of the few, or, as it became in Ceauşescu's case, the obsession of one man. Romanian nationalism became, therefore, a means of tyranny rather than of popular expression, a debasement rather than an inspiration. Brought down to this condition, the Romanian people, with notable but few exceptions, became defenseless against a ruler who eventually perfected terror, and never hesitated to use it. After a while, many people simply became mesmerized by fear. Already at the end of the 1970s, for example, there was a common belief that all ashtrays in restaurants were wired. Only a very tiny percentage of them were. But that did not matter: the aim of terror was accomplished. No one—until December 1989—could break through the barrier of fear. And terror needed, and created, paranoia. Many visitors to Romania agreed that this was the outstanding characteristic of society. It traveled from the top downward and then spread out.

Most degrading of all was the active or passive acquiescence in Ceauşescu's personality cult, an ever-growing monstrosity, constantly demanding sustenance and never failing to receive it. The unending examples of the credulity-snapping adulation of Ceauşescu need not be repeated.[19] Occasionally, they had their gallows-humor side as when one court jester, forgetting his history—or remembering it—came close to comparing his idol with Genghis Kahn.[20] But behind all the nausea and the nonsense was a serious and, again, a sinister intent. Anneli Ute Gabanyi describes it as follows:

> The elaborate ritual organized every year to pay homage to Ceauşescu on his birthday has by now lost any semblance of spontaneity. Praise for Ceauşescu proceeds along strictly prescribed patterns. The "Great Leader" and "Most Beloved Son of the Fatherland" is, for example, portrayed as a providential figure, a part of "Romanian mythology," the incarnation of all national virtue, and the historic culmination of national aspirations and goals. His adulators present him as a man of superhuman, if not godlike, qualities: epithets such as "the genius," "the titan," and even "the demigod" point to the clearly hagiographic aspect of the Ceauşescu cult. His birthplace, Scorniceşti, has become the site of a nationwide pilgrimage that underlines the cult's quasi-religious undertones. The party-directed campaign, as Ceauşescu him-

self confided to his French biographer Michel-Pierre Hamelet, is "a matter of organization and perspicacity"; it is clearly trying to tap deep-rooted national feelings, aligning itself with the political culture of a peasant society that has embarked on a road of modernization.[21]

There was much more to the personality cult, therefore, than simple sycophancy, although most of its practitioners were nothing but sycophants. Those who orchestrated it knew what they were doing. The sites were set higher, or deeper, than just tickling the Conducător's fancy. The whole vast exercise could also be seen in terms of "homogenization." The term means, or implies, wholeness. The whole state became one person. And that person was Ceaușescu.[22]

An English journalist could not have put it more aptly when he wrote: "James Frazer's 'Golden Bough,' the classic study of primitive blood kinship and ritual, is of more use than Lenin, or indeed of the CIA, in predicting the future of this European dynasty."[23] In the event, not even Frazer could have foreseen the fate of the Ceaușescu family.

In the course of the 1980s the most obvious manifestation of the merging of leader and national destiny was the rebuilding of large parts of Bucharest in the Conducatorial image. The architecture was horrible enough, described variously as "Stalinist-fascist," "pharaonic," or—most accurately—"Ceaușescu-Bloody." But much more horrible than the buildings that went up was the barbaric indifference to those that had to come down. They included parts of the nation's cultural, religious, and architectural heritage. Just as bad, they included many small cottages whose inhabitants were dumped into the concrete hovels the new order was providing for them. Nothing Ceaușescu ever did had quite the same mix of hideousness, pretentiousness, philistinism, and banality.[24]

It would be a mistake to forget Elena in all this. She played her own dominating role in the Romanian tragedy, exercising an influence on her husband that some considered to be decisive at times. Certainly they were a very close couple, mostly inseparable. Occasional glimpses tended to confirm that Elena was the more determined and forceful of the two. She was usually the more strident. It is worth noting that in a traditionally male-dominated society like the Balkans, women have often played a dominating familial and political role, and the second half of this century was no exception. Queen Frederika of Greece, Lyudmila Zhivkova in Bulgaria, Nexhmije Hoxha, Enver's fearsome spouse and watchdog over his legacy—in Albania, not to mention Mirjana Marković-Milošević, stronger wife of Serbia's "strong man," have all been good examples. But none played as big, sinister, or disastrous a role as Elena. In the last few years of their rule and of their lives, as they grew more isolated, they fed each other's sense of unreality, more so than all the pomp and paraphernalia of the personality cult. Each saw the other as having almost a divine role, as Romania's supreme patriarch and matriarch. Some of their last words illustrate this, absurdity vying with pathos. Just before her execution Elena called out to the firing squad: "Think, children, how for 20 years I was like a mother to you. Don't forget all I have done for you."[25] Ceauşescu, himself, being driven by a police sergeant to the army post when he was arrested, was asked: "Why did you cut down the television program to two hours?" He answered: "So as not to tire the working people. So that the working people should rest properly and be fit for work the following day."[26] The firing squad emptied between 180 and 200 bullets into their bodies. No political scientist could do justice to their last days. No historian either. It would need an Ibsen or a Euripides.

The Counterattack Against Reform

Ceauşescu opposed Gorbachev from the start. First, he resented, on nationalist grounds, the new Soviet leader's early attempts to infuse efficiency into the East European system though multilateralism. This had been standard policy for a quarter of a century and could be regarded as being in the spirit of sovereignty generated under Gheorghiu-Dej. When Gorbachev Mark II appeared, it might have been expected that Ceauşescu would now have welcomed the new laissez-faire approach. But he recognized that the real danger to himself lay in the virus of reform now loose in Eastern Europe, and from then on his stand increasingly hardened against any reformism. At a Central Committee plenum in November 1985, just a few months after Gorbachev's accession, he referred to numerous "errors and warpings" in the implementation of the policy already laid down, but refused to concede that the policy needed revising in any way. He described the new 1986–90 economic plan as a "new offensive" on the road to communism. Rejecting any departure from "socialist principles," he criticized ideas coming from "abroad," advocating their "renewal" or even their "discontinuance."[27]

He continued this rejection of reform right to the end, each pronouncement on the subject shriller than the last. But, toward the end, he did not just stop at defending the frontiers of Romania from the threat of reform. He tried to counterattack, not just with criticism, but with demands for action. In the summer of 1989, not long before the end, he tried to initiate joint Warsaw Pact measures to contain the forces of reform that were now sweeping through the alliance. He appears to have been active in this regard at the

Warsaw Pact summit in July 1989. What had particularly incensed him were the developments in Poland, where communism had been routed and Solidarity was about to form the first postwar democratic government.[28] What kind of action Ceauşescu was proposing was never divulged. Perhaps he himself did not know. Some understood him as wanting military action, but there is no proof of this. But, whatever he wanted, it was a long way from the line of August 1968 when he had stood alone against the invasion of Czechoslovakia and the Brezhnev Doctrine. The Brezhnev Doctrine was (almost) dead. Long live the Ceauşescu Doctrine!

The truth was that the once sturdy patriotism had become a deranged nationalism. Nowhere was this more evident than in the determination to pay off Romania's hard currency debt. Standing at between $10 billion and $11 billion in 1981, it had unquestionably become a serious problem. But Ceauşescu chose to tackle it by throttling imports and maximizing exports regardless of the increased suffering he was inflicting on the already pauperized population. He was successful in his aim. At the end of March 1989 he was able to announce that the debt had been virtually paid off—an extraordinary achievement in terms of statistics.[29] Many hoped, and the Romanian people had certainly a right to expect, that Ceauşescu would now let up, giving the consumer the relief and reward he deserved. In no way. The new goal was *industrial modernization*, to be achieved largely by the same economic policy as had paid off the foreign debt. It is too much to say that this decision was the beginning of the end for Ceauşescu. The uprising in Timişoara in December sprang from a complexity of causes. But had the victory over the debt been followed by a humanity toward those who had suffered for it, the mood of the country might have been different. By 1989, however, Ceauşescu, never strong on humanity, was now far beyond it, answerable only to his own fanaticism.

He was squeezing the country beyond endurance, at the same time making claims for domestic economic performance that deceived nobody but himself. Romanian statistics had always had the worst reputation in Eastern Europe, but now they began surpassing even themselves in fantasy. Nowhere more so than in agriculture. For example, the regime claimed a grain harvest of 32 million tons for 1987 when weather conditions were known to have been bad in Southeastern Europe and when judging from the previous year's figures the amount claimed would have been impossible to reach. In 1989 the figures soared. Ceauşescu put the grain harvest figure at 60 million tons when it was something like 16 million.[30] All this at a time when many foodstuffs were severely rationed or totally unobtainable, and people were freezing for lack of fuel.

By 1989 the effect on the economy of such misrule was evident. For example, his throttle on imports meant that certain industries, notably chemicals, some of whose products had export potential, were denied many of the simplest spare parts. On the huge state farms cattle were given substandard feed which lowered milk production. Pesticides and herbicides were forbidden—not on ecological grounds—but to save hard currency. Tourism, once a most promising money-spinner, deteriorated through lack of investments. The number of West German tourists, with precisely the kind of hard currency Ceaușescu wanted to lay his hands on, dwindled from about a quarter of a million in the mid-1970s to about 20,000 in 1988.[31]

In the most primitive kind of economic policy imaginable, everything was subordinated to paying off the debt. The result was that no matter how healthy Romania's foreign bank balance came to look, the country was pauperized. There was a certain logic, however inhuman, when he said that, after the debt, must come modernization. But paying off the debt in the way he did made modernization all the more illusory, because existing plants had run to rack and ruin in the process. Nicolae Ceaușescu, therefore, ruined Romania's economy, its society, and its reputation. Few leaders have left such a legacy.

Dissent and Opposition

Whatever opposition there was in Romania was minimal by the standards of East-Central Europe—Poland, Hungary, Czechoslovakia, and the GDR. Some of the reasons for this have been discussed. Many Romanians have been pained by this fact, but many also have had the honesty to admit it. Mircea Dinescu, for example, estimated there might have been one dissident for every 2 million people.[32] After the extraordinary uprising that toppled Ceaușescu, it would be easy to imagine that prior resistance had been widespread. But it had not been. Attempts to prove that the uprising was prepared beforehand, perhaps with the connivance of Moscow, continue to enjoy some currency. But they have failed because they are spurious, based on partial investigation or distorted information.

But the Ceaușescu misrule was not without its opponents, and the terror it exercised only served to highlight how courageous they were. Resistance within the party itself was the least of Ceaușescu's worries— which is not to say it was totally nonexistent. It seems to have been most serious during 1985 when the new breeze began to blow from Moscow and when there was widespread feeling that it was time to ease up on the Romanian consumer. At the November 1985 Central Committee plenum mentioned earlier, Ceauşescu referred openly to domestic reform sentiment, indicating that it reached high levels in the party. He hinted at opinions in favor of expanding private property, presumably in agriculture. "I would not say," he added, "that there are not some people who think along (reformist) lines but who do not say so openly."[33]

There were, in fact, some suggestions at this time, usually in the specialist press, that more private ownership might be just what the economy needed. There was also passive opposition in the countryside to forced deliveries being imposed *before* the peasants had seen to their own needs. More serious from the regime's point of view was the sympathy some local officials had for this opposition.

But through terror, corruption, and demoralization Ceauşescu contained whatever opposition might have existed inside the regime. It was not until March 1989 that a serious show of defiance was made from within the establishment, and this was by emeritus-rank former leaders. Their names are worth recording: Alexandru Bîrlădeanu, one of the architects of the independent economic policy beginning in the 1960s; Corneliu Mănescu, former foreign minister, erstwhile president of the United Nations General Assembly; Constantin Pîrvulescu, aged ninety-four, former Politburo member, the party's "Grand Old Man," whose outburst against Ceauşescu at the Twelfth Party Congress in 1979, in full view of the television cameras, had become legend; Gheorghe Apostol, one of Gheorghiu-Dej's old henchmen, who had actually been party first secretary in 1954 and 1955; Silviu Brucan, an old party intellectual, former ambassador to Washington and to the UN in New York; and Grigore Răceanu, the least-known of the six, a respected old party stalwart.

Their letter of protest, smuggled abroad and then broadcast back, sharply criticized Ceauşescu's misrule and the isolation into which it had led Romania.[34] It was written, though, from the viewpoint of seasoned communists, profoundly disappointed, but still communist. It had a narrow perspective, reflecting a philosophy certainly not shared by the mass of the population. But it was still a landmark event in Romanian history. Even for many noncommunists it was a break in the clouds. As for the nearly 4 million members of the party itself, the letter said what most of them felt. It was also an act of courage. Its signers may have hoped their age, infirmity, and standing would exempt them from revenge, but all of them were brutally interrogated, placed under house arrest, and denied necessary medicines. In the case of Răceanu the Nazi custom of *Sippenhaft* was applied: his son, Mircea, a distinguished diplomat, was "suspected" of treason, dismissed, and humiliated.

In Romania's intellectual milieu, the high level of artistic attainment stood in sharp contrast to the low level of courage and self-respect. This was nothing new for the Romanian intellectual community as a whole. These people never had been the "conscience of the nation." Too many intellectuals were high on cynicism and low on responsibility. It was not just the few who fed Ceauşescu's personality cult. It was the many who did nothing but take their salaries and allowances and immersed themselves in their ghetto of intrigue, backbiting, petty one-upmanship, and parochial cleverness.

There were, though, exceptions who put their colleagues to shame. The dogged modern language teacher in Cluj, for example, Doina Cornea, who was hounded, persecuted, and subject to every kind of chicanery. She brought to mind the feisty little Gdansk shipyard crane driver, Anna Walentinowicz, whose dismissal in 1980 led to the strike that gave birth to Solidarity. Neither was very practical once the fight had been won and the problems of building anew beset them. But both had already rendered inestimable service to their countries. There were a few writers, some of them former convinced communists, even Stalinists, who courageously stood up for decency and were punished for it. No star, though, shone more brightly than that of Ana Blandiana. The poet of the uprising, however, the man who expressed the exaltation of a nation recovering its soul, was Mircea Dinescu. For his previous courage and integrity he deserved that opportunity. He seemed to combine his estimable talents and qualities with a sense of what was politically practical, realizing in the heady days after Ceauşescu's death that there would be no freedom without restraint, or democracy without compromise.

The sorry showing of the Orthodox Church in the struggle against tyranny was truly embarrassing, though not surprising. There were indeed close similarities between the body of the Church and the official body of the intellectuals. The "fat slumbers" of both, as Edward Gibbon had put it in a similar context, rendered both contemptibly ineffective.[35] But notable exceptions, like Father Gheorghe Calciu, who was not ready to render anything to a Caesar like Ceauşescu, did something to salvage the honor of a thoroughly discredited institution. Outside the official Church, the numerous Romanian Baptists, unfettered by tradition (and with good underground contacts with their American supporters), practiced Christianity and suffered for it. Romania's once large Jewish community, sunk now to 50,000 at most, was not generally persecuted. Most of those Jews who had wanted to emigrate had been allowed. The community's leader, the rabbi Moses Rosen, became a well-known figure in the West, especially in the

United States. He kept on the right side of Ceauşescu, who turned a blind eye to some of his activities and a deaf ear to some of his statements (uttered abroad) in the hope of preserving his Western reputation. Rabbi Rosen did a lot of good. Now he could do better.

It was the workers who, until the December Uprising, had resisted most. The most celebrated strike in Romanian communist history occurred in the Jiu Valley coalmines in southern Transylvania in August 1977. (Strikes in Romania were officially regarded as subversion. In countries like Poland, Hungary, and Yugoslavia, they were simple expressions of dissatisfaction, so numerous as to be part of everyday life.) The miners demanded the restoring of social benefits that had been withdrawn, better food supplies, and no reprisals. (These demands were not dissimilar to those of the Donbas miners in the Soviet Union in 1989.) They locked up an official delegation, headed by a Politburo member, sent from Bucharest to talk with them. Ceauşescu eventually came, shouted at the miners and was shouted back at, promised them what they wanted, and assured them about reprisals. Neither the promises nor the assurances were kept. Food was rushed to the mines, but there was no sustained improvement after the strike. Later, the miners' leaders were arrested, imprisoned, and forbidden ever to return to the Jiu Valley.[36]

There were a few reports of scattered strikes in the early 1980s, in the open-cast mines and quarries in 1981, for example, in the Motru Basin in the southwest of the country, and in mines in Maramureş in northern Transylvania in 1983. In 1986 when the effects of Ceauşescu's foreign debt strategy were really beginning to bite, unrest became more frequent. Instances occurred in the two Transylvanian cities of Cluj and Turda in November of that year, triggered by the reduction of food rations in cases of norm nonfulfillment in industry. Again, the pattern of response was the same as it had been in the Jiu Valley: officials rushed to the scene (though not Ceauşescu this time); promises of redress; some attempts to keep the promises; backsliding when the trouble died down; reprisals.

In February 1987 there was a strike in a large factory in Iaşi, Moldavia, one of the few cases of unrest in a mostly Romanian ethnic center. This was immediately followed by strikes and demonstrations by students at the University of Iaşi, a traditional stronghold of militancy dating from the inter-war period. Once the unrest in the city was ended, the students seem to have been left alone, but a larger number of striking workers were dismissed soon afterward.

The Iaşi incidents were just the prelude to the serious unrest in Braşov, in Transylvania, Romania's second largest city, in November 1987. What apparently began as a protest by workers against being herded like sheep into voting stations, developed into a full-scale demonstration protesting the lack of food and freedom. The violence of police countermeasures led to rioting in which considerable damage was done to property, including local party buildings. The paucity of Western reporting prevented a clear picture being gained of the scale of the Braşov riots. There was apparently unrest in other cities that went totally unreported. The regime response to Braşov was the introduction of a genuine reign of terror, accompanied by a typical piece of Ceauşescu vindictiveness: the further reduction of food rations in the affected areas. Terror kept the lid on for another two years. But Braşov prepared the way for Timişoara. Ceauşescu might be able to batten the country down for some time yet, but all it needed from now on was the right constellation of forces and events to burst the hatches open.[37]

From International Acclaim to Isolation

One of the elements in this constellation was the increasing isolation of Ceauşescu's Romania. Twenty years after enjoying a strong international reputation, with Ceauşescu being sought after as an ally, associate, or intermediary, now both the country and its leader had become global pariahs.

If only to put Romania's subsequent fall from grace in proper perspective, it is worth recalling the distinction of those earlier years. Ceauşescu won the admiration of the free world, and of many in the less than free world, by his courage in August 1968. He carried Romania's name (and his own) around the world, visiting countries of all sizes in all places. (He even vied with Tito as Europe's top political tourist.) He would have liked Romania to join the nonaligned group of nations, but that was incompatible with the country's bloc commitments, which he could not openly flout. So he consoled himself with associate or observer status in practically every developing-country group that would have him—and in his early years he was quite a prestigious catch on the Third World circuit. Like Tito, Ceauşescu could be criticized for his incessant globe-trotting. It was often more ego trip than anything else, not to mention the time and money involved. But the travel had a genuine purpose: to make Romania a more difficult target for Soviet wrath by becoming a world champion of medium, small, and developing states. For a time it also appeared that a Bucharest-Belgrade axis was developing, two medium-sized communist states with similar defensive concerns regarding Moscow and similar European and world interests. They even combined in the joint production of a military aircraft which, happily for all concerned, never had to take to the skies in combat.

But after peaking in the mid-1970s, Romanian-Yugoslav cooperation descended gently to a plateau of formality. The construction of the Iron Gates dam project on the Danube remains its lasting monument.

Ceauşescu also knew, however, that neither Third World declarations nor any special relationship with Belgrade was a substitute for real diplomacy.[38] Maintaining and expanding Romanian independence of action essentially lay in beneficial relations with three countries: China, the Federal Republic of Germany, and the United States. (France under Charles de Gaulle was a fleeting, flamboyant fourth. But the general's ignominious retreat back to Paris from a visit, ironically enough, to Bucharest in May 1968 to face the student revolution was an appropriate reminder to Romania, and everybody else, that France's reach was exceeding its grasp.) It was in relations with the Federal Republic that the first major Romanian break with the Soviet-coordinated Western policy had occurred. Romania defied Soviet dictates and broke bloc unity by establishing diplomatic relations with Bonn in January 1967. This began a cordial and profitable relationship for Romania that continued well into the 1980s.

But important though the West German connection was for Romania, the Bucharest government realized that the diplomatic support of the United States would probably be essential if its independence from the Soviet Union were to be sustained. China had been of immense value as an intrabloc bargaining chip while the Sino-Soviet dispute ran its course, but, once the schism was final, this value was greatly reduced. On the global scale it was the Washington connection that counted. The American government, for its part, was happy to have a foothold in Eastern Europe, a small but not negligible acquisition in the zero-sum game of the Cold War.

Bearing in mind the sensitivities of the Romanian situation vis-à-vis the Soviet Union, Washington handled Bucharest with care. Still, the relationship had its spectacular moments. President Nixon visited Romania in 1969, as did President Ford on his way to the Helsinki conference in 1975. Ceauşescu visited the United States three times, in 1970, 1973, and 1978, the enthusiasm of his reception progressively declining with each visit. The most tangible—although eventually controversial—mark of U.S. goodwill was the granting of most favored nation (MFN) status to Romania in 1975, only the second country to receive it after Poland in 1960. Economically, it did not mean much, but MFN's political symbolism was considerable, which made it keenly sought after by most East European countries.

When MFN was granted in 1975, some Americans were having misgivings about Ceauşescu's domestic record. As in the case of Poland in 1960, when the reward for good conduct was eventually granted, the conduct had already begun to deteriorate. Similarly, Ceauşescu's personality cult was already established; so were what some Romanians were soon describing as his "Caligulan eccentricities." This all went along with the steady reversal of what a few years before had seemed a more liberal attitude to human rights. Indeed, in a very short time it was clear that all the earlier hopes of liberalization had been illusory. Western, particularly U.S., attitudes to Ceauşescu's Romania therefore began to harden. The "Romanian deviation," a once laudatory expression for Bucharest's rejection of Soviet dictates, now came to signify a contempt for international standards of public decency.

Although never central to American foreign policy, relations with Romania became hotly debated on the periphery. Those favoring the continuance of MFN argued that Romania's foreign policy was still at variance with that of the Soviet Union on some important global issues and that Bucharest remained a realpolitik asset. Even on the human rights issue some evidence suggested that fear of losing MFN had at times stayed Ceauşescu's hand. The threat to take away the carrot was a stick in itself.

These arguments were rejected by those who maintained that any support for Ceauşescu had now become immoral and was tarring the United States with the same brush he had so liberally applied to himself. Besides, it was self-defeating politically because whatever realpolitik use Romania may once have had was now exhausted. Its government was now despised, not admired. As for independence from Moscow, economic necessity, it was alleged, was steadily pushing Romania back toward dependence.

The clamor for the United States to change its policy was growing when Ceauşescu effectively ended the dispute by bowing Romania out of it. He announced in February 1988 that Romania would not seek a renewal of MFN status when it expired the following July. The move came after particularly intense U.S. pressure for an improvement in Romania's human rights record. It surprised almost everybody, particularly in Washington, where both advocates and opponents of MFN for Romania suddenly found themselves combatants without a cause.

The whole question of American relations with Romania continued as a subject of debate right up to the fall of Ceauşescu and even beyond. The issues were often clouded by emotion, much hyperbole, and not a little political self-vindication. The truth was that, long before it bowed out of MFN, Ceauşescu's Romania had become worthless as an international asset. It would have been wiser to have booted Romania out of the international comity of nations much earlier. President Reagan should have done it when he came to power. Instead, he gave Romania a new lease on life as an exploitable object in the crusade against "the Evil Empire." Allowing for a customary State Department excess of prudence, it was not so much the doves who clung to Ceauşescu as the hawks. Long before Ceauşescu was dropped by Washington (or dropped himself), he ceased to count for anything, plus or minus, in Moscow. There were even those who thought Brezhnev was actually grateful for his existence because it made him shine by comparison!

Romania's political relations with the Soviet Union remained cool as always, but new impulses had been evident in economic relations since the turn of the 1980s. They were caused by Romania's deteriorating economic situation, particularly regarding the national resource in which it had once been so uniquely blessed: mineral oil. Romania remained a considerable oil producer, but domestic sources were falling off and increasing supplies had to be imported to feed the huge oil refining industry that had been developed since the early 1970s. In the mid-1980s domestic oil output stood at about 11 million tons, while imports were about 12 million. Almost all of this oil went into the huge new refineries and was then exported. Although Romania's refineries were operating at far less than capacity, it was a money-spinner on international markets—at least till the crash in oil prices—helping to battle the foreign debt. As imports from its Middle Eastern suppliers became more difficult, Romania turned to the Soviet Union for relief, and the latter was ready to oblige. Soviet supplies in 1983 were estimated at 1.5 million tons, and twice that amount was reportedly offered for 1985. Romania paid for these supplies in part by sending a large volume of foodstuffs. But a large amount of Romanian oil industry equipment was also going to the Soviet Union, and Moscow was believed to be asking Bucharest to begin investing in its oil extraction in newly opening fields.[39]

None of this meant that Romania was edging back to Moscow politically or was surrendering the semi-independent status it had enjoyed for nearly twenty-five years. It was a question of mutual economic advantage, and both sides recognized it as such. In any case, with the arrival of Gorbachev, mutual economic advantage notwithstanding, the personal relationship between him and Ceauşescu became one of mutual revulsion. Gorbachev's first official visit to Romania only occurred in May 1987, about twenty-five months after he had come to power. Not surprisingly, Bucharest was the last Warsaw Pact capital to be officially visited by the new Soviet leader. The visit went off correctly, though not cordially. In October 1988 Ceauşescu made an official visit to Moscow. It appeared that during these two top-level meetings, and probably at meetings over a long period between less senior Soviet and Romanian officials, the Soviet side did attempt to impress Bucharest with the inescapable need for change. In this respect Gorbachev appeared to be casting aside his Mark II, laissez-faire approach (Romania certainly invited exceptions in this regard). But, if that indeed was the Soviet intention, it failed entirely.[40] Ceauşescu was incorrigible, and Gorbachev appears to have given up on him. All the indications suggested that he welcomed his fall, almost regardless of the consequences.[41] Romania had always been of less importance to the Soviet Union than any other East European country, but this in no way explained the apparent relief with which Moscow greeted Ceauşescu's overthrow and death.

But if Romania's relations with the Soviet Union became more frigid than ever, with Hungary they descended almost to a war footing. They had never been good, but the rural systematization campaign especially made them fall precipitately. Few, if any, Hungarian villages had been affected by this, but the threat seemed real in 1988 and 1989 and the Budapest regime was thoroughly concerned. Obviously, there was much sincere concern in Hungary's attitude, and the mounting number of refugees crossing the border from Transylvania was proof enough of the increasing desperation of many of Romania's citizens of Hungarian nationality. But the issue tended to be blown out of proportion in Budapest (see chapter 5). In the new vividness of Hungarian public life, Transylvania and the original sin of all Romanians were good politics, with Ceauşescu uniquely fitted for the role of demon king. In the worst fantasies he was invested with both nuclear potential and chemical warfare capability—*plus* the intention to use them.[42] It was all a heady brew, but a dangerous one, too. It was whipping up deep, historical Hungarian resentments and, with the fall of Ceauşescu, raising hopes about the situation in Transylvania that were doomed to be disappointed.

The Spirit of Timişoara

It was both ironical and poignant that the fate of Romanians and Hungarians should be intertwined in the fall of Ceauşescu and the bloody, heroic events that led to the new dawn in Romania. The uprising began in Timişoara (Hungarian Temesvar), capital of the ancient Banat, a city with a strong population mix of Romanian, Hungarian, and German (as well as a considerable Serb minority). Visitors to Romania during November and December, including the journalists and delegates to the Romanian Communist Party congress (Ceauşescu's last, grimmest, and most stubbornly reactionary congress), spoke of a restiveness in the air. Neighboring Bulgaria had thrown aside Todor Zhivkov the previous month. The rest of Eastern Europe and the Soviet Union were in ferment. It was getting to be time for a change in Romania, too. All that was needed was the right moment, the right incident, the right person.

They came together in Timişoara. A "turbulent priest," the Reverend László Tökés, a Hungarian Reformed Church pastor, a man of both courage and deep humility, was being evicted from his house by the police. Tökés, an outspoken defender of human freedom and Hungarian rights, had been persecuted for a considerable time and his case had received much publicity in Hungary itself.[43] A crowd of Hungarians in Timişoara, protecting Tökés, were assaulted by the police on December 17 and violence ensued. Romanians joined in to help, and the uprising started. Many observers feared that this might be another of those local incidents, largely confined to Hungarians, that flared up and then was brutally put out. But it spread to Bucharest and many other cities and acquired an unmistakable Romanian hallmark. The Timişoara rioting had become the Romanian Uprising.[44] It was over in less than a week, with the Ceauşescus executed on Christmas Day. But those few days were as tense and nerve-racking as any since the Hungarian Revolution thirty-three years before. For a couple of days, perhaps more, it looked as if the many Ceauşescu loyalists among the *Securitate*, well-armed and well-trained, and with nothing (or everything) to lose, might defeat the poorly equipped army and the people.[45] The result, however, was different from 1956 in Hungary. The darkness that had shrouded Romania for many years lifted.

But the first few months of Romania's freedom were far from reassuring. At times it looked as if the country might be moving through anarchy into another dictatorship. The "Spirit of Timişoara" that had united Romanians and Hungarians in their uprising against Ceauşescu soon evaporated. Ugly race riots broke out in Transylvania. For many Romanians, too, their revolution had been hijacked by a communist cabal, under Ion Iliescu. Iliescu had indeed served under Ceauşescu, but he had been prominent only till 1971. In fact, his fall from grace coincided with Ceauşescu's descent into Avernus. Until then, the latter's rule had seemed full of promise. It was similar with many of Iliescu's colleagues. They were tainted but, like many others in Romania, not greatly compromised by their past actions. As for any hijack, this was more by default than anything else. Unlike any other East European country, including Bulgaria, there were no coherent opposition forces to pick up the pieces left by Ceauşescu. Iliescu and the National Salvation Front, therefore, stepped into a void. Had they not done so, the entire uprising might have failed.

Moreover, despite the fraud in the free elections in May 1990, Iliescu was clearly backed by the majority of Romanians. But he began his presidency badly, widening still further the historic gulf between intellectuals and the rest of the population, and eliciting universal censure for the primitive way he suppressed the antigovernment rioting in June 1990. He remained, though, by some margin, the ablest figure on the Romanian political scene. He still had a chance to show his leadership qualities. But he and his colleagues were on notice, and their margin for error was narrower. Their regime had both authoritarian and democratic aspects. Characteristics of the old order certainly persisted, as did huge numbers of its former lackeys. But it was essentially different from the past. The real danger now was that, whatever this regime might be, it had no coherence. Its writ meant practically nothing, while the economic situation worsened rapidly. And— perhaps most depressing of all—political life in Romania was again being vitiated by malevolence, calumny, fantastic rumor, paranoia, and irresponsibility. Things were indeed getting back to normal.

9 Yugoslavia and Albania: The Eclipse of National Communism

Yugoslavia: Impending Disintegration

This chapter was written almost ten years to the month after Josef Broz Tito died. During that decade, especially toward the end of it, the world with which Tito had been familiar, the world that had given his life coherence, purpose, and inspiration, had all but vanished. The world communist system was in a state of disintegration. So was the Soviet Union, to which for the first half of his life he had given his loyalty and, even after 1948, a kind of inverted loyalty. In most of Eastern Europe popular revolutions, bloodless except for Romania, had swept away communism. And in his own country, "Tito's Yugoslavia," as the world came to know it, communism had become irrelevant, federalism damaged beyond repair, even its unity threatened. Some veteran communists survived to suffer the collapse of their life's work. Tito was spared that by a few years. In 1980 when he died, his achievement still stood.

But even then it was far from secure. Tito himself was the main institution holding it together. Socialist Yugoslavia had not become a viable organism any more than royal Yugoslavia was one between the wars. Already in 1980 it was showing signs of disruption and decay. "Apres moi, le déluge" fitted Tito every bit as much as it did Louis XV.

The Six Myths of Yugoslavia

Although this chapter cannot attempt a full analysis of the failure, it can suggest its root cause. Tito's Yugoslavia was based on six myths, powerful and sustaining at first, but later fading into impotence and disillusion:

(1) Tito himself. Tito's greatness as a warrior-statesman cannot be denied. His personality, leadership, wartime victory, establishment of Yugo-

slavia, and successful defiance of Stalin secure his place in history. But his achievements, together with his own personal inclinations, invested him with an aura of sacred indispensability that harmed rather than helped Yugoslavia. For Yugoslavia's future it was self-defeating.[1]

(2) The "Club of 41." The wartime, partisan legend. Again, as an inspirational force in the early days of the republic, this was creative and binding. The break with Stalin—the very thought of it, let alone doing it—would have been impossible without this myth. But in the ensuing years a once living legend became a fossilized relic, a cramping, not a creative, tradition. Old partisans clotted the arteries of Yugoslav public life long after they should have settled into the well-deserved quiet of their own private repose.[2]

(3) Socialism. There was nothing specifically Yugoslav about this: the myth that socialism represented the shortest, surest route to human prosperity and happiness. In Yugoslavia, "reformed" though it claimed to be, it did nothing of the sort.

(4) Self-management. The ideological myth. This was Yugoslavia's own contribution to the "treasure house" of Marxism-Leninism. It was a short-lived propaganda triumph and a long-lived economic catastrophe. In the artificial prosperity of the 1960s and 1970s its deficiencies could be hidden. Later, when it was too late, they could not. Self-management gave Yugoslav socialism a global reputation for enlightenment it did not deserve.[3] In many respects it was as dogmatic as anything in either Eastern Europe or the Soviet Union.

(5) Federalism. The notion that federalism, combined with socialism, could overcome ethnic differences in a multinational state by making them irrelevant. In 1962 Tito himself was saying that the national problem in Yugoslavia had been overcome.[4] Already in his own lifetime there was to be ample evidence that this was not true. After his death, the tragic absurdity of this claim became manifest.

(6) Nonalignment. This was Tito's illusion, a mixture of geopolitics and grandeur. Even before his death most Yugoslavs recognized it as unsustainable. It was now becoming a choice between East and West—and most Yugoslavs were in no doubt what the choice had to be: the West, in general; Western Europe, in particular.

These myths had become unsustainable several years before Tito's death, but his charisma hid the truth from most of his countrymen and from the outside world. There were signs, though, that he himself was not unaware of the dangers. But his greatest disservice to his country was the way he chose to counter them. The only way he knew was, not forward to real systemic change, but back to Leninism. Tito remained a Leninist throughout his life. The single remark that best revealed his true political convictions was made regarding the sixth congress of the Yugoslav League of Communists in 1952. It was this congress that recommended the party withdraw from active, everyday direction of the political life of the country into a guiding, teaching, arbitrational role, persuasive rather than coercive. Some eighteen years afterward, Tito said he had "never liked the sixth congress."[5] It went against the grain of everything that meant sense and order to him.

It should not have been surprising, therefore, that when faced with the greatest crisis Yugoslavia had experienced in its entire history up to then—the Croatian crisis of 1971—his reaction, almost by reflex, was to try to strengthen party authority, mainly by purging "liberals" and "revisionists." This led to party purges, not only in Croatia, where many liberals as well as nationalists were rooted out, but in Serbia and other parts of the federation, most notably Macedonia. It is worth stressing that until this time the "liberal-conservative divide" in Yugoslavia had not been simply along north-south lines.[6] Reform communism—something roughly similar to the Prague Spring's "socialism with a human face"—had been strong in southern (or southeastern) republics like Serbia and Macedonia. But Tito effectively eliminated it. Had he not done so the course of Yugoslav history might have been different. The communist leadership in Serbia might have remained in the hands of liberals like Marko Nikezić and Latinka Perović, whom Tito got rid of—in the face of serious opposition from within the Serbian Central Committee. Later, the Serbian party fell further into the hands of increasingly hard-line nationalists who helped bring on the most recent, perhaps terminal, crisis in Yugoslavia's postwar history.

But Tito's return to Leninism, through strengthening the party, did not stop with the purges of the early 1970s. His policy from then on until his death was to strengthen party control at the expense of all other possible centers of authority. He broke the worker self-management system in 1976 by a reform in which the Basic Organization of Associated Labor (BOAL) replaced the enterprise as the main unit of self-management. There could now be several BOALs in one enterprise, and within a few years Yugoslavia was teeming with BOALs.[7] The self-management system was destroyed through fragmentation. It probably deserved to be destroyed anyway, for its inability to generate reinvestment was only the most serious of several weaknesses it had revealed in the more than twenty years of its existence; but the main beneficiary from its destruction was the Communist Party at the local level. The party, contrary to the original intention, had always kept an important role in the workings of self-management. Now its overall authority was strengthened even more. Two years earlier the country's new constitution, a massive document, more a primer for living than for lawmaking, had made Yugoslavia a de facto confederation by reducing the federal structure "almost entirely to an apparatus for agreement" among the republics and provinces.[8] But as the center in Belgrade was weakened, the party organizations in the republics were strengthened. Thus in just two years the party from the republic level downward recovered much of its lost strength. Tito's Leninism triumphed, but as it did so the unity of the Yugoslav state was gravely weakened. More than ever the political power was entrenched in Ljubljana, Titograd, Zagreb, Sarajevo, Skopje, and in Belgrade (in its function of capital of Serbia, *not* of Yugoslavia). The trend toward separatism, already gathering pace, was now boosted by the accretion of party power in the republican capitals. Centrifugal tendencies in Yugoslavia were running unchecked.

The Revival of Serbian Nationalism

Tito's last important act before he died—another disservice to his country—was his promulgation in 1978 of the "collective leadership" system, to go into operation at his death. No clear, or acceptable, heir apparent had emerged, and Tito in any case became anxious to preempt anyone from gaining too much power after his death. But the real aim of the new "collective leadership" system was to establish and preserve strict equality in party posts among the Yugoslav nations as well as equality in the executive organs of federal government. After Tito's death, it was decided that the posts of president of the Yugoslav state and of the Yugoslav League of Communists (the party) would be *rotated annually* on an ethnic basis. Therefore, a new head of state and federal party leader from a different republic or province from the previous one would be elected every year. "As a consequence," Viktor Meier wrote, "the political institutions of the country became inhibited in their functions and to a large extent faceless."[9] After 1980 the contrast with the Tito period was almost impossible to exaggerate. After a leader whose name and face were familiar the world over, there followed a carousel of figures and faces about which even the majority of Yugoslavs knew little and came to care less. As long as Tito lived, foreigners were interested in Yugoslavia. After he died, they became indifferent. But the Yugoslavs themselves could not become indifferent to the consequences of Tito's miscalculations. Those mistakes were steadily destroying the country.

The threat to Yugoslavia's survival in the late 1980s had two sources: national and economic. They became so intertwined as to be inseparable, mutually reinforcing to a degree that many, both inside and outside the country, considered to be fatal.

The national threat to Yugoslavia became increasingly associated with the dissatisfaction and the ambitions of Serbia. Most Serbs resented this association as an oversimplified, unfair interpretation of a complex situation. Those familiar with the Serbs' history, their contributions and their sufferings in the cause, not only of their own freedom, but that of other European nations, often felt sympathy for their protests and aggrieved contentions. It was not their fault that they found themselves appearing to resist the course of both history and historical justice. A beacon of Balkan freedom in the nineteenth century, the "nation of state" in the first Yugoslavia, they found themselves in Tito's Yugoslavia pressed into a position of increasing weakness, relative both to their own past and their pretensions arising from it. Two concepts of Yugoslavia came into collision here—the Serb concept and that of the other Yugoslav nations. The Serbs had seen—and many of them instinctively still saw—Yugoslavia mainly (merely) as an extension of Serbia. In this sense they were enthusiastic Yugoslavs. In royal Yugoslavia, originally the "Kingdom of the Serbs, Croats, and Slovenes," they not only provided the royal house but also the overwhelming part of the governmental bureaucracy and officer corps. Included in Serbia itself were parts of Yugoslavia that after 1945 became separate republics and provinces: Macedonia, Vojvodina, Kosovo, Montenegro, and most of Bosnia-Hercegovina. In the new Yugoslavia many Serbs assumed that, even if the former dominance were not completely restored, Serbia would remain Yugoslavia's "nation of state." Instead, they became convinced that a totally opposing concept was beginning to govern: "strong Yugoslavia, weak Serbia." This concept, held by most non-Serb Yugoslavs, was predicated on the belief that if Yugoslavia were to be an equitable and viable state, the power, pretensions, and size of Serbia needed to be curbed.

Many Serbs came to suspect that Tito had all along subscribed to this second concept.[10] He was not a Serb; he was of Croat-Slovene parentage. His chief assistant for forty years, Edvard Kardelj, was Slovene. The chief Serb in his entourage, Alexander Ranković, had been purged in 1966. Moreover, Serbs suspected (not entirely without evidence) that the Yugoslav Communist Party historically had been anti-Serb and that this had been built into the very foundations of the new Yugoslavia. As proof, they pointed, not just to the hiving off of Serbian territory to re-create Montenegro or to create Macedonia, but to the administratively curious decision to divide the remaining Serbia into Serbia proper and the autonomous provinces of Vojvodina and Kosovo, both of which were granted considerable decision-

making powers at the federal level, bypassing Serbia proper. Serbian grievances on this score were immeasurably exacerbated by the new federal
constitution of 1974, which assured these two provinces virtual home rule
and gave them the veto power at the federal level, bringing them very close
to full republican status.

Vojvodina, a former Hungarian province with a once very large German
community which, after World War II, shrunk to about five thousand, was
dominated by Serbs with more than half the total population. The Hungarian community now numbered less than 20 percent. Odd, therefore, that
it should be deemed worthy of autonomous province status. Many Serbs
thought so, too. But Vojvodina was the least of their worries. The Serb
majority ensured that Serbs were well treated—as was the Hungarian minority, better than anywhere else in the territories lost at Trianon. The
creation of a whole Serbian provincial bureaucracy based on Novi Sad, the
capital, was another source of Serbian consolation.

Kosovo was totally different. In terms of Wilsonian self-determination
principles, the Serbian case here was very weak. By the end of 1989 the
Albanians in the province were in a nine-to-one majority. But in Eastern
Europe the principle of self-determination had only been accepted by those
who benefited from it. Those who did not pointed to traditions and com-
plications making the system unworkable and often unfair. For Serbs—all
Serbs—Kosovo had to be a clear and hallowed exception to the self-
determination principle. It was the original Serbian heartland, the seat of
the great medieval Serbian empire, and the site of the battle of Kosovo in
1389 which marked the end of that empire and the beginning of Ottoman
domination over Serbia lasting until early in the nineteenth century. But no
bald recital of facts can convey what this territory and that lost battle mean
to Serbs. It is a cultural, emotional, psychological, and tribal passion that
non-Serbs may understand, but can never feel. It is also worthy of great
respect and sympathy. The ceremonies marking the six hundredth anniversary of the battle, in June 1989, were profoundly moving.[11] To it is now
added the pathos associated with a great nation in frustration and at bay.
Other nations possess similar overriding passions for similar reasons: the
Jews in Israel, for example, and the Afrikaners in South Africa. And some
parts of all these nations also share a negative characteristic: a sense of racial
superiority over the nations with which they live on the same territory. Many
Serbs have always regarded the Muslim Albanians as infidels and as inferior—practically subhuman. This attitude sharpened the tension in Kosovo,
introducing dangerous elements of the irrational and uncontrollable.

Not that the Kosovo Albanians did not themselves contribute to the antipathy. The behavior of some was brutal and primitive—typical, though, of a nation, long humiliated, now sensing that its hour had struck. The Albanian Kosovars were the fastest-growing population in Europe, and their numerical preponderance over the Serbs living in Kosovo increased as more Serbs migrated into Serbia proper. According to the Serbs, this migration was mainly caused by intimidation, terror, rape, and robbery. There was some truth in their charges, but the number and goriness of the incidents were willfully exaggerated in Belgrade.

The existence of Albania, bordering on Kosovo, and the memory of the state of Great Albania during World War II which united Albania and Kosovo, also raised fears among the Serbs. The communist government in Tirana was always circumspect in its references to Kosovo, strongly disclaiming any irredentist ambitions. Few Kosovars, in any case, nurtured any hopes of reuniting with Albania as long as such a tyrannical regime ruled there. But the situation could change dramatically in Albania; the year 1989 had shown just how dramatically it could change elsewhere. If the communist regime were to fall in Tirana, or be replaced by a regime still communist, but reformist, or become reformist itself, then support for union could grow in Kosovo. The situation would be analogous to that in Soviet Moldavia. As long as Ceauşescu ruled in Romania, there was no incentive for the Romanian-Moldavians to want reunion with Romania. As soon as Ceauşescu fell, the situation radically changed. Many Albanians, in both Kosovo and Albania proper, keep Great Albania in mind. Whatever its auspices might have been during World War II (and few Albanians minded the Italo-German patronage at the time), it was the fulfillment of the Albanian national dream. Another analogy is relevant here—this time with Slovakia. The puppet clerical-fascist state established during the war by the Nazis was a good example for nobody, and many Slovaks were ashamed of it. But it was the first Slovak state, and neither Slovakia nor Slovaks were ever the same again.[12]

Many Serbs fearfully remembered the enthusiasm in Kosovo over the cooperation with Albania that was allowed in the late 1960s after the fall of Ranković, the "hammer" of the Albanians during his period as federal interior minister in the 1950s. And one of the reasons why they (and other Yugoslavs, too) opposed demands from Kosovo for full republican status was because that could give Kosovo the legal right to secede from the federation and join Albania. No one could ever be sure that Albanians would never want this. A friend of mine knew one of the few senior Yugoslav federal civil servants of Albanian nationality. This man—sophisticated, cosmopolitan, Yugoslav—made an official visit to Tirana in 1986.

When asked his impressions of what is unquestionably the most retarded metropolis in the whole of Europe, he replied that he had never in his life felt more at home—and less Albanian.

It was Kosovo, then, that focused and sharpened Serb grievances. What Serbs were waiting for was a leader who could embody, articulate, and dramatize those grievances. He appeared in the unlikely person of Slobodan Milošević.[13] A senior federal bank official before he catapulted himself to political fame, Milošević was well known to members of the Western banking community who negotiated loans and payments agreements in Belgrade. He struck them as a competent enough bureaucrat; none of them suspected the inner flame that lay concealed, awaiting its cause. Milošević, the classic people's tribune, told the Serbs what they wanted to hear with a simple, direct eloquence. To compare his speeches with those of any of his Yugoslav contemporaries was like comparing night and day. Though Milošević's speeches were imbued with Serbian patriotism, he also declared himself strongly for Yugoslavia ("What kind of Yugoslavia?" asked the Slovenes, Croats, and sundry others). He seldom ranted, and often seemed at pains to be fair to his opponents. His demagogy lay in his ability to stir audiences by depicting the problems that worried them, but without suggesting solutions that even remotely took into account the complexities of the situation. His modesty of manner could be disarming, and his almost Spartan life-style contrasted with the corruption festering throughout Yugoslav public life.

Milošević was already Serbian party leader when he engineered a political coup at a Serbian Communist Party plenum in September 1987 that ensured the downfall of Ivan Stambolić, the respected president of the republic of Serbia, who steered a moderate course in politics and on the national question.[14] Milošević emerged as Serbia's "strongman," the first such since King Alexander I, Yugoslavia's monarch in the interwar kingdom. He pursued a ruthless course of purging his opponents, subordinating the till then liberal Belgrade press to his political will, and introducing into Serbian politics his own brand of populist nationalism. A strong whiff of "Peronism" now floated through the Belgrade streets and the Serbian countryside. The mass of Serbians loved it, as did most party apparatchiks. Many intellectuals did, too, pouring out their praise in the purplest of prose.

Having consolidated his hold on Serbia itself, Milošević now proceeded with the second and more dangerous part of his policy. He virtually assumed the patronage of all Serbs, not just in Serbia, but throughout Yugoslavia. In doing so, he swept aside what one writer has called "the Titoist 'feudal' principle that had firmly tied each leadership to a particular territory, and began to speak for all Serbs."[15] The danger in this lay in the fact that the Serbs, who constituted about 38 percent of the total Yugoslav population, were spread throughout several parts of the entire country. Only 40 percent of them lived in Serbia proper. Some 24 percent of them lived outside Serbia itself and the two autonomous provinces of Vojvodina and Kosovo. Some 32 percent of the population of Bosnia-Hercegovina were Serb, and nearly 12 percent in Croatia. Serbian nationalists also claimed that most of the citizens of the republic of Macedonia were Serb. Many Serbs outside Serbia now began to look to Milošević for support and eventual protection (not totally unlike many Germans outside the Third Reich in the 1930s looked to Adolf Hitler). As for Milošević, he took steps to associate some of them more closely with Serbia proper.

His principal method was intimidation through demonstration. The streets became his corridors of power. As a result of well-planned demonstrations of Serbs in key cities, the party regimes in Vojvodina, Montenegro, and finally Kosovo itself were replaced by leaders amenable to Serbian hegemony. Serbia then regained, through ostensibly constitutional means, the control over Vojvodina and Kosovo it had lost under the 1974 constitution. In Montenegro a regime more obedient to Serbia emerged from the changes. But the success in Kosovo turned out to be questionable, Milošević's high-handed tactics worsening an already tense situation. Anti-Serb feeling in Kosovo erupted into violence several times in Yugoslavia's history. In 1981, within a year of Tito's death, rioting led to probably between forty and fifty deaths. Seven years later when Milošević maneuvered Azem Vllasi, Kosovo's party chief, out of office in preparation for his attempt to regain full control over the province, there were strikes and demonstrations leading to clashes with the authorities. In early 1989 there were more strikes, clashes, and fatalities. Subsequently, the Serbian authorities, now back in command of Kosovo province, arrested Vllasi for subversion and brought him to trial in January 1990. It proved to be a serious miscalculation. Vllasi, a tribune of ability and standing, became a Kosovar hero and potential martyr. Strikes and violence resumed, and again many were killed. Kosovo looked as if it might become a permanent battlefield.[16]

Milošević's miscalculation worked against him. Already during the second part of 1989 he had suffered a series of tactical political defeats at the federal level and in Serbia itself. His political conservatism, together with his dictatorial tendencies, was losing him followers.[17] There was reason to believe he was trying to subvert political stability in Bosnia-Hercegovina.[18] Even for some Serbs this was going too far. For other Serbs his opposition to the federal government's economic program smacked of dogmatic immobilism. Liberals demanding a multiparty system, which the federal Yugoslav party had now decided to support, were becoming more assertive. They were already looking beyond communism, however reformed or human, toward a parliamentary democracy of the West European type. They were now *following* Eastern Europe, just as thirty years before East European communist reformers would have liked to follow Yugoslav revisionism. A ferment was brewing. Whatever became of it, it was all making Milošević suddenly look very old-fashioned. More Serbs seemed to be concluding that nationalism alone was no longer enough. In late 1989 Milošević was triumphantly reelected president of Serbia on a popular vote. But many were now asking how long his triumph would last.

"Civil Society" in Slovenia

"Land of contrasts" was always one of the tourist cliché's about Yugoslavia, an effective one in bringing millions of Westerners across its borders. More recently the same theme has attracted small bands of dedicated political scientists, seeking and finding a contrast in Yugoslavia between two possible courses of development for the East European states: the high road, toward a civil society; or the low road, toward ethnic and national divisiveness. (This subject is discussed in chapter 10.) In Yugoslavia the two contrasting avenues had opened up in the same country: Serbia projected national divisiveness, Slovenia the "civil society." The train journey from Belgrade to Ljubljana now brought greater contrasts than ever.

There were other similarities and contrasts. If in ethnic divisiveness Yugoslavia was a microcosm of what the Soviet Union was becoming, then Slovenia was to Serbia what Estonia, or more recently Lithuania, was to Russia.[19] Slovenia was much smaller and culturally, economically, and politically more developed than Serbia. It also had a totally different historical and international orientation. And, like Estonia, it was declaring itself empowered and, if need be, ready to secede from the federation to which it belonged. (Indeed, it was easier for Slovenia because, unlike that of Estonia, its population was almost totally homogeneous: some 90 percent Slovene.)

Very briefly, the "civil society" concept in Slovenia began as "socialism with a human face," of the Prague Spring variety, and then moved ineluctably toward liberal democracy. The Slovene party leader, Milan Kučan, originally had in mind political democratization (not necessarily democracy) and a market economy.[20] His concept included toleration of "alternative" youth movements and other political groups under the umbrella of the Communist Party. But Kučan soon found, as Mikhail Gorbachev also was soon to find (and as Alexander Dubček would have found in 1968, had the Prague Spring been allowed to become summer) that, once that path is joined, progress on it is swift and impossible to regulate.

By the middle of 1990 Slovenia had become the constitutional, liberal democracy that Hungary became through its parliamentary elections in March 1990. How many steps it was from leaving Yugoslavia was open to question. Not many, it seemed, unless relations with Serbia showed signs of improvement. It was one of the ironies of Yugoslavia's history that Slovene-Serb relations should have come to this.[21] In royal Yugoslavia, Slovenia had been an ally of Serbia and saw itself protected, and even fulfilled, in Yugoslavia. "Even the worst Yugoslavia," its famous clerical leader, Anton Korošec, used to say, "is better than none."[22] Now the Slovenes were more choosy.

What had led to the postwar disillusionment? Economic considerations had long been the basis of Slovene dissatisfaction. With just under 10 percent of the total Yugoslav population Slovenia accounted for about 20 percent of the gross national product and produced 30 percent of Yugoslavia's total exports.[23] Together with Croatia, Slovenia had always complained that it was footing much more than its fair share of the bill for the overall development of Yugoslavia. Ljubljana had been fighting a continuous battle since the early 1960s over this with the federal capital in Belgrade. While Yugoslavia was in a relatively prosperous state the dispute was containable. But during the 1980s, as the economic crisis worsened, what had once been irritants now became serious aggravations. The Slovenes became incensed, for example, over a revised federal currency law of 1985 that they saw as particularly working against them.

With these economic grievances and mounting Serbian criticism of the growing political freedoms in Slovenia, many Slovenes were beginning to question their own place in Yugoslavia. Some politically articulate young Slovenes had already made up their minds. Thoroughly westernized, their prime aim was to make Slovenia a liberal democracy, outside Yugoslavia if it could not fit inside. One Yugoslav academic put it neatly: "If Yugoslavia cannot adapt itself to European democracy, then there is no place for us any more in this country."[24] Kučan and the majority wing of the Slovene party were carried along on this tide. They did not want secession but, as one Slovene privately remarked, they wanted "one hundred percent independence inside Yugoslavia." By the end of 1989 Slovenia declared it had the right to secede, and Serbia and Slovenia had broken off economic and cultural relations. In January 1990 the Slovenian delegation walked out of the 14th congress of the league of communists of Yugoslavia, called in the hope of slowing the slide toward disintegration.[25] In February the Slovenian Communist Party declared itself independent of the league of communists of Yugoslavia. One of the last unifying factors in Yugoslavia as a whole, the federated Communist Party, had been irreparably damaged. The only hope for a political armistice between Slovenia and Serbia—and thus a halt to the slide—lay in the signs that the Milošević bandwagon might be slowing down in Serbia itself. If these signs proved deceptive—if Milošević were to gain more power rather than lose it—then Slovenia would try to leave the federation and Yugoslavia could be facing perhaps its terminal crisis.

Emotions were running very high. Many Yugoslavs, even some of those suspicious of Milošević, were also suspicious of the Slovenes. They resented their alleged "tight-fistedness" and their sense of superiority. Though admitting they might be Slavs, many Yugoslavs hardly considered them South Slavs.

Croatia the Key

Few would say the Croats were not South Slavs—at least in the sense of Croatia not being essential to Yugoslavia. The key to Yugoslavia's foundation, existence, and future lay in the Serbia-Croatia axis. The failure of the first Yugoslav state was due to the Croatian unwillingness to accept Serbian supremacy. During World War II Croatia achieved an independence of sorts with the creation of its puppet kingdom, under Italo-German patronage. It was a catastrophe that the first Croatian state since 1102 was such a ghastly criminal concoction, perpetrating its own brand of genocide, mainly against the Serbs. This cast a blight on Croat-Serb relations in Tito's Yugoslavia that has never really lifted, poisoning relations between the two nations in a myriad of both specific and indefinable ways. And yet both nations have known that as long as Yugoslavia survived they were thrown together within its framework. They both also knew that separation would be extraordinarily difficult. Even after the wartime genocide, nearly 12 percent of Croatia's population was made up of Serbs. They have constituted both a hostage to, and a guarantee of, Yugoslavia's survival. Slovenia, almost ethnically homogeneous, has had no such vital link with Yugoslavia's fate.

It was typical of the Croat-Serb relationship that each nation thought itself badly served by Tito's Yugoslavia. As already mentioned, many Serbs thought it had been a deepening conspiracy against Serbia culminating in the Kosovo and Vojvodina injustices in the new constitution of 1974. But the Croats saw it, not only as economically exploitative in the same sense the Slovenes did, but also as curbing Croatia's right of self-expression. The

Slovenes were also making the same complaint in the course of the 1980s, but theirs had nothing like the cultural depth, the national resentment and passion, and the obsessive conviction of superiority, of the Croats' complaint. The Croats could not forget the crisis of 1971 when nationalism and liberalism joined forces to inspire a patriotic surge that was turned back by Tito. The same Croats then collapsed into an orgy of despair, recrimination and self-disdain, not just because they had collapsed but because they had collapsed so easily.

Croatia then went into a hibernation of the spirit. With the purge of its liberals by Tito, Croatian politics became conventional and conservative. Dogmatism and caution took over where dynamism and flair had left off. Croatian intellectuals who, more than in any other Yugoslav republic, set the pace of political life, lapsed into another long period of brooding introspection. (There was a similarity with the Czechoslovaks—especially Czechs—after 1968. But many Czech intellectuals rallied during the 1970s to become the center of opposition to "normalization" and most Czechs, throughout, at least maintained a wry humor that contrasted with the bitterness to be found in Zagreb.) This hibernation lasted about seventeen years. Only when Yugoslavia began to bubble with crisis-ridden ferment in Kosovo, Serbia itself, and Slovenia, did Croatia itself start stirring, too.[26] The Zagreb press, as lively and certainly more sophisticated than anywhere else in the country, took sides on the issues of the day, generally supporting the Slovenes and the Kosovars against the Serbs and warning against the Milošević "menace." The Croat party and state leadership, in the meantime, had gradually cast off its slough of dogmatism and become more pragmatic and responsive.

What worried Croats most was the increased stridency of some Belgrade politicians, intellectuals, and newspaper editors in their references to Croatia itself. Most disturbing of all was Milošević's policy of regarding Serbs throughout Yugoslavia as being part of Serbia's patrimony. Croats watched with alarm as Serbia regained control over Vojvodina and Kosovo, and seemed to be trying to subvert the authorities in Bosnia-Hercegovina. They also believed rumors of Serb attempts to do the same thing in Macedonia. But what they feared most of all were Serbian encroachments on the Serbs in Croatia itself. And there was reason for their fear. Though rumors inevitably exaggerated the situation, there was enough hard evidence to suggest that in 1988 emissaries from Serbia proper began agitating among sections of Croatia's Serbian community.[27] Some of this was done clandestinely. But there were also well publicized cases of minor Serb "invasions" with resultant demonstrations, often with nationalist excesses. Official sources in Belgrade, including the well-drilled press, hotly denied anything sinister in these events. But Croats were not convinced. Many felt increasingly vulnerable and unprotected, repeatedly pointing out that about 25 percent of the police in Croatia were Serb. Short memories went back to the Croat-Serb tensions inside Croatia in 1971, longer went back to the tragedies of World War II. Could it be, that, after the sideshows of Kosovo and Slovenia, Yugoslavia was preparing for the "big one": the squaring-off between Serbia and Croatia? This was the apocalypse some were fearing.

It appeared to have arrived in August 1990 when ethnic Serbs in the area around Knin tried to arrange a referendum vote for an autonomous status. Their fears had been increased by the recent victory in Croatia's first free elections of the Croat National Party under Franjo Tudjman, a politician with a fiery anti-Serb record. The referendum was called off and the danger (it could have led to civil war) averted. But for how long?

The Economic Impasse

At the beginning of June 1989 the Yugoslav National Bank, after careful artistic preparation and inevitable bureaucratic delay, brought out its 100,000 dinar note (bill). It was in response to the galloping inflation that had already overtaken Yugoslavia, designed specifically to stem the tide of smaller banknotes that was flooding the economy. When the 100,000 dinar bill appeared it was worth about eight dollars. But as one German expert put it, "The dinar's fall was quicker than the bureaucracy." In two months the worth of the 100,000 dinar bill had fallen to about $5.[28] In early August, therefore, the Bank brought out its 2,000,000 dinar bill. It was worth about $90 when it appeared.

One year earlier, such a 2,000,000 dinar bill would have brought about $850. Yugoslav inflation had approached South American proportions and showed no signs of abating. Yugoslavs who knew their history, or remembered what their fathers or grandfathers had told them, were comparing it with that of the Weimar republic—and shuddering about the possibility of similar political consequences. There were no photographs yet of the Yugoslav currency being pushed around in wheelbarrows, but it was common to see it being carried in bulging plastic shopping bags.

As the dinar became valueless hard Western currencies, particularly the West German Deutsche-Mark (DM), became the real currency of the land. Yugoslavia took second place only to the GDR as a West German DM country. And there were plenty of Marks about, remitted by the several hundred thousand Yugoslav *Gastarbeiter* in the Federal Republic.[29] Already in June

1989 the Yugoslav authorities took official cognizance of the situation by allowing Yugoslav tourist establishments to make direct charges in hard currency instead of going through the motions of using dinars.

All this made Yugoslavia a very cheap country for Western tourists, who could afford to wrestle with the arithmetical problems of the dinar with good humor. But for the majority of ordinary Yugoslavs it was no laughing matter. The living standards of many had sunk to the level of thirty years before, the average monthly salary being the equivalent of about $180. In the two "have" republics, Slovenia and Croatia, real incomes were higher than the average, but in the poorest of the "have not" republics, Montenegro and Macedonia, above all in the autonomous province of Kosovo, incomes were much lower. Ingenuity, resilience, urban links with the land, were helping stave off acute hunger for many, but toward the end of 1989 some were wondering how long even this small consolation could last. Even bread, the staple Yugoslav food, was becoming too dear for many. The breadshelves in the foodshops were filling up with so much unsold bread that, for the first time ever, the authorities decreed that yesterday's bread could be sold after 2 P.M. at a 30 percent reduction.[30] Those few citizens who may still have remained unconvinced of crisis were now persuaded.

"Will the Marković government stumble over a loaf of bread," the Yugoslavs were asking.[31] Ante Marković, a highly respected Croatian economic official and former factory director, had formed a government, after his predecessor, Branko Mikulić, had resigned (for lack of success) with his whole cabinet at the end of 1988. If Mikulić's move was unprecedented, so was the economic mess he left behind. He had become premier in May 1986 with a reputation for competence and forcefulness. But even allowing for the daunting nature of the task he assumed, Mikulić was an acute disappointment. Where flexibility and market reform was needed, he rigidly sought to apply out-dated concepts of economic reorganization. In 1982 the Yugoslav party had accepted a "Stabilization Program" providing for extensive reform, including the introduction of market principles and freedom for private initiative. The government of Milka Planinc tried hard to implement the "Stabilization Program" in both letter and spirit, but was frustrated by the still strong conservative group within the party leadership opposed to the market and other "capitalistic innovations."

Mikulić, Planinc's successor, turned out to be a reactionary in terms of economic reform. His answer to the growing crisis was simply a modification rather than a transformation of the command economy. His anti-inflation program in the fall of 1987 was based on a freeze of both prices and wages. The public, with no confidence in the regime's policies, responded with strikes and demonstrations. When the freeze was lifted prices shot up, wages followed and the Yugoslav economy was much worse than when Mikulić had begun. In the end he lost everybody's confidence, including his own.[32]

Economic and Political Reform

The first few months of Marković seemed to be almost as disastrous as the last few months of Mikulić. Inflation continued to gallop, social tensions mounted, and there was fierce political opposition, particularly in Serbia, to his policies. But by the end of 1989 there were some real signs of improvement. Marković had established a relation of trust with the International Monetary Fund (IMF) on the strength of his belief in liberal economics and his determination to impose them. Yugoslavia's foreign debt actually went down in 1989, by $1 billion from $22 billion. There was a marked improvement in foreign trade and foreign investments increased remarkably: in 1989 they totaled $400,000,000, higher than for the previous twenty-two years. Industrial productivity increased, as did foreign currency reserves. Marković's most courageous step was to make the dinar fully convertible and peg it in to the German Mark. The immediate impact was encouraging: it bolstered confidence in the dinar to some extent. Marković was even promising to get inflation down to 13 percent by the end of 1990 from its present several thousand percent.[33]

Could social tensions be contained while the therapy was working? It was the same question for Yugoslavia as it was for the other East European countries. The standard of living would continue to fall for many months. Since more than a third of the country's 27,600 enterprises were running at a loss there were going to be massive closures as the reforms began to bite. Some were estimating that two million workers would lose their jobs in the next two years.[34] There was still a real danger that a combination of communist reaction and worker resentment would defeat them.

But, paradoxically perhaps, there was more hope for real economic improvement in Yugoslavia at the beginning of 1990 than there had been for several years. Despite the hardships he was putting them through, many Yugoslavs respected Marković and he had also done something to improve Yugoslavia's prestige abroad. Foreign aid was beginning to flow into the country again. The political system, too, was becoming liberalized, and pressure for more liberalization was growing. The multiparty system had sprouted throughout the country and had been approved at the federal level. Even in Serbia, the one party rule principle collapsed and Milošević was forced to adapt to the changes. The truth was that communism and the communist parties were increasingly seen as anachronistic to Yugoslavia's problems and the tide was running against those who thought otherwise.

Questions About the Military

The military had always had a more privileged and respected position in Yugoslavia than in any European communist country, even Poland. It enjoyed a special reputation not only as the defender of the country's borders but also for its unity and integrity. As other centripetal factors in public life faded or disappeared the importance of the military increased correspondingly.

But, though the military had pursued an active role in politics, it had abjured an interfering one. More recently, however, many Yugoslavs had begun asking whether this could not change in view of threatening disintegration. There had been some signs that it might; in particular the situation in Slovenia and later in Croatia, was causing particular worry. Already in March 1988 the Military Council had met in Belgrade and expressed concern about "counterrevolutionary" and "antimilitary" activity in Slovenia. The military followed up this declaration by apparently devising some contingency plan for intervention in case disorder broke out there. The Slovene leadership, under Milan Kučan, was incensed when news of this preparation was revealed. It was nowhere near as incensed, however, as the vast majority of the Slovene population, who saw the episode primarily in national terms: the Serb-dominated army officer corps conspiring against them. The excitement subsided, but the military later showed its muscle by arresting and convicting, before an army court, three young Slovene journalists and a noncommissioned officer for purloining alleged military secrets with the intention of publishing them.[35]

During 1989 many senior military officers spoke out against the political chaos and economic decline in Yugoslavia as a whole, admonishing their civilian counterparts to act more decisively and pull their socks up generally.[36] Some of their phraseology suggested threats of interference and were widely reported in Yugoslavia and abroad. But the political attitude reflected in these warnings—as far as it could be detected—was not one of bunker conservatism. Most of the military leaders welcomed political and economic reform and indirectly gave the Marković government much needed support. But, though supporting political "pluralism" in principle, the military were drawing the line at a multiparty system. Therefore, as support for this system mounted, and its introduction became only a matter of time, it would be crucial to Yugoslavia's future to see how the military reacted. The military, like many other Yugoslavs, saw the disaggregating threat the multiparty system would present to Yugoslav unity. Parties would form on ethnic, or national, rather than political lines. Thus each republic would have its own peasant party, democratic party, social democratic party, and so on. In the case of Slovenia, the military condemned—as did many Yugoslavs generally—the constitutional amendments asserting the republic's right of secession. What would the military do if Slovenia ever acted on that right? Would an institution whose whole existence and reputation had been predicated on its saving the federation, sit by and rationalize its deliberate disintegration? Or would the *federal* character of the army change, its largely Serb officer corps becoming, as many feared, an arm of the republic of Serbia rather than of Yugoslavia? Military leaders were still insisting they would not intervene in politics. But under any circumstances?

The International Context

At the end of 1989 Yugoslavia hosted the world conference of non-aligned countries. It was a much different affair than when Tito was striding the world stage and Yugoslavia basked in the warmth of Third World admiration. Now the Third World despised Yugoslavia and most Yugoslavs were saying openly what they had always thought about the Third World. It was certainly the last such gathering Yugoslavia would ever host. Now its eyes were elsewhere—mostly toward the West, at least as far as intellectual opinion in *all* the republics was concerned.

The Slovenes and Croats, as could have been expected, were foraging busily in the West. They were members of an organization for cooperation among Alpine countries or regions, known as Alpen-Adria. This also included Bavaria, parts of Austria and of Italy, and Hungary. Many observers, even some of Alpen-Adria's members, did not take this association all that seriously. But the Croats, and particularly the Slovenes, did. For them it was a valuable foothold in the West. In 1989 the Yugoslav federal government joined an informal grouping that included Italy, Hungary, and Austria, and was later extended to Czechoslovakia. Many Yugoslavs also were now interested in some of the schemes (or dreams) of "Danubian cooperation" that were being revived as the East European states recovered their independence and their history.

Yugoslavia's relations with the Soviet Union improved notably under Gorbachev, who finally convinced Belgrade of Moscow's abiding respect for its independence and integrity. And, even if Gorbachev had personally not convinced them, the independence achieved by the Soviet Union's erstwhile East European satellites as a result of Gorbachev's policies, finally did. Earlier speculation, therefore, by several Western writers (including this one) that Moscow might seek to take advantage of Yugoslavia's weakness by enticing it back toward, or into, its sphere of influence, was decisively overturned by events.[37] Indeed, such was the switch from East-West confrontation to cooperation, that some Western observers had gone on to suggest a degree of Western-Soviet *cooperation* to stabilize the situation in Yugoslavia. But now, if only because of the dramatic increase in Moscow's domestic preoccupations, such a possibility also seemed highly unlikely.

What, then, could Yugoslavia's future international orientation be? Here speculation easily drifts into fantasy. But 1989 in Eastern Europe had made fantasy permissible, even respectable. Yugoslavia was drifting either toward anarchy or moving toward a difficult but orderly confederative arrangement. Under the latter the republics would be virtually conducting their own foreign policy. In that case Slovenia and Croatia would gravitate westward. Slovenia, on better terms with Austria as a result of more understanding over the Slovene minority in Carinthia, would become closely connected with Vienna. Italy, as some of its leading politicians were now advocating, could now step over its fascist shadow and pursue a more active policy in Southeastern Europe. It might then assume a friendly patronage over Croatia, despite the inhibiting memories of World War II.

But where would Serbia go—proud, poor, and aggrieved? Why not toward Russia? Whatever became of the Soviet Union, Russia would remain, or again become, a major power. In Moscow in 1990 there was a horror of foreign entanglements. But the emerging Russia *would* have a foreign policy. However strong and credible international institutions became, there was no reason to believe that the nation-state concept would not continue to be an important component in international relations. Renewed Russian interest in the region, therefore, could be complemented by a revival of pro-Russian and pan-Slavist sentiment in Serbia, and Montenegro (Soviet comment on Kosovo had always been strongly pro-Serb). The situation could be even further complicated by the reemergence of Macedonian nationalism. Dismissed by Bulgarians, Greeks, and most Serbs as not constituting a real nation, the Macedonians were now bent on showing everybody that they were. They not only resisted Serb encroachment on their sovereignty but were demanding recognition for Macedonian minorities in Bulgaria and Greece. They also were bullying their own large Albanian minority. Indeed, they were behaving like a historical nation.

Recycling even more history, what were the eventual possibilities of Turkey increasing its interest in the Kosovo, Macedonian, and even Bosnian Moslems (not to mention the Bulgarian Turks and Albanian Moslems)? Turkish hopes of entering the European Community, despite Ankara's brave showing in the 1990 Iraqi crisis, were bound to be disappointed. This, combined with its eventually declining importance to NATO, could lead to a further repudiation of the Atatürk "European" legacy and a reversal, perhaps not to Islamic fundamentalism, but more to Turkic self-absorption, to an Ottoman nostalgia that was already noticeable. The scramble for clients and patrons in the Balkans could be on again.

In the next few years, therefore, with Yugoslavia no more, Turkey rejected, the Soviet Union transformed, Pax Sovietica no more, and the certainties bred of East-West confrontation dissolved, the Balkans will become "re-Balkanized." But, before lapsing into plus ça change despondency, we should ponder three possibly reassuring factors: (1) future international frameworks and arbitration could help dull the edge of disputes; (2) there would not be the same monstrous predators lurking as there were before 1914 and between World War I and World War II; (3) the Balkan peoples, though not forgetting their grievances, had not forgotten the horrors into which their grievances had led them in the past. These three factors gave hope that history could resurface without the cataclysms for which it was once responsible. "The Eastern Question," that drawn-out imperialist melodrama of the nineteenth century, might be returning to the Balkan stage. But it would be different. The minor actors' roles would be much the same but the big actors who made it so famous—and dangerous—would largely be missing, or at least the characters they played would be different.

Albania: The Perils of Isolation

On November 27, 1989, when most East European countries were in the throes of revolutionary upheaval, The New Yorker carried a cartoon depicting a tranquil though not too prosperous, obviously Balkan, scene—mountainous with a few rural huts under a high-clouded sky. The caption was, "Meanwhile, in Albania. . . ."

The point, and the poignancy, of the New Yorker's comment were not lost either on the many who ignore Albania or the few who do not. Insulated by its neo-Stalinism, Albania seemed impervious to the shocks and shifts affecting the rest of Eastern Europe and, by all appearances, seemed likely to continue that way. The alarms caused by rumors at the beginning of 1990 of bloody demonstrations in several Albanian cities turned out to be mainly

Serbian concoctions eagerly snapped up by parts of the news-hungry Western media. Albania remained generally quiet.[38]

But it was no longer the quiet of the graveyard. Under Enver Hoxha's successor, Ramiz Alia, both head of state and party secretary-general, subtle but important changes had been taking place in Albanian public life that might accelerate and pave the way for quicker change. The media, for example, had become freer to an extent that Hoxha would have barely recognized, let alone approved. Occasionally, indirect calls for change could be detected. The youth of Albania were becoming slowly but inexorably Westernized—again more slowly than elsewhere, but unmistakably. Lamentations in the media about youthful degeneration were exaggerated, but the lamentations themselves reflected a changing situation.

Cultural life was immeasurably freer than five years before. More realism and less socialist realism was now the hallmark of Albanian literature. Writers still had to be careful, and some were still rapped didactly over the knuckles. But the penalties were now less serious and the whole environment was friendlier. Albania's great man of letters, Ismail Kadare, always difficult to touch, even under Hoxha, because of his international reputation and his advertising value for the Tirana regime, seemed anxious to bring Albanian culture into the European mainstream. But the real recent sensation in Albanian literature was a novel by Neshat Tozaj, *The Knives*, published in November 1989, which modestly but clearly criticized past actions of the *Sigurimi*, Albania's secret police, the regime's instrument for subduing the population and perpetuating itself.[39]

Political Change?

Again the progress should not be exaggerated. Though obviously becoming frayed at the edges, the Hoxha legacy was still largely intact. Hoxha's widow, Nexhmije, a formidable dowager in the Balkan tradition, jealously guarded it, as apparently did parts of the powerful defense establishment. So did the old Hoxha leadership team, still largely in place. Their legitimacy depended on its safekeeping. So, for that matter, did Ramiz Alia's. He had been Hoxha's protégé, with the latter so determined to anoint him as his successor that he had Premier Mehmet Shehu, the man most likely to succeed, framed and disposed of in 1981 on charges that made Stalin's political trials seem unimaginative.[40]

Alia strongly dissociated himself and his regime from Gorbachev's perestroika, which was officially regarded as nothing but a continuation of the revisionism begun after Stalin. Perestroika was leading back to capitalism and was a confession of the kind of total failure that Albania, still true to Marxist-Leninist principles, had managed to avoid. So the argument went, and so it was parroted by the Albanian leadership. There were important variations, though, nuances suggesting (perhaps signaling) an acceptance of the need, not just for quicker, but also more systemic change. Alia, himself, announced political reforms, involving pluralism and greater electoral choice, in January 1990. They still emphasized one-party rule and the command economy.[41] But they looked like the beginning of a breakthrough. Foto Çami, Politburo member and Central Committee secretary for ideology, with a strong power base in the Tirana party organization, drew attention to himself during 1989 precisely for the boldness of his variations on the conservative theme—often not so much from what he said but from what he did not say. He gave the impression of a man waiting for the inevitable and the opportunity it would give him. It seemed that Çami, or others, would take the plenum in January 1990 and make it a turning point in Albania's post-Hoxha era.

But though change had now come to be expected, no one was prepared for the bizarre manner in which it was made attainable in July 1990. Aware of the ferment that had produced revolutions in other parts of Eastern Europe, sensing the relaxation at home, and obviously knowledgeable of the tactics that had started the downfall of the East German regime, many Albanians flooded into Western embassies in Tirana. They were allowed to leave for the Western country of their choice; Albanian isolation had been pierced irreparably.

Economic Survival

If *basic* change came, it would come through the economy, through its weaknesses and its failure to feed and clothe ordinary Albanians. Albania was a poor country, but not exactly a pauper. It had considerable oil and natural gas deposits. It was the world's third largest exporter of chrome, and also a big nickel exporter. Its own energy supplies came mainly from hydro-electric power, small volumes of which it exported to Greece, Yugoslavia, and even Austria. It also exported some agricultural produce.

With a rational economic policy Albania could have become a relatively prosperous country. But, identifying heavy industry with socialism, Albania embarked on the post-World War II road to perdition. After forty-five years of communist rule, with smokestack industries producing unsalable rubbish and unceasing pollution, Albania needed reform as much as any other former Stalinist satellite. Officially it was still sticking to the classic tenets of Stalinist economic policy, but there were a few signs of rationality, particularly in the specialist press. Most pressing of all, however, were reforms in agriculture. These could affect the very survival of the nation. After the Albanian in Kosovo, the Albanian population in Albania proper was the fastest-growing in Europe. It was now about 3 million; by the end of the century it would be 4 million. Albania is a small country with large parts of it uncultivable. It could sustain such a population increase only if it grew (and distributed) more food. It would not do this until it gave its peasants the right incentives through extensive privatization. There were growing signs that Alia was aware of the problem, but he needed to scratch much deeper than the surface.[42]

Albania also needed economic help from abroad. One of Enver Hoxha's last acts was to have the taking of foreign loans constitutionally proscribed. (It was one of Ceauşescu's last acts in Romania, too.) It was difficult to see how this self-defeating prohibition could be openly repudiated in the near future. But even if it stayed on the statute book, it need not be an insuperable obstacle. Albania was, in any case, already taking small commercial credits from abroad,[43] and after the events of 1990 was likely to take more. In this and most other respects, what Albania needed was "de-Enverization." It could not be done frontally, unless by popular revolution. Though much less unlikely than before, this could still be a little way off. In the meantime, the only recourse was to "de-Enverization from above." This, in fact, had already begun. But it needed to be quickened and broadened. There was not much time for Eastern Europe's last fully communist regime.

Window to Western Europe

At the beginning of 1990 it was more than ten years since Albanian-Chinese relations had come to a halt, and Albania appeared to be totally alone in the world, without a patron for the first time in its history. But Albania maintained diplomatic relations with over a hundred countries, and in 1983, five years after the break with China, it signed a commercial agreement with Beijing, which had none of the patron-client characteristics of the former association. With the two superpowers, there were also signs of a less unbending attitude. Normal diplomatic relations with both no longer seemed so far off at the beginning of 1990.

But it was Albania's window to Western Europe that promised the most. Hoxha had opened the window a little before he died in 1985; this was especially true of Italy, with which contacts had always remained correct. In 1983 a thrice-monthly ferry service between Durres and Trieste was inaugurated which, while far from a money-spinner, was of symbolic political importance. French business delegations began appearing in Tirana. But it was with West Germany that the most promising opportunities obviously lay. Contacts began in the late 1970s and picked up sharply during the 1980s with the late Franz-Josef Strauss, the Bavarian minister-president, leading the West German drive. In October 1987 Tirana created a minor sensation by establishing diplomatic relations with Bonn. Work began on a program of economic cooperation, and Albania appeared likely to reap considerable benefit from its diplomatic coup.[44]

On his accession to power, Alia began trying to get Albania more accepted among its Balkan neighbors. With Turkey there was no need to expend much effort; relations with the former imperial power had always been good. Greece was another matter. Here, relations had been bedeviled by nationality and territorial disputes. But there had been promising contacts in the early 1980s after the coming to power in Athens of the left-wing Papandreou government. After Hoxha's death, relations between the two countries improved remarkably, despite the opposition of conservative and clerical forces in Greece. In 1987 the technical state-of-war that had lasted forty-seven years was finally lifted, which opened the way for exchanges of high-level visits.[45]

Alia's biggest break with precedent lay in his conversion to multinational regional cooperation in the Balkans. (Hoxha had condemned the very notion out of hand.) He began modestly in December 1987 by sending delegates to a Balkan conference on the environment, but in February 1988 the Albanian foreign minister, Reis Malile, an able diplomat, attended a regional foreign ministers' conference sponsored by Yugoslavia. The relationship continued: Albania had become a member of the Balkan club.

But, however brisk Albania's relations with Western Europe or with Greece, its future depended on its relations with Yugoslavia. Nationalism had continued, despite the victory of communism in many parts, to be the most powerful dynamic in Balkan relations. It still poisoned Yugoslav-Albanian relations, as it had done from the beginnings of Albania's statehood in 1913. The two countries maintained diplomatic relations; Yugoslavia remained Albania's biggest trading partner and was essential to its existence. Yet the hatred persisted, not so much between Albania and Yugoslavia as a whole, as between Albania and Serbia. And the crux of this was Kosovo. Even when Kosovo was quiet, it remained a festering sore. When it erupted, as it did after Tito's death, it brought the old antagonism to the surface. At the end of the 1980s and into the 1990s, with Kosovo perpetually in ferment and Serbian nationalism triumphant, the scene seemed set for confrontation. (So it did, to a lesser extent, in Macedonia where the Albanian minority—20 percent of the population—were treated as inferior intruders. In other parts of Yugoslavia there was much sympathy for the Kosovars, but this was usually a measure of the antipathy to Serbia.)

The future looked set for even worse relations between Albania and Serbia, the Albanians incensed at the repression in Kosovo, the Serbs hypersensitive to anything that remotely smacked of Albanian irredentism.[46] And, if Yugoslavia continued to disintegrate and its individual republics cast aside even the few remaining constraints, then the danger of irrationality was all the greater. Serbia was much the stronger, but Albania, strategically located at the entrance to the Adriatic and with a population whom nothing stirred more than sympathy with Kosovo and the black memories of Serbia, would never be a mean proposition. Again, re-Balkanization! And some of the constraints staying the hand of other countries in the region might not have the same effect on Serbia and Albania. All the more need for an international body, not just counseling restraint, but compelling it.

10 The Prospects Before Them

The old order is dying, the new cannot yet be born. In the period between, morbid realities assert themselves.—Antonio Gramsci

In prison, you develop in a very narrow space with well defined limits: It is in that space that you can move freely; that life has a meaning; the meaning is that there is a glimmer of light at the end of the tunnel, the light of freedom which you hope to regain. But suddenly you walk out of the prison door and find yourself in a space which seems to have no limits; suddenly you are seized with indecision, you lack confidence and aims, you vacillate in an unknown undelineated world. . . .—Václav Havel

The revolution euphoria is fading fast. The public is beginning to ask—what next?—Mladá Fronta (Prague)

Obviously, when this book was being written, the dust had not settled on 1989. No one knew how long it would take before it did; some were already despairing of it ever happening. What was already clear, though, was that the problems facing the new Eastern Europe were daunting. Many would not be solved before the century was out. Some would persist into the next century. Some would never be solved; at best they might be managed or contained.

Eastern Europe was indeed living between two ages in 1990. The former age—the communist era—was over; the new age—the democratic era(?)—had not yet begun. But it was not Eastern Europe alone that was thus suspended. In varying degrees the whole of Europe was. The Soviet Union certainly was. But so was Western Europe, facing up to the problems posed by the reunification of Germany. Just five years earlier a kind of stability had prevailed throughout Europe. The Soviet Union, though visibly weakening, gave no sign of the turbulence to come. Nor did any of the East European countries. And Western Europe, built on the basis of the European Community, in general, and on the Franco-German rapprochement, in particular, seemed set for further stable growth. That might yet turn out to be the case: a united Germany could be a constructive European and world force. But the suddenness with which German reunification was thrusting itself on the world scene was unsettling. Just as the different parts of Europe were living between two ages, so were the alliance systems that had kept, however uneasily, the peace in Europe for forty years. The Warsaw Treaty Organization was in total disarray, while the future of the North Atlantic Treaty Organization was uncertain. The old European order was changing in its entirety. Eastern Europe was just part of the general uncertainty.

The numerous problems facing the East European states could be grouped under nine headings. The problems were interactive, and, though some were more serious than others, they were all likely to affect the attempts of the East Europeans to put those newly won freedoms on a solid basis.

The Value System

Nothing was more vital to Eastern Europe's future health than the value system, or the political culture, that the new polities would develop. Broadly speaking, two quite different paths appeared to be beckoning. One was toward what has become popularly known as the "civil society," a polity based on law, constitutionality, and liberal values. The other was the retrograde path toward traditional ethnic divisiveness. In Eastern Europe in 1990 there were both bright hopes of the one and grim prospects of the other.

It was the contrast between *East-Central Europe* and *South-Eastern Europe* (the two terms that should now replace *Eastern Europe*) that presented itself in this context. Leaving aside the special case of the GDR, in the process of being absorbed into the successful West German democracy, the three other former "Northern Tier" states—Poland, Czechoslovakia, and Hungary—had the real potential for developing the "civil society." Poland and Hungary had dispensed with communism in constitutional style. Their new leaders, European in culture, understanding of constitutional practice and moderation, tempered in active opposition before coming to power, were aware of their opportunities, responsibilities, difficulties, and limitations. So were the new Czechoslovak leaders, who had come to power by a much quicker, more direct route, but who were nonetheless as constitutionally oriented as any of their Polish or Hungarian counterparts. No one who had the privilege of hearing President Václav Havel's address to the

U.S. Congress on February 21, 1990, could have any doubt about the spirit
and intent of Czechoslovakia's new leadership. The Czechoslovak democratic tradition, the lessons of Tomáš Masaryk, were all there—refined,
perfected, matured.

But in the case of all the East-Central European countries it was a
mistake to assume that it was necessary to look solely to the precommunist
era for the democratic or constitutional tradition. The preceding pages
should have made clear that, first in Poland, but then in Hungary and
Czechoslovakia, elements of the civil society—dissident groups, semiau-
tonomous groups of different kinds—emerged, survived, and prospered,
especially after the mid-1970s. Whatever pretensions the regimes in these
countries may have had to totalitarianism had evaporated long before 1989.
Just as Soviet domination could never eradicate nationalism in Eastern
Europe, so communist totalitarianism often wilted in the face of resilient
society. It was the communist, not the precommunist, experience that made
the difference between Poland and Romania in the early 1990s. The Polish
experience in the interwar years was no more democratic than the Romanian. But after Stalin's death in 1953 Polish society became incomparably
freer than the Romanian. *And it was this freedom that made the subsequent
difference.*

Poland and Hungary were both fortunate in having no acute ethnic
national problems. Neither country had been a stranger to them in the past,
and neither had been exemplary in its efforts to solve them. Poland before
World War II had huge German, Jewish, Ukrainian, and White Russian
communities. The Holocaust, postwar expulsions, and Soviet annexations
had largely removed them. Now Poland, for the first time in its history, was
virtually without minorities. Hungary, whose territory before World War I
was numerically dominated by minorities, lost them, and much more besides, through the Treaty of Trianon in 1920. Now, though not quite without
minorities, it was without the problems associated with them. Czechoslovakia was different. Despite the attainment by Slovakia of federal status in
October 1968, the only bloom of the Prague Spring that survived, the last
word on the Czech-Slovak relationship had almost certainly not been heard.
Slovak nationalism reemerged with speed and force in early 1990. And in
Slovakia itself there was still a large Hungarian community numbering over
550,000. The potential for ethnic divisiveness was very much still there. But
there was reason to hope that the problems could be contained by goodwill
and civilized political behavior. The democracy of the first Czechoslovak
republic had treated the Slovaks unwisely, and it never had a chance of
resolving its German and Hungarian minority problems because of the

predatory irredentism of Nazi Germany and Hungary. The new rulers could learn from the mistakes of the past. And whatever Germany and Hungary might now be, they were not irredentist predators.

In South-Eastern Europe, the old "Southern Tier," the situation was quite different. Yugoslavia was one big nationality problem. In Romania, though problems relating to the German community looked capable of peaceful solution, those affecting the Hungarian minority could bedevil, not only Romanian-Hungarian relations, but the internal development of Romania itself. Citizens of Romania, Romanian and Hungarian alike, joined in the uprising that felled Ceauşescu, but the "spirit of Timişoara" did not last long. Recriminations, repudiations, and violent incidents began to proliferate. It was difficult to allocate blame, but the nub of the problem was that the Hungarians were demanding a status most Romanians considered privileged and were not prepared to concede. Ceauşescu's crazed messianism might be gone forever, but Romanian nationalism was very much there to stay, and few governments in Bucharest, with their eye on the ballot box, would be prepared to concede more than what the voters consider a "civilized minimum." And the Romanian view of this was quite different from the Hungarian.

And in Bulgaria, the Turkish problem, exacerbated by the old communist dictatorship, still remained. One of the heartening aspects of its development after November 1989 was the unity between communists and the democratic opposition on the need to give minority rights to the Turkish community. But the uproar this decision aroused showed how difficult and emotionally laden the problem was. (However much hard-line old regime elements stage-managed some of the uproar, it did have considerable spontaneous support.) And then there were the more than 200,000 Bulgarian Turks who had gone to Turkey, and stayed, in the summer of 1989. They would continue to be a heavy burden on relations between Ankara and Sofia. In the meantime, the Turkish population, already five times larger (50 million to 10 million), would be growing much faster than the Bulgarian. It could also be getting more nationalistic (see chapter 9). None of this bode well for Bulgaria.

Such problems as these would be beyond even the most mature society and democratically experienced body politic. The fact that the Yugoslav, Bulgarian, Romanian (let alone the Albanian) were neither of these only compounded the problem. What Bulgaria, Romania, and Yugoslavia were still faced with was the legacy of imperialism—Byzantine, Ottoman, Habsburg, tsarist, and then Soviet—that stretched over six hundred years. East-Central Europe had also grappled—unsuccessfully—with the legacy of imperialism, but this had been largely lifted from its shoulders by World War II and its aftermath. It was this difference rather than any greater political maturity (however much this may have existed), that gave the East-Central Europeans such an advantage over their fellow Europeans to the south.

A further word is necessary on this civil society–ethnic contrast: It is by no means clear-cut and complete. Obviously, as has been shown in the Czechoslovak case, ethnic divisiveness can also be present in states most likely to achieve the civil society. Also, developments in Romania and Bulgaria in the first half of 1990 were to show that ethnic divisiveness was by no means the only bar to the civil society. Even without the Hungarian problem, President Iliescu in Romania, for example, was not likely to be much of a Jeffersonian. Nor in Bulgaria was Premier Lukanov, one of whose first actions after triumphing at the polls in June 1990 was to pay his respects at the tomb of Georgi Dimitrov. The truth was that the Bulgarians and Romanians were behind the nations of East-Central Europe in societal maturity and democratic awareness. The 1989 revolutions for them meant the overturning of dictatorships and removing the worst stains of communist rule. In the political vacuum that followed the overturning of these dictatorships, reform communists took over, almost by default, and were then confirmed in the elections that followed—the irregularities of which by no means decisively affecting the result. Romania and Bulgaria now both had socialist/reform rule which, despite the setbacks, was evolving toward democracy. Yet they also had this extra (enormous) problem of ethnic divisiveness which, alone, would certainly delay—and might destroy—the prospect of the civil society.

"Pollution of the Mind"

This was the term frequently used by Václav Havel, referring to the moral, intellectual, and political deformation that the contrast between communist fiction and actual fact had inflicted on individuals and society as a whole. This handicap could be cured only slowly. The practice of saying one thing and meaning another would not suddenly discontinue once the communists were driven from office; it could take a generation to eradicate. The problem was more psychological than political. Many younger East Europeans, schooled in communist theory and practice, genuinely failed to see the problem here, tending to confuse anticommunism with democracy. But those who saw an easy solution to this problem were part of the problem themselves.

Nor was it just this spiritual and moral corruption that had to be rooted out. There was the material corruption that had penetrated all aspects of the everyday human interaction. In fact, the inefficiency of the system had often made corruption essential. It now affected not just the countries with an Ottoman or Phanariot legacy but also a country like Czechoslovakia, which earlier had owned a proud record of civic and bureaucratic honesty.

Problems of Power and Politics

Descending to the plane of more practical problems, those concerning political power were among the most pressing. Free general elections took place throughout Eastern Europe in 1990, except in Poland, where they had been held in June 1989. They all went at least part of the way toward answering the basic, crucial question of how stable, or unstable, Eastern Europe's first democratically elected governments in more than forty years would be. How long would they last? Would the new governments be able to set up viable democratic and legal institutions?

One feature that puzzled and disheartened many observers was the political apathy of many citizens. In some countries, most notably Poland, there was little demonstrable enthusiasm for the newly won political process. Voter turnouts were low, and many young people especially were almost hostile to what they considered the "paraphernalia" of democracy. For the mass of citizens, economic considerations were clearly uppermost. It seemed that, until the economies improved, few East Europeans would become political animals. And even then . . .?

A related problem, the solution of which would brook no delay, was now the most explosive. What members of the former communist bureaucracies should be retained by the new democratic governments to facilitate transition and reconstruction? What criteria should be used in this selection? It is the problem every country has faced during the transition from dictatorship to democracy, and it is never solved without controversy. In the Federal Republic of Germany, Konrad Adenauer was severely criticized for allegedly holding over too many former Nazis in his administration. He appeared to adopt three criteria of selection: crime-free, contrite, and competent. The new East European governments seem to be adopting the same criteria. But how sound or objective would they be? Competence is easy to judge; it was also essential in the economic sphere. But crime-free and contrite? The whole issue became emotionally charged. The bitterly anticommunist public had criteria obviously different from governments trying to combine equity with efficiency. With many citizens the line between calling to account and settling accounts was impossible to draw. The opportunities for demagogy were immense.

Generally speaking, though, the new governments throughout Eastern Europe would do well to stick to their policies of calculating magnanimity to all but the criminal and incompetent among the old bureaucracies. Many former communists could serve the new order efficiently, diligently, and wholeheartedly. What was needed was a *healing* policy aimed at dressing the wounds inflicted by communist rule and bridging the divisions which that rule had created.

It would be damaging, therefore, if the divisions created by communist domination were immediately replaced by new divisions inherent in unbridled competitive politics. As I argue later in this chapter, a democratic political consensus is best suited to steer East European society through the shoals of economic reform. Similarly, such a consensus might be best to bring calm to Eastern Europe after forty years of communist rule and the turbulence of 1989. This is not to negate the need for political democracy, Western-style. It is rather to prepare for it—to build an economic, social, political, and psychological basis for it. And consensus politics can easily evolve into competitive politics. Take Solidarity in Poland, a phenomenon which was developing almost organically into two, perhaps three, parties. The same is now true of the Civic Forum in Czechoslovakia, even the National Salvation Front in Romania. Opposition groups, too, such as the one in Bulgaria, will evolve in a similar way. In a few years the political landscape will be quite different from what it was in 1990. It is to be hoped that by that time the foundations for stable democracy will have been laid.

The problem was compounded by the fact that these countries had been not just communist states, but communist *police* states. In all the states concerned, most members of the old security apparatus had simply gone back into the woodwork. But many citizens were not prepared to let them stay there, and some, especially in Romania, where the *Securitate* had been a virulent instrument of terror, feared they would come back. The last days of the GDR were also being marked by astonishing revelations about the fearful ubiquitousness of the *Stasis*. Even more emotional and divisive was the question of those who had, over the past forty years, cooperated in some form with the secret police. It was becoming clear that many people had. Many East Europeans, therefore, some of them high in the new order, went about in constant fear of exposure. The evil of the old system would continue to blight the new. Who was who, and when, was becoming a lethal inquiry. More than anything else, this issue dramatized the moral dilemma of society and the individual in their relationship to an abhorrent government.

There were differences among the East European countries in the handling of this problem; and again the division tended to be on North-South lines. The Solidarity-led government in Poland was actually boxed in by law to rather more "stabilizing generosity," as one Pole privately observed, than turned out to be necessary. The preelection agreement "ensuring" 65 percent of the seats in the Sejm to the Communist Party and its presumed allies turned out to be no obstacle to Solidarity forming a government. But conceding the defense and interior ministries to communists, as well as the presidency to Jaruzelski, turned out to be overly cautious. Many Poles began criticizing their founding fathers of democracy for being color-blind: they thought the light was red when it was actually green. In Czechoslovakia, Havel's initial magnanimity toward the ancien régime was imbued with both character and calculation. But it was by no means fully shared by all his compatriots, in either the Czech Lands or Slovakia. In Romania the issue looked as if it was leading to chaos—perhaps not surprisingly in view of the terror the *Securitate* had used. There the issue went right to the top of the provisional regime that had succeeded Ceauşescu. The Romanians demonstrating in the streets against their revolution being hijacked had reasons for frustration. But it seemed to be leading them into a situation where some of the fruits of the famous victory over Ceauşescu might be wasted. One of the most serious dangers to the unfolding of democracy in Romania and elsewhere in Eastern Europe comes not from former stalwarts of the old regime. They realize the game is up, or very soon will be. It comes from the impatience and intolerance of those considering themselves democrats who can bring themselves to accept the democratic process only when it goes in their favor.

Romania, in particular, looked in poor shape to live up to the requirements of the new era. Its opposition leaders were clearly below the general East European level, including the Bulgarian. And its governmental leaders, despite their clear electoral victory in May 1990—or because of it?—were showing little capacity for democratic conciliation. President Ion Iliescu's handling of the serious disturbances in Bucharest the following June was deplorable from every point of view. The rioters behaved lawlessly and should have been dealt with by the force and the process of law. Bringing in the miners to smash the rioters suggested revolutionary terror rather than civilized justice. Not only was it inhumane, it was also politically self-defeating, fragmenting further a society that had been fragmented enough. And for Iliescu it could be a precedent both politically and personally dangerous. One day the miners come to help him. Some day they might come to get him.

Before finally leaving the political landscape of 1990, it is worth risking a backward glance at the fate of Eastern Europe's once almighty communist parties. The glory had indeed departed. To begin with, all, except the Bulgarian, heavily lost membership. The Polish United Workers' Party disbanded at the end of January 1990 and split into the Social Democracy of the Polish Republic and the Social Democratic Union, both offshoots seeking respectability in the folds of social democracy. In October 1989 the Hungarian Socialist Workers' Party became the Hungarian Socialist Party with the prime minister, Miklós Németh, resigning from it and becoming an independent. The Czechoslovak premier, Marián Čalfa, also resigned from the Czechoslovak Communist Party and became an independent. The Bulgarian Communist Party became the Bulgarian Socialist Party. The Romanian party simply ceased to exist. The East German Socialist Unity Party (SED) tacked on "Party of Social Democracy" (PSD), becoming SED-PSD, with emphasis on the latter. Nor were the former ruling parties losing only their power and their names. They were losing their huge financial and material assets. Indeed, it sometimes seemed that they fought harder to retain these assets than anything else.

What of their future? Here again, even after allowing for the huge differences between Bulgaria and Romania, Eastern Europe seemed to be dividing on North-South lines. The new Bulgarian Party went on to win a mandate in the free elections held in June 1990. In Romania the Salvation Front, the phoenix that rose reformingly from the ashes of communism, was clearly endorsed at the polls. Further north, in East-Central Europe, the new leaders of the new parties made a good impression. But they had no chance of power in the near future. Except in Poland, however, they were not annihilated at the polls, as some observers had expected. The new-look Socialist Unity Party–Party of Social Democracy, under its new, personable, capable (and Jewish) leader Gregor Gysi got over 16 percent at the East German elections in March 1990, the Hungarian socialists over eight percent in April, the Czechoslovak communists 13 percent in June. They would play a role in opposition. And, depending on how successful over the long term the East European revolutions turned out to be, they might not be in opposition forever. But one thing was sure: If they ever came back to power they would be totally different from what they had been. They would have to be.

Problems of the Economy

Some East European economies were in a worse state than others, but none, except perhaps the Czechoslovak, was far from collapse. Conditions seemed likely to worsen rapidly, partly because of the apparent collapse of intra-Comecon trade. Previously agreed mutual orders were simply not being delivered. Halfway through February 1990 Hungary, for example, had not received a single shipment of goods from the GDR.

Their parlous condition raised a whole cluster of questions. Some concerned possible help from the West, including Japan. By the middle of 1990 there was agreement on only one thing in this context: the help promised so far was not enough. This was the view not only of the East European governments themselves but of many detached Western observers who were critical of the West European and American efforts. No one wanted to repeat the crazy credit cycle of the 1970s, when billions of untied Western credits poured into Eastern Europe only to be squandered and later transmuted into the crippling debt burden. But this often seemed to be the Western excuse for doing nothing. There was certainly much *talk* in the West. Discussion ranged across the whole gamut of possible forms of assistance. These included the feasibility of a new Marshall Plan, this time for Eastern Europe; the rescheduling, even forgiveness, of hard currency debts (Poland's stood at $40 billion, Hungary's at $17 billion, Bulgaria's $10 billion, the GDR's $10 billion); new government loans for specific purposes; official loan guarantees for commercial credits—a favorite German form of assistance; investment; takeovers of East European companies or joint ventures; technical aid, advice, know-how, and business consultancies. There was an almost bewildering array of possibilities, and, apart from the numerous Western marauders in for a quick "killing," the West's concern was genuine. The establishment of the European Bank for Reconstruction and Development in Paris was certainly a step in the right direction. But there still seemed to be little Western appreciation of the immensity and complexity of Eastern Europe's difficulties—of the disaster of the communist legacy. And far too few Westerners seemed to be aware of the momentous opportunity history was offering and the likely consequences of squandering it.

Even more important than the volume and type of Western aid would be the way the East Europeans themselves set about reforming their own economies. The immensity of their task beggared description. Apart from the obvious economic damage wrought by state socialism, the social devastation had been incalculable. There was no middle class, no artisan class, no private peasantry except in Poland.

There was practically no entrepreneurial ethos and little work ethos. What there *was* plenty of was a socialist Parkinson's Law ethos that had made bureaucracies big and bloated. No one could have put it better than an unidentified officer of the former East German secret police, *Stasi*, in an interview with the West German paper *Die Welt* on June 1, 1990:

> I like to quote the joke which we used to tell each other about the Indian maharaja who buys a bear for his son and has to hire someone to take care of the bear. Then he finds out that this man also has to have a break sometimes; so he gets a relief. Two men need a boss. A whole apparatus develops. After many years the bear dies, and, many years afterwards, the maharaja notices that he has a hole in his budget. He founds the Bear Caretaking Main Administration. He summons the boss and says: My dear friend, the bear has been dead for 10 years, and you still have the whole apparatus. The boss answers: But, Maharaja, we are such a good team, we do not need the bear. In a figurative sense this describes the socialist system.

All countries were now bent on introducing the market mechanism and on carrying out extensive privatization, despite the enormous difficulties entailed by these changes, especially the latter. But there the similarities ended. The Polish government toward the end of 1989 agreed on a speedy full-scale conversion to capitalism. But by the middle of 1990 the Poles were the only East Europeans opting for the "shock therapy," and in this regard a fateful generalization could be hazarded. While Spain stood as a precedent for a successful political evolution from dictatorship to democracy, there existed no such precedent for the transition from state socialism to market capitalism. This fact made the Polish experiment so vital. If that experiment failed, slowed down or was slowed down, canceled or drastically modified for whatever reason, then the political as well as the economic future of Eastern Europe might be endangered. The only chance the East European economies stood of recovering and eventually creating wealth was in this capitalist conversion. And it was on the ability to establish a sound economic basis to create wealth, *and then to have it distributed fairly*, that the future of civil society in Eastern Europe rested. Perceptive observers of human nature, from Aristotle to Bertolt Brecht, are unanimous on this point: the good life begins with a full stomach.

At first, Poland once again seemed to be showing the way. Its "shock therapy" economic reform, involving a quick break with socialism and a dash for capitalism, was put in place in 1990 by a Solidarity-led government that had legitimacy and strong public support. A political consensus seemed to exist that could induce the nation to bear the painful social consequences of draconian reform. But then Wałęsa deliberately disrupted the consensus (see chapter 4), ostensibly in the name of competitive politics and pluralism. His could be a move for which Poland will pay dearly. Successful economic reform might be crippled, thereby postponing, perhaps indefinitely, the full achievement of the civil society. A democratic political consensus is necessary for economic reform. Premature political pluralism, by politicizing economics, could derail and ruin needed changes. Having previously set such a good example for Eastern Europe, Poland seemed now in danger of setting a bad one. It was not a question of principle, but of priorities.

The Environment

Reference was made in chapter 2 to Eastern Europe's ecological disaster. In mid-1990 conditions were getting worse rather than better, dragging Eastern Europe into a pit from which there might be no escape. This was true in spite of the fact that concern was growing. One of the symptoms of reunification fever in the Federal Republic of Germany was the shock and horror at realizing the extent of the problem in the GDR. West German television carried scenes of devastation most of its viewers would never have considered possible. It was another huge item to go on the bill of reunification, perhaps the most urgent item of all.

But East Germany would be taken care of—in this as well as in other respects. What about the rest of Eastern Europe—Poland, northern Bohemia and Moravia, many parts of Romania? How could Romania, for example, on its own, carry through the reforms necessary for even the most rudimentary social services, *and* the wealth necessary to save the environment? The same question could apply in varying degrees to all the East European countries.

What could be foreseen, without too much perspicacity, was that the environment would be left till last, which meant indefinite neglect. Eventually, the winding down of most of the smokestack industries throughout the region—a basic part of any economic reform—would ease the problem. Banning the use of brown coal, responsible for so much of the pall hanging over several countries, would help immensely. These would represent big steps toward mastering the problem, but they would take time and be very expensive.

It was too much for the East Europeans themselves. Massive Western help would be needed—more than could ever be provided. Even so, it was toward the environment that Western help could probably be most efficaciously directed. Nongovernmental sources, private foundations, could play the major role, partly unencumbered by the delays, disruptions, and the labyrinthine bureaucracy of the governmental process. Helping the environment was also less complicated than trying to help the East European economies. The targets were obvious and the controversy over types, amounts, and recipients much less involved. The politics, as well as the political implications of such aid, would be much less convoluted. If Westerners were looking for a quick, life-supporting, and lifesaving way to help, the environment was it. By the middle of 1990, there was no time to lose.

The Urge to Emigrate

One of the ironies of the new East European situation was the urge to emigrate. Emigration to Western Europe and beyond had become a flood. The flood, soon to include Soviet citizens, would become a tidal wave, one of the West's biggest social problems in the early twenty-first century.

Their reasons were not difficult to find. They were not restricted to material desires—better wages, conditions of work, etc., however much these may have played a role. They extended to a simple desire to leave what had been a stifling atmosphere, to have an opportunity to stretch physically and emotionally after having been denied so long. Nowhere had this been stronger than in the GDR with its "Berlin Wall complex," developed since August 1961. Only psychologists could perhaps fully grasp the harm done to East Europeans, particularly East Germans, by the injuries communist rule had inflicted on them. The desire to flee once the opportunity presented itself simply could not be resisted. The 2,000–3,000 East Germans moving to West Germany each day captured the most attention in the early months of 1990, but the situations in Poland and Hungary were also cause for concern. Travel regulations for several years before 1989 in both countries had been liberalized, and the emigration from Poland had caused the communist regime, the Roman Catholic episcopate, and the Holy See great concern. All three institutions issued similarly worded admonitions against it. But with little effect. Throughout Eastern Europe the surge to leave was the same. Emigration and the political apathy described earlier were different sides of the same coin.

Among those leaving were some of the best and the brightest. Their country needed them, but, often exercising rights now savored for the first time, they still were leaving. Many genuinely intended to come back. Give them a few months, or a year or two in the West, time to live and learn and then they would return, placing their newly found skills and their experience at their country's disposal. So the protestations went. But, however sincere they were, the chances of many coming back were slim. Some might be good ambassadors for their country and serve it well from abroad. But they were lost to it, and their loss would be felt, comprehensively.

Relations with the Soviet Union

Soviet-East European relations were briefly discussed in chapter 2, particularly the Gorbachev revolution in Soviet policy. Now, in 1990, it seemed that Soviet policy toward the region it had once dominated was at a standstill. For one thing, the Gorbachev leadership was preoccupied with its own domestic difficulties pertaining to the economy, the nationalities, and the innovations necessary to bring Soviet institutions in line with new political realities. For another, policy toward Eastern Europe was no longer a question solely of alliance leadership or, as it had been in some respects, a virtual extension of domestic policy. Whether Moscow liked it or not, policy toward Eastern Europe had now to be considered within an all-European framework, more recently against the background of approaching German reunification. It was, therefore, complicated, unsure, subject to sudden change. There was little coherence about it.

All the East European countries, however, with the exception of Bulgaria, were united in the desire to put as much distance between themselves and the Soviet Union as they could. Many citizens of the countries concerned, their emotions outpacing their realism, wanted to sever all ties. For them the matter harbored no difficulty or brooked no delay.

Their new leaders, however, realized the complexities of the issue and had so far resisted the temptation of playing to the public mood. For the most part, they seemed likely to continue doing so. The GDR presented the most difficult long-term problem. Although about to be absorbed into the Federal Republic, the problem of its future affected the whole future European security arrangement. How quickly would some or all of the 375,000 Soviet troops stationed on East German territory be withdrawn? The Soviet Union finally agreed that reunited Germany could be a member of NATO, but important questions remained to be resolved about Germany's position in the new security order. Although the GDR might be disappearing into Germany, its memory would affect the new European system.

In Poland, Czechoslovakia, and Hungary the issues seemed simpler and the prospects for a steady reappraisal of Soviet relations much better. None of these countries were anywhere near as pivotal for the future of Europe as the GDR. All three wanted Soviet troops off their territory as soon as possible. With Hungary, strategically unimportant, there would be little difficulty. Even with Czechoslovakia, on what used to be known as the Warsaw Pact's "front line" in Central Europe, the initial difficulties would soon be overcome. In the case of Poland the matter was becoming complicated. It was not just that as long as some Soviet troops remained in East Germany, some would need to stay in Poland. It was now about reunited Germany, the Oder-Neisse border, the Polish historical dilemma. Some Soviet troops remaining in Poland might not be a reminder of the past, but insurance for the future.

The future of the Warsaw Pact was becoming more problematical each day. Its need was being questioned, and new "relevancies" conjured up for it were far from convincing. Its most obvious use in 1990 was diplomatic: East-West negotiations—for example, on European arms reduction—demanded its existence as a negotiating partner! The East European states wanted withdrawal and dissolution, but they realized there were legal, military, technical, and logistical questions to be considered.

Early in 1990 it had also seemed that, despite the obvious weakening of the Soviet Union and the domestic preoccupations of its leaders, it would still remain a great, even dominating, power. It would, therefore, be prudent not to antagonize the Soviets, not to assume too much independence too soon. The Soviet Union would have legitimate, enforceable security interests in Eastern Europe.

But this reasoning failed to take into account two things: the strong revulsion in Moscow to any further East European commitments of any kind and, more important, the rapid disintegration of the Soviet Union that began to threaten in the second half of 1990. With the possible exception of Byelo-Russia, every part of the Soviet Union bordering onto Eastern Europe was in the midst of nationalist upheaval, demanding autonomy with a view toward independence. The East European states were faced with something quite new: not a threateningly strong Soviet Union but a threateningly weak Soviet Union. Take, for example, an eventually independent Ukraine—an uncomfortable prospect for Poland, Hungary, Czechoslovakia, and Romania. Or worse still, civil strife in the Ukraine between an independence-minded western part and a Russified eastern part. Take the prospect of hundreds of thousands of migrating Soviet citizens trying to move through Eastern Europe to the West. Thus the Soviet Union, now in its weakness as once in its strength, could still demand not only the attention of East Europeans but also careful handling by them. Eastern Europe simply could not get rid of the gigantic neighbor to its east.

But this was for the future. What was more urgent was the future of Comecon and economic cooperation. What happened to the Council for Mutual Economic Assistance could make the difference between survival and collapse for some sectors of the East European economies. It was one of the most piercing ironies of East European communist history that Comecon, derided as one of the most inefficient organizations ever devised, would never seem so necessary as when it was finally giving up the ghost. It was mentioned earlier that, by the middle of February 1990, there had been no shipments of goods to Hungary from the GDR since the beginning of the year. The GDR might, of course, be a special case because of its own particular *Zusammenbruch,* but reports from all the countries of the region indicated dangerous slowdowns in trade. And Comecon trade, whatever its lunacies, was vital. What was needed was a certain transitional stabilization. Again, it was the "between-two-ages" syndrome. Comecon was dying, but nothing was replacing it. The Soviet Union was in no position to stabilize the situation. It was far too early for Western countries, singly or through the European Community, to have any effect. Obviously, it was also too early for the East European states to begin helping themselves. This threat of economic breakdown, heightened now by the tension in the Middle East, was becoming the biggest threat to Eastern Europe's short-term future.

Would the Soviet Union want to stabilize the situation even if it could? Again it was ironic, but there were signs that in the twilight of its hegemony in Eastern Europe, Moscow was putting into practice the "get-tough" policy it had been threatening in the early 1980s when its mastery seemed unassailable. It was, for example, cutting its oil supplies to the dependent East Europeans and making other aspects of bilateral trade increasingly difficult for its smaller partners. (This in addition to the haggles over the possible future of Comecon discussed in chapter 3.) Was this simply a reflection of the Soviets' own economic plight, or was Moscow, as far as it was able, deliberately reminding its former clients of just how dependent they were on the old firm? Dependent they certainly were and were likely to remain. The responsible leaders of the new democratic states saw this as a constraint. But, as mentioned, it was not the only one. Again, the fate of the East European countries and that of their great neighbor to the East were bound up; and this would continue.

Relations with the West

One of the more lasting achievements of Soviet domination in Eastern Europe was to make East Europeans feel closer to the West and/or more European than ever before. This was perhaps not so difficult to do in the case of East-Central Europe, but in South-Eastern Europe's case it had indeed been an achievement. Europe had little relevance for, or resonance with, Serbs or Montenigrins—barring a very small number of urban intellectuals whose intimacy with Western Europe had been close. In Romania there was a strong, traditional, intellectual link with France, but this had practically no impact on most citizens. In Bulgaria (and in Greece, the cradle of European civilization) Europe was something very remote. The few young men going to Germany or France from Bulgaria before 1939 for their higher education were said to be "going to Europe" for their studies, a fabled land very much on the fringes of their map. Indeed, of all the Western countries, it was America, the land of immigration and opportunity, that meant more to most East (including East-Central) Europeans as a whole than "Europe." Many families had relatives who had emigrated, from whom they heard and perhaps even occasionally saw. Those who had no such familial contacts certainly heard about America. And in the 1930s, Hollywood was already beginning to exert its cosmic magical influence.

As any existing illusions about communism began to fade, the Westward gravitation among the East European societies became increasingly marked. In Hungary, Poland, and in the very last years of the GDR, travel became liberalized; many visited Western Europe, and some even penetrated to the United States. West German television in the GDR, Hungarian television in some parts of Hungary and Czechoslovakia, Western radios all over the region, constantly put the West before the eyes and ears of the mass of East Europeans. Not everything depicted was flattering, but the audiences seldom used their critical faculties. As the East continually failed them, they could not have enough of the West. When the collapse came in 1989, they were ready to fall into the arms of the West—literally in the case of the East Germans, culturally, economically, psychologically, politically in the case of the others.

It was difficult to overstate this fixation. Some visitors to Eastern Europe after the collapse were staggered by the "Europa-complex" of politicians and intellectuals alike. Any content analysis of speeches, interviews, articles in the East European press would have shown how, after domestic considerations, it was Europe that dominated: the determination to join (or "rejoin") the European mainstream; to "rise to the standards" of European civilization; above all, to be accepted by Europe. It was exhilarating and often touching, and very understandable. But it had the potential for frustration, disappointment, even disillusion. The hopes were too high, the expectations too great. The West, however sympathetic to their liberation, was simply not going to welcome the "former" East Europeans with the readiness and generosity they unquestionably deserved and naively expected. Most of the many East Europeans to whom I conveyed this reality responded with varying degrees of incomprehension. Czechs found it particularly hard to believe that this "resumption of history" would be all that difficult. There was a danger that perceived rejection would lead to destructive introspection, to the self-pity to which East Europeans were traditionally prone. If full acceptance were not immediately possible, the West could at least show understanding, patience, and, above all, respect.

The American role could be a special one. Nowhere in the world was the prestige of the United States so high. The East Europeans—Bulgarians as well as Poles; Romanians as well as Czechoslovaks; "Southern Tier" as well as "Northern Tier"—wanted an American presence. In just what form they were not quite sure: economic, if possible, but also culturally and educationally in the broadest sense possible. As mentioned (see chapter 1), America dominated the imagination of so many young East Europeans. The response to American offers of educational help at all levels, to the introduction of America Houses in their cities, for example, to any initiatives reflecting American interests and concerns, would be overwhelming. Once again, there was a great historical opportunity to be taken here—or to be lost.

As to more prosaic specifics, the new East European democracies were moving toward membership of global commercial financial organizations such as GATT, IMF, and the World Bank. In Europe, Hungary was leading the way in seeking and gaining membership in the Council of Europe, the West European Union (WEU), and applying for associate membership of the European Community. For Hungary, as well as for other applicants such as Poland and Czechoslovakia, this looked like a difficult and protracted process. First, the Community itself had finally to make up its mind between "deepening" and "widening." Only if the "widening" philosophy prevailed would there be any hope for East Europeans before the end of this century. But, above all, the East Europeans themselves needed to put their economic house in order, through "capitalistic" reforms that were bound to hurt. Once that real, permanent improvement became evident, then would be the time for serious negotiations. A transitional (probationary?) period of EFTA (European Free Trade Area) status was being suggested before entry to the Community itself. There could be several means of access. But they would all be long and arduous. Indeed, until and unless the East European states—the Soviet Union, too—could get their economies to some level of efficiency, there could be no real thought of rejoining Europe. It would continue to be a lopsided partnership, a North-South type relationship, with some East European countries in a Third World status. Rejoining Europe in the cultural and political senses might not be too difficult—economically and technologically it would be more than hard.

For many thoughtful East Europeans the Conference on Security and Cooperation in Europe (CSCE)—the "Helsinki Process"—nebulous though it still was, and no remedy whatsoever for their economic ills, had strong attractions. It probably had as much to do with self-respect as anything else. At least they were members of CSCE—founder-members. There was no need to apply for membership in this club. The same went for the Soviets, of course, from whom the East Europeans were so anxious to distance themselves. Still, most East Europeans recognized Russia (Soviet or whatever else it became) as part of Europe. And a democratic Russia, even a Gorbachev Russia, would be acceptable. In any case, better in than out. And CSCE guaranteed a place for *the United States*, too.

In fact, a CSCE framework, with both the United States and the Soviet Union as full, participating members, began to look more attractive when German reunification burst onto the European scene. Some states—Hungary, for example—were not unduly worried about the prospect of German reunification. Neither were Romania or Bulgaria. In fact, all three looked to a reunited Germany as a potential source of economic aid. But Poland, particularly, and Czechoslovakia, greater Germany's prospective neighbors and recent victims of Nazi Germany, were concerned. CSCE might have no powers of compulsion, but it might be a force for containment, a link, too, with the European states in the West which, while cooperating with the new Germany, would also need to contain it.

Cooperating with Each Other

In a Polish-language radio interview in January 1990 Zbigniew Brzezinski revived the idea of a federation between Poland and Czechoslovakia. This was more necessary than ever, argued Brzezinski, in view of the looming prospect of German reunification. It was not a new idea, having been first mooted in the early 1920s and then during World War II.

It was the response itself to Brzezinski's suggestion—rather than any support for or opposition to it—that was telling. It set off a lively debate in both countries which was joined by some, and followed with great interest by others, in Hungary. In Poland the response was generally favorable. Several prominent journalists expressed enthusiasm for the idea, and opinion in official circles, though more cautious, was receptive. On the Czechoslovak side there was caution to the point of coolness. Czechoslovak (particularly Czech) memories of relations with Poland were less than happy. The Polish seizure of Těšín (Cieszyn) in September 1938, completing the carve-up of Czechoslovakia after the Munich agreement, and then the Polish role in the Soviet-led invasion thirty years after—memories like these made Czechs somewhat wary of Polish offers of cooperation. Many Czechs still

maintained that Poles were incapable of cooperation and the spirit of compromise that should be the true basis for it.

Czechoslovakia's new foreign minister, Jiří Dienstbier, initially damp-
ened enthusiasm for the federation proposal by arguing that his country was
interested in a "pluralistic" Europe, not in creating new blocs. Statements
like these reflected the strong Czechoslovak desire to get back into the European mainstream. They also echoed the long-standing belief that Czechoslovakia, because of its unique geographical location in the heart of the conti-
nent, had a special linking, bridging role to play. It had been an idea of
Masaryk and of Edvard Beneš—tragically in the latter's case because, trusting Stalin, he had persisted in imagining Czechoslovakia could play this
role after World War II. The new leaders in Prague argued that now the
international situation was different, and they were conducting a diplomatic offensive to reassert this traditional ambition.

The reaction to the Polish-Czechoslovak federation proposal was il-
lustrative because it reflected attitudes and prejudices shared by many East
Europeans about cooperating with each other. Some of these factors:

(1) Mutual national suspicions based on history. Czechoslovak suspicions of Poland, even more so of Hungary. Lingering Hungarian bitterness
over dismemberment by the Treaty of Trianon as far back as 1920. Lingering
Bulgarian bitterness over dismemberment by the Congress of Berlin as far
back as 1878. Mutual Serb-Croat suspicions. . . . The list was almost end-
less.

(2) Mutual national dislike—seldom based on the past and disarmed by
the present. Poles and Hungarians historically have had a mutual respect for
each other. Among the rest it was often usually hatred, suspicion, and
contempt. Forty years of socialism and the brotherhood of men had only
solidified these sentiments.

(3) Yearning to become part of the West. This has been a recurrent theme
throughout this book. It affected all the East European states to some degree.
Acceptance in the West was considered more urgent and important than
cooperation in the East.

(4) Every country "a special case." This particularly affected the East-
Central European countries—Czechoslovakia, Poland, and Hungary. Each
country saw itself as somehow "set apart" from the rest. The Czechoslovak
case has been mentioned. The Polish case was based on size (territory and
population); geopolitics; and Poland's twentieth-century role against imperialism and totalitarianism. The Hungarians, straddling five countries—
Hungary itself, Romania, Yugoslavia, Czechoslovakia, and the Soviet Union,
saw themselves (rather mistily) in some future *pivotal* role.

And yet, in spite of obstacles in the way of meaningful cooperation, the issue would not go away, as seen in the excitement over Brzezinski's suggestion. It was because the *need* was there, as strong in Eastern Europe in 1990 as it had been in Western Europe after 1945. Nor were there the national difficulties in Eastern Europe much different from those standing in Western Europe's way nearly a half century before. But in Western Europe the centuries-old suspicions and hatreds had largely been superseded by cooperation and growing trust. The determination not to let the past happen again had prevailed.

Could the same happen in Eastern Europe? Many East Europeans were already doubting it. Many Westerners, too, were back in the business of seeing East Europeans as historically accident-prone, irrevocably doomed to second-rate status, to an "uncivil society." But they were prejudging and oversimplifying a complex situation. In their brief periods of independence in modern times the East European states had done badly—individually (except for Czechoslovakia) and collectively. They did badly because they never had a chance: a wretched imperial inheritance; a web of intertwining nations that only the cataclysms of World War II separated—and even then not fully; economic backwardness compounded by global economic depression; a self-destructive social system; Great Power predators like Nazi Germany and Fascist Italy, and, after the war, Soviet Russia. Now on several of those counts the situation looked better. Above all, there were no lurking predators. The Soviet Union was licking its own wounds and, whatever *rational* fears might exist about a reunified Germany, they could not include its being a predator.

The East Europeans, therefore, seemed to have more chances of success than in the past (and less excuses for failing). In this light the efforts of Hungarian, Czechoslovak, and Polish intellectuals to discover (or rediscover) a Central European identity should be seen, along with the massive revival of the theme of *Mitteleuropa* both in East-Central Europe and in West Germany. These efforts had already spawned a huge literature of mixed quality. But, quality apart, the basic problem seems to have been that most Germans writing on the subject ignored East-Central Europe, and most East-Central Europeans ignored Germany. Nothing very new, perhaps, but not very promising either. If *Mitteleuropa* was itself to have any validity for the twenty-first century, this was *the* chasm that had to be bridged. Many East-Central Europeans were aware of the problem. Some of these were now members of the democratic leaderships of their own countries (or very close to them). Their cause in Western Europe and the United States had been carried by several publicists, most notably by Timothy Garton Ash, who wrote about them and the whole question of "Central European identity" with brilliance, sympathy, insight, and wisdom. But Garton Ash's work went beyond journalism and publicity. It assumed the role of mission, one that first looked quixotic but was to be crowned with almost unbelievable success. No Briton since R. W. Seton-Watson early in this century had done more for the liberties of East-Central Europeans than Garton Ash.

What realistic hopes, then, did exist for effective cooperation in Eastern Europe? There was a greater disposition than ever to try; that in itself was something. Hungary was anxious to join Czechoslovakia and Poland in a new "little entente." As mentioned in chapter 9, there are numerous new ideas for Danubian association, with Hungary again among the initiators. Hungary was crucial both in the role it could play and the history it had to live down. Between the wars the "little entente," composed of Czechoslovakia, Romania, and Yugoslavia, had been directed against Hungary and its virulent irredentism. In World War II Hungary totally lost its international reputation, and since then, with some considerable success under János Kádár, it steadily redeemed it. It was now genuinely set on a course of cooperation, a cooperation that would bring out the best in Hungary and bridle the worst. With both Germany and Hungary renouncing their pasts and intent on cooperation, not ascendancy, and with the Soviet Union back in its tent, Eastern Europe was indeed off to a fair start.

Speculation about the role of Austria in the new East-Central Europe continued to grow. Austria in some respects seemed the ideal East-West pivot. It was now keen on full membership in Europe through the European Community. Some Community members opposed its application, and if they prevailed, Austria's entry would certainly be delayed and might fail. If it eventually succeeded, then Austria might become a conduit for states like Hungary to approach membership. As it was, Austria and Hungary were now linked in healthier and friendlier association than they ever were in the Habsburg era. Austria had been the envy of all the East European states for many years. There was little ill-will against it on account of Habsburg domination. Having seen what other empires could be like, most East Europeans looked back even fondly on Austrian rule. What was needed now was some political will in both government and society. "Putting the balls back in the Ballhausplatz," as one irreverent Viennese put it, needed a national decision. Austria could never finance the East European states, but it could help foster and guide their futures.

What would come of all this? By the end of the twentieth century would the East European states be on the way to a new, more promising phase in their history? Would they at last be able to insist on the principle of "nothing about us without us," with themselves as the subjects, not the objects, of international relations? There were going to be many disappointments. Old weaknesses were already showing. But the chances looked better than ever before of East Europeans becoming Europeans and paying their dues to the new Europe. The problems were still enormous in every respect. But the first decisive step—even in Romania and Bulgaria—had been taken in 1989. With their own exertions, and with the West's example and assistance, the East Europeans could take the chance that history offered.

They could take the chance history offered, or they could fall to the temptations it invited. By 1990 everything that had been wrought in Eastern Europe in the twentieth century seemed to be unraveling. Certainly, the results of World War II were: Soviet domination; socialism itself; the division of Germany; the Cold War; the two opposing alliances. But much that emerged from World War I was also facing liquidation or dismemberment: the Soviet Union preeminently, but Yugoslavia also. This was not leading just to hope, on the one side, or uncertainty, on the other. For some East Europeans it was leading to a dangerous restiveness. With so much history unraveling, perhaps the rest of it might be up for grabs, too! Trianon, for example; the integrity of Czechoslovakia; borders in the Balkans; parts of the Soviet Union. It was all very understandable, but it would lead away from a promising future back into a wretched past. It was up to the East Europeans themselves. They were not masters of their own fate, but this choice was very much theirs.

Appendix: Chronology of Main Events in Eastern Europe, Yugoslavia, and Albania, 1989

████████████████████████ The year 1989 was so momentous that even the relatively action-packed diary that follows will be too sparse for many. Obviously, an element of the arbitrary—idiosyncratic, perhaps—was at work in the choice, but hopefully it gives some impression of, and feel for, the mounting excitement and sense of drama—almost of inevitability.

The "East European" entries (i.e., affecting Bulgaria, Czechoslovakia, the GDR, Hungary, Poland, and Romania) were culled from information appearing in Radio Free Europe research papers. Milan Andrejevich supplied the Yugoslav material, and Louis Zanga the Albanian.

Eastern Europe: 1989

January 3	The East German news agency, ADN, announced that East Germans had made approximately 7 million visits to the "West" in 1988. Visits to West Germany had increased from about 2.2 million in 1987 to 2.79 million in 1988; visits to West Berlin had risen from 2.8 million to 3.96 million. ADN also said that 242,000 visits had been made to other "nonsocialist" countries.
January 5	Lech Wałęsa told a press conference in Gdansk that Solidarity's weapons remained arguments rather than strikes, but that this could change if the government failed to restore the union's legal status.
	Starting on January 5, Elena Ceauşescu's birthday on January 7 was lavishly celebrated by the media, in a series of articles, commentaries, and poems that continued for a week.
January 6	At a meeting on foreign trade with ministry officials and enterprise managers in Bucharest, President Ceauşescu said that socialism was "marvelous" and that there was no need to discuss its improvement beyond the "firm implementation of science and new technology [and] maintaining and developing the revolutionary spirit."
January 9	The Prague authorities banned the January 15 dissident commemoration for Jan Palach, the student who burned himself to death in a

public protest on January 16, 1969. Václav Havel said that he had received an anonymous letter in which a student had threatened to set himself on fire in Wenceslas Square in Prague on January 15. Havel issued an urgent appeal against the threatened suicide. He was questioned by the police about the letter.

January 12   The Bulgarian Ministry of Internal Affairs announced that several leading members of the Independent Association for the Defense of Human Rights in Bulgaria had been arrested on January 11 on suspicion of spreading false rumors intended to create mistrust toward the government.

January 15   The Romanian delegation leader at the Helsinki CSCE review conference in Vienna said that Romania accepted the final document but did not feel obliged to honor all its specifications on human rights, some of which would promote interference in the internal affairs of sovereign states.

An estimated five thousand people tried to commemorate the twentieth anniversary of Jan Palach's suicide in Wenceslas Square in Prague. Police and units of the people's militia dispersed the crowd using dogs, tear gas, and water cannon. Ninety-one demonstrators were detained.

January 16   More than eight hundred young people gathered in the center of Leipzig in an attempt to stage a demonstration protesting restrictions on the freedom of expression in the GDR. Police used force to break up the demonstration, and more than a hundred people were detained.

Police again used dogs, tear gas, and water cannon against small groups of demonstrators and passersby in Wenceslas Square, Prague. Fourteen activists were detained, among them Václav Havel.

January 16–18   Continuing its tenth plenum, begun in December 1988, the Polish Central Committee debated the state of the party and trade union pluralism. Politburo member and Prime Minister Mieczysław Rakowski proposed that the party legalize Solidarity, but only on the condition that the union declare itself a "component of socialism," support the government's reform program, and abstain from activities that would destabilize the country. The plenum appraised a resolution on political and trade union pluralism.

January 17   There were further police actions in the center of Prague.

January 18   Some five thousand demonstrators gathered in Wenceslas Square, shouting such slogans as "Freedom!" and "Where is Mr. Havel?" and "We want to live like human beings." Police did not interfere.

Hungary's Gypsy minority announced formation of an independent organization, the Democratic Association of Hungarian Gypsies, and wanted recognition as a nationality and representation in the Hungarian National Assembly.

January 19   French President Mitterrand began the second day of his state visit to Bulgaria by breakfasting at the French embassy with twelve members and sympathizers of the Discussion Club for the support of perestroika and glasnost.

For the fifth day in a row a demonstration occurred in the center of Prague. Security forces attacked the crowd, making over 280 arrests, injuring fourteen people, and severely beating many others.

In an address to a Socialist Unity Party (SED) gathering in East Berlin, Erich Honecker said the Berlin Wall would remain in place for as long as there were reasons for its existence.

In his speech to the final session of the Helsinki Review conference in Vienna, Soviet Foreign Minister Shevardnadze said that the 50,000 Soviet troops that were being withdrawn from Eastern Europe would take their tactical nuclear weapons with them.

Polish Party leader General Wojciech Jaruzelski held a press briefing to discuss the results of the party's tenth plenum. He said that, if Solidarity agreed to respect the "legal order of the socialist state," all other conditions for legalization were open to discussion. The Polish Central Committee's resolution on pluralism, which was reported to have passed by a vote of 143 to 32 with 14 abstentions, was made public. It said that the CC agreed to lift a ban on independent unions, provided they respected the Polish constitution, obeyed the law, and supported economic development and production.

January 20   Demonstrators again gathered in the center of Prague. The police did not attack the crowd, which eventually dispersed voluntarily.

January 21   Czechoslovak police mounted a huge operation to thwart a pilgrimage to Jan Palach's grave, near Prague. More than four hundred people were detained as they tried to make their way to the cemetery.

January 26   *Sofia News* reported that, in order to reduce air pollution in the capital, the Sofia city council had ordered thirty factories to shut down or drastically reduce their production by June 1989.

It was reported that 692 Czechoslovak cultural figures had signed a letter to Prime Minister Ladislav Adamec demanding the release of Václav Havel and other activists from custody and denouncing police actions against demonstrators. The letter called for a dialogue between leadership and society.

The Hungarian government agreed to allow the exhumation and reburial of Hungary's leader at the time of the 1956 revolt, Imre Nagy, and of his associates. The government said that it would be up to the families of the deceased to decide whether they wanted public burials or if a monument should be erected at the grave site.

The Hungarian government approved the draft of a law on strikes that would allow workers to go on strike as a final resort in protecting their interests.

The archbishop of Lyons said that Cardinal Franciszek Macharski of Cracow had informed him that the group of Carmelite nuns who had set up a convent at Auschwitz would move to a new location away from the site of the former death camp.

January 27 — Prime Minister Adamec accused Czechoslovak Primate Cardinal František Tomášek of supporting illegal activities and encouraging political confrontation. In his letters to Adamec, the cardinal had criticized the use of force against peaceful demonstrators.

January 28 — The Foreign Office in London officially protested the police manhandling of the British ambassador to Romania who was thereby prevented from visiting Doina Cornea, the Romanian dissident.

February 2 — The leading ethnic Turkish members of the Independent Association for the Defense of Human Rights in Bulgaria were expelled from the country.

February 3 — Czechoslovak CC Secretary Jan Fojtík ended an official visit to East Berlin. He was received by Erich Honecker. Both sides pledged to increase cooperation in the ideological sphere.

North Korea recalled its ambassador from Budapest. The move was in protest at Hungary's establishment of full diplomatic relations with South Korea on January 29.

February 4 — The Czechoslovak Party daily, *Rudé Právo*, stated that preferential investments and special subsidies to Slovakia were being discontinued and that identical criteria of economic performance would be applied throughout the country in the future.

The Polish party ended a conference devoted to ideological matters. While the conference discussed the need to "accelerate the devolution of a centrally governed society," delegates agreed that the party had to retain its "leading role."

February 6 — The long-postponed roundtable talks in Poland between Solidarity and the regime began in Warsaw. They were immediately adjourned till mid-March. Three main working commissions were set up and would begin meeting in the next few days. These were to deal with economic matters, trade union pluralism, and political reforms.

February 9 — At a meeting with representatives of the Czechoslovak news media, CPCS Secretary General Miloš Jakeš and chief ideologist Jan Fojtík attacked independent groups and ruled out the possibility of a dialogue with "antisocialist forces."

February 10–11 — An extraordinary meeting of the Hungarian Central Committee was called to discuss the political situation created by Politburo member Imre Pozsgay's statement of January 28 on the need to reassess the

1956 Hungarian revolt. The Central Committee also formally endorsed the idea of a multiparty system in Hungary.

February 11   A group of Bulgarian intellectuals and artists applied to register an independent trade union called *Podkrepa* (Support).

February 15   A Polish journal published a report on the Katyn massacre written in 1943. The report offered proof that some four thousand Polish officers were murdered by Soviet NKVD forces at Katyn in 1940. Two days later Radio Moscow, commenting on the report, said that if its data were accurate, then only the NKVD was responsible for the massacre.

February 17   Polish students demonstrated for the legalization of the Independent Students' Association. Police used force to disperse the Cracow demonstration.

February 18   Czech Prime Minister František Pitra made an official visit to Bavaria and attended a conference on ecological cooperation.

February 20–21   The Bulgarian Politburo met with "representatives of the intelligentsia." Todor Zhivkov made an introductory speech on the theme: "The Restructuring of Our Society—Recognition and Responsibility for the Intelligentsia."

A two-day session of the Hungarian Central Committee approved the draft of Hungary's new constitution, which omitted mention of the leading role of the party.

February 21   Playwright Václav Havel stood trial in Prague and was sentenced to nine months in prison. Western governments and cultural organizations expressed their outrage and called for his immediate release.

February 24   Czechoslovak General Secretary Miloš Jakeš proposed the setting up of an international "consultative body" to promote joint environmental actions in Central Europe.

It was announced in Budapest that in January more than 13,000 refugees from Romania had been registered in Hungary.

February 27   At the premiere of two plays by Václav Havel in Warsaw, which was attended by Prime Minister Rakowski, opposition activist Adam Michnik read an appeal for Czechoslovak authorities to end repression and begin a process of "reconciliation with the nation."

An editorial in *Neues Deutschland* said that the GDR would pursue its own brand of "socialism in the colors of the GDR," which included maintaining the party's leading role, state-run industry, and subsidized prices.

February 28   A French association was set up for "adopting" some 2,100 Romanian villages to protect them from destruction. The creation of this association followed similar action initiated by Belgian circles on February 4.

March 3   A Polish working group on the environment produced a draft report that said Poland's ecological situation was disastrous.

March 5   It was announced that in the future Radio Free Europe correspondents would be able to work without restrictions in Hungary.

March 8   Student rallies were held in Warsaw, Cracow, and several other cities to mark the anniversary of the "March events" of 1968.

                 A resolution unanimously adopted by the Council of Europe's Standing Conference of Communities and Regions of Europe called for increased worldwide concern at the fate of Romanian villages threatened with demolition under the rural resettlement program.

March 9   Tentative agreement was reached by the Polish roundtable working group on political reform on the creation of a second parliamentary chamber and the future status of the president. Elections to the new chamber (to be called the senate and have only limited powers) were to be free and democratic. The opposition side reportedly agreed to accept 35 percent of the seats in the Sejm, on the condition that free competition would be permitted for these seats. Of the remaining seats, 60 percent were to remain in the hands of the PUWP and its two allies; and 5 percent were to be allocated to pro-regime Catholic groups. The president, who would have extensive powers, was to be selected jointly by the two chambers of parliament. A government spokesmen announced that elections to the Sejm and the senate had been set tentatively for June 4 and 18.

March 11   In a move unprecedented in the history of the Romanian Communist Party, six once prominent RCP members sent an open letter to Ceauşescu criticizing him for failing to observe the 1975 Helsinki Final Document, for discrediting socialism, and for ruining the economy. The letter also accused Ceauşescu of ignoring and abusing human rights and of effectively suspending the constitution. The signatories were former RCP First Secretary Gheorghe Apostol, former Politburo member and RCP founder Constantin Pîrvulescu, former Deputy Prime Minister and Politburo member Alexandru Bîrlădeanu, former Foreign Minister Cornel Mănescu, former ambassador to the United States and the United Nations Silviu Brucan, and veteran RCP member Grigore Răceanu.

                 The Hungarian opposition movement, the Democratic Forum, concluded its first national conference by adopting organizational statutes and electing a presidium.

March 13   Several hundred people demonstrated in Leipzig demanding exit permits to resettle in West Germany. A number of demonstrators were detained, and security officials tried to obstruct West German television teams filming the incident.

March 14   The Romanian prosecutor general's office announced that the *Securitate* had uncovered a "grave act of treason against the country and the people's interests" by Mircea Răceanu, a former diplomat and the son of one of the signatories of the protest letter from RCP veterans to Ceauşescu. Răceanu, the office said, had engaged in spying for an unnamed foreign power and would be tried for espionage and treason.

March 17	Father Hristofor Subev, a Bulgarian Orthodox priest, informed Radio Free Europe that an independent Committee for Religious Rights, the Freedom of Conscience, and Spiritual Values had been founded and had applied for official registration.

In an open letter to Ceauşescu that reached the West, the well-known poet Dan Desliu protested Ceauşescu's systematic violation of the Romanian constitution, his promotion of a cult of himself and his family, his ideological dogmatism, and his regime's mismanagement of public affairs.

In an interview published by the Paris daily *Libération*, the Bucharest poet Mircea Dinescu protested the Romanian regime's repressiveness and ideological dogmatism and expressed the hope that reforms similar to those introduced by Mikhail Gorbachev in the USSR would eventually be adopted in Romania.

March 18–20	Rural Solidarity in Poland held a national congress in Warsaw attended by more than four hundred delegates from forty-six voivodships.
March 21	It was announced that a Warsaw court had granted legal registration to the Social Fund for Workers' Solidarity, the independent health fund set up by Solidarity to make use of a grant of $1 million from the U.S. Congress.

An appeal hearing in Prague reduced Václav Havel's prison sentence from nine to eight months and prescribed a milder form of confinement than the original "strict regime" imposed at his original trial in February.

March 23	The revived Independent Smallholders' Party in Hungary held its first national congress and elected a provisional leadership.
March 24	Romanian Deputy Prime Minister Stefan Andrei conferred in Ruse (Bulgaria) with Bulgarian Minister of Foreign Economic Relations Andrey Lukanov on bilateral economic cooperation. The Bulgarian media said that ecological issues had also been discussed; but the Romanian media failed to mention this. The city of Ruse had been severely afflicted by cross-border chemical pollution from Romania in recent years.
March 27	Radio Warsaw reported that about a thousand people staged a demonstration in Szczecin for better environmental protection and a referendum on the issue of nuclear power. The march had been authorized by the local authorities.

March 28–29   High-ranking officers of the East German and West German armed forces held a two-day meeting in Hamburg to discuss NATO and Warsaw Pact defense policies and disarmament. The discussion, organized by the West German Institute for Peace Studies and Security Policy, was the first of its kind.

March 29   Radio Prague said that President Gustáv Husák would soon be released from the hospital but would continue to receive medical treatment at home. Husák suffered a stroke earlier in the month.

March 31   The U.S. weekly *Forbes Magazine* accused Bulgaria of laundering more than $2 billion a year for Turkish heroin dealers and earning up to $10 million annually for the service. Similar charges were published by the New York newspaper *Newsday* on April 1; the paper also said that Turkish gangsters were operating heroin laboratories in Bulgaria. The charges were immediately denied by the Bulgarian embassy in Washington and subsequently by official sources in Sofia. On April 7 a U.S. State Department spokeswoman confirmed the charges, but said there was no evidence that high-level Bulgarian officials were involved.

April 1   The Polish weekly *Polytika* reported that Lech Wałęsa's popularity had risen from 24 percent in May 1988 to 79 percent in March 1989, making Wałęsa the second most popular public figure in Poland behind Cardinal Józef Glemp. Public approval of Solidarity, the paper reported, had increased from 22 percent in May 1988 to 70 percent in March 1989 and trailed only the Church in this respect.

April 3   Some four thousand people, including members of Hungary's former aristocracy, attended a requiem mass in the Mátyás Cathedral in Budapest in honor of the country's last queen, the late Empress Zita of Austria. The mass was conducted by Catholic Primate Cardinal László Paskai.

April 5   The Polish roundtable talks ended with the signing of an agreement. General Czesław Kiszczak opened the final session by saying that "here we are closing a chapter in our history and opening another one." He said the talks had made it possible to "outline a common vision of a reformed political system based on a civic society in the state of socialist parliamentary democracy." Lech Wałęsa began his speech with the words "there is no freedom without Solidarity." While expressing concern lest the roundtable agreement remain a collection of unfulfilled "lofty declarations," Wałęsa praised the talks for providing the "indispensable minimum for entering the realm of democratic changes."

               Radio Budapest reported plans to erect two monuments to victims of the 1956 Revolution. The plans called for one monument to those executed after the 1956 trials and another to those who were not executed but suffered other judicial wrongs.

April 6   Radio Budapest announced that a partial withdrawal of Soviet
                   troops from Hungary would begin on April 25 and end in late June. It
                   was expected that approximately ten thousand of the 62,000-strong
                   Soviet force would be affected.

                   In an interview with Radio Free Europe, Wałęsa said that Solidarity
                   would not limit itself to trade union activities after legalization but
                   would continue to spearhead a "great movement for reform" until
                   Poland was truly democratic.

                   The East German party daily *Neues Deutschland* published the May
                   Day slogans for 1989. For the first time, the slogans did not contain a
                   reference to the Soviet Union.

April 13   West German Chancellor Helmut Kohl said in a television interview
                   that the political situation in Romania had become intolerable for
                   ethnic Germans.

April 14   The Romanian Central Committee ended a three-day plenum meet-
                   ing in Bucharest. In his opening speech Ceauşescu announced that
                   Romania had finished paying back its foreign debt the previous
                   month.

April 15   A Hungarian "reform circles" meeting was attended by an estimated
                   six hundred representatives of reformist groups in the HSWP. Some
                   participants advocated a split of the party, but Imre Pozsgay and
                   Reszö Nyers both told the meeting that any party split at this time
                   would be detrimental to reform.

April 17   A Warsaw voivodship court extended legal registration to the inde-
                   pendent Solidarity trade union.

                   The Soviet news agency TASS announced that the Soviet Union
                   would begin to withdraw about ten thousand of its troops and a
                   thousand tanks from the GDR on May 11. The withdrawal would be
                   completed by August 15.

                   Former Czechoslovak Party First Secretary Alexander Dubček gave
                   an interview to Hungarian television in which he strongly criticized
                   the former Hungarian party leader János Kádár for supporting the
                   1968 invasion of Czechoslovakia.

April 17–18   Czechoslovak General Secretary Miloš Jakeš officially visited Mos-
                   cow, where he held talks with Soviet President Gorbachev. During a
                   press conference Jakeš said that he did not "intend [to allow] the
                   political rehabilitation or return to political activity of Alexander
                   Dubček."

April 18   An international meeting on freedom of information opened in Lon-
                   don. The meeting was part of the follow-up process to the 1975
                   Helsinki Accords and was attended by representatives of all thirty-
                   five signatories to the accords.

April 19 Solidarity leader Lech Wałęsa traveled to Rome with a delegation of Solidarity representatives. Wałęsa said he intended to thank Pope John Paul II for his support and ask for a papal blessing for Poland's "difficult road toward reform."

April 20 The Warsaw voivodship court extended legal registration to Rural Solidarity.

Otto Reinhold, director of the Social Sciences Academy of the East German CC, held talks in Prague with Czechoslovak Presidium member Jan Fojtík. They reportedly discussed closer ideological cooperation.

April 21 East German Politburo member Hermann Axen was received in Bucharest by Ceauşescu. Axen was on an official visit lasting several days.

Several hundred people wearing gas masks staged a demonstration against air pollution in Budapest.

April 25 A public opinion poll in Czechoslovakia on restructuring revealed that 80 percent of the two thousand people interviewed supported restructuring, but that 75 percent said that it should be implemented more quickly. The prevailing view was that "much was being said and nothing was changing."

April 28 Otto von Habsburg began his first ever official visit to Hungary.

May 4–5 The Bulgarian Party Central Committee held a two-day plenum on agrarian policy. Todor Zhivkov presented a report, "On Agrarian Policy Under the Conditions of *Perestroika*," that outlined proposals for removing central managerial controls, reorganizing rural workers into "firms," and introducing a system of private leasing in remote and mountainous areas.

May 5 A statement by 531 Czechoslovak artists, protesting that they had been harassed after signing a petition on behalf of Václav Havel, was made public.

May 6 Radio Budapest rebroadcast speeches by former Prime Minister Imre Nagy and former Defense Minister Pal Maléter for the first time since the 1956 Soviet invasion.

Four Bulgarian ethnic Turks began a hunger strike to protest the compulsory changing of Moslems' names and the BCP's policy of national assimilation.

May 7 Local government elections were held throughout the GDR. It was officially reported that 98.95 percent of the votes had been in support of the official candidates. A number of civil rights groups protested alleged irregularities in the counting of the ballots and said that the no-vote tally should have been much higher than the official figure.

In Leipzig the police detained about a hundred people overnight after they had attempted to demonstrate against improper conduct in local government elections. More than eight hundred people gathered in Leipzig's central square to take part in the protest.

May 8

Over five hundred people demonstrated in Leipzig to protest the local elections and the arrests made on May 7. The police detained sixteen protesters.

The first issue of the Polish opposition's *Gazeta Wyborcza* [Election News] was published.

May 8–9

The Hungarian Central Committee held a two-day plenum, which voted to relieve former HSWP General Secretary János Kádár of his posts as party president and CC member.

May 11

Polish Industry Minister Mieczysław Wilczek said that the Nowa Huta steel mill would have to be modernized to protect the environment. The interests of Cracow, Wilczek said, should be put ahead of those of the Nowa Huta mill.

May 12

In an interview with Radio Budapest, Chairman of the Hungarian National Assembly Mátyás Szürös said that Romania was governed by a "nepotist, dictatorial system" with "Byzantine and Balkan" elements, which made it difficult to handle on the basis of European ethical norms.

May 16

Radio Budapest quoted Lieutenant General Ilie Ceauşescu, the brother of the Romanian president, as saying that an openly hostile situation had developed between Hungary and Romania. Ceauşescu had written in a Romanian military journal that Hungary was copying Hitler's methods by complaining about the situation of Hungarians in Romania to divert attention from its domestic problems.

May 17

Romanian President Ceauşescu made an official visit to Czechoslovakia.

Václav Havel was released from prison after serving only half of his eight-month sentence. Former First Secretary Alexander Dubček visited the playwright at his home in Prague.

The Polish Sejm approved a law giving legal status to the Catholic Church. The legislation guaranteed the Church's rights to carry out religious, educational, and charitable work and to govern its own affairs, such as making appointments to clerical offices.

May 19–20

Thousands of ethnic Turks staged protest demonstrations in Bulgaria against the government's national assimilation policy. Similar demonstrations began occurring in several parts of the country.

May 20–24

Bulgaria began to expel the initiators and leaders of the ethnic Turkish hunger strikes.

May 22	Polish head of state and party First Secretary General Wojciech Jaruzelski made a one-day visit to East Germany. Jaruzelski and his East German counterpart, Erich Honecker, signed an accord settling a territorial dispute involving the Pomeranian Bay. The agreement altered the water boundaries between the two countries.
May 25	Turkish president Kenan Evren called a "mini-summit" at his residence in Ankara to discuss Turkey's response to the ethnic minority protests in Bulgaria.
May 29	Bulgarian president and party leader Todor Zhivkov said on Bulgarian television that all "Bulgarian Moslems" who wanted to would be allowed to go to Turkey. He appealed to the Ankara government to open its borders.
June 2	The Hungarian parliament approved the government's decision to suspend construction work on the Hungarian part of the Gabčikovo-Nagymaros hydroelectric project with Czechoslovakia. The project had been a subject of controversy for over a year, with ecological groups stepping up their protests.
June 2–7	Bulgaria expelled hundreds more ethnic Turks for supporting the protest movement against the government's assimilation policy. Some went directly to Turkey and others to Yugoslavia and Austria. On June 7 a Turkish Foreign Ministry spokesman said that almost three thousand deportees had arrived in Turkey since May 6.
June 4	The first round of elections to the Polish Sejm and senate was held. Turnout was moderate; about 62.11 percent of more than 17,200,000 eligible voters cast ballots.
June 6	The Polish election results tallied by the Solidarity Citizens' Committee showed that its candidates had won 92 of 100 seats in the senate and 160 of 161 available seats in the Sejm.
June 8	The East German parliament unanimously approved an official statement on events in China. It said that "violent and bloody excesses of anticonstitutional elements" had prevented the solution of domestic problems "consistently sought" by the leadership and forced "the use of armed forces to restore order and security."
June 14	The Hungarian tripartite roundtable talks began between regime and opposition representatives and representatives of pro-regime and conservative organizations.
	Rudé Právo declared Czechoslovakia's support for China's crackdown on student demonstrations, saying the Chinese leadership had shown more than enough patience.
June 15	The Hungarian daily *Magyar Hirlap* said that many more Romanians were seeking refugee status in Hungary as a springboard to a third

country. An estimated 30,000 people had fled to Hungary, both legally and illegally, over the past two years. Among these, the proportion of ethnic Hungarians had fallen from 84 percent in 1988 to 63 percent in the first five months of 1989.

June 16
The reburial of Imre Nagy and his associates was held. Hundreds of thousands of people paid tribute to them at Budapest's Heroes' Square.

June 17
Czechoslovak party Presidium member Jan Fojtík told a rally in Slovakia that, in Hungary, "counterrevolutionary forces" were at work behind the slogan of regenerating socialism.

June 18
Only 25 percent of those eligible voted in the second round of the Polish Sejm and senate elections. Eight of the nine Solidarity candidates won their races, giving the opposition 161 seats in the Sejm and 99 of 100 in the senate.

June 19
The Polish Main Statistical Office reported that in the first five months of 1989 prices rose 78.2 percent. The average monthly wage in the socialized sector of the economy was 106.7 percent higher in May 1989 than a year earlier. Pensions rose only 67.9 percent in the same period.

June 19–21
East German Foreign Minister Oskar Fischer paid an official visit to Albania, the first visit by a Warsaw Pact foreign minister to Albania since it broke its alliance with Moscow in 1961.

June 21
The Hungarian media said that Romania was building a wire fence two meters high along part of its border with Hungary, with ditches on both sides apparently as a barrier to vehicles. Five days later the Hungarian media reported that the Romanians were dismantling the fence.

June 22
Bulgarian Deputy Foreign Minister Ivan Ganev said that 150,000 "Bulgarian Moslems" had received passports to go to Turkey and that a further 100,000 applications were being processed.

June 23
Todor Zhivkov paid a twenty-four-hour working visit to Moscow and met with Soviet leader Gorbachev for talks.

June 23–24
At a Hungarian Central Committee meeting, the top ranks of the Communist Party were reorganized. Rezsö Nyers was elected as HSWP chairman and as a member of the four-man party Presidium; the three others were to be Imre Pozsgay, Károly Grósz, and Miklós Németh. The move meant that Grósz was effectively demoted from party leadership.

July 1
The prime ministers of Poland, Czechoslovakia, and the GDR signed a tripartite agreement on environmental protection in Wrocław. The accord outlined areas of cooperation among the three countries with

special emphasis on air and water pollution, and it provided for an expansion of technical and scientific exchange.

July 2   Over 200,000 Czechoslovak Catholics took part in an annual pilgrimage to a shrine outside the Slovak town of Levoča.

July 3   In an article entitled "Your President, Our Prime Minister" in *Gazeta Wyborcza*, Adam Michnik argued that Solidarity ought to form Poland's next government in exchange for the union's support for a communist presidential candidate.

July 4   The Bulgarian Politburo announced a reorganization of some Central Committee departments. The Department on Culture was to be headed by Todor Zhivkov's son, Vladimir.

July 6   The Prague Institute for Economic Forecasting said that the Czechoslovak authorities were afraid of the instability that might result from far-reaching reforms and were implementing only halfhearted economic changes which would have no positive effect.

The death of former HSWP General Secretary János Kádár was announced.

The Hungarian Supreme Court legally rehabilitated executed Prime Minister Imre Nagy and his associates.

July 7   Czechoslovakia, Bulgaria, the GDR, and the USSR concluded an agreement with Vietnam on importing demobilized Vietnamese soldiers from Cambodia as temporary workers in undermanned sectors of their economies.

July 7–8   The Warsaw Pact Political Consultative Committee held a regular meeting in Bucharest. It ended by adopting a joint declaration on security in Europe and issuing a communiqué. The documents affirmed the right of member states to select their own domestic policies and criticized attempts by the West or other communist states to interfere in pact members' internal affairs.

July 8   Erich Honecker left the Warsaw Pact summit meeting in Bucharest early because of acute illness.

July 9   U.S. President George Bush traveled to Warsaw.

July 10   In an address to the Polish parliament, President Bush unveiled his plan for economic assistance to Poland. This included requesting that the U.S. Congress grant $100 million to revitalize Poland's private sector, urging the World Bank to make available loans of $325 million to improve agricultural and industrial production, and providing $15 million for environmental protection in Cracow.

World Jewish Congress President Edgar Bronfman opened the World Jewish Congress' first East European office in Budapest. Bronfman was awarded the Order of the Banner, Hungary's highest distinction for foreigners.

July 11 President Bush visited Gdansk. He had lunch with Solidarity leader Wałęsa at Wałęsa's home and gave an address at the monument commemorating workers killed during the disturbances in 1970.

July 11–12 President Bush paid an official two-day visit to Hungary, where he met party officials as well as representatives of the opposition, delivered a major address at the Karl Marx University in Budapest, and signed agreements on economic and cultural cooperation.

July 14 A small group of American Jews climbed onto the grounds of a Carmelite convent located at the site of the Auschwitz concentration camp. They claimed that the convent, which was to have been moved to another site in February, desecrated the memory of Jews killed in the Holocaust. Construction workers forced the protesters to leave.

July 15 At their meeting in Paris the leaders of the world's seven major industrial democracies (G7) issued a declaration supporting economic and political reform in Eastern Europe and calling for an international conference to coordinate Western aid to Poland and Hungary.

July 17 European Community Foreign Ministers met in Brussels to discuss preparing a coordinated aid program for Poland and Hungary.

Poland and the Vatican issued a joint communiqué announcing the restoration of diplomatic relations.

July 19 The U.S. Senate unanimously voted to condemn the Bulgarian government for its treatment of its ethnic Turkish minority and voted $10 million in aid to Turkey to pay for food, shelter, clothing, and medical care for the refugees from Bulgaria.

The Polish National Assembly elected General Wojciech Jaruzelski to the newly created post of president by a vote of 270 to 233, with 34 abstentions and 7 invalid ballots. Jaruzelski received the absolute minimum necessary for victory.

July 25 According to Czechoslovak dissident sources, the dissident petition "Just a Few Sentences," urging more freedoms, had been signed by close to 12,000 people.

General Jaruzelski met with Solidarity leader Wałęsa for about two hours to discuss the next Polish government. Wałęsa rejected Jaruzelski's offer for the opposition to take part in a coalition government.

A regional court in Opole, Poland, rejected an application for official registration by an association representing the local German minority.

July 26 The Vatican announced four episcopal appointments in Czechoslovakia, breaking a long deadlock on the subject with the Prague government.

July 29

Reports reached the West that more than a hundred East Germans had taken refuge in the West German embassy in Budapest in an attempt to win permission to emigrate to the West.

August 2

By a vote of 237 to 173 with 10 abstentions, General Czesław Kiszczak was approved as Polish prime minister after being nominated by President Jaruzelski.

August 3

Romania recalled its ambassador in Budapest for consultations as a protest against a recent Hungarian television interview with ex-King Michael of Romania. In the interview the former king criticized some aspects of Romanian domestic policy.

Western newspapers reported that at least eighty East Germans were "occupying" the West German mission in East Berlin in the hope of securing an emigration visa to West Germany. Another 130 were said to be in the West German embassy in Budapest.

August 4

It was announced that "guaranteed genuine" pieces of the dismantled iron curtain from the Hungarian border with Austria were to be produced and marketed by a joint venture set up by a Hungarian firm and a firm in Vienna.

August 7

Lech Wałęsa said that Solidarity, the United Peasants' Party, and the Democratic Party should form a coalition government, excluding the Communist Party. This was after premier-designate Kiszczak ran into difficulties forming a government.

Czechoslovak Deputy Prime Minister Matěj Lucan held talks with Cardinal František Tomášek on his offer to mediate between the leadership and the opposition.

August 9

Leaders of the Polish Communist Party's traditional allies, the United Peasants' Party and the Democratic Party, announced that they were willing to hold talks with Solidarity about forming a new coalition government.

August 10

Cardinal Franciszek Marcharski, archbishop of Cracow, issued a statement saying that plans to move a Carmelite convent from the site of the Auschwitz concentration camp had been blocked because of an atmosphere of aggression created by some Jewish groups.

August 11

Jewish groups issued protests against Cardinal Macharski's statement.

August 14

In an interview with *Newsweek*, Ceauşescu accused the six former party officials who wrote an open letter in March, criticizing his policies, of being agents of foreign countries. Ceauşescu specified that one was an agent of the Soviet Union, one an agent of the United States, one of Great Britain, and one of France. Ceauşescu added that they had made deals to act on behalf of those countries.

West Germany closed its embassy in Budapest to the public because it was filled to capacity with East Germans hoping to emigrate.

Erich Honecker, making his first appearance after falling sick after a gall bladder attack, defended the record of his regime and warned people seeking to emigrate that life in the West was full of problems. Addressing workers at a high-tech firm he said, "the human fate of socialism will not allow itself to be distorted by those in capitalist strongholds who consider it normal that mass unemployment, housing shortages, and new forms of poverty exemplify their 'free' system."

The homes of four of Slovakia's leading human rights activists, Ján Čarnogurský, Miroslav Kusý, Hana Ponicka, and Anton Selecký, were searched. All four were accused of incitement, and Čarnogurský and Kusý were detained. They were later charged with "incitement."

August 15 — Solidarity leader Wałęsa told reporters that the opposition was prepared to form a government that would leave the ministries that control the "physical continuity of the state" in communist hands.

An appeal by Václav Havel became public in which he asked Czechoslovaks not to resort to street protests on the August 21 anniversary of the 1968 invasion, citing fears the authorities would use demonstrations to provoke street violence. Instead, Havel urged, citizens should sign the petition "Just a Few Sentences."

August 17 — Leaders of Jewish and Polish groups in the United States called for an end to the dispute over the Carmelite convent at the site of the Auschwitz concentration camp.

August 19 — President Jaruzelski nominated Tadeusz Mazowiecki to become the new Polish prime minister. Five days later Mazowiecki was confirmed by the Sejm.

August 21 — Between two thousand and ten thousand people, including protesters from Hungary, Poland, and Italy, demonstrated in central Prague on the anniversary of the Warsaw Pact invasion. Police broke up the march and arrested 320 Czechoslovak citizens and fifty foreigners. Smaller rallies took place in Brno, Olomouc, and Gottwaldov.

August 22 — Turkey closed its borders to ethnic Turkish refugees from Bulgaria. More than 310,000 ethnic Turkish refugees had arrived since May.

August 23 — West Germany said that more than three thousand East Germans had fled into Austria from Hungary during August. A West German Foreign Ministry spokesman said that the embassy in Vienna had processed over two thousand refugees in the past four days.

August 25 — Hungarian Prime Minister Németh and Foreign Minister Horn paid a surprise visit to West Germany, meeting for more than four hours with West German Foreign Minister Hans-Dietrich Genscher. The

East German refugee problem reportedly headed their agenda, but few details were released.

August 27   Poland's primate, Cardinal Józef Glemp, addressed the controversy over the Carmelite convent on the site of the Auschwitz concentration camp. Glemp called for "a dialogue in honesty and truth" and urged Jews not to talk to Poles "from a position of a nation elevated above all others" and not to make impossible conditions. Glemp stressed that the nuns at Auschwitz wanted to be a symbol of human solidarity embracing the living and the dead. Actions against the nuns, Glemp said, offended the feelings of all Poles. He criticized the group of American Jews that had staged a protest by scaling the convent walls in July.

August 28   *Gazeta Wyborcza*, the Polish Solidarity paper, ran an editorial criticizing Cardinal Glemp for statements he made about Jews during a sermon at Czestochowa on August 27.

August 31   Hungarian Foreign Minister Horn paid a visit to East Berlin to discuss the problem of East German refugees in Hungary.

September 1   Bulgaria's new passport laws came into effect liberalizing travel to the West.

September 5–6   Czechoslovak Prime Minister Ladislav Adamec visited Romania and discussed economic cooperation with top Romanian officials, including Ceauşescu.

September 9   Cardinal Glemp postponed his projected pastoral visit to the United States because of "unconducive circumstances," an apparent reference to the controversy over the Carmelite convent in Auschwitz.

September 10   Hungarian Foreign Minister Horn announced on Hungarian television that his government would allow all GDR citizens who so desired to leave for West Germany via Austria. Horn said that Hungary was temporarily suspending its 1969 agreement with the GDR that obliged both parties to prevent each others' citizens from crossing into third countries without valid visas.

The official East German press agency ADN accused Hungary of violating international law and of "engaging in the organized, subversive trading of human beings."

September 12   The Soviet Foreign Ministry spokesman Genadii Gerasimov said that the USSR was ready to cooperate with the new Polish government and develop mutual relations.

September 16   Polish Finance Minister Leszek Balcerowicz told *USA Today*, an American national newspaper, that rescuing Poland's economy depended on simultaneously imposing budget austerity and creating a market economy.

Poland's Primate, Cardinal Glemp, acknowledged that any dialogue between Catholics and Jews required the removal of the Carmelite convent from the grounds of the Auschwitz concentration camp. Three days later the Vatican announced that the removal would take place.

September 19   West German officials said that more than 17,000 East Germans had arrived in West Germany from Hungary since Hungary opened its border.

September 20   Manfred Gerlach, chairman of the Liberal Democratic Party and deputy chairman of the GDR Council of State, urged the country's leaders not to "block new ideas, but to track them down and bring them into play."

September 21   The East German Interior Ministry denied legal registration to the opposition group New Forum on the ground that its "subversive platform" and "antistate policies" were contrary to the GDR's constitution.

September 25   In what was described as the biggest spontaneous demonstration in the GDR for many years, thousands of people marched in Leipzig, calling for reforms. Among their slogans was a demand for the legalization of New Forum. Security forces detained dozens, but were said to have acted with unusual restraint.

September 26   Radio Prague announced that more than a thousand East German refugees at the West German Embassy in Prague hoped to get a permit to emigrate to the FRG.

September 28   Police dispersed a demonstration by several hundred people in Prague calling for more freedom and democracy.

September 29   Figures released in Bonn showed that of some 100,000 East Germans who had settled in the Federal Republic so far this year, one-third— more than 35,000—had done so without permission from GDR authorities.

Polish Finance Minister Balcerowicz outlined the government's economic plans to the Sejm. He said that Poland could expect aid from the West only if it agreed to take painful steps to improve its economy. Balcerowicz said that the government's first steps would be designed to fight inflation. Poles could expect hardships as a result. Enterprises would find their operations more difficult and some would go bankrupt. In the long term the government would act to dissolve state monopolies, privatize enterprises, end state subsidies, and control wage increases.

October 2   Between 10,000 and 15,000 people marched through the center of Leipzig demanding democratic reforms and the legalization of New Forum and other opposition groups.

October 3	It was announced in Bonn that the GDR had agreed to let East German refugees in Prague resettle in the Federal Republic, using the same procedure followed two days earlier when some six thousand were allowed to leave in East German trains, being "expelled" during the passage through the GDR. By this time the number in the embassy was put at around 11,000.
October 5	More than seven thousand East German refugees left the compound and the vicinity of the West German Embassy in Prague and were transported to West Germany.
	Soviet President Gorbachev arrived in East Berlin to take part in the GDR's fortieth anniversary celebrations.
October 7	Riot police broke up demonstrations for reform by thousands of people in East Berlin, Leipzig, Potsdam, and Dresden. Church sources said that up to seven hundred demonstrators had been arrested.
October 8	Huge crowds of demonstrators took to the streets in East Berlin, Dresden, Leipzig, Potsdam, and other cities, mostly to be answered with police brutality and arrests.
October 9	As many as 70,000 people demonstrated peacefully in Leipzig for reform and dialogue in the biggest single protest in the GDR since 1953. It was apparently during this demonstration that a group of prominent Leipzig citizens prevailed on the police not to open fire on the crowds.
October 10	The Hungarian Socialist Workers' Party ended its congress. The communists decided to change the party's name to the Hungarian Socialist Party. It chose the chairman of the dissolved HSWP, Rezsö Nyers, as its president.
October 16	Approximately 100,000 East Germans demonstrated peacefully in Leipzig for reform and dialogue. The police did not intervene. Massive demonstrations took place in other East German cities.
	The CSCE conference on the environment opened in Sofia. It had been preceded by a demonstration organized by the Bulgarian ecological group *Ecoglasnost*, which continued demonstrations throughout the conference.
October 18	The SED Central Committee held a special session at which Erich Honecker, for health reasons, resigned from all his posts. He was replaced by Egon Krenz, former CC secretary for security affairs.
October 19	Speaking at a party meeting in Dresden, local party chief Hans Modrow said that the political situation in the GDR "requires deep change." He went on to urge the GDR to learn from Soviet-style reforms: "Experiences gathered in the Soviet Union should also be used in the course of . . . renewal."

October 23   As many as 300,000 people marched in the streets in Leipzig and
                thousands poured into the streets in at least four other cities in the
                most widespread show of peaceful protest in East Germany's forty-
                year history.

October 24   The West German government reportedly decided to provide Poland
                with up to DM 3 billion in credit guarantees. The government also
                decided, it was reported, to write off part of a DM 1 million credit
                granted in 1975 and let Poland pay the rest in zloty.

                The European Parliament asked the European Community to budget
                $300 million ($100 million more than had been proposed already by
                the twelve-member governments) to support reforms in Poland and
                Hungary in 1990.

October 25   The French government announced it had approved an emergency
                three-year aid plan for Poland worth about $640 million. The govern-
                ment said its main goal was to modernize the Polish economy by
                creating an investment fund that would be supplied with credits.

                The Japanese Foreign Ministry announced that Japan had signed an
                agreement to allow Poland to extend its debt repayment schedule for
                about $396.5 million in loans.

                Czechoslovak Prime Minister Adamec ended an official visit to Aus-
                tria, where he met with Austrian Chancellor Vranitzky. Adamec
                accused Austrian media of "organizing demonstrations in Czecho-
                slovakia" and ruled out any dialogue with the opposition. He de-
                scribed Václav Havel as a "zero." Almost all members of the Czech
                Philharmonic announced that they would support the earlier deci-
                sion of their artistic director, Václav Neumann, and boycott Czecho-
                slovak television and radio to protest the persecution of their col-
                leagues who signed the "Just a Few Sentences" petition.

                Ceauşescu said Romania's grain crop yields in 1989 were expected to
                exceed 60 million tons, promised substantial increases in other
                crops over 1988, and forecast high meat consumption quotas for next
                year.

October 26   Police attacked, beat, and detained more than twenty activists of the
                independent *Ecoglasnost* group who had been collecting petition
                signatures in a small park in central Sofia.

                Ceauşescu addressed a plenary meeting of the National Council of
                the Socialist Democracy and Unity Front. He said that capitalism
                was historically bound to disappear sooner or later and that attempts
                to move nations from the socialist road would be blown away "as
                snow is blown away by the wind."

October 26–27   The Warsaw Pact's foreign ministers met in Warsaw. On Poland's
                suggestion, ministers responsible for foreign trade and economic
                cooperation also attended. Polish Foreign Minister Krzysztof Sku-

biszewski opened the session by expressing his hope that it would contribute to the democratization of relations within the pact and to the creation of "a single, indivisible Europe." Skubiszewski said the Polish government wanted to maintain friendly ties with its Warsaw Pact allies "on the principle of equal rights."

October 28 | According to Western sources, 10,000 to 20,000 demonstrators gathered in Prague to commemorate the seventy-first anniversary of an independent Czechoslovakia. Police used force to disperse the crowd.

October 30 | More than 300,000 people marched in Leipzig. Tens of thousands of protesters also staged rallies in Schwerin, Magdeburg, Karl-Marx-Stadt, Cottbus, and Poessneck.

Some 460 Poles, mostly relatives of officers murdered in 1940, traveled to the site of the Katyn massacre. Former U.S. national security adviser Zbigniew Brzezinski joined in the memorial mass held at the site.

November 1 | Soviet leader Gorbachev and new GDR leader Egon Krenz held three hours of talks in Moscow.

November 3 | Six *Ecoglasnost'* members in Bulgaria delivered an environmental petition with some 12,500 signatures to the National Assembly, while approximately five thousand people, shouting "democracy" and "glasnost'" and singing patriotic folk songs, gathered outside the building. This was the first independent demonstration in more than forty years of BCP rule.

November 4 | As many as 1 million people demonstrated for reforms, freedom of speech and assembly, and free elections in East Berlin. It was the largest demonstration in East German history.

November 5 | Another eight thousand East Germans crossed into West Germany via Czechoslovakia, bringing the total number of refugees to have used this route since November 3 to 15,000.

November 7 | The entire East German Council of Ministers formally handed its resignation to the *Volkskammer*.

November 8 | The entire East German SED Politburo resigned, only for a new one to be appointed three hours later. It consisted of eleven members, of which four were newcomers, including Hans Modrow. Krenz continued as general secretary.

Author Christa Wolf appealed on GDR television to urge would-be emigrés to stay in the country. She was reading a statement signed by five unofficial groups including New Forum and the Social Democratic Party.

November 9 | The East German Council of Ministers decided to open the GDR's borders to the West. The new regulations allowed all East Germans to apply for visas for private visits to the West; they also said the authorities had been ordered to grant approval on a short-term basis. Second, the new rules called for authorities to issue emigration papers without delay to would-be emigrés. Finally, persons emigrating could now use any border crossing to West Germany.

Masses of jubilant East Germans surged toward Berlin Wall crossing points to visit West Berlin. The East German border authorities stopped checking visas for people passing into the Western sector of the city and asked merely for personal identification.

West German Chancellor Helmut Kohl arrived in Warsaw for a scheduled six-day visit. The following day he interrupted his visit because of the opening of the East German border and returned to Bonn. On November 11 he returned to Poland.

November 10	East and West Germans gathered on top of the Berlin Wall, on the Western side of the Brandenburg Gate. Thousands of East Berliners came to the West.

A one-day plenum of the Bulgarian Central Committee accepted the unexpected resignation of 78-year-old Todor Zhivkov as BCP secretary-general. Foreign Minister Petur Mladenov succeeded Zhivkov.

The Hungarian Prosecutor's Office ordered a retrial investigation in the case of Cardinal József Mindszenty, who was convicted of treason and other charges in a show trial in 1949 and sentenced to life in prison.

November 11 — Romanian opposition activist Doina Cornea began a hunger strike in her hometown of Cluj to protest the arrest of writer Dan Petrescu and to mark the second anniversary of workers' protests in Braşov on November 15, 1987.

November 11–12 — Foreign ministers of Hungary, Austria, Italy, and Yugoslavia met in Budapest and pledged to step up regional cooperation.

November 12 — German Chancellor Kohl and Polish Prime Minister Mazowiecki attended a bilingual religious service at Krzyzowa in Silesia. About three thousand people attended, some of them carrying banners in German.

November 13 — At least 200,000 people marched in Leipzig calling for free elections and protesting the leading role of the party. There also were protests in Dresden, Cottbus, Halle, Neubrandenburg, and Schwerin.

The GDR *Volkskammer* elected Politburo member Hans Modrow as prime minister. Modrow, who was district party first secretary in Dresden, succeeded Willi Stoph.

November 15 — Solidarity leader Wałęsa addressed a joint session of the U.S. Congress as only the second non-American who was not a head of state or government to be invited to do so. Wałęsa noted that nearly five decades of communist rule had "led the Polish economy to ruin, to the verge of utter catastrophe."

November 16   Hungary formally applied to become the first East European member of the Council of Europe.

November 17   The Bulgarian National Assembly unanimously approved the release of Todor Zhivkov as State Council head and elected BCP Secretary-General Petur Mladenov as his replacement.

An authorized rally in Prague, attended by some 50,000 people, to commemorate the death of a Czech student fifty years ago at the hands of the Nazis, turned into a pro-democracy and antigovernment demonstration. Police riot troops responded with unprecedented violence.

November 18   The next day Czechoslovak actors and students called for a one-week boycott of all theater performances and university classes and urged a two-hour general strike on November 27 to protest police brutality in Prague.

November 19   At least 20,000 people took part in a demonstration in Prague calling for the resignation of CPCS General Secretary Miloš Jakeš.

November 20   More than 200,000 people demonstrated in Prague for an end to communist rule. Many thousands also protested in other Czechoslovak cities.

Romania's Communist Party opened its Fourteenth Party Congress in Bucharest. In his opening speech Ceauşescu firmly rejected the reform path followed in other socialist countries.

November 21   More than 200,000 people again demonstrated in Prague, while student strikes were reported to have been spreading throughout the country. Václav Havel announced to the crowd in Wenceslas Square in Prague that representatives of the new Civic Forum had met earlier in the day with Prime Minister Adamec, who promised a dialogue with the opposition.

The Czech Philharmonic as well as employees of Czechoslovak Radio and Television, the National Gallery, and other institutions joined the protest against the police violence.

More than 5 million East Germans had visited West Germany since the GDR opened its frontiers on November 9.

November 22   More than 200,000 people demonstrated in Prague for democracy and the resignation of the leadership. A message from Alexander Dubček was read to the crowd. Another huge rally was reported from the Slovak capital of Bratislava. Virtually all university and college students were on strike.

November 23   Demonstrations continued all over Czechoslovakia. In Prague the crowds amounted to some 300,000. About 50,000 people gathered in Bratislava to hear Dubček, who made his first public speech in twenty-one years.

November 23–27 | Polish Premier Mazowiecki made his first official visit to the Soviet Union. Mazowiecki held talks with Soviet President Gorbachev and with Soviet Prime Minister Nikolai Ryzhkov. Gorbachev told Mazowiecki that "it might surprise some people that I wish you success."

November 24 | Miloš Jakeš resigned as Czechoslovak party secretary-general and was replaced by Karel Urbánek.

November 25 | Hundreds of thousands of people rallied in Prague to listen to Havel, Dubček, and other opposition figures. Massive demonstrations took place in many other Czech and Slovak cities.

November 27 | A two-hour general strike took place in cities and towns all over Czechoslovakia. In Prague, Bratislava, and other places, it was followed by mass rallies. Prime Minister Adamec held talks with the opposition.

About 200,000 East Germans demonstrated in Leipzig to press for democratic reform and free elections. A similar demonstration, organized by the opposition group New Forum, took place in Halle involving tens of thousands of people.

November 28 | The Polish government announced that Poland intended to restore diplomatic relations with Israel early in 1990. Israeli Vice-Premier Shimon Peres had arrived in Poland the previous day.

November 29 | Three days after the national referendum on the Hungarian presidency, it was announced that the margin of victory for the "yes" votes on the issue of when and how to hold the presidential election was 0.07 percent, or about six thousand votes. As a result, the president of the republic would be selected by the National Assembly after the new general elections in March 1990. The result of the referendum doomed Imre Pozsgay's chances of the presidency.

November 30 | East Germany joined Poland and Hungary in condemning the Soviet-led August 1968 invasion of Czechoslovakia.

December 2–3 | Presidents Bush and Gorbachev met at Malta.

December 2 | The new Bulgarian party Politburo and government condemned the 1968 Soviet-led invasion of Czechoslovakia.

A Romanian court ruled that ethnic Hungarian pastor Lászlo Tökés must leave his congregation and his house within six days. The clergyman was charged with "profiteering in food and aid deliveries."

December 3 | The whole East German Politburo and cc (including Krenz) resigned at a special session of the cc. A working group was set up to run party affairs until the party congress scheduled for December 15–17.

December 4 | Hundreds of thousands of demonstrators took part in a rally in Prague to denounce communist domination of the proposed new

Czechoslovak government. There also were demonstrations in other cities.

The West German Interior Ministry said that more than 133,000 East Germans had resettled in West Germany in November. Another 6,700 arrivals were registered in the first three days of December.

December 6   Egon Krenz handed in his resignation as State Council chairman and chairman of the National Defense Council of the GDR.

December 7   Nine independent organizations joined together to found the Union of Democratic Forces in Bulgaria (UDF). The UDF later announced that it would campaign for political pluralism, a market economy, and observance of the rule of law in Bulgaria. Zhelyu Zhelev was elected as UDF chairman and Petur Beron as secretary.

Czechoslovak opposition leader Václav Havel said that he would accept the state presidency if that was the only way out of the crisis.

Czechoslovak Prime Minister Adamec resigned, and his First Deputy Prime Minister Marián Čalfa was named to form a new federal government.

The CPCS Presidium expelled former Secretary General Miloš Jakeš from the party.

December 9   An extraordinary East German SED congress elected Gregor Gysi as the new party chairman.

It was announced in Budapest that general elections should be held in the second half of March 1990.

In an interview published by the Hungarian daily *Magyar Hirlap*, Nina Andreeva, Soviet hard-line opponent of Gorbachev's reforms, praised Ceauşescu's anti-market-economy policies in Romania.

December 10   Some 50,000 to 100,000 people joined a pro-democracy demonstration in Sofia organized by the UDF. UDF Chairman Zhelev was cheered as he called for roundtable talks between the BCP and the opposition.

The head of the Baťa shoe enterprise, one of Czechoslovakia's most successful businesses which moved to Canada after the 1948 communist takeover, offered to return and modernize Czechoslovak shoe factories.

December 16–17 Foreign news agencies reported on clashes between police and demonstrators in the western Romanian town of Timişoara. Disturbances began when police tried to evict pastor Lászlo Tökés from his home and were confronted by several hundred of his supporters. Several thousand more people reportedly then joined them in marching on public buildings in the center of town, chanting anti-Ceauşescu slogans. Troops reportedly moved into the area to help the police quell disturbances.

December 18   Ceauşescu left Bucharest on a scheduled official visit to Iran. He returned three days later.

December 18–20   Clashes continued in Timişoara and reportedly extended to the Romanian cities of Arad, Oradea, Cluj, and Braşov.

December 21   An officially sponsored meeting to support Ceauşescu's policies and condemn the situation in Timişoara began in Bucharest. But the meeting turned into an anti-Ceauşescu demonstration. The shouting of hostile slogans forced Ceauşescu to cut off his speech for several minutes. Several thousand people, mostly pupils and students, were surrounded by police and tanks. Police began firing on the trapped crowd.

December 22   A state of emergency was declared in Romania. It also was announced that Minister of National Defense Vasile Milea had committed suicide after having been "unmasked as a traitor." Soon after, demonstrators began to assault official buildings in Bucharest. The army did not open fire, as ordered by Ceauşescu, and many soldiers fraternized with the demonstrators.

It was later announced that Romania was now ruled by a National Salvation Front, headed by a 39-member council which promised a turn to democracy.

December 25   Nicolae and Elena Ceauşescu were tried by a military tribunal, sentenced to death, and executed by a firing squad.

The Soviet government recognized Romania's National Salvation Front.

December 26   The Council of the National Salvation Front appointed Ion Iliescu its president.

December 29   A special joint session of the Czechoslovak Federal Assembly unanimously elected Václav Havel as the first Czechoslovak noncommunist president since 1948.

Yugoslavia: 1989

January 10–13   *Montenegrin leaders resign.* Following two days of protests, on January 10 and 11, some 120,000 Montenegrin workers and students succeeded in bringing about the collective resignation of the republic's top party and state officials. Late on January 11 the Montenegrin Central Committee accepted the resignation of its Presidium, and on January 13 the republic's State Presidency's resignation was accepted by the republic's National Assembly. The protesters had demanded the resignation of all the republic's political leaders, whom they blamed for Montenegro's economic malaise. The protests and resignations in Montenegro were by and large local matters and appear to have been motivated by local social concerns.

January 11 and
February 16

The Slovenian Democratic Alliance and the Social-Democratic Alliance of Slovenia hold founding conventions in Ljubljana. On January 11 an independent political association, the Slovenian Democratic Alliance, held its founding convention. The group's platform called for establishment of a parliamentary democracy and the sovereignty of the Slovene state. The Social-Democratic Alliance of Slovenia held its founding convention on February 16, fourteen months after announcing its formation. In December 1988 it had become the first political group to openly declare its intention of working to create a Western-style parliamentary democracy in Yugoslavia.

January 30–
February 1

The twentieth plenum of the Central Committee of the Yugoslav League of Communists (LCY). The plenum was held to clear up many unfinished party affairs left over from the Seventeenth CC Plenum in October 1988. Amid growing tension and heated disputes, two high-ranking military officers lashed out against the sharp divisions within the party. They described the conflicts as pushing the country "onto the rocks of catastrophe." Nothing of substance was produced in the way of solutions to the country's crisis. The plenum seems to have clearly set the stage for further political and national polarization in Yugoslavia.

February 3–
March 30

Unrest in Kosovo. The latest unrest in the autonomous province of Kosovo indicated how ineffective the country's leaders had been in dealing with what was regarded by many Yugoslavs as the country's gravest issue. For the past two months Kosovo had witnessed civil unrest, strikes, the introduction of special measures involving the Yugoslav Peoples' Army to stem the tide of unrest, and (what had been feared for some time) the escalation of physical violence. After February 3 the unrest became largely politically motivated. It was in response to recent rulings and decisions made by Yugoslavia's top party and state leaderships related to the November 1988 demonstrations by ethnic Albanians and the removal of a former president of the Kosovo party, Azem Vllasi, from the federal party's Central Committee. According to official sources, from March 27 and 28 two policemen and twenty-two demonstrators were killed and twenty-two injured. The violence was triggered by the approval of the Kosovo legislature of amendments to the Serbian constitution which increased Serbia's control over its province. On March 28 Serbia's National Assembly promulgated the amendments.

March 16

The new federal government. On March 16 the Yugoslav Federal Assembly endorsed the installation of the country's ninth prime minister and tenth government since the promulgation of the federal constitution of 1946. The new nineteen-member government, officially called the Federal Executive Council (FEC), was to be headed by the Croat Ante Marković, who replaced Branko Mikulić. Mikulić had resigned on December 30, 1988, making his government the first to resign under pressure in the postwar period. Marković's cabinet was a mixture of veteran politicians, army generals, professional businessmen, and industrial managers, and it represented a balance between liberal economic reformers and political conservatives. The government would be dominated by the traditionally more powerful republics of Croatia, Serbia, and Slovenia.

April 2   In a direct election by secret ballot the Slovenian public chose a 38-year-old economist, Janez Drnovsek, to represent Yugoslavia's most economically developed and politically liberal republic in the eight-member Yugoslav State Presidency. It was the first time that either a State Presidency member or any top official had been elected by the general public. Direct elections determining representatives in the State Presidency were later held in Montenegro (April 9), Bosnia-Hercegovina (June 25), and Macedonia (June 25).

April 25–27   *Communists in Montenegro elect Young Reformers.* From April 25–27 Montenegro held its first extraordinary party congress; it was Yugoslavia's first regional party to hold a congress prior to the League of Communists' Extraordinary Fourteenth Congress scheduled for mid-December 1989. Montenegro's party congress elected an entirely new 65-member CC, which in turn elected its eleven-member Presidium on April 28. The new CC and Presidium included members who helped organize the demonstrations in October 1988 and January 1989 that toppled the republic's top state, party, and government leaders. The average age of the new Presidium was thirty-eight, and the CC average was about forty. The new leaders promised to push through far-reaching market-oriented reforms and to establish a greater degree of political pluralism desired by the public. The congress also demonstrated that Montenegro was moving away from traditional Yugoslav policies toward reform.

May 29–   *Tensions escalate between Serbia and Slovenia.* Over the past year
June 20   Serbia and Slovenia took significant steps to redefine their national interests within multinational Yugoslavia. In the process, both sides became aware of their growing incompatibility. On May 22 Serbian leader Slobodan Milošević called Slovenia's views on Kosovo "primitive and incompatible with the culture of present-day Europe" and "as a fascistic display of irrational hatred." Slovenes had frequently labeled Milošević a "Stalinist" and described his May 22 attack as "insulting and malicious." On June 16 the Constitutional Commission of the Slovenian National Assembly adopted amendments to the republic's constitution. The most controversial was a clause claiming the right to secession. On June 20 the Presidium of the Slovenian party's Central Committee announced that Slovenia would walk out of the Fourteenth Extraordinary LCY Congress if it was outvoted on important issues such as Western-style political pluralism. The Slovenes would then function as an independent communist party within Yugoslavia.

June 28 *Milošević's speech at Kosovo Polje.* This speech on the six hundredth anniversary of the defeat of the Serbian Army by the Ottoman Turks was relatively mild for a man known as an aggressive and uncompromising politician. Some aspects of his speech were tough-sounding, however. He openly assailed past leaders of Serbia, without mentioning names, blaming them for the failed policies concerning Kosovo. He also said: "Today, six centuries later, we are again fighting a battle and facing battles. They are not armed battles, although such things cannot yet be excluded."

July 19 *Macedonia's constitutional amendments adopted.* The Macedonian National Assembly passed amendments to the republic's constitution. While the main goals were economic, the chief effect was to worsen the already bad inter-ethnic relations with Macedonia's large Albanian minority. The most controversial amendment redefined the republic's statehood defining Macedonia as "the national state of the Macedonian nation." It amended the 1974 constitution, in which Macedonia was defined as a "state of the Macedonian people and the Albanian and Turkish minorities." Local municipalities dominated by ethnic Albanians expressed strong opposition to some of the amendments and interpreted them as chauvinistic.

July 30 and 31 *The twenty-fifth plenum of the LCY Central Committee.* The LCY plenum produced nothing but a stream of accusations and complaints that revealed all the old differences. The plenum was intended to discuss solutions to the persistent problem of inter-ethnic conflicts, but it left matters worse off.

September 4–7 *Yugoslavia hosts nonaligned summit.* The ninth summit of the Nonaligned Movement was held from September 4–7 in Belgrade, the second time the summit had been hosted in that city. Yugoslavia took over as chairman of the movement until 1992.

September 27 *Slovenia adopts constitutional amendments.* The Slovenian National Assembly met to approve amendments to its republic's constitution. Among the most controversial was the explicit assertion of the republic's right to self-determination, which was taken to mean the right to secession. Despite repeated warnings from the federal government, assembly, party, State Presidency, and the military, Slovenia passed the amendments. Another controversial amendment granted Slovenia the right to declare a state of emergency in the republic. The amendments also prepared the way for Slovenia to introduce laws liberalizing electoral procedures and guaranteeing the public's right to organize political groups.

November 29– December 1 *Worsening relations between Serbia and Slovenia.* A rally of Serbs and Montenegrins from all over Yugoslavia, scheduled for December 1 in Ljubljana, was called off by its organizers after the Slovene authorities banned it on November 21. The rally was to be called "the meeting of truth about the events in Kosovo." On November 29 the Serbian Socialist Alliance urged the breaking of all economic, institutional, and cultural ties with Slovenia. According to the Yugoslav media, the continuing dispute between the two republics had prompted the most severe political crisis in Yugoslavia since World War II.

December 11–13 *Eleventh Congress of the Croatian party.* The congress adopted a far-reaching political program that favored the introduction of multi-party elections, encouraged all forms of ownership, called for the abolition of capital punishment, and recommended an end to democratic centralism.

December 18–20 *Federal government's economic reform program.* On December 18 Yugoslav Prime Minister Ante Marković unveiled a far-reaching reform package. The program called for economic and political reforms and recommended constitutional amendments that would give the federal government more power over macroeconomic policy. The program was passed on December 20 by both chambers of the Federal Assembly following three days of heated debate. The program was designed to combat runaway inflation (2,600 percent in December 1989). The political and constitutional changes would lead to what was described as a new kind of "market socialism." The backbone of the economic program was a monetary reform calling for a new "heavy" dinar worth 10,000 of the old units and convertible with all Western currencies. It also called for a freeze on prices and wages until June 30, 1990, lighter monetary and budgetary controls, and a strict application of bankruptcy and liquidation laws that forbade state subsidies for loss-producing enterprises and banks. The Marković program also called for freeing the economy from political interference; "political pluralism" would be guaranteed, although the program did not explicitly refer to a multiparty system.

Albania: 1989

January *Deputy foreign ministers of the Balkan states meet in Tirana (January 19–21).* The meeting of foreign ministers ended with the adoption of an extensive program of inter-Balkan cooperation, including the decision to hold the next conference of foreign ministers in Albania (October 1990). The Albanians' special effort to make the conference a success was further evidence of its intent to abandon its isolationist policy. The country's mounting economic problems and its perennial conflict with Yugoslavia were some of the reasons why it had been forced to seek greater international cooperation.

February *Extensive changes made in leading party and government posts.* President and party leader Ramiz Alia declared that the changes in government and party posts were a step to give new impetus to the economy. Although the changes may have been seen as a first crack in Alia's "monolithic" leadership, it seemed that it was the country's poor economic performance that forced Alia to resort to the measure.

A party Central Committee plenum made important decisions affecting the organization, finances, and management of agriculture. The plenum called for the purchase of a large amount of foreign agricultural machinery, new forms of wages and pricing, productivity incentives, and greater decentralization. These changes were prompted by the need to improve living standards.

April

Gorbachev's reforms condemned. Albania's second most powerful leader, Foto Çami, condemned Soviet leader Mikhail Gorbachev's reforms in a speech about perestroika in the USSR. At the same time Çami admitted the need for changes in Albania, but he claimed that they should be suitable to the country. Earlier, Çami had made some proposals to end the lack of creativity in the arts. He called for greater experimentation and said that artists should not be afraid of "making mistakes."

August

Mother Theresa's visit. Nobel Peace Prize winner Mother Theresa paid a "private" visit to her native country, Albania. A visit by a world-famous missionary to a country claiming to be atheistic was obviously a significant event, another sign of Albania's creeping back into the world. Foreign commentators speculated that the visit also might encourage the Albanian leadership to introduce a more tolerant religious policy.

September

Internal policies softened. The Eighth Central Committee Plenum introduced a new program of changes calling for the gradual softening of the country's rigid internal policies, shaking up bureaucracy, and "democratization" of the country's life.

November

Secret police criticized. A new novel, *The Knives* by Neshat Tozaj, attacked the secret police, the *Sigurimi.* Reviewing the book, Albania's internationally famous writer, Ismail Kadare, supported the book's point of view and condemned violations of human rights in Albania. Kadare had become the leading proponent of the democratization in Albania.

Notes

1 Millennium Becomes Memento Mori

1 Milovan Djilas, *Conversations with Stalin* (New York: Harcourt, Brace and World, 1962), p. 114.

2 The settlement reached at the Diet of Augsburg in 1558, whereby the religion—Catholic or Protestant—of a territory was decided according to the religion of its ruler.

3 For the prewar order, see Joseph Rothschild, *East-Central Europe between the Two World Wars* (Seattle: University of Washington Press, 1974). For the early postwar years, see Hugh Seton-Watson, *The East European Revolution* (New York: Praeger, 1956).

4 Zbigniew K. Brzezinski, *The Soviet Bloc: Unity and Discord* (revised and enlarged ed.; Cambridge, Mass.: Harvard University Press, 1967), passim. See also J. F. Brown, *East Europe and Communist Rule* (Durham, N.C.: Duke University Press, 1988), passim. An excellent shorter study is Joseph Rothschild: *Return to Diversity: A Political History of East Central Europe Since World War II* (New York: Oxford University Press, 1989).

5 R. V. Burks, *The Dynamics of Communism in Eastern Europe* (Princeton, N.J.: Princeton University Press, 1961), passim.

6 The best treatment of this aspect of anti-Semitism is by Paul Lendvai, *Anti-Semitism in Eastern Europe* (London: Macdonald, 1971).

7 For the role of Western media in Czechoslovakia, see Timothy Garton Ash, "The Prague Advertisement," *New York Review of Books*, December 22, 1989, and especially "The Revolution of the Magic Lantern," *New York Review of Books*, January 18, 1990. See also Carl Builder and Steven C. Bankes, "The Etiology of European Change" (unpublished paper, Rand Corporation, Santa Monica, Calif., February 1990).

8 See chapter 2, p. 48.

9 *Kommunist* (Moscow), no. 14, 1955, p. 127.

10 Brzezinski, pp. 271–309.

11 See William E. Griffith, *Albania and the Sino-Soviet Rift* (Cambridge, Mass.: MIT Press, 1963).

12 See Kenneth Jowitt, *Revolutionary Breakthroughs and National Development: The Case of Romania, 1944–1965* (Berkeley: University of California Press, 1971); David Floyd, *Rumania: Russia's Dissident Ally* (New York: Praeger, 1965).

13 *Pravda,* March 27, 1959, quoted in Brzezinski, pp. 451–452.

14 Brown, p. 272.

15 On the "Khrushchev Sixties," see ibid., passim.

16 For an excellent critique of the convergence theories that was totally vindicated by future events, see the concluding chapter by Zbigniew Brzezinski in his book with Samuel P. Huntington, *Political Power: USA/USSR* (New York: Viking Press, 1964).

17 See Charlotte Saikowski and Leo Gruliow (eds.), *The Documentary Record of the 22nd Congress of the Communist Party of the Soviet Union* (New York: Columbia University Press, 1962), pp. 14–31.

18 See Carol Skalnik Leff, *National Conflict in Czechoslovakia: The Making and Remaking of a State, 1918–1987* (Princeton, N.J.: Princeton University Press, 1988).

19 The best book on the Prague Spring remains—and is likely to remain—H. Gordon Skilling, *Czechoslovakia's Interrupted Revolution* (Princeton, N.J.: Princeton University Press, 1976).

20 This point is well made by Philip Windsor, *Change in Eastern Europe* (London: Royal Institute of International Affairs, 1980).

21 See Brown, pp. 85–93.

22 Ibid., pp. 46–51.

23 Ibid., pp. 51–53.

24 For an excellent study, see Henrik Bischof, *Umweltschutz-probleme in Osteuropa* (Bonn: Friedrich-Ebert-Stiftung, February 1986).

25 The two best books on Solidarity remain Timothy Garton Ash, *The Polish Revolution: Solidarity* (New York: Scribners, 1984); and Abraham Brumberg (ed.), *Poland: Genesis of a Revolution* (New York: Random House, 1983).

26 Thane Gustafson of Georgetown University made several of these points in contributions to a Sovset electronic mail discussion in early 1990.

27 See Brown, pp. 18–28.

28 *Der Spiegel* (Hamburg), December 25, 1989.

29 *Foreign Affairs,* vol. 68, November 1, 1989.

30 For an excellent analysis of the attitudes and morale of Polish youth, which has some applicability to East European youth generally, see Tadeusz Szawiel and Rafal Zakrzewski, "Die Polnische Jugend Ende der achtziger Jahre," *Frankfurter Allgemeine Zeitung,* August 29, 1989.

31 The best essay on the decline of the Soviet East European system is by Timothy Garton Ash, "The Empire in Decay," *New York Review of Books,* September 29, 1988, October 13, 1988, and October 27, 1988. These, and other brilliant essays, were published in book form as *The Uses of Adversity: Essays on the Fate of Central Europe* (New York: Random House, 1989).

32 Ronald Linden, "The Dynamics of Change in Eastern Europe," Radio Free Europe Research Report, internal distribution, December 30, 1989.

33 Ibid.

34 Interview with *Wochenpresse* (Vienna), March 16, 1990.

2 Gorbachev's Policy Revolution

1 For an expanded version of this discussion, see J. F. Brown, *Eastern Europe and Communist Rule* (Durham, N.C.: Duke University Press, 1988), pp. 30–32.

2 Zdeněk Mlynář, *Night Frost in Prague* (New York: Karz, 1980), pp. 239–240.

3   Brown, pp. 32–33.

4   Ibid., pp. 41–43.

5   Ibid., pp. 57–59.

6   See Ronald D. Asmus, *East Berlin and Moscow: Documentation of a Dispute*, Radio Free Europe Research, vol. 9, p. 3 (August 31, 1984).

7   For a fuller discussion of these three phases of Gorbachev's policy in Eastern Europe, see J. F. Brown: "Hope and Uncertainty in Eastern Europe," *SAIS Review*, Winter-Spring 1990, vol. 10, no. 1. See also John Van Oudenaren, "The Soviet Union and Eastern Europe: New Prospects and Old Dilemmas," in William E. Griffith (ed.), *Central and Eastern Europe: The Opening Curtain?* (Boulder, Colo.: Westview Press, 1989), pp. 102–130; Melissa A. Dawson, "The Soviet Reaction to Eastern Europe," unpublished paper, Rand/UCLA doctoral program in political science, June 6, 1990.

8   A Politburo memorandum on the subject in November was discussed privately by official sources in Moscow. See the speech by Central Committee department deputy head Alexander Kapto at the Nineteenth CPSU Conference, published in *International Affairs*, no. 11, November 1988; also interview with Oleg Bogomolov in *Komsomolskaia Pravda*, July 29, 1988.

9   Mikhail Gorbachev, *Perestroika* (New York: Harper and Row, 1987), p. 163.

10 *Pravda*, April 11, 1987.

11 Polish Television Service, July 16, 1988.

12 Moscow Television Service, July 6, 1989.

13 *Die Welt* (Hamburg), April 24, 1989.

14 Deutsche Presse Agentur (dpa), August 28, 1989.

15 Interview in *Izvestia*, July 23, 1989.

16 See Jim Hoagland, "Gorbachev, Honecker Represent Different Faces of Communism," *Washington Post*, October 8, 1989.

17 On Gorbachev warnings, see R. W. Apple, Jr., "Prague Reports a Soviet Warning on Foot-Dragging," *New York Times*, November 16, 1989. On the attempted "coup," see, for example, Reuters news agency from London, May 30, 1990, quoting BBC television.

18 See chapter 7, p. 197.

19 The most balanced appraisal of the claims and denials is by Jonathan Eyal, "Rival Versions of Uprising Back Claims to Power," *Guardian* (London), January 5, 1990. The dispute, however, continued and seemed the kind that would never be settled conclusively. For a firsthand contribution to the discussion, opening up the controversy again, see the interview with Major Michail Lupoi, the first officer to go on television on December 22, 1989, to say the army was with the people. *L'Unità*, March 1, 1990.

20 Dr. Andranik Migranyan, of the Institute for the Study of the World Socialist Economies, Moscow, discussed this with me during his visit to Los Angeles in January 1990.

21 In the early part of 1990 this fear was expressed by "reformers" and "conservatives" alike in the Soviet Union.

22 For example, Lech Wałęsa, "We agreed that the President [Jaruzelski] should be a communist because our membership in the Warsaw Pact, among other things, was at stake." *L'Unità* (Rome), August 22, 1989.

23 There was considerable private speculation on this point in NATO circles in Brussels, Bonn, and Washington.

24 Interview given at Montecatini, Italy, to the Italian News Agency, ANSA, September 8, 1989.

25   See Jackson Diehl, "Ligachev Praises Hungary's Daring Reforms," *Washington Post,*
     April 26, 1987.

26   For the GDR, see TASS, September 16, 1989; for Czechoslovakia, TASS, March 12, 1989.

27   Fedor Burlatsky was already drawing this distinction in April 1989. Conversation
     with me in Berkeley, California.

28   Private conversations in Moscow, November 1989.

29   Shevardnadze also considerably increased the foreign ministry's influence in defense
     and arms control policy. See John Van Oudenaren, *The Role of Shevardnadze and the
     MFA (Ministry of Foreign Affairs) in the Making of Soviet Defense and Arms Control
     Policy* (Santa Monica, Calif.: Rand Corporation, September 1989).

30   The foreign ministry official responsible for coordinating this group was Vladimir
     Shustov, a relatively young but experienced diplomat, very much in the new Shev-
     ardnadze "mold."

31   See Vladimir Sobell, "Mikhail Gorbachev Takes Charge of Comecon," Radio Free
     Europe Research, Background Report, December 20, 1985. See also Mary Elizabeth
     Sperry, "CEMA Scientific-Technical Cooperation: The Struggle Between Cohesion and
     Viability," unpublished paper, Santa Monica, Calif., Rand/UCLA Center for Soviet
     Studies, Spring 1988.

32   Rezsö Nyers, for example, spoke of the desirability of developing a "smaller subre-
     gional, market in the East with those countries interested in market reform" *Figyelö,*
     February 19, 1989.

33   "Euthanasia for Comecon," January 11, 1990.

34   Ibid.

35   For a perceptive brief study of the decline of the Pact, see Daniel N. Nelson: "The
     Military Demise of the Warsaw Pact" (Washington, D.C.: Carnegie Endowment for
     International Peace, 1989).

36   Imre Szokai and Csaba Tabajdi, "The Changing Hungarian Socialist Model: A Change
     in the Orientation of Hungarian Foreign Policy," *Magyar Nemzet,* August 10, 1989.

37   This idea was amplified in a report in the *Frankfurter Allgemeine Zeitung,* August 10,
     1989.

38   Interview in *Frankfurter Rundschau,* June 3, 1989. See also Vlad Sobell, "Austria,
     Hungary, and the Question of Neutrality," Radio Free Europe Research, Background
     Report, August 24, 1989.

39   Interview in the *Washington Post,* September 19, 1989.

40   These comments on Poland and the Warsaw Pact have been taken from the excellent
     review by Thomas S. Szayna, *Polish Foreign Policy Under a Non-communist Govern-
     ment* (Santa Monica, Calif.: Rand Corporation, November 1989). For a thoughtful
     Polish view on the Warsaw Pact, see Wojtek Lamentowicz, "Warsaw Pact: End of the
     Empire," *Tygodnik Solidarność,* December 15, 1989.

41   Soviet Television, July 8, 1989.

42   For a perceptive article, partly but by no means wholly overtaken by events, see Mark
     Kramer, "Beyond the Brezhnev Doctrine: A New Era in Soviet-East European Rela-
     tions, *International Security,* Winter 1989/1990.

3   *Poland*

1   For a fuller discussion of this period, see J. F. Brown, *Eastern Europe and Communist
    Rule* (Durham, N.C.: Duke University Press, 1988), pp. 158–182.

2 On Gomułka's "distinctiveness," see Zbigniew Brzezinski, *The Soviet Bloc: Unity and Discord* (Cambridge, Mass.: Harvard University Press, 1967), pp. 333–357.

3 On the treaty, see Brown, pp. 167–168.

4 See, for example, his interview in *Przegląd Tygodniowy*, May 21, 1989.

5 For a brief review of Jaruzelski's role in the 1980s, see J. F. Brown, "Poland Since Martial Law" (Santa Monica, Calif.: Rand Corporation, December 1988).

6 Roger Boyes in *The Times* (London), December 18, 1986, wrote: "Martial Law had two functions: to crush Solidarity and any direct competition to the communist party, and to allow General Jaruzelski to outflank the anti-reformist old guard of the state apparatus."

7 *Trybuna Ludu*, June 1, 1983.

8 See chapter 4, pp. 99–100.

9 Boyes, *The Times*, December 18, 1986.

10 See Brown, "Poland Since Martial Law," pp. 5–6.

11 See "Third Priest Dies in Unexplained Circumstances," Radio Free Europe Research, Polish Situation Report, August 22, 1989.

12 See, for example, Brown, *Eastern Europe and Communist Rule*, pp. 191–192.

13 Ibid., p. 199.

14 Abraham Brumberg, "New Deal for Poland," *New York Review of Books*, January 13, 1987.

15 Bernard Margueritte cites these figures in his excellent "Polen: 1986: Realitäten und Perspektiven," *Europa-Archiv*, vol. 20, 1986.

16 Włodzimierz Rydzkowski and Krystyna Załadkiewicz, "Poland's International Debt: Prospects for Repayment," *East European Quarterly*, June 1989, p. 217.

17 Ibid., p. 218.

18 On the hardening of the Soviet economic line, see Brown, *Eastern Europe and Communist Rule*, pp. 153–155.

19 See chapter 1, pp. 31–32.

20 See Brown, *Eastern Europe and Communist Rule*, pp. 119–120.

21 See Brown, "Poland Since Martial Law," pp. 14–15.

22 On the effects of the amnesty, see Abraham Brumberg, "Poland: The New Opposition," *New York Review of Books*, February 18, 1988.

23 Some of the more important oppositional groups are mentioned in Brown, "Poland Since Martial Law," pp. 18–23.

24 The referendum is well-analyzed by Brumberg, "Poland: The New Opposition."

25 The most thorough study of Polish attitudes, putting them in their historical perspective, is by Hans-Henning Hahn, "Zur Dichotomie von Gesellschaft und Staat in Polen—Genese und Aktualität eines Grundmusters des politischen Mentalität," Berichte des Bundesinstituts fur ost-wissenschaftliche und internationale Studien (Köln, 20-1989).

26 For the developments in Poland, as well as in Hungary and Czechoslovakia, from the beginning of 1988, the brilliant and magisterial analyses of Timothy Garton Ash in *New York Review of Books* are best. See "The Empire in Decay," September 29, 1988; "Reform or Revolution," October 27, 1988; "Revolution: The Springtime of Two Nations," June 15, 1989; and "Revolution in Hungary and Poland," August 17, 1989.

27 A good deal of credit for holding the Solidarity side together during the roundtable talks with the regime, for drafting Solidarity's position, and for the whole success of the opposition during 1988–89 should go to Geremek. For good insight into his

thinking, see his interview with Véronique Soulé in *Libération* (Paris), August 22, 1989.

28   See Radio Free Europe Research, Polish Situation Report, "Walesa Victorious in Television Debate," December 16, 1968.

29   Inflation was to rise meteorically in 1989. But prices had been rising rapidly throughout the 1980s. Between 1983 and 1988, bread, for example, had risen 369 percent, milk 269 percent, pork 247 percent, beef 222 percent. *Polytika*, December 31, 1988.

30   See Jan B. de Weydenthal, "Politics in Poland After the Round Table Agreement," Radio Free Europe Research, Background Report, April 26, 1989.

31   For a remarkable analysis comparing and contrasting developments in Poland and Hungary, see A.O., "Polen and Ungarn-Parallelen, Unterschiede," *Neue Zürcher Zeitung*, October 22–23, 1989.

32   For events leading up to the election, the election itself, and its aftermath, there is no better piece of reporting than Lawrence Weschler's "A Reporter at Large—A Grand Experiment," *New Yorker*, November 13, 1989.

33   See Bernard Guetta, "La longue marche de l'opposition polonaise," *Le Monde*, August 24, 1989. On Mazowiecki, see Sylvie Kauffmann, "Tadeusz Mazowiecki: la fermeté et la prudence," *Le Monde*, August 20–21, 1989.

34   On Wałęsa's political shrewdness and sense of timing, see John Lloyd, "Lech Walesa—A Shrewd Grasp for the Substance of Power," *Financial Times*, August 19, 1989.

35   See Pol Mathil, "Jaruzelski sans lunettes: l'homme aux deux visages," *Le Soir* (Brussels), June 9, 1989.

36   "Geremek Quoted Calling for Ouster of Communists," Reuters (Warsaw), January 16, 1990.

37   There were many obituaries for the old Polish party. One of the most apt was by Stefan Dietrich, "Sozialdemokraten über Nacht—Das Begräbnis der polnischen Kommunisten," *Frankfurter Allgemeine Zeitung*, January 30, 1990.

38   Deutsche Presse Agentur (dpa), January 23, 1990.

39   See, for example, Jacek Syski, "Polish Myths and Realities," *Polytika*, December 8, 1989.

40   Victor Keegan, "Poland Sails into Uncharted Waters," *Guardian*, January 31, 1990.

41   The most crisply informative of the numerous articles on the new Polish economic strategy is Peter Norman and Stephen Fidler's "Poland Makes a Dash for Economic Liberalization," *Financial Times*, September 28, 1989.

42   Radio Free Europe, Daily Analysis, RFE/RL Daily Report no. 75, April 18, 1990.

43   See M. Sc., "Rasche Zunahme der Arbeitslosigkeit in Polen," *Neue Zürcher Zeitung* (Fernausgabe), February 8, 1990.

44   This analysis of the Polish ruling group is based mainly on M. Sc., "Andauerndes Vertrauen in die polnische Regierung," *Neue Zürcher Zeitung* (Fernausgabe), January 25, 1990.

45   The Polish economic program was essentially devised by Balcerowicz. Professor Jeffrey Sachs of Harvard University received much (well-deserved) publicity for his role as adviser, but Balcerowicz, and not he, was the master planner. Balcerowicz also received considerable publicity; see his interview in *Der Spiegel* (Hamburg), January 29, 1990.

4 Hungary

1 For Kádár's appeal, see Charles Gati, "The Kádár Mystique," *Problems of Commu-nism*, May–June 1974.
2 See J. F. Brown, *Eastern Europe and Communist Rule* (Durham, N.C.: Duke University Press, 1988), pp. 200–208; Charles Gati, "Reforming Communist Systems: Lessons from the Hungarian Experience," in William E. Griffith (ed.), *Central and Eastern Europe: The Opening Curtain?*, (Boulder, Colo.: Westview Press, 1989), pp. 218–241.
3 Kádár first publicized this slogan in 1961; *Népszabadság*, December 10, 1961.
4 See Brown, pp. 203–205.
5 See chapter 1, pp. 13–14.
6 It should be mentioned that Alexander Dubček, the deposed leader of the Prague Spring, more than twenty years later severely criticized Kádár for not having stood out against the invasion, arguing that had he done so, Brezhnev might have called it off. Series of interviews with Hungarian television during April 1989, see Radio Free Europe Research, Czechoslovak Situation Report, "Dubček's Interview in Hungary," May 5, 1989.
7 See chapter 1, p. 28.
8 See Brown, pp. 125–126, and 141–145.
9 See John M. Kramer, "Soviet-CEMA Energy Ties," *Problems of Communism*, July–August 1985.
10 See Laura d'Andrea Tyson, "Economic Adjustment in Eastern Europe" (Santa Monica, Calif.: Rand Corporation, 1984).
11 Perhaps the most prominent of these was János Kornai. See, for example, his article, "The Hungarian Reform Process: Visions, Hopes, and Reality," *Journal of Economic Literature*, vol. 24, December 1986.
12 For a good glimpse into Pozsgay's thinking, and ambitions, see his interview in *Marxism Today* (London), May 1989, and his interview with Rudolf L. Tökés in *The New Leader*, June 12–26, 1989.
13 One of the most important developments in this evolution were the establishment of the Hungarian Democratic Forum in September 1987 at a meeting in Lakitelek that was also attended by Pozsgay. "Democratic Forum Proposed by Populist Writers and Other Intellectuals," Radio Free Europe Research, Hungarian Situation Report, No-vember 28, 1987. See also Jiri Pehe, "Independent Movements in Eastern Europe," Radio Free Europe Research, Background Report, November 17, 1988.
14 For Kádár's previous adroitness on this issue, see Brown, p. 224.
15 The following points are based almost exclusively on Charles Gati, "Reforming Communists Systems . . .," in Griffith (ed.), *Central and Eastern Europe*, pp. 230–234.
16 For a remarkable analysis of the impact of the Gorbachev revolution in Hungary, see A.O., "Ostmitteleuropas Abfall von Moskau: Rückwirkungen der Perestroika-das Beispiel Ungarns," *Neue Zürcher Zeitung* (Fernausgabe) February 18–19, 1990. (This article is an abridged version of a lecture given at the University of Zurich on February 5, 1990.)
17 See Brown, pp. 419–444.
18 See Douglas Clarke, "The Romanian Military Threat to Hungary," Radio Free Europe Research, Background Report, July 27, 1989.
19 See J. F. Brown, "The View from Vienna and Rome," in Lincoln Gordon, *Eroding*

Empire: Western Relations with Eastern Europe (Washington, D.C.: Brookings Institution, 1987), pp. 269–279.

20 For a brief biography of Grósz, see Brown, *Eastern Europe and Communist Rule*, pp. 487–488.

21 See George Schöpflin, Rudolf Tökés, and Iván Volgyes, "Leadership Change and Crisis in Hungary," *Problems of Communism*, September–October 1988.

22 János Szentágothai, former president of the Hungarian Academy of Sciences; *Magyar Nemzet*, January 11, 1989.

23 See Sylvie Kaufmann, "La Hongrie exorcise son passé," *Le Monde*, June 17, 1989.

24 For the significance of this move, see Alfred Reisch, "Hungary in Transition: A Commentary," Radio Free Europe Research, Background Report, July 21, 1989. For a remarkably insightful analysis of Hungarian developments at this time, with apt comparisons to Poland, see Urs Schoettli, "Ungarn in Umbruch," *Neue Zürcher Zeitung* (Fernausgabe), June 10, 1989.

25 On Nyers, see Henry Kamm, "Budapest Encore: Old Socialist Elected," *New York Times*, October 10, 1989.

26 See note 12.

27 See "HSWP Reform Circles Hold National Conference Prior to Party Congress," Radio Free Europe Research, Hungarian Situation Report, September 1, 1989.

28 For an inventory of the emerging groups and parties, see Zoltán D. Bárány, "Hungary's Independent Political Groups and Parties," Radio Free Europe Research, Background Report, September 12, 1989.

29 For a fair appreciation of Kádár, see Georg Paul Hefty, "Der Kommunist ist gescheitert, der Patriot hat bleibende Verdienste," *Frankfurter Allgemeine Zeitung*, July 7, 1989.

30 Sándor Csóori, personal conversation, December 1988.

31 Schöpflin et al., "Leadership Change and Crisis in Hungary." See also three articles in Radio Free Europe Research, Hungarian Situation Report, July 9, 1989: "Reforming the National Assembly: The Electoral Process"; "Reforming the National Assembly: Parliamentary Work"; "Political Reform: Revising the Constitution."

32 Carl E. Buchalla, *Süddeutsche Zeitung*, June 13, 1989. See also A.O., "Imre Nagy's Rückkehr in Ungarns Geschichte," *Neue Zürcher Zeitung*, June 17, 1989.

33 See "The Negotiations Between the Party and the Opposition: The Differing Goals," Radio Free Europe Research, Hungarian Situation Report, June 23, 1989.

34 Ibid.

35 The recommendations of the Berend committee were published in *Figyelö*, May 4, 1989. They included a big reduction in CEMA trade, aggressive reprivatization of economic assets, and free transfer and sale of land. The more conservative proposals of the Csaki committee appeared in *Társzadalmi Szemle*, special edition, April 1989.

36 Radio Budapest, June 14, 1989.

37 Associated Press (Budapest), August 12, 1989.

38 See Tibor Fényi, "Wohin kippt Ungarns 'runder Tisch'? Machtfülle für den Staatspresidenten als Kernfrage der Verhandlungen," *Die Presse* (Vienna), August 28, 1989.

39 See Radio Free Europe Research, Hungarian Situation Report, May 30, 1989. On July 14, 1989, Radio Budapest reported that the party's Central Committee had decided to reduce the *nomenklatura* authority of itself and the Politburo from 1,200 positions to 435.

40 Henry Kamm, "Hungarian Party in Money Scandal," *New York Times*, September 7, 1989.

41 This issue was much discussed and it characterized the atmosphere of glasnost that had developed in Hungary that, despite the subject's sensitivity, the discussions were widely reported. See, for example, the interview with major-General János Sebök, army officer and a National Assembly deputy, Radio Budapest, June 10, 1989.

42 The following is based mainly on Judy Dempsey, "Fudging in Hungarian Poll Deal," *Financial Times*, September 20, 1989.

43 On the Workers' Guard, see "The Workers' Guard: A Threat to Hungary's Reforms," Radio Free Europe Research, Hungarian Situation Report, July 27, 1989.

44 Jiří Dienstbier; interview with *Die Volkskrant* (Amsterdam), March 2, 1990. On Horn, see Dempsey, "The Man Who Let the East Germans Go," *Financial Times*, September 18, 1989. For an excellent eyewitness report on the different moods in Hungary during the fall of 1989, see Steven W. Popper, "Slouching Towards Budapest: A Trip Report" (Santa Monica, Calif.: Rand Corporation, November 1989).

45 For an incisive analysis of this decision, see A.O., "Ungarns Entscheidung," *Neue Zürcher Zeitung* (Fernausgabe), September 13, 1989.

5 The German Democratic Republic

1 Radio GDR II, August 19, 1989.

2 On adverse comments about the situation in Poland and Hungary, see, for example, Otto Reinhold in *Einheit* (no. 1, 1989), p. 54; Harry Nick in *Neues Deutschland*, March 25–26, 1989.

3 See B. V. Flow and Ronald D. Asmus, "The Eleventh SED Congress," *Radio Free Europe Research Background Report*, April 30, 1986.

4 *Stern* (Hamburg), April 8, 1987; reprinted in *Neues Deutschland*, April 10, 1987.

5 Speech at Twelfth SED plenum, December 1988, *Neues Deutschland*, December 2, 1988.

6 Quoted in *Der Tagesspiegel* (West Berlin), May 24, 1989.

7 See chapter 2, p. 46, for an elaboration on this point. For an excellent, brief review of Soviet-East German relations, see Norman M. Naimark, "Soviet-GDR Relations: An Historical Overview" (Köln: Bundesinstitut fur ostwissenschaftliche und internationale Studien, no. 51, 1989).

8 For an expert critique of the GDR's economic performance under Mittag, see the interview with Wilma and Rolf Merkel in *Die Zeit* (Hamburg), September 29, 1989.

9 John M. Kramer, "Soviet-CEMA Energy Ties," *Problems of Communism* (July–August, 1985).

10 *Neue Zürcher Zeitung* (Fernausgabe), March 27, 1985.

11 Josef Joffe, "The View from Bonn: The Tacit Alliance," in Lincoln Gordon, *Eroding Empire: Western Relations with Eastern Europe* (Washington, D.C.: Brookings Institution, 1987), p. 157.

12 Analysis of the Central Intelligence Agency, *East European Economies: Slow Growth in the 1980s*, vol. 2; Foreign Trade and International Finance, Selected Papers Submitted to the Joint Economic Committee, Congress of the United States (Washington, D.C.: U.S. Government Printing Office, 1986).

13 See Manfred Melzer and Arthur A. Stahnke, "The GDR Faces the Economic Dilemmas of the 1980s: Caught Between the Need for New Methods and Restricted Options," in *East European Economies: Slow Growth in the 1980s*, vol. 3: Country Studies on Eastern Europe and Yugoslavia, pp. 132–135 and p. 166.

14 See "What It Takes to be Boss," *The Economist*, February 22, 1985.

15 *Der Spiegel* (Hamburg), February 26, 1990.

16 See Brown, p. 234. See also David Childs, *The GDR: Moscow's German Ally* (London: George Allen and Unwin, 1983); A. James McAdams, *East Germany and Détente: Building Authority After the Wall* (Cambridge: Cambridge University Press, 1988).

17 Brown, p. 255.

18 *International Herald Tribune*, December 13, 1988, quoted by Barbara Donovan, "East Germany in the Gorbachev Era," internal Radio Free Europe Research Analysis, July 1989.

19 See Ronald D. Asmus, "The GDR and Martin Luther," *Survey* (London), vol. 28 (summer 1984); also "The Portrait of Bismarck in the GDR," *Radio Free Europe Research Background Report*, July 24, 1984.

20 The best analysis of this episode is by Ronald D. Asmus, "East Berlin and Moscow: The Documentation of a Dispute" (Munich: RFE Occasional Papers, Radio Free Europe, 1985).

21 McAdams, p. 119.

22 On this point, see Timothy Garton Ash, "Which Way Will Germany Go?" *New York Review of Books*, January 31, 1985. See also Ferdinand Hurni, "Deutscher als die Bundesrepublik?" *Neue Zürcher Zeitung* (Fernausgabe), July 27, 1987.

23 Brown, pp. 252–254.

24 Barbara Donovan, "Inter-German Relations: Political and Cultural Aspects," *Radio Free Europe Research Background Report*, May 8, 1987.

25 Daniel Vernet, *Le Monde*, November 11, 1989.

26 Brown, pp. 255–258. See also Vladimir Tişmaneanu, "Nascent Civil Society in the German Democratic Republic," *Problems of Communism*, March–June 1989.

27 See Donovan, "East Germany in the Gorbachev Era."

28 Some observers saw the whole episode as a victory for Honecker. See A. James McAdams, "The New Logic in Soviet-GDR Relations," *Problems of Communism*, September–October 1988.

29 From what was subsequently revealed about the venality and self-serving characteristics of at least part of the SED leadership, it can be assumed they were also acting very much in their own interests. But the two, particularly by the actors involved, are seldom easy to separate.

30 *Neues Deutschland*, April 2, 1988.

31 See Donovan, "East Germany in the Gorbachev Era."

32 *Neues Deutschland*, December 2 and 3–4, 1988.

33 *Junge Welt*, October 29, 1988.

34 *Neues Deutschland*, November 24–25, 1988.

35 *Neues Deutschland*, February 11–12, 1989.

36 Stephan Hermlin, *Der Spiegel*, February 6, 1989, quoted by Donovan, "East Germany in the Gorbachev Era."

37 Wolfgang Herger, elected Politburo member and CC secretary after the fall of Honecker. The reason for the collapse, according to Herger, was that the SED leadership forgot one of its old, cherished slogans: "to learn from the Soviet Union is to learn how to win." Quoted by Timothy Garton Ash, "The German Revolution," *New York Review of Books*, December 21, 1989.

38 A good, brief, portrait of Modrow was published in the *Süddeutsche Zeitung* (Munich), November 9, 1989.

39 Deutsche Presse Agentur (dpa), June 8, 1989. Krenz was criticizing the condemnation of the Chinese massacre by Oskar Lafontaine, prime minister of Saarland.

40 The significance of this episode, against the background of the general weakening of the regime, is analyzed by Albrecht Hinze, "Die SED in der Isolation," *Süddeutsche Zeitung*, November 13, 1989.

41 See chapter 2, note 16.

42 Subsequent SED publicity made Krenz the main hero of this incident. It appears, however, that he was persuaded to intervene by a group of citizens of which Kurt Masur, director of the Leipzig Gewandhaus Orchestra, was one of the most prominent. See *Frankfurter Allgemeine Zeitung*, November 21, 1989; also Ash, "The German Revolution."

43 See Barbara Donovan, "The Berlin Wall Comes Tumbling Down," Radio Free Europe Research, Background Report, November 20, 1989.

44 See chapter 4, note 22.

45 Of the many editorials and analyses written on this event, none is better than Hermann Rudolph, "Der Zusammenbruch," *Süddeutsche Zeitung*, December 12, 1989. On the future of the GDR, written just before its collapse became evident, see Dieter Schröder, "DDR im Post-Sozialismus," *Süddeutsche Zeitung*, December 9, 1989.

6 Czechoslovakia

1 *Nová Mysl*, no. 1, 1983.

2 *Hospodářské Noviny*, no. 47, November 26, 1982.

3 H. Gordon Skilling, "Czechoslovakia Between East and West," in William E. Griffith (ed.), *Central and Eastern Europe: The Opening Curtain?* (Boulder, Colo.: Westview Press, 1989), p. 243.

4 Vlad Sobell, "The Running Battle with Labor Discipline," Radio Free Europe Research, Czechoslovak Situation Report, May 13, 1985.

5 Vladimir V. Kusin, "Husák's Czechoslovakia and Economic Stagnation," *Problems of Communism*, May–June 1982. See also Kusin's *From Dubček to Charter 77* (New York: St. Martin's Press, 1978).

6 In 1988 the Czechoslovak net debt was estimated at $4.2 billion, the lowest in Eastern Europe except for Romania. The Czechoslovak per capita debt was $270, the Polish $900, the Hungarian $1,470. *Libération* (Paris), September 19, 1989.

7 *Statistické Přehledy* (Prague), no. 5, May 1987, pp. 143 and 151.

8 J. F. Brown, *Eastern Europe and Communist Rule* (Durham, N.C.: Duke University Press, 1988), pp. 302–303.

9 Kusin, "Husák's Czechoslovakia."

10 Václav Vertelář, quoted by William Echikson and Elisabeth Pond, "Experiments in Eastern Europe," *Christian Science Monitor*, January 8, 1986.

11 Ibid.

12 For a brief biographical sketch of Štrougal, see Brown, pp. 483–484.

13 For a review of Komárek's earlier articles, see Vlad Sobell, *Fundamental Change in the Economic Mechanism Advocated*, Radio Free Europe Research, Czechoslovak Situation Report, June 27, 1985.

14 *Rudé Právo* (Prague), June 19, 1985.

15 *Borba* (Belgrade), November 23–24, 1985.

16 Ibid.

17   See Economic Commission for Europe, "East-West Joint Ventures" (New York, 1988). See also Leslie Colitt, "West Woos Orders from Prague," *Financial Times*, September 17, 1985.

18   *Nová Mysl*, no. 11, 1985.

19   Brown, p. 305.

20   *Rudé Právo*, March 26, 1986.

21   Ibid., March 25, 1986.

22   Bilak comprehensively responded to perestroika in *Rudé Právo* on February 20, 1987, an article immediately carried by the East German party daily, *Neues Deutschland*. It also was significant that Ivan Hlivka, a well-known hard-line official at the International Department of the Central Committee, wrote an article in *Rudé Právo* of February 29, 1987, on the "new thinking" in the international communist movement without mentioning Gorbachev by name and referring only vaguely to Soviet international policies.

23   *Die Welt* (Hamburg), February 10, 1987.

24   See "Husák Reluctantly Confirms New Course," Radio Free Europe Research, Czechoslovak Situation Report, April 6, 1987.

25   The entire Gorbachev visit to Czechoslovakia is covered in the complete issue of Radio Free Europe Research, Czechoslovak Situation Report, May 4, 1987.

26   Ibid.

27   The entire program was published in a supplement of the economic journal, *Hospodářské Noviny*, no. 13, March 27, 1987.

28   *L'Unità* (Rome), May 20, 1987.

29   Vlad Sobell, " 'Restructuring' versus 'Normalization': A Transient Accommodation," Radio Free Europe Research, Czechoslovak Situation Report, June 12, 1987.

30   Radio Prague, July 28, 1987.

31   *Rudé Právo*, August 13, 1987.

32   See Richard Davy: "Czechoslovakia Under Jakeš," *World Today* (London), April 1988.

33   *Frankfurter Rundschau*, January 22 and 26, 1988. The interview was reported in *Rudé Právo*, January 22, 1988, but with all obviously controversial parts excluded.

34   In Griffith (ed.), "Central and Eastern Europe: The Opening Curtain?," p. 252.

35   Kusin, "Husák's Czechoslovakia."

36   This discussion of Charter 77, VONS, and other opposition groups in Czechoslovakia is based on H. Gordon Skilling, "Independent Currents in Czechoslovakia," *Problems of Communism*, January–February 1985.

37   See the analyses under the general title, "Saints Cyril and Methodius," in Radio Free Europe Research, Czechoslovak Situation Report, April 19, 1985.

38   *L'Unitá*, January 10, 1988.

39   See Radio Free Europe Research, Czechoslovak Situation Report, "Dubček's Interview in Hungary," May 5, 1989.

40   See Radio Free Europe Research, Czechoslovak Situation Report, "Support for Petition for Democratization Grows Despite Fierce Official Attacks," August 12, 1989.

41   *Gazeta Wyborcza* (Warsaw), July 25, 1989.

42   *Rudé Právo*, July 27, 1989.

43   Radio Free Europe Research, Czechoslovak Situation Report, "Petition Calling for Democratization Angers Prague," July 11, 1989.

44   See Radio Free Europe Research, Czechoslovak Situation Report, "Fojtík Defines CPCS

Stand on Reform," September 20, 1989. See also Viktor Meier, "Der Prager 'Beton-bunker' zunehmend unsicherer," *Frankfurter Allgemeine Zeitung*, August 24, 1989.

45 Interview with Radio Free Europe (Munich), September 1, 1988.

46 The following discussion of the changes, their background, and their implications is based mainly on Radio Free Europe Research, Czechoslovak Situation Report, October 14, 1989, which is entirely devoted to the changes.

47 The best discussion of the political "block" on systematic economic reform in Czechoslovakia is by Françoise Lazsare, "Tchecoslovaquie: la peur du choix," *Le Monde* (Paris), August 15, 1989.

48 See, for example, his speech on "Miners' Day" in Prague on September 2, 1989, *Rudé Právo*, September 4, 1989.

49 Reuters (from Prague), July 6, 1989, quoting Vladimír Dlouhý, deputy director of the Institute for Economic Forecasting. Dlouhý was to become head of planning in the new democratic government.

50 Reuters (from Prague), August 30, 1989.

51 Ibid.

52 *Mladá Fronta*, January 2, 1990.

7 Bulgaria

1 For general histories of Bulgaria under communism, see William A. Welsh, *Bulgaria* (Boulder, Colo.: Westview Press, 1986). For the earlier communist period, see J. F. Brown, *Bulgaria Under Communist Rule* (New York: Praeger, 1970). See also Paul Lendvai, *Eagles in Cobwebs: Nationalism and Communism in the Balkans* (New York: Doubleday, 1969), pp. 206–262; J. F. Brown, *Eastern Europe and Communist Rule* (Durham, N.C.: Duke University Press, 1988), pp. 316–336.

2 For the "Great Leap Forward," see Brown: *Eastern Europe and Communist Rule*, pp. 320–321; for the agro-industrial complexes, pp. 325–326.

3 This was the so-called "July Concept"; see p. 187.

4 For details, see *Neue Zürcher Zeitung* (Fernausgabe), April 5–6, 1985, quoting figures provided by the Vienna Institute for Comparative International Economics.

5 Statement by Ivan Iliev, head of the State Planning Commission, *Rabotnichesko Delo*, December 13, 1985.

6 For the end of 1984 the net debt was put at only $0.7 billion, *Neue Zürcher Zeitung* (Fernausgabe), November 30, 1985. Judging from statements made after the fall of Zhivkov, these figures had always been grossly distorted. The gross debt for 1989 was being put at $8 billion (Bulgarian Telegraphic Agency—BTA—December 11, 1989). The *Frankfurter Allgemeine Zeitung*, January 20, 1990, put the debt at $10 billion.

7 For a detailed account of Bulgarian economic progress for 1985 and the first quarter of 1986, see PlanEcon Report, vol. 2, no. 24, June 13, 1986.

8 For a fuller account of this episode, see J. F. Brown, "Conservatism and Nationalism in the Balkans: Albania, Bulgaria, and Romania," in William E. Griffith (ed.): *Central and Eastern Europe: The Opening Curtain?* (Boulder, Colo.: Westview Press, 1989), pp. 283–314.

9 *Frankfurter Allgemeine Zeitung*, April 19, 1986.

10 In the summer of 1989 the State Department confirmed media reports—for example,

Newsweek, August 14, 1989—about the secret police's involvement in drug smuggling.

11   See Ronald D. Asmus, *East Berlin and Moscow: The Documentation of a Dispute* (Munich: RFE Occasional Papers, Radio Free Europe, 1985).

12   A *Financial Times* (London) survey of September 7, 1984, quoting Wharton Econometrics, said that in the previous three years Bulgaria had made a profit of $2.2 billion on the re-export of refined or chemically processed Soviet oil. For the most authoritative survey of Bulgaria's trade during the communist period, see J. M. Montias, "Industrial Policy and Foreign Trade in Bulgaria," *East European Politics and Societies,* vol. 2, no. 3, Fall 1988.

13   See "A Review of Bulgarian-Soviet Relations," Radio Free Europe Research, Bulgarian Situation Report, November 7, 1985.

14   Harry Schleicher, "Frühjahresputz mit vagen Oberbegriffen," *Frankfurter Rundschau,* April 7, 1986.

15   *Rabotnichesko Delo,* July 29, 1987.

16   Agence France Press (AFP), August 18, 1987; see "National Assembly Approves Further Major Government Changes," Radio Free Europe Research, Bulgarian Situation Report, August 21, 1987.

17   Tass (in English), October 16, 1987.

18   Stephen Ashley, "The Mounting Hysteria in the Media," Radio Free Europe Research, Bulgarian Situation Report, March 9, 1989.

19   According to diplomatic sources in Sofia, Alexandrov was invited to, and attended, the official reception at the Soviet Embassy in Sofia marking the seventy-first anniversary of the October Revolution in November 1988, much to Zhivkov's displeasure.

20   Ashley, "The Mounting Hysteria in the Media."

21   See the excellent article by Richard Crampton, "The Intelligentsia, the Ecology, and the Opposition in Bulgaria," *World Today* (London), vol. 46, no. 2, February 1990.

22   The best treatment of *preustrojstvo* is by Ld, "Preustrojstwo—Bulgariens Reformvariante," *Neue Zürcher Zeitung,* June 14, 1989.

23   *Rabotnichesko Delo,* January 11, 1989.

24   Ibid., July 27, 1989. See also "Toward Genuine Reform or Mock Perestroika?," Radio Free Europe Research, Bulgarian Situation Report, September 1, 1989.

25   Reuters, February 22, 1989. See also "Bulgaria's Stalinists and Victims of Stalinism," Radio Free Europe Research, Bulgarian Situation Report, October 5, 1989.

26   C., Sr., "Schleppendes politischer Umbau in Bulgarien," *Neue Zürcher Zeitung,* July 18, 1989.

27   The Turkish exodus in 1989 received enormous publicity abroad, unlike the forced changing of Turkish names in 1984–85. One of the best articles was by Wolfgang Günter Lerch, "Für viele eine Flucht in Ungewisse: Der Exodus der Türken aus Bulgarien," *Frankfurter Allgemeine Zeitung,* August 5, 1989. See also "The Social and Economic Problems Caused by the Exodus," Radio Free Europe Research, Bulgarian Situation Report, October 5, 1989.

28   The intricacies of the plot against Zhivkov still need a full explanation. An excellent immediate report was by Judy Dempsey, "One Vote Toppled Zhivkov in Longplanned Palace Coup," *Financial Times,* November 16, 1989. For the best historical background to the coup, see Christophe Chiclet, "La Bulgarie aussit choisit le changement," *Le Monde Diplomatique,* December 1989.

29 In the welter of comment, mostly highly critical, often ill-informed, on Zhivkov after his fall and subsequent disgrace, the best-balanced was by Peter Bender, "Immer Langsam voran. . . . ," *Die Zeit* (Hamburg), December 1, 1989.

30 Dempsey, "One Vote Toppled Zhivkov."

8 Romania

1 J. F. Brown, *Eastern Europe and Communist Rule* (Durham, N.C.: Duke University Press, 1988), p. 263.

2 Cyrus Sulzberger, who enjoyed pre-World War II Bucharest, once asked General Hans Speidel, later to become chief of staff of NATO, "which among all the non-German troops [in World War II] were the best soldiers: the Finns, the Croats, the Hungarians? 'None of them,' he said, 'the Rumanians. Give them good leadership, and they are as good as any you'll find.'" C. L. Sulzberger, *A Long Row of Candles: Memoirs and Diaries (1934–1954)* (Toronto: Macmillan, 1969), p. 74.

3 Rebreanu's book was first published in Romania as *Răscoala* in 1932. An English translation, *The Uprising*, was published in London in 1964 by Peter Owen.

4 Quoted by Carl E. Buchalla, "SZ-Gesprach mit Mircea Dinescu," *Süddeutsche Zeitung* (Munich), January 11, 1989.

5 For the most recent authoritative study, see Daniel N. Nelson, *Romanian Politics in the Ceauşescu Era* (New York: Gordon and Beach, 1988). Also the excellent essay by Larry L. Watts, "Romania 1944–1989: Nationalism, Patrimonial Communism, and Delegitimation" (unpublished manuscript, Santa Monica, Calif.: Rand Corporation), November 1989.

6 See J. F. Brown's two-part article, "Rumania Today," *Problems of Communism* (January–February, March–April 1969). Part I of the series is called "Towards Integration," and Part II, "The Strategy of Defiance."

7 For a short review of Ceauşescu's personality and policy, nothing equals Jan Krauze's three articles in *Le Monde* (Paris): "Le Style, c'est l'homme," February 28, 1984; "Vingt-deux millions de fourmis et quelques cigales," February 29, 1984; "Quelques murmures isolés dans le foule," March 1, 1984.

8 Brown, *Eastern Europe and Communist Rule*, p. 276.

9 Professor Kligman has discussed these ideas several times with me. I am indebted to her for readily sharing her knowledge of, and insights into, contemporary Romania.

10 *Scînteia*, March 4, 1988.

11 See "An Underground Essay on Urban and Rural Development," Radio Free Europe Research, Romanian Situation Report, February 3, 1986. For the best introduction to the "systematization" scheme, see Michael Shafir, "The Historical Background to Rural Resettlement," Radio Free Europe Research, Romanian Situation Report, August 23, 1986.

12 *L'Express* (Paris), May 28, 1987.

13 Figures taken from Romanian Statistical Yearbook, 1986 (Bucharest: Central Directorate of Statistics, 1986), pp. 10 and 12.

14 A good article illustrating this sensitivity, as well as the hypocrisy of regime propaganda, is Christoph von Marschall, "Das Regime präsentiert heile Dörfer," *Süddeutsche Zeitung*, November 15, 1989.

15 For a perceptive, moving, and beautifully written account of a German woman's

experiences in Romania and the reasons for her decision to leave, see Helga Höfer, "Wenn Heimat zur Fremde wird," *Süddeutsche Zeitung*, April 22, 1989.

16   There had been a notable case of Romanian-Hungarian working-class unity in the Jiu Valley miners' strike as early as 1977. (See Vladimir Socor, "Eyewitness on the 1977 Miners' Strike in Romania's Jiu Valley," Radio Free Europe Research, Background Report, August 13, 1986.) The uprising in Timişoara in December 1989 was, of course, the high point of unity. Within weeks the old hatreds and prejudices had resurfaced.

17   Information from Gail Kligman, see note 9.

18   See John Kifner, "Bucharest Says It Disbanded Feared Secret Police," *New York Times*, February 22, 1990. Kifner puts *Securitate* numbers at "between 10,000 and 20,000 operatives and many more informers at its peak."

19   See, for example, Waldemar Fromm, " 'In uns lebt die Partei in jeder Ader'—vom Eigenlob der Sprache/Ceauşescu und seine Hofdichter," *Frankfurter Allgemeine Zeitung*, September 29, 1989. For the most amusing (and frightening) review of the adulation, see "An A to Z of the Personality Cult in Romania," Radio Free Europe Research, Romanian Situation Report, February 2, 1989.

20   See "Veiled Comparison Made Between Ceauşescu and Genghis Khan," Radio Free Europe Research, Romanian Situation Report, November 6, 1986.

21   See "Ceauşescu's Personality Cult—an Analysis," Radio Free Europe Research, Romanian Situation Report, February 6, 1987.

22   See Nicolas Tertulian, "Rumänien zwischen Stalinismus and Faschismus," *Neue Zürcher Zeitung* (Fernausgabe), March 18/19, 1990.

23   Roger Boyes, "Shadows Round a Despot," *The Times* (London), August 8, 1989.

24   For one of the best reports on the demolition, see Barbara von Ow, "Bulldozer erzwingen eine 'Neue Zeit,' " *Süddeutsche Zeitung*, July 8, 1989. For an excellent description of the depressing character of Bucharest under Ceauşescu, see C., Sr., "Unwirtliches Bukarest: Modernisierungswahn des Conducător," *Neue Zürcher Zeitung* (Fernausgabe), December 23, 1989.

25   Reported by Buchalla, *Süddeutsche Zeitung*, January 11, 1990.

26   Radio Bucharest, January 3, 1990.

27   *Scînteia*, November 21, 1985.

28   For a good roundup on this subject, see "Ceauşescu Denounces Reforms as Antisocialist, Calls for Warsaw Pact Joint Steps to Contain Them," Radio Free Europe Research, Romanian Situation Report, August 4, 1989.

29   Radio Bucharest, April 14 and 17, 1989.

30   Figures quoted by Thomas Ross, reporting an interview with the new Romanian economics minister, General Atanasie Stanculescu. *Frankfurter Allgemeine Zeitung*, February 8, 1990.

31   Deutsche Presse Agentur (dpa), January 3, 1990.

32   Quoted by Florin-Gabriel Marculescu, "Self-Dissolution," *România Liberă*, January 10, 1990.

33   *Scînteia*, November 21, 1985.

34   See "Former Senior RCP Officials Protest Ceausescu's Policies," Radio Free Europe Research, Romanian Situation Report, March 29, 1989.

35   The Orthodox patriarch, Teoctist, who had had few rivals in sycophancy to Ceauşescu, resigned in January 1990. See Dan Ionescu, "Crisis in the Romanian Orthodox

Church," Radio Free Europe Research, Background Report, January 22, 1990. Teoctist, however, was subsequently reinstated.

36 Brown, *Eastern Europe and Communist Rule*, p. 287.

37 For analyses of these events and for Ceauşescu's rule at the local level generally, see Daniel N. Nelson's articles: "Le fiasco politique de la Roumaine," *Revue d'études comparatives est-ouest*, September 1989, and "Ceauşescu-Kult und lokale Politik-bereiche in Rumänien," *Osteuropa*, 1989. See also the same author's *Elite-Mass Relations in Communist Systems* (New York: St. Martin's Press, 1988).

38 This discussion of Romanian international relations is based on J. F. Brown, "Conservatism and Nationalism in the Balkans: Albania, Bulgaria, and Romania," in William E. Griffith (ed.), *Central and Eastern Europe: The Opening Curtain?* (Boulder, Colo.: Westview Press, 1989), pp. 283–314.

39 See Olaf Ihlau, "Seine Allmacht, Der Conducător," *Süddeutsche Zeitung*, July 8, 1989.

40 See "Nicolae and Elena Ceauşescu Visit the USSR," Radio Free Europe Research, Romanian Situation Report, November 9, 1988.

41 Shevardnadze visited Bucharest as early as January 6, 1990. See his interview in *Izvestia*, January 9, 1990. See also Celestine Bohlen, "As Communist Rule Fades, Rumanian-Soviet Ties Grow," *New York Times*, December 30, 1989.

42 See Douglas Clarke, "The Romanian Military Threat to Hungary," Radio Free Europe Research, Background Report, July 27, 1989.

43 On the Reverend Tökés, see A.O., "Die Verfolgung Kritischer Bürger in Rumänien," *Neue Zürcher Zeitung*, October 27, 1989.

44 On the controversy over whether the uprising was spontaneous or prepared, see chapter 2, note 19; see also p. 210.

45 For an excellent account of the uprising, see Robert Cullen, "Report from Romania," *New Yorker*, April 2, 1990. See also Pavel Campeanu, "The Revolt of the Romanians," *New York Review of Books*, February 1, 1990.

9 Yugoslavia and Albania

1 Grudgingly fair and insightful, Milovan Djilas's *Tito: Eine Kritische Biographie* (Vienna: Molden, 1980) is still the best guide.

2 Paul Lendvai shows the best feel for the "Club of 41," its ethos, and its grip on political life in his *Eagles in Cobwebs: Nationalism and Communism in the Balkans* (Garden City, N.Y.: Doubleday, 1969), pp. 61–65.

3 For a serious study of the self-management system, see Harold Lydall, *Yugoslav Socialism: Theory and Practice* (Oxford: Clarendon Press, 1984).

4 Duncan Wilson, *Tito's Yugoslavia* (Cambridge: Cambridge University Press, 1979), p. 141. Wilson's book and Dennison Rusinow's more comprehensive *The Yugoslav Experiment, 1948–1974* (London: C. Hurst, 1977), despite a relative optimism about Yugoslavia's future that may have been unjustified, are notable for their knowledge, wisdom, and grasp.

5 *Politika* (Belgrade), August 29–30, 1970, referred to by Rusinow, pp. 281 and 312.

6 See J. F. Brown, *Eastern Europe and Communist Rule* (Durham, N.C.: Duke University Press, 1988), pp. 352–356.

7 Ibid., pp. 356–358.

8 Rusinow, p. 330.

9 Viktor Meier, "Yugoslavia: Worsening Economic and Nationalist Crisis," in William E. Griffith (ed.), *Central and East Europe: The Opening Curtain?* (Boulder, Colo.: Westview, 1989), p. 266.

10 See Christopher Cviic, "The Background and Implications of the Domestic Scene in Yugoslavia," in Paul S. Shoup (ed.) and George W. Hoffman (project director), *Problems of Balkan Security: Southeastern Europe in the 1990s* (Washington, D.C.: Wilson Center Press, 1990), pp. 93–95.

11 Conversations about Kosovo and Serbia with Professor Ronelle Alexander of the University of California at Berkeley have been most enlightening, and I am very grateful to her.

12 On Kosovo from an Albanian standpoint, see J. F. Brown, "Conservatism and Nationalism in the Balkans: Albania, Bulgaria, and Romania" in Griffith (ed), pp. 285 and 287.

13 Few contemporary East European politicians have received as much attention as Milošević. Few Western sources can be as revealing as the interview he gave to *Le Monde* published on July 12, 1989. For a good depiction of the controversy surrounding Milošević, see Maren Köster-Hetzendorf, " 'Warum muss dieser Kretin hier überall hängen?.' " *Die Presse* (Vienna), December 28, 1989.

14 Meier, in Griffith (ed.), p. 272.

15 Cviic, in Shoup and Hoffman, p. 92.

16 See Carl E. Buchalla, "Politische Opfer auf der Bühne des Nationalismus," *Süddeutsche Zeitung*, October 28–29, 1989.

17 See Milan Andrejevich, "Growing Opposition to Milošević in Serbia," Radio Free Europe Research, Background Report, December 15, 1989.

18 See Milan Andrejevich, "Serbia Accused of Interfering in Bosnian Affairs," Radio Free Europe Research, Background Report, October 19, 1989.

19 See Celestine Bohlen, "Restive Yugoslav Areas Weigh Their Options," *New York Times*, April 6, 1990.

20 Meier, in Griffith (ed.), pp. 269–272.

21 See Milan Andrejevich, "Serbia Urges Breaking Ties with Slovenia," Radio Free Europe Research, Background Report, November 30, 1989.

22 Quoted by Cviic, in Shoup and Hoffman, p. 96.

23 Meier, in Griffith (ed.), p. 269.

24 Professor Ivan Urbančić, of the University of Ljubljana, quoted by Olaf Ihlau, "Zehn Jahre nach Tito's Tod. Der Anfang vom Ende in Jugoslawien?" *Süddeutsche Zeitung*, February 6, 1990.

25 See Judy Dempsey, "Serbs Rally to Ghosts of Tito and Lenin," *Financial Times*, January 24, 1990.

26 See Johann-Georg Reissmuller, "Auch in Kroatien Kommt Bewegung," *Frankfurter Allgemeine Zeitung*, December 1, 1989.

27 For a review of how this problem developed, see C., Sr., "Polemik um Kroatiens serbische Minderheit," *Neue Zürcher Zeitung*, December 3–4, 1989.

28 Carl E. Buchalla, "Das Land der notleidenden Millionäre," *Süddeutsche Zeitung*, August 14, 1989.

29 For an estimate of the foreign remittances, see "Foreign Remittances from Yugoslavs Working Abroad, 1974–1988," *Yugoslav Survey* (Belgrade), vol. 30, no. 2, 1989.

30 Buchalla, "Das Land der notleidenden Millionäre."

31 Ibid.

32 For an excellent survey of Yugoslavia's political-economic crisis, see Roland Schön-feld, "Das jugoslawische Dilemma," *Europa-Archiv* (Bonn), no. 15–16, 1989.

33 See "Jugoslawien zwischen Stabilisierungspolitik und System Reform: Ein Gespräch mit Ministerpräsident Ante Marković," *Neue Zürcher Zeitung* (Fernausgabe), March 25–26, 1990.

34 Milan Andrejevich, "Yugoslavia in 1989," Radio Free Europe Research, Background Report, November 29, 1989.

35 Meier, in Griffith (ed.), pp. 271–272.

36 See, for example, Milan Andrejevich, "Military Leaders Issue Stern Warnings to the Central Committee of the LCY," Radio Free Europe Research, Yugoslav Situation Report, February 3, 1989.

37 See Brown, *Eastern Europe and Communist Rule*, pp. 362–367.

38 Western reports have persisted, however, of disturbances in Shkodër. National Public Radio in Washington, D.C., on March 28, 1990, quoted an eyewitness on a demonstration there on January 11. Her report must be taken as credible.

39 See Louis Zanga, "Novel Criticizes Albanian Security Services," Radio Free Europe Research, Background Report, November 15, 1989.

40 See Brown, *Eastern Europe and Communist Rule*, p. 377.

41 See Peter Humphrey, "Albania Opts Reforms with a Socialist Face," *Independent* (London), February 24, 1990. See also Kerin Hope, "Hints of Reform in Albanian Doublespeak," *Financial Times*, March 6, 1990; Louis Zanga, "Alia on the Defensive," Radio Free Europe Research, Background Report, February 2, 1990.

42 See J. F. Brown, "Conservatism and Nationalism in the Balkans, in Griffith (ed.), pp. 310–311.

43 According to Reuters, reporting from Tirana on February 19, 1990, the Albanian government had begun allowing foreign investment, but no foreign ownership would be allowed. The news agency quoted a government adviser as saying: "Foreigners will be welcome to invest their technology and know-how, while we invest our labour and materials, and we will share the profit and the risks. We can repay the foreign investors through the product."

44 See Brown, "Conservatism and Nationalism in the Balkans," in Griffith (ed.), p. 307.

45 See Patrick Moore, "Noisy Neighbors in the European House: Albanian-Greek Relations," Radio Free Europe Research, Background Report, January 15, 1990.

46 For a fair, sensitive analysis of Albanian-Yugoslav relations over Kosovo, see Arshi Pipa, "The Political Situation of the Albanians in Yugoslavia, with Particular Attention to the Kosovo Problem: A Critical Approach," *East European Quarterly*, vol. 23, no. 2, Summer 1989.

Bibliography

The bibliography for my book, *Eastern Europe and Communist Rule* (pp. 545–553), has provided the basis and background for this book. It need not be repeated here. As mentioned in the Foreword, the Radio Free Europe Research and Analysis Department's reports have been used extensively, as have the BBC's world monitoring bulletins and the Foreign Broadcast Information Service (FBIS) reports for Eastern Europe.

The German-language press has been indispensable, notably the *Neue Zürcher Zeitung*, the *Süddeutsche Zeitung*, the *Frankfurter Allgemeine Zeitung*, and *Die Zeit*. So also have *Le Monde*, *Le Monde Diplomatique*, *Libération*, the *Financial Times*, the *New York Times*, the *Washington Post*, the *Economist*, and the *New York Review of Books*. Occasionally, the *New Yorker* has had incomparable reportage.

The following books, published since work was completed on *Eastern Europe and Communist Rule*, have been helpful in the writing of this work. They are merely a handful, not because of my limited reading capacity, but because most would-be chroniclers and interpreters of the events were still reeling under the shock when this manuscript was completed.

Ash, Timothy Garton, *The Uses of Adversity: Essays on the Fate of Central Europe* (New York: Random House, 1989).

Brzezinski, Zbigniew, *The Grand Failure: The Birth and Death of Communism in the Twentieth Century* (New York: Scribners, 1989).

Dawisha, Karen, *Eastern Europe, Gorbachev, and Reform: The Great Challenge* (Cambridge: Cambridge University Press, 1988).

De Nevers, Renée, *The Soviet Union and Eastern Europe: The End of an Era* (London: I.I.S.S. Adelphi Papers, no. 249, March 1990).

Eyal, Jonathan (ed.), *The Warsaw Pact and the Balkans: Moscow's Southern Flank* (Basingstoke: Macmillan, 1989).

Gati, Charles, *The Bloc That Failed: Soviet-East European Relations in Transition* (Bloomington: Indiana University Press, 1990).

Grémion, Pierre, and Pierre Hassner (eds.), *Vents d'est: vers l'Europe des Etats de droit?* (Paris: Presses Universitaires de France, 1990).

Griffith, William E. (ed.), *Central and Eastern Europe: The Opening Curtain?* (Boulder, Colo.: Westview Press, 1989).

Holzman, Franklyn D., *The Economics of Soviet Bloc Trade and Finance* (Boulder, Colo.: Westview Press, 1988).

Kaufman, Michael T., *Mad Dreams, Saving Graces: Poland, a Nation in Conspiracy* (New York: Random House, 1989).

Kittrie, Nicholas N., and Ivan Volgyes (eds.), *The Uncertain Future: Gorbachev's Eastern Bloc* (New York: Paragon House, 1988).

Lendvai, Paul, *Hungary: The Art of Survival* (London: I. B. Tauris, 1988).

Liebowitz, Ronald D. (ed.), *Gorbachev's New Thinking: Prospects for Joint Ventures* (Cambridge, Mass.: Ballinger, 1989).

Magris, Claudio, *Danube* (translated by Patrick Creagh) (New York: Farrar, Straus & Giroux, 1989).

Nelson, Daniel N., *Romanian Politics in the Ceauşescu Era* (New York: Gordon and Breach, 1988).

Nelson, Daniel N., *Elite-mass Relations in Communist Systems* (New York: St. Martin's Press, 1988).

Rothschild, Joseph, *Return to Diversity: A Political History of East Central Europe Since World War II* (New York: Oxford University Press, 1989).

Shafir, Michael, *Roumania: Politics, Economics, and Society* (London: Frances Pinter, 1988).

Shoup, Paul (ed.), and George Hoffman (project director), *Problems of Balkan Security: Southeastern Europe in the 1990s* (Washington, D.C.: Wilson Center Press, 1990).

Zeman, Zbyněk, *Pursued by a Bear: The Making of Eastern Europe* (London: Chatto & Windus, 1989).

Index

About the Author

J. F. (Jim) Brown was educated at Manchester University
(England), the University of Michigan, and Columbia University.
After serving as a Flying Officer in the Royal Air Force and after
short periods first in teaching and then in industry, he joined the
staff of Radio Free Europe in Munich in 1957. He worked with
RFE for twenty-six years, becoming head of research in 1969 and
station director in 1978. He resigned in 1983. From 1984 to 1986
he was Senior Associate Member of St. Anthony's College,
Oxford. He was a visiting fellow at the RAND/UCLA Center for
Soviet Studies (1987–88). In 1989 he was visiting professor of
political science at the University of California, Berkeley. He is
now a senior staff member at the RAND Corporation, and teaches
at the University of California at Los Angeles.

He is the author of *The New Eastern Europe* (1966), *Bulgaria
under Communist Rule* (1970), and *Eastern Europe and
Communist Rule* (Duke, 1988) as well as numerous chapters and
articles on communist affairs. He is now preparing a book on the
Balkans and the major powers.

Mr. Brown's home is in Oxford.

Library of Congress Cataloging-in-Publication Data
Brown, J. F. (James F.), 1928–
   Surge to freedom : the end of Communist rule in Eastern
Europe / J. F. Brown.
   Includes bibliographical references and index.
   ISBN 0-8223-1126-7 (cloth). — ISBN 0-8223-1145-3 (paper)
   1. Europe, Eastern—History—1945–1989.   I. Title.
DJK50.B78   1991
947.084—dc20   90-44883 CIP